'Robb describes his latest offering as "an adventure history", and with good reason. Rather than attempting a conventional biography, he takes the reader on a dizzying exploration of 400 years of Parisian history ... Robb may be a fine historian, but he can also spin a rattling good yarn ... *Parisians* is as audaciously written as it is meticulously researched. Robb is both a fine historian and, above all an enthusiast for his subject' 'Book of the Week', *Daily Mail*

'Robb writers beautifully, and possesses the novelist's ability to think himself into another's head ... Marvellously evocative' *Scotsman*

'There is much of the architect in Graham Robb. He creates huge, substantial works but also has the eye, ear and word for the detail ... *Parisians* is ambitious in scale, precise in language and inspired in its conception and realisation ... and a worthy addition to the catalogue of a writer who may just be the most original, most accomplished non-fiction writer of his generation' *Sunday Herald*

'Enjoyable and entertaining ... Robb imagines, novelises and even cinematises his Parisian vignettes' *Financial Times*

'Following Robb's last hugely successful book, *The Discovery of France*, he returns to the capital and shows us that the Eiffel Tower, the Louvre, the Café de Flore and Montmartre are the merest sideshows in a darker, stranger, more fragmented history, sprinkled with mystery and magic ... Every chapter contains a surprise, written up in a rich and supple prose ... and this is a deeply engrossing, ingenious and rewarding book ... I thought I knew Paris well. But Graham Robb has shown me, quite chillingly, that I hardly know it at all' RUPERT CHRISTIANSEN, 'Book of the Week', *Sunday Telegraph*

'A treasure trove of historical journeys in Paris ... Paris has never been so fascinating' *Psychologies*

PARISIANS

Also by Graham Robb in Picador

BALZAC

VICTOR HUGO

RIMBAUD

STRANGERS
Homosexual Love in the
Nineteenth Century

THE DISCOVERY OF FRANCE

GRAHAM ROBB

PARISIANS

An Adventure History of Paris

PICADOR

First published 2010 by Picador
an imprint of Pan Macmillan, a division of Macmillan Publishers Limited
Pan Macmillan, 20 New Wharf Road, London N1 9RR
Basingstoke and Oxford
Associated companies throughout the world
www.panmacmillan.com

ISBN 978-0-330-53623-3

1 3 5 7 9 8 6 4 2

A CIP catalogue record for this book is available from
the British Library.

Typeset by SetSystems Limited, Saffron Walden, Essex
Printed in the UK by CPI Mackays, Chatham ME5 8TD

Visit **www.picador.com** to read more about all our books
and to buy them. You will also find features, author interviews
and news of any author events, and you can sign up for e-newsletters
so that you're always first to hear about our new releases.

TO MY PARENTS

GORDON JAMES ROBB
(1921–2000)

JOYCE ROBB,
née Gall

Contents

[ix]

Contents

List of Illustrations

[xi]

Section Two

ILLUSTRATIONS IN THE TEXT

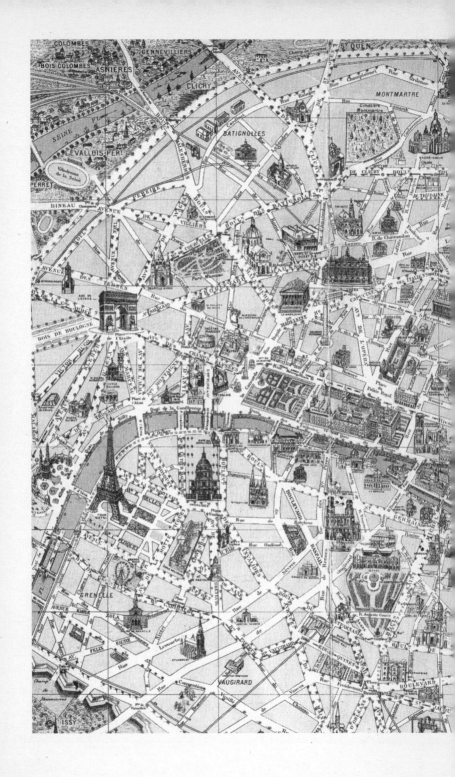

DEPARTURE

By the time I reached Paris, the Bastille had disappeared. The map supplied by the tourist agency clearly showed a 'Place de la Bastille' in the east of the city, but when I emerged from the Métro at the station called 'Bastille', there was nothing to see but an ugly green column. Not even the vestige of a ruin remained. On the base of the column was a date in dirty gold lettering – 'JUILLET 1830' – and an inscription praising citizens who had died in the defence of 'libertés publiques'. The French Revolution, I knew, had taken place in 1789. Evidently, this was some other revolution. But if the King and the aristocrats had been guillotined, who had massacred the defenders of liberty in 1830? The monument offered no explanation. Later, an older boy at school told me of yet another revolution, which I had missed by only seven years.

For my birthday, my parents had given me a week's holiday in Paris. The package included a room in a small hotel near the École Militaire, some clues to monuments and cheap restaurants, a voucher for a boat-ride on the Seine, and a coupon to be redeemed at the Galeries Lafayette for a free gift. My suitcase contained what seemed an excessive amount of clothing, some emergency provisions, and a second-hand copy of the works of Charles Baudelaire. This was my guide to all the mysteries and indefinable experiences that filled the space between the famous sights. I read the 'Tableaux parisiens' and the chapter on 'L'Héroïsme de la vie moderne': 'Parisian life is bursting with wonderful, poetic subjects: the miraculous envelops us; we breathe it in like the atmosphere, but we do not see it.' Deciphering Baudelaire in a café near the Tour Saint-Jacques, with the rain blurring the faces on the street, dissolving the Gothic stones into misty air, I was quite certain that I could see it.

During that week, I made a number of other interesting discoveries. I found the little cottage across the river from the Eiffel Tower where Balzac had hidden from his creditors to write *La Comédie Humaine*. I climbed up towards the white dome of the Sacré-Cœur, and found a provincial village full of cheerful cafés and artists all forging the same paintings. I walked through the Louvre for hours, forgetting to eat and remembering almost nothing. I found medieval streets that were paved with sand, and pondered graffiti that seemed to have been written by highly educated people with serious political opinions. I walked past limbless beggars in the Métro, and, in *quartiers* not mentioned in the pocket guide to Paris, I saw women of the kind described in 'Tableaux parisiens'.

On the first day, after trying to practise the language I had understood to be French, I decided that Paris was best experienced in a state of silent contemplation. It turned out to be possible to walk from one side of the city to the other in half a day, and I did this several times, until I began to plan my days by marking numbers on the bus-map. By the end of the week, numbers 27, 38 and 92, and most other routes that ran buses with open rear platforms, were old acquaintances. I left the boat-ride to the last day, and slept through part of it. When I boarded the airport bus at Les Invalides with a bulging case of second-hand books, some of which I suspected of being priceless treasures, I had seen so many sights that I felt only slightly guilty about leaving my free gift uncollected at the Galeries Lafayette.

One of the most important discoveries came too late to be of use. On the plane home to Birmingham, an American gentleman struck up what he must have hoped would be a conversation. He asked if I had seen something called the Latin Quarter. I told him I had not (though I later found out that I had). 'Well,' he said, 'you'll have to go back! If you haven't seen the Latin Quarter, you haven't seen Paris.'

The following year, I returned with enough money for two weeks, determined to find a job, which I did, after three weeks, and then stayed for six months. Later, I came to know Paris well enough to realize that I would never really know it. The sight of a heavy *porte cochère* closing on an inner courtyard seemed to be a characteristically Parisian sight. I made some Parisian friends, most of whom had not been born in Paris but who were proud to think themselves Parisian. They showed me places I was never able to find again on my own, and they shared a certain Parisian *art de vivre*: sitting in traffic jams as a form of *flânerie*, parking illegally as a defence of personal liberty, savouring window displays as though the streets were a public museum. They taught me the tricky etiquette of pretending to argue with waiters, and the gallantry of staring at beautiful strangers. As a student, I read novels and histories, and tried to match the information to the visible facts. I learned to distinguish one revolution from the next. Eventually, I was able to explain the column in the Place de la Bastille, and I could even understand some of the political graffiti. But there was always something cumbersome and incongruous about this deliberately acquired knowledge. It was the baggage of a historical tourist. I read all seven thousand entries in Jacques Hillairet's *Dictionnaire historique des rues de Paris*, and gazed at all the photographs, but in the open air of Paris, the most brazenly illuminated monument was still a labyrinth on many levels. Even when my French had improved enough for eavesdropping, the crowds on the boulevards and the faces at windows were reminders that a changing metropolis with a population of millions can never be comprehended by a single person.

THE ADVENTURES that follow were written as a history of Paris recounted by many different voices. The book begins at the dawn of the French Revolution, and ends a few months ago. There are also some excursions to the medieval and prehistoric past. It traces the spread of the city from the island in the Seine that was the home of the Parisii tribe to the mushrooming suburbs that inspire more fear today than when they were patrolled by highwaymen and wolves.

The idea was to create a kind of mini-Human Comedy of Paris, in which the history of the city would be illuminated by the real experience of its inhabitants. Each tale is true, and each is complete in itself, but there are also correspondences and crossroads, both literal and mysterious, which serve as landmarks in time and space. Certain districts and buildings reappear at different stages, seen through different eyes, transformed by events, obsessions, visionaries, architects and the passing of time.

No completely accurate map of Paris existed until the end of the eighteenth century, and few people wandered far from their own *quartier*. Even today, the discovery of Paris, or of any great city, entails a degree of disorientation and distraction. A pattern of streets, a certain topographical texture, a combination of climate, smell, building-stone and the flurry of humanity create a particular sense of reality. Every vision of the city, however private or eccentric, belongs to its history as much as its public ceremonies and monuments.

A single viewpoint would have turned these representative adventures into a scripted tour. Narrative devices and perspectives were naturally suggested by a place, a historical moment or a personality. Each tale was written with a flavour of the time in mind; it demanded its own explanations and imposed its own forms of courtesy to the past. Descriptions of the architectural transformations of Paris, the development of its police force and government, its infrastructure and housing, its recreations and revolutions, are there primarily because they serve the purposes of the tale. Nothing has been artificially inserted, and no one – except Baron Haussmann, Adolf Hitler and some Presidents of the Republic – discourses on the evolution of the drainage system or the transport network.

A tourist who follows an uncharted course like a train of thought, only later, after retracing the puzzle of streets on a map, recognizes how much knowledge can adhere to the accidental experience. I have tried to replicate the convenient, mnemonic effect of a long walk, a bus ride or a personal adventure, to create a series of contexts to which more detailed information can be attached. Almost every historian of Paris notes the impossibility of giving a complete account of the city, and I am quite confident of having made this impossibility even more obvious than usual. This book is not intended as a substitute for analytical histories of Paris, some excellent examples of which are currently in print. But it is not as remote from traditional history as it might first appear. It required as much research as *The Discovery of France*, which was devoted to the other eighty-five per cent of the population, and the intention was not to treat hard-won historical data as an amorphous mass of modelling clay. Above all, it was written for the pleasure of thinking about Paris, and I hope that it will be read for the same purpose, which is why an impartial historian should point out that, in the time that it takes to read this book, it would be possible to decipher every gravestone in the Père-Lachaise cemetery, sit at every *terrasse de café* between the Place de l'Étoile and the Place de la Sorbonne, ride a dozen different buses from departure to terminus, or examine every book-box from the Quai de la Tournelle to the Quai Malaquais.

ONE NIGHT AT THE PALAIS-ROYAL

EVERY WEDNESDAY MORNING, at seven o'clock in summer and eight o'clock in winter, the water-coach left the town of Auxerre on its hundred-and-thirty-mile journey to Paris. In winter especially, it was the safest, most comfortable route from Burgundy and the south. It took just three days to sail down the Yonne and the Seine to Paris, where it came to rest among the spires and domes in the heart of the old city. A large, flat-bottomed boat painted green and divided into compartments with portholes and a spacious room lined with benches, the water-coach held up to four hundred human passengers and as many animals, bound for markets along the river or for the dinner tables of cousins in the city. There was a galley serving soups and stews for those who came without enough provisions, and, on either side, two half-turrets known as *les bouteilles* (the latrines), for those who paid ample homage to the vineyards along the banks.

Wealthy travellers who had lurched along the post-roads for countless leagues found the voyage a delightful adventure, once they had grown accustomed to the company of soldiers, travelling sales-men, wandering musicians, monks and peasants, and the army of wet-nurses who left their babies at home and went to sell their breast-milk in the capital. A poet who made the journey a few years before this story begins imagined himself 'aboard one of those vessels laden with creatures of every species destined to populate some recently discovered territory overseas'. Passengers who found a quiet vantage point in that Noah's Ark behind the coiled ropes and the piles of luggage observed the peculiar effect of a landscape that seemed to glide past the motionless boat like a painted backdrop. In those long hours of idleness and gentle progress, in the cheerful promiscuity of social ranks, some passengers experienced a sudden rejuvenation. Men who were eager for the sights of Paris, and curious to test the reputation of Parisian women for congeniality and charm, often found themselves sentimentally attached long before they had glimpsed the towers of Notre-Dame.

Among the passengers who boarded the service from Auxerre on the morning of 7 November 1787 was a young artillery lieutenant from a regiment recently posted to Valence. He was eighteen years old, afraid of nothing except embarrassment; a little too short for his long leather boots, but fierce enough to demand instant reparation from any man who dared to call him Puss in Boots to his face. The inspector of his military school at Brienne had described him with something approaching admiration:

> Upright and thoughtful; conduct most regular; has always distin-guished himself in mathematics; possesses a fair knowledge of history and geography; weak in social accomplishments; will make an excellent sailor.

As an avid reader of Jean-Jacques Rousseau, the young man was not insensitive to the charms of a river journey, but he was far too conscious of the honour of his uniform to indulge in the sort of dalliance that made the voyage seem all too short to some of his fellow passengers: when he was sent to join his regiment in Valence, he alone in the party of young officers had not taken advantage of the night in Lyon to visit a brothel. In any case, though he was impatient to discover Paris, he had more serious matters on his mind.

He had just returned home for the first time since leaving for school eight years before. His father had died after wasting several years and part of the family's fortune by suing his own relatives. When he saw the house again, he felt no grief at the old man's passing, but when he found his mother performing domestic chores, humiliation struck him like a slap in the face. The family had legitimate and ancient claims to nobility, but the government in France treated them as though they were ignorant peasants. They had been granted a subsidy for planting mulberry trees and introduc-ing silk production to their backward region, but now that they had invested their money in the scheme, a nameless servant of the Crown had withdrawn the subsidy. Since the older brother was taken up with fruitless legal studies, it was left to him to negotiate with the authorities in Paris.

It had been a long journey up from the Mediterranean, on roads that were already showing the effects of an early winter. It was only now, as he resigned himself to the leisurely andante of a river journey, that he began to think of the city that lay ahead.

He had seen Paris once before, as a cadet, at the age of fifteen, with three of his classmates and a monk from the school at Brienne. There had been just enough time to buy a novel on the *quais* and to say a prayer at Saint-Germain-des-Prés before they were delivered to the École Royale Militaire, from where, in twelve months, he had seen precisely nothing of the city, except the parade ground on the Champ de Mars. But of course, he had heard about Paris and its splendours from his family and his fellow officers. He had read about its monuments and treasures in histories and geographical dictionaries. He had studied its defences and resources like a foreign general planning an invasion.

He remembered his readings and his comrades' half-true tales as he watched the satellite towns of Vitry and Choisy-le-Roi come into view, and the Bercy plain beginning to widen to the north. He stood on the foredeck, looking ahead like the captain of a ship, silent and severe among the pigs and the chickens in baskets, and the children playing at his feet. He felt the boat catch the current of the sea-green Marne as it joined the Seine at Alfort and broadened the brown river into a majestic thoroughfare. Here, the first steeples of Paris could be seen in the distance, and the deep water had yet to be sullied by the effluent of drains and factories. There were long rafts of floated wood steered by wild-looking men in wolfskin cloaks, and boats bringing passengers and paving stones from Fontainebleau. Washerwomen began to appear along the banks. He saw a tree-lined road on which carriages were running, and long wooden sheds where barrels of wine from Burgundy and the centre of France were rolled up to the waiting wagons.

This time, he knew what he was seeing – a city that had grown up like a thousand villages, stifled by privilege and petty competition.

There should have been a proper port to rival London instead of those rickety landing-stages. The government should build huge granaries and warehouses to feed the people in times of need. A city that barely knew how to keep its population alive had no right to compare itself to ancient Rome, still less to be sniffy about provincials.

Now, low houses ran along both banks. The water-coach entered the channel to the south of the uninhabited Île Louviers that was covered with enormous piles of firewood as though the Gaulish forests had only recently been cleared. Behind it stood the tall houses of the Île Saint-Louis, and, behind them, rising out of the river mist and the chimney-smoke like the stern of a great ship, the buttressed mass of Notre-Dame.

The lieutenant disembarked with the other passengers at the Quai de la Tournelle, and pointed out his trunk to a porter from the hotel where he intended to stay. Then, having previously studied the map and committed the route to memory, he set off across the Pont au Double and entered the medieval maze of the Île de la Cité. After getting lost in the cul-de-sacs and the chapel closes, he found the other bank and threaded his way through the crowded streets to the east of the Louvre. He crossed the Rue Saint-Honoré – the main thoroughfare running east to west across the Right Bank – and turned up the Rue du Four-Saint-Honoré, at the point where the heavy stench of the river gave way to the vegetable smells of Les Halles.

The Rue du Four-Saint-Honoré was a street of furnished hotels, patronized mainly by men who came to do business at the central markets. The lieutenant went to the Hôtel de Cherbourg, next door to the Café du Chat-Qui-Pelote. The hotel register (which has long since disappeared) showed that he stayed in room nine on the third floor, and that he signed his name in its native, Italianate form rather than in the French form that he later affected.

When his trunk was delivered, he settled in, and, in that city of six hundred thousand souls, savoured the delight of being alone. In the house where he lodged in Valence, people ambushed him when he left his room each morning and when he returned in the evening; they stole his time and scattered his thoughts with polite conversation. Now, he was free to think and explore, to compare his own experiences with the books he had read, and to find out for himself whether or not Paris deserved its lofty reputation.

EVEN WITHOUT the handwritten account that forms the basis of this story – a brief, incomplete description of one night's adventure – it would have been easy to guess the principal object of the lieutenant's curiosity. In those days, there was only one place that every visitor to Paris wanted to see, and any traveller who published an account of his trip and omitted to mention it, or pretended to have shunned it as a place of debauchery, cannot be trusted as a guide to the city. The streets in its vicinity were said to be the busiest in Europe. By comparison, the other sights of Paris – the Louvre and the Tuileries, Notre-Dame and the Sainte-Chapelle, the Bastille, the Invalides, the grand squares and gardens, the Pont Neuf, and the Gobelins tapestry works – were almost deserted.

In 1781, the Duc de Chartres, a pleasure-seeking, fashionably liberal cousin of the King who was chronically short of cash, began to turn the grounds of his royal residence into an amazing bazaar of economic and erotic activity. Wooden galleries were erected along one of the rows of arcades that formed the stately courtyard. They looked (if such a thing had existed) like a railway station implanted in a palace. Shopkeepers, charlatans and entertainers occupied the galleries even before they were finished in 1784, and, almost overnight, the Palais-Royal became an enchanted city-within-a-city that never closed its gates. According to Louis-Sébastien Mercier, 'a prisoner could live there without getting bored and would dream of freedom only after several years'. It was known, half-humorously, as 'the capital of Paris'.

No one who saw the Palais-Royal in 1787 could doubt the progress of industry and the benefits of modern civilization. There were theatres and puppet shows, and nightly firework displays in the gardens. The galleries and arcades housed over two hundred shops. Without having to walk more than a few hundred feet, a man who cared nothing about cost or the honesty of shopkeepers could buy a barometer, a collapsible rubber raincoat, a painting on a pane of glass, a copy of the latest banned book, a toy to delight the most despotic child, a box of rouge for his mistress and some English flannel for his wife. He could rummage in mountains of ribbon, gauze, pompons and satin flowers. In the slow-moving crowd, he could find himself pressed up against a strangely attractive woman, her bare shoulders glaring in the lamplight, and move on, a moment later, his pockets completely empty. If he was sufficiently rich, he could lose his money in a gambling house on the first floor, pawn his gold watch and embroidered coat on the second, and console himself with one of the ladies who lived in rented rooms on the third.

There were restaurants fit for emperors, fruit stalls with exotic fruits from the suburbs of Paris and wine merchants selling rare liqueurs from non-existent colonies. Everything that made a person beautiful could be bought at fabulous prices: lotions and ointments that whitened the face, eradicated wrinkles or showed up the blue veins on a breast. A feeble old *chevalier* could leave the Palais-Royal a twinkling Adonis, with lustrous teeth, a glass eye of any colour, a black toupee under his powdered perruque and new calf muscles in his silk stockings. An ill-favoured girl in want of a husband could make herself desirable, at least until the wedding night, with false shoulders, hips, cleavage, eyelashes, eyebrows and eyelids.

There were fancy boutiques in which the clothes of gamblers and libertines were displayed in glass partitions, poorly lit to hide their stains, and sold to clerks and *petits maîtres*. There were public latrines where, for a modest fee, a customer could wipe his bottom on the day's news. The Palais-Royal catered to every taste, and, it was said, created tastes that had never existed before. A guide that was published shortly after the lieutenant's visit recommended Mme Laperrière, 'above the baker's shop', who specialized in old men and whips, Mme Bondy, who supplied the foreign and the very young (recruited from the most reputable convents), and Mlle André's fashion store – though 'one should never spend a night there, because Mlle André applies the principle that "at night, all cats are grey"'.

Despite his abhorrence of a place where everyone felt free to stare at everyone else, and despite his aversion to crowds, the lieutenant seems to have made some preliminary forays into the palace gardens – perhaps in the morning, when ragged women rooted in

the shrubberies and drains for dropped coins and trinkets, or at
noon, when people set their watches by the cannon that was fired
by the rays of the sun through a powerful lens. During one of
these reconnaissance expeditions, he visited Jean-Jacques Rousseau's
favourite coffeehouse, the Café de la Régence on the square in front
of the palace, where chess-players sat at marble tables in a gigantic
hall of mirrors and chandeliers. In Valence, he enjoyed a certain
reputation as a chess-player. At the Café de la Régence, he marched
his pawns across the board, deployed his knights with an occasional
flash of brilliance, apparently indifferent to his losses, and always
furious to find himself in checkmate.

The Hôtel de Cherbourg stood just five streets from the Palais-
Royal, along the Rue Saint-Honoré. On his way back to the hotel
from the Finance Ministry, where he spent hours each day in
antechambers to learn the outcome of his family's appeal, he often
passed the iron railings that ran along the galleries. Eventually, he
began to explore the galleries, always later in the day, after dark – to
satisfy his curiosity and to fill a gap in his knowledge (though he felt
that too much was made of the matter, and that it was commonly
approached in a frame of mind that made it impossible to profit
from the experience). The Palais-Royal was, after all, a place where
a man of philosophy and sense could make some valuable observations. As he wrote a year or so later in an essay on happiness,
entered in a competition that was held by the Académie de Lyon,
'the eyes of Reason preserve us from the precipices of Passion'. At
the Palais-Royal, he was able to witness the illusory pleasures of
bachelorhood and the deleterious effects of the modern contempt for
family life. A man might go to the Palais-Royal to see the savages
from Guadeloupe, or 'la Belle Zulima', who had died two centuries
ago but whose exquisite body was perfectly preserved; but he might
also see those civilized monsters who had turned the natural desire
for health, happiness and self-preservation into a brutish quest for
animal satisfaction.

On the night in question, the lieutenant had spent almost two
weeks in Paris, far from his family and comrades. He was no further
advanced with the subsidy for the mulberry groves, though he had
acquired some useful ideas on the subject of administrative reform.

He felt the need of some distraction. He walked past the Palais-Royal and the Bibliothèque du Roi towards the tree-lined boulevards and the theatre where the actors of the Comédie Italienne performed their comic operas. The 'Italiens' was popular with lovers of light music and humorous innuendo, but also with gentlemen in search of a companion for the night, who appreciated the convenience of finding the ladies already arranged by price, from the expensive *balcons* to the cheap *amphithéâtres*.

On the bill that night was a historical operetta called *Berthe et Pépin*. It was a subject to stir the imagination of an ambitious young officer. By acts of astounding bravery, the diminutive Pépin le Bref impressed the soldiers who dubbed him 'the Short'. Such was his political skill that he had himself crowned King of the Franks by the Pope at Saint-Denis. After imprisoning his brother in a monastery, King Pépin subdued the Goths, the Saxons and the Arabs, and marched victoriously across the Alps into Italy. Pépin, rather than his son Charlemagne, was the first ruler of a European empire.

The operetta was based on an amorous interlude in Pépin's life. Having inadvertently married a tyrannical woman pretending to be Berthe of Laon, Pépin happens upon the real Berthe in the forest of Le Mans. 'Big-Footed Berthe' (so called because of her club foot) has sworn never to reveal her true identity, except to save her virginity. By threatening her maidenhood, Pépin discovers her to be his true queen, and the pair return in triumph to Paris. The main dramatic interest, to an audience chiefly preoccupied with sex, was the pursuit of a club-footed maid by a short and lusting king.

By the end of the performance, the young lieutenant was in a state of agitation that can easily be imagined. The evening was far from over, and all around him people were talking excitedly about the night ahead. He had no desire for cheery company, yet the thought of dining alone at the Hôtel de Cherbourg was repellent. He left the theatre and pulled his coat about him as the winter wind blew down the boulevard. People and carriages were rushing about as though the day had just begun. Impelled by a sudden resolution, he set off down the Rue de Richelieu towards the galleries and arcades where a thousand lamp-lit dramas were acted out every night.

An hour or so later, he returned to room nine in the Hôtel de

Cherbourg. This time, he was not alone. When his visitor had gone, he sat down to record his observations in a large notebook. He never completed his account, but he kept the notebook, perhaps because it recorded an event of such importance in his young life.

Years later, when his life was in danger, he placed the notebook in a cardboard box covered with grey paper, and had it sent to his uncle for safe-keeping. It is fortunate that the manuscript has survived. So many people visited the Palais-Royal, yet so few left any honest account of their dealings there, that the value of the manuscript as a historical document far outweighs its biographical significance.

Thursday, 22 November 1787. Paris, Hôtel de Cherbourg.

I had left the Italiens and was striding along the avenues of the Palais-Royal. Stirred by the vigorous sentiments that characterize my soul, I was indifferent to the cold. But as my imagination cooled, I felt the chill of the season, and took shelter in the galleries.

I was standing on the threshold of those iron gates when my eyes fell on a person of the female sex. From the time of day, the cut of her clothes and her extreme youth, I deduced without hesitation that she was a whore.

I looked at her, and she stopped, not with that martial air of the others, but with an air that was perfectly in keeping with her physical appearance. I was struck by this concordance of manner and demeanour. Her timidity emboldened me, and I spoke to her – I who feel more keenly than any other man the odiousness of her profession and who have always considered myself soiled by a single glance from one of those creatures ... Yet her pale complexion, her frail physique, and her gentle voice caused me to act without delay. Either, I told myself, this person will be of use to me in the observations I wish to make, or else she is simply a dolt.

'You must be very cold', I said, 'How can you force yourself to walk these avenues in such weather?'

'Oh, Monsieur, hope is my spur. I must finish my evening's work.'

The dispassionate manner in which she uttered these words, and her composure in answering my enquiry, won me over, and I walked at her side.

'You appear to possess a weak constitution', I observed, 'I am surprised that you have not tired of this profession.'

'Indeed, Monsieur, one must do something!'

'That may be, but is there no profession better suited to your state of health?'

'No, Monsieur; one must earn a living.'

I was delighted to see that she was at least answering my questions. None of my earlier attempts had met with such success.

'To brave the cold as you do, you must come from a northern country.'

'I come from Nantes in Brittany.'

'I know the region ... You must do me the pleasure, Mademoiselle, of recounting to me the loss of your virginity.'

'An officer took it from me.'

'Does that anger you?' I asked.

'Oh yes, of that you may be certain.' (As she spoke these words, her voice had a charm and richness I had not previously detected.) 'You may be certain of that, Monsieur. My sister is now well established, and there is no reason why I should not have been so too.'

'How did you come to Paris?'

'The officer who degraded me, and whom I hate with all my heart, abandoned me. I was forced to flee my mother's indignation. A second man presented himself. He brought me to Paris, where he deserted me. He was succeeded by a third, with whom I have lived these three years. Although he is a Frenchman, his business affairs have called him to London, where he is now . . . Let us go to your lodgings.'

'But what shall we do there?'

'Come, Sir, we shall warm ourselves up and you shall satisfy your pleasure.'

I was not about to be overcome by scruples. I had provoked her so that she would not run away when I put to her the proposition I was preparing to make, my intention being to feign the honourable designs that I wanted to prove to her I did not harbour . . .

At this point, the lieutenant laid down his pen. No doubt the rest of the evening's adventure scarcely lent itself to the style of prose he had learned in sentimental novels. And perhaps, as he wrote and became entangled in his phrases, he realized that he was not the principal actor in his play, and that there was more to that arduous profession than he had supposed.

The observer had been observed and analysed long before he made his first approach. She had seen him walking in the crowd in his blue uniform, self-conscious and proud, not quite as elegant as he would have liked, and clearly not from Paris. He wore his virginity like an advertising board. Such a man would appreciate a shy young whore who was dignified in her predicament – and prepared to hold a conversation in the cold. He needed a woman skilled in the art of love who would make him feel that he was leading the dance and teaching her the steps.

The lieutenant shifted uncomfortably in his chair. There was indeed much to be learned at the Palais-Royal. He had shown by his actions more than by his words that he could profit from the lessons: too much time refining tactics and preparing the ground. He had turned the loss of his virginity into a campaign, when all it took was a few sous and five minutes of his time.

He stayed on at the Hôtel de Cherbourg for another few weeks. In one sense, it was a wasted journey. He failed to secure a subsidy for the mulberry groves, which seemed to him a predictable outcome in a city of shopkeepers and libertines. He wrote a few letters and the first paragraph of a history of Corsica: 'Though I have scarce reached the age [here, there is a gap in the manuscript], I have the enthusiasm that a more mature study of men often eradicates from the heart.' Doubtless he became better acquainted with the sights of Paris, but he left no other record of his observations. If he returned to the Théâtre des Italiens in December, he would have seen *The Lover Put to the Test*, or *The Invisible Woman*, but not *The English Prisoner*, which was premiered two days after he boarded the boat for Montereau on Christmas Eve. He may also have returned to the Palais-Royal, but the crowds were so dense, and an engaging girl from Brittany was rarely short of customers. It is unlikely that he ever saw his first lover again.

The woman herself is known to us only from the lieutenant's account. Even that small amount of detail is unusual. Official statistics show that of twelve thousand seven hundred prostitutes in Paris who knew their place of birth, fifty-three came from her part of Brittany, but no names are attached to the figures – other than the usual *noms de guerre*: Jasmine, Abricote, Serpentine, Ingénue, etc. – and there is nothing to corroborate her tale of disgrace and abandonment.

Perhaps her companion, if he existed, returned from London and rescued her from the Palais-Royal. Or perhaps, like the wife of Balzac's Colonel Chabert, she was picked up in the galleries 'like a hackney cab', and installed in an elegant *hôtel*. Two years after the young lieutenant's visit, when the Palais-Royal became a centre of revolutionary activity, she might have joined her sisters-in-arms in the historic meeting around the fountain, when 'the demoiselles of the Palais-Royal' vowed to publish their grievances and to demand fair remuneration for their patriotic labours:

> The confederates of all parts of France who are joined together in Paris, far from having reason to complain of us, will retain a pleasant memory of the lengths to which we went to welcome them.

She was better placed than prostitutes in other parts of the city to survive those difficult years. When François-René de Chateaubriand returned from English exile in 1800, after passing through a ravaged landscape of silent churches and blackened figures in neglected fields, he was amazed to find the Palais-Royal still ringing with sounds of jollity. A little hunchback was standing on a table, playing a fiddle and singing a hymn to General Bonaparte, the young First Consul of the French Republic:

> By his virtues and attractions,
> He deserved to be their father!

If she was eighteen when she met Lieutenant Bonaparte, she would then have been nearing the end of her professional life. (Most prostitutes in Paris were aged between eighteen and thirty-two.) After the Revolution, life became harder. Whenever General Bonaparte attended the Théâtre Français and parked his carriage near the Palais-Royal, soldiers were sent to 'purge' the brothels, lest the First Consul be exposed to embarrassing overtures. Later still, when the young lieutenant had conquered half of Europe, married an Austrian princess and made his mother the richest widow in France, the whores of the Palais-Royal were fined, imprisoned, medically inspected or sent back in disgrace to their native provinces.

But even Napoleon Bonaparte had little effect on 'the capital of Paris'. According to an English traveller, it remained 'a vortex of dissipation where many a youth is engulfed'. Its fame spread through-out the empire and beyond. In the depths of Russia, Cossacks talked of it as a place of legend, and when armies from the east crossed the frontiers of the crumbling empire, officers inspired their troops with tales of the Palais-Royal, insisting that, until he had seen that palace of debauchery and tasted its civilized delights, no man could call himself a man, or consider his education complete.

THE MAN WHO
SAVED PARIS

1

THOUGH THEY took place in a city whose every twisted street and shuttered window had a tale to tell, one might have expected the sequence of catastrophic events that began on 17 December 1774 to have left some lasting trace in the history of Paris. For several years, they threatened to overshadow all the wars, revolutions, plagues and massacres that ever blackened the thirteen square miles that lie between Montmartre and the Montagne Sainte-Geneviève. Yet almost two hundred years have passed since any historian has even mentioned them. Perhaps this will turn out to be the lesson of the tale: so many people chose to live in a city that poets habitually described as Hell because it offered the priceless blessing of oblivion. The perpetual turmoil of Paris carried everything away, like the rain that rushed the sweepings of a hundred thousand households into the Seine.

The first sign of something untoward came on a Saturday after-noon, a week before Christmas Day in 1774. The main customs gate on the southern edge of the city was clogged up with the usual heavy traffic. Paris was filling its markets and shops for the holiday ahead, and even that late in the year, travellers had to expect long delays before they could enter the pandemonium and begin the final descent towards the smoke-shrouded steeples.

Customs officers exacted payment on everything that entered the city. Every vehicle, passenger and piece of luggage had to be searched for 'any article contrary to the King's orders'. Pedlars and milkmaids, foot-weary peasants pulling handcarts stacked with winter vegetables, mud-caked passengers from the north-bound diligence were all forced to wait in each other's company.

Some of them sat in the garden of a nearby windmill drinking excise-free wine; others stood at the barrier exchanging news and gossip. That afternoon, a group had gathered to watch wine barrels being unloaded from a cart. A wheelwright was heating up his forge to repair a broken axle. The carter, who had left Orléans before dawn, had run into a large hole on the last stretch of road before Paris. Anywhere else in France, a pot-hole – even one deep enough to drown a horse – would have passed without comment, but this hole had appeared without warning in the great road south to Orléans. In the distant days when Paris was a town of huts on an island in the river Sequana, the road had been plied by the high-speed chariots of the Gauls, and it was along the same magnificent avenue that the legions of Labienus had launched a devastating attack on the armies of the Parisii tribe in 52 BC. Now, in 1774, it was the busiest stretch of highway in the kingdom. Sometimes, when the traffic wasn't held up by livestock, more than ten vehicles passed through the customs gate in an hour.

It was a fact of tremendous significance to those who witnessed the event that this part of the road was called the Rue d'Enfer. No one knows how the street acquired its sinister name. It may originally have been a Gaulish word for 'fair', or the verbal remnant of something made of iron – perhaps a gate that had marked the limits of the city. Many people said that the street was known as Hell because so much shouting and swearing was heard in the *quartier*, but, as others pointed out, that would have to have been the name of almost every street in Paris. Others still, believing that names were clues to the future as well as to the past, associated it with an ancient prophecy which said that, one day, all the temples, taverns, convents and heretical schools of the Latin Quarter would be swallowed up by an infernal abyss. Educated people, however, preferred a more scholarly derivation:

Etymologists assert that in the days of the Romans, the Rue Saint-Jacques was the *Via Superior*, while this street, being the lower of the two, was the *Via Inferior* or *Infera*. And so it was that, by corruption and contraction, it assumed the name ENFER.*

At about three o'clock that afternoon, the crowd at the customs barrier saw a sight that might have settled the matter once and for all: the roofs of the buildings on the Paris side changed their angle slightly in relation to the skyline. A second later, there was the sound of a giant heaving a great sigh and stretching his limbs. The cattle that had passed through the gate panicked and backed into the barrier. A man was seen running with a hood pulled over his head. Behind him, a cloud was billowing up from the road, and the buildings on the street beyond the Rue d'Enfer suddenly came into view. Along the eastern side of the Rue d'Enfer itself, extending towards the centre of Paris for what proved to be one quarter of a mile, a gaping trench had opened up and swallowed all the houses.

Predictably, the chasm was identified as 'the Mouth of Hell', and, in view of what had happened, only the most pedantic etymologist could have doubted the true, satanic origin of the street's name.

2

A LITTLE MORE than two years after the incident in the Rue d'Enfer, a luxuriously upholstered sedan chair was bobbing and weaving along the Rue de Grenelle through the heart of the Faubourg Saint-Germain. A light rain had fallen in the night and turned the sandy streets to mud. The new Inspector of Quarries was on his way to his first appointment. He stared out of the mud-flecked window of the sedan, remembering the days when he had roamed the noble Faubourg on foot. He had studied those grand facades, pausing to sketch a frieze or an *œil-de-bœuf* window, wondering how

* Hurtaut and Magny, *Dictionnaire historique de la ville de Paris et de ses environs* (Paris, 1779). This ingenious explanation is no longer considered reliable, and the origin of the name is now officially 'obscure'.

the architect had managed to fold the stables and the service quarters into a rhomboidal plot and still create a courtyard wide enough for any visitor to lose his nerve before he reached the front door. He had made jottings of corbels and porticos, spattered by the water that flowed from the mouths of copper dolphins, under the insolent scrutiny of doorkeepers dressed like kings.

To Charles-Axel Guillaumot, whose views are known to us from his many pamphlets, and whose character is in some respects a key to the following events, Paris had always been a city of closed doors. Its coat of arms – a ship and a motto borrowed from the ancient corporation of Seine boatmen: *Fluctuat nec mergitur* ('Buffeted but not about to sink') – might as well have been a *porte cochère* instead of a ship: a solid barrier of oak and iron, with the motto from Dante's *Inferno*, 'All hope abandon, ye who enter here!'

More than once, as a young architect in Rome, he had been dragged in from the street by a nobleman who wanted to expose to an artist's enlightened gaze the treasures that lay behind his crumbling facade. In Paris, a man who begged admittance to a masterpiece of domestic architecture but who lacked the necessary qualifications – a title and a pair of white cuffs – would invariably be turned away by a snooty servant with the blessing of his master. Sometimes, he had seen the ridiculous mask of rouge and white lead sneering from an upper window.

Italy had proved its superiority by opening its artistic competitions to all the nations of Europe, and by awarding him, Charles-Axel Guillaumot, the architectural Prix de Rome when he was only twenty years old. Though his parents were French, the accident of his birth in Stockholm, where his father had been a merchant, had disqualified him from every scholarship that was open to Frenchmen. He had been forced to fight his way out of obscurity with nothing but genius and determination. His foreign origin had at least preserved him from the preposterous arrogance that enabled a Frenchman to believe that a cathedral that had to be propped up like a decaying hovel was the equal of a Greek temple. It was no coincidence that his architectural studies had been best appreciated by a man who was forced to live in exile. 'Your observations are as enjoyable as they are instructive', Voltaire had told him in a letter.

I still take an interest in Paris, as one does in old friends, whom one loves along with all their faults – crooked streets, markets in the middle of the road, houses and even fountains without water! It is a consolation to know that the monastic orders have all the space they need. No doubt everything will be put right within the next five or six hundred years. In the meantime, I wish you all the success that your great talent deserves.

The sedan chair had skirted the slime-green walls of Saint-Sulpice, and was climbing the Rue de Tournon towards the Luxembourg. This was not a part of Paris to which he himself had made a noticeable contribution, and he might reasonably have felt a twinge of resentment at the obvious defects of certain monuments. At this late stage in his career, his most profitable work had been his wooing of Mlle Le Blanc, whose undisputed charms included the fact that she was the daughter of the city's chief architect. Even as the son-in-law of M. Le Blanc, Guillaumot had struggled to make a name for himself. He had built some châteaux in the provinces, and an abbey on the ruins of a monastery at Vézelay, but in Paris, he was known chiefly as an architect of barracks. His talent for shoring up other men's shoddy work had brought him some lucrative but inglorious commissions.

He had married Mlle Le Blanc sixteen years before. Now, in his late forties, he was a tall, stony-faced man with a head that could easily be pictured as a skull. He wore his wig a long way back on his scalp, perhaps in order to expose the full elevation of his brow. The effect was slightly forbidding, but in certain lights there were hints of timidity and gloominess suggestive of profound and frequent meditation, and even a certain generosity of spirit that wanted only recognition to flourish. His passions ran too deep to be visible, and he rarely expressed them, except in print. He had two daughters, several protégés and powerful connections, and saw no professional need for friends.

Even on this day of a new beginning, Charles-Axel Guillaumot was more thoughtful than excited. He fully expected his designs to be stunted by small-minded people and miserly budgets. 'Unhappy is the Artist,' he had written, 'for even before his idea achieves perfection, it is warped by ignorance and envy.' He was already planning a devastating pamphlet, *On the Harm that is Done to Architecture by Ill-Informed and Exaggerated Attacks on the Expenditure Occasioned by the Construction of Public Monuments*, and he was not entirely optimistic about the post that he was about to take up. Ominously, the sedan was lowered to the ground at the end of the Rue de Vaugirard. Something was blocking the road ahead. The King had appointed him to the post on 4 April. Thanks to the incredible slowness of the Ministry, it was now the 24th, and he was obviously destined to be late for his first meeting.

His intention was to inspect the site of the 1774 collapse, and to gauge the solidity of the work carried out by one of the King's architects, M. Dupont. On the day after 'the Mouth of Hell' had opened in the Rue d'Enfer, Dupont had had himself lowered into the trench to a depth of eighty-four feet. By the light of a flaming torch, he had seen a gallery extending north along the line of the street towards the Seine. It appeared to be an ancient quarry, dug by miners who had known nothing of the art of excavation. At several points, the gallery was obstructed by the peculiar formations known as *fontis*. A *fontis* is a cavity that develops when the roof of a subterranean gallery caves in. An arched void forms, and, as rocks tumble in, the cone of rubble migrates upwards. The rounded top of the rubble pile, known as the *cloche*, is usually seen only when the sinkhole has broken through, and when whatever structures had enjoyed the illusion of solidity abruptly vanish from the face of the earth.

The walls of rubble had been consolidated by masons dangling on the end of long cables. Only one man had fallen in, but after spending three hours in the darkness, imagining things that could not possibly exist, he had been winched to safety and recovered after a few days. The street was reopened to traffic in a surprisingly short time, and Dupont had been congratulated on his swift and effective operation. The new *Dictionnaire Historique de la Ville de Paris* had devoted a special section to him, using terms that some might have found a little extravagant:

Men such as the Sieur Denis [they meant Dupont] are a precious boon to Society. He has proved by his example that intrepidity in the preservation of Citizens is not the sole prerogative of the military professions, and that other breeds of men are ready to step into the breach to safeguard the lives of their Compatriots.

Beyond the end of the Rue de Vaugirard, the square where the Rue de La Harpe came up from the Seine was filled with carriages. The Rue d'Enfer had been closed off by the Highways and Buildings Police, and even a sedan would have been unable to get through. Charles-Axel levered himself out of the chair and squeezed through the crowd. At the junction of the Rue Saint-Hiacinte and the Rue d'Enfer, he showed the gendarme his copy of the King's decree. It stated that 'le Sieur Guillaumot' was to 'visit and reconnoitre the quarries dug in the City of Paris and adjacent plains so as to determine the encroachments and excavations that might injure the solidity of its foundations'. The agent ascertained that the gentleman possessed the proper credentials – he wore an embroidered coat and gave off a pleasant smell of flowers – and ushered him through the barrier.

Some people had gathered on the eastern side of the street, just before the convent of the Feuillans des Anges Gardiens. A man of Guillaumot's experience had no need to ask what had happened. A faint odour hung in the air, which he recognized immediately. It was as though a cellar door had just been opened for the first time in centuries. The walls along the street appeared to be intact, but on the other side of a *porte cochère*, the slumped elevations of a stable block were an unmistakeable sign. He entered the courtyard and saw a neatly defined sinkhole with a diameter of about twenty feet. Placing one foot on the rim, he peered down into the pit. He estimated the distance from street-level to the top of the *cloche* to be fifteen feet. The *fontis* itself might extend another seventy or eighty feet.

It was only when he saw the engineers he had arranged to meet at the site of the earlier collapse that he was struck by the significance of the new hole. It had appeared at least half a mile closer to the centre of Paris than the subsidence of 1774. This was not the vague and rubbly zone of shacks and windmills by the customs barrier; it was Paris itself, with its monuments and spires. From where he stood, he could see the dome of the Val-de-Grâce, the towers of half a dozen churches, and, further down the street, on the line of the old

Roman road, the dome of the Sorbonne and the towers of Notre-Dame.

The possibility that the Rue d'Enfer was sinking was remarkable enough in itself, not to mention the fact that the geological formations beneath the street had waited, so to speak, for the very day on which he assumed his duties as Inspector of Quarries. A superstitious man might have imagined that those ministerial delays had been engineered by some unknown power, and that the gradual fissuring and collapse of each successive stratum had been timed to produce a catastrophe on Thursday 24 April 1777. But Charles-Axel Guillaumot had lived in Paris long enough to know that coincidences were everyday events. The source of his agitation lay within, in the memory of those long years when his genius had been stifled and confined. He stood on the edge of the hole, as stones went skittering down into the darkness, and contemplated that gaping wound in the city's foundations as an explorer might gaze on the shores of a new continent.

3

A FEW DAYS into the preliminary exploration of the quarry beneath the Rue d'Enfer, Guillaumot was not surprised to be told by some of the miners of a mysterious trail of footprints. In one of the vaulted cavities, the dust of ages had been disturbed as though by the swishing of a long tail. A worker who wore a sachet of crushed garlic and camphor around his neck (the miners' trusted defence against the effects of noxious gas) told M. Guillaumot of a shadowy form he had seen fleeing along the tunnel. It had left behind 'a funny smell'. Other miners subsequently described the figure as 'green' and 'very fast', from which it was inferred that the creature could see in the dark.

Even the most recent event always seemed to be attached to an ancient legend. Though no subterranean being had been reported before, it was said that anyone who saw *L'Homme Vert* would certainly die or lose a relative within the year. An uncle of one of the miners passed away barely a month after work began, and so the legend was obviously true …

For the first phase of consolidation, he divided his workers into three teams. The 'Excavation' team, composed of migrant workers, was to clear the galleries of rubble. Then the 'Masonry' team would reinforce the roof with pillars, using the stone that had been dug out by the excavators. Inspection pits were sunk at regular intervals from the street, causing road closures and general indignation. Finally, the 'Cartography' team would create a map of the underground labyrinth on a scale of 1:216 – which meant that the map of abandoned quarries would be more detailed than any map that had ever been produced of the streets of Paris.

The most serious obstacles were the numerous *cloches*. Removing one of those towering mounds of rubble was a risky operation, and so the masons, following the architectural plans supplied by Nature and refined by M. Guillaumot, turned each *cloche* into a beautiful, swirling cone of stonework that might have been copied from a strange, inverted cathedral. A lesser architect would have filled the void with rock and sand; Guillaumot created spacious vaults and porticos. Tunnels that had been clumsily hacked out by ignorant hands were dressed with freestone and dignified with coursed limestone walls. On smooth surfaces that would have graced a daylit avenue, salient frames were carved and inscriptions inserted – either painted or engraved – to indicate the place in the sequence of consolidations, the architect of the work ('G' for Guillaumot), and the date.

$$25 \cdot G \cdot 1777$$

For the rest of 1777, and throughout the following year, Charles-Axel Guillaumot matched his tunnels to the streets above. He dug twin galleries beneath the house-fronts on either side of the street, leaving the consolidation of the buildings to their owners. (This was, in part, because a landlord legally owned all the earth beneath his house: he could, if he so wished, try to dig a cellar all the way to hell.) But there was also a certain satisfaction in mirroring the streets and creating a subterranean image of the city. The street names were etched on stone plaques; a *fleur de lys* indicated the proximity of a convent or a church. Only a few outlying *quartiers* had numbered their houses (for the purposes of billeting), and so Guillaumot devised his own numbering system, and applied it so consistently that in that unpopulated world where every wall bore the initial G., a man could find his way more easily than in the congested labyrinth above.

For the first time since his student days in Rome, he found himself in a state of near-contentment. He had feared that the Inspector of Quarries would be little more than a glorified stonemason, but as the work progressed, he saw all around him the indestructible evidence of his own genius. Eighty feet below the Latin Quarter, he knew the silent joy of a man who devotes himself, body and soul, to a single passion.

In view of the accusations that were soon brought against him, it is as well to note that he was the unwavering friend of any man, however humble, who shared his passion. Twice a day, the miners were allowed to breathe the air and to feel the warmth of the sun. One of the miners, an old soldier, chose to spend his hours of freedom underground, carving a replica of Fort Mahon, which he had helped to capture from the British in 1756. One day, he was chiselling away at his model when the roof fell in. Guillaumot ordered a monument to be raised to his memory:

Here, after braving the battle's fury for thirty years, this courageous veteran met his end, and died as he had lived, serving King and Country.

A poet was commissioned to write a eulogy to the work of consolidation. Since the work was far from over, it might be said that the Inspector of Quarries was tempting fate. Yet the subject of the eulogy was not the architect himself but the redemptive art he practised:

Without that art whose great power bears its weight,
The vast metropolis and all its palaces of stone
That make their ancient cradle creak and groan
Would have vanished into the bowels whence they came.

IT WAS PROBABLY inevitable that ignorance and envy would try to undermine his work. Dupont, whose consolidations had proved inadequate, tried to stir up rebellion among the miners by telling them that they were underpaid. In the echoing corridors of the Ministry of Finance, he whispered that M. Guillaumot was squandering public money, wasting millions of livres on needless masterpieces when they might have been spent on sanitation, roads and national defence.

Guillaumot paid less attention to these rumblings than perhaps he should. But they reached his ears at precisely the time when a terrible truth was dawning, compared to which his rival's machinations were nothing but a spider's web in a bottomless abyss.

4

WHEN THE SEPARATE sections of the underground map were pieced together, Charles-Axel saw the city's past spread out before him like a gallery of historical paintings. The Gauls and the Romans had dug their building stone from open quarries near the Seine. Eventually, they had burrowed into the hills to the north and south, following the ancient bed of the river. As the city spread from the island to both banks, the quarries deepened, and Paris began to devour its own foundations – sand for glass and smelting, gypsum for plaster, limestone for walls, green clay for bricks and tiles. Giant wheels had once lined the Rue Saint-Jacques: a horse that walked three miles in a circle could winch up a six-ton block of limestone. Some of the best building stone, which had gone to make Notre-Dame, the Palais-Royal and the mansions of the Marais, had come from beneath the Rue d'Enfer. The miners had dug away as much stone as they dared, leaving just enough to support the roof. Years later, other miners had found the worked-out quarries, and dug down to lower layers. The floor of each quarry then became the roof of yet another mine, so that now, instead of finding solid rock beneath the tunnel floor, Guillaumot encountered vast cavities buttressed only by a few teetering piles of stone.

Far below the surface, he could hear the rumble of carriages above. It was perhaps at such a moment that he comprehended the full horror of the situation: the enormous weight of all the streets and houses of the Left Bank was supported by nothing but slender pillars of limestone.

The irreparable destruction of half of Paris would have been a disaster to rival the Great Lisbon Earthquake. But there was also another, more intimate threat. During his long hours in the underworld, his perception of the task had changed. Now, his own architectural wonders underpinned the city. They, too, would be annihilated if those feeble props gave way.

In the circumstances, he might be forgiven for the manner in which he swept aside the obstacles that were placed in his path by the envious Dupont.

Having established himself as the man who could save Paris, Guillaumot was able to call on the assistance of policemen and spies. Some of the miners and miners' widows who had been persuaded to petition the King for higher wages were sent to jail. Dupont himself was placed under surveillance. His home was searched, and he was threatened with exile to a remote province. He was asked to consider the unpleasantness of being 'left to rot in a dungeon of the Bastille'. When he felt the ground give way beneath his feet, he signed a document that was, according to Guillaumot, 'written in his own hand, freely, and at his own home', announcing his immediate retirement, and acknowledging that Charles-Axel Guillaumot was a man of unimpeachable honour.

THROUGHOUT THE NEXT ten years, even in the deepest, most dangerous galleries, the miners sometimes saw the tall figure of M. Guillaumot walking the silent streets of his subterranean realm, his face as pale as though it were painted with white lead. No one questioned his decisions, and no one tried to reduce his budgets. Every line that he traced on sheets of drawing-paper turned into solid reality. While the King's rebellious ministers grumbled at the continuing expense of Versailles, Guillaumot was quietly constructing the largest architectural ensemble in all of Europe. If those galleries had been placed end to end, they would have reached the edge of the Massif Central, two hundred miles away. More cartographers were employed on the map of the underworld than had worked on

Cassini's map of the entire kingdom. When he uncovered a mile-long section of the Roman aqueduct that had fed the baths on the Rue de la Harpe, he rebuilt and improved it, connected it to the repaired Médicis aqueduct that led to the Luxembourg and the Palais-Royal, adorned it with finely sculpted corbels, and created a dark triumphal avenue for the city's fresh water.

Far from the light of day, Guillaumot attained a state of professional fulfilment in which the very notion of happiness had become irrelevant. His comprehension of the city's past now exceeded anything that could be found in books. He amassed a collection of curious stone animals, and some intriguing formations that he took to be petrified fruits. There was no doubt in his mind that where he walked there had once been an ocean. One of the miners, a Breton sailor, claimed to have recognized the remnants of a ship in a layer of compacted silt. Perhaps more than two thousand years ago, a great flood had brought boulders of porphyry and granite from the south. Men who had lived there long before the Gauls must have seen their settlement destroyed by an unimaginable catastrophe.

He had seen with his own eyes what little remained of the city the Romans had called Lutetia – a shattered aqueduct, some brick walls and conduits, a few coins and broken busts. He knew that his own creation would outlive the city. When the centuries had turned the Louvre and the Tuileries to dust, the works of Charles-Axel Guillaumot would be the only evidence that Paris had once been great.

All his subterranean kingdom lacked was a population.

THEN, ONE DAY, across the river, the inhabitants of the Rue de la Lingerie found their cellars overrun with decomposing corpses. The Cimetière des Saints Innocents had been founded in the ninth century, just outside the city. It had remained in use for nine hundred years. As the graveyard filled up, the ground had slowly bulged, and, at last, one of the retaining walls had given way.

Guillaumot at once recommended that all nine centuries' worth of putrefaction be transported to an ossuary that he proposed to install in the consolidated quarries. The plan was adopted. It was decided in addition that all the other corpses that were polluting the city should be moved to the same place.

Beyond the Enfer customs barrier was a street called La Tombe-Issoire. It owed its dismal name to an ancient funerary slab, which local people identified as the tomb of a Saracen giant called Isouard who had threatened Paris in the days of the crusades. It was there, beneath the street, that Guillaumot prepared a three-acre site, with an entrance in the Rue d'Enfer. In memory of Rome, he called his ossuary the Catacombs.

The biggest ever relocation of dead Parisians began in 1786. For more than a year, the inhabitants of several *quartiers* were kept awake by blazing torches, chanting priests, and carts that sometimes dropped portions of human body along the route. It was a fifteen-month-long procession in which the whole history of Paris was represented. There were nuns from convent graveyards and lepers from cemeteries that had once lain outside the city walls. The victims of the Saint Bartholomew's Day massacre were lumped together with the Catholics who had killed them. Some of the oldest bones came from unrecorded burial grounds. They were the remains of men and women who had died before Saint Denis had Christianized the city in the third century. It was said that the number of skeletons that made the journey to La Tombe-Issoire was ten times greater than the living population of Paris.

Guillaumot waited for the dead millions to arrive before completing his masterpiece. At Montrouge, beyond the Place d'Enfer, the skeletons were tipped into a hole. A dangling chain scattered the bones as they fell, and prevented them from blocking up the shaft. At the bottom, they were arranged in columns and courses. There were walls of tibias and femurs, decorative friezes of skulls, 'and other ornamental arrangements in keeping with the character of the place'. Such was the architectural splendour of the necropolis that the horror of death was stifled by the multitude.

A FEW YEARS AFTER that great procession of the dead, when the Revolution had turned Paris into a hell on earth, the Catacombs received the anonymous bones of aristocrats who had perished in the great upheaval. Guillaumot himself spent that chaotic period in a prison cell, a victim of slander, disgruntled workers and his close association with the former regime. But he had the imperishable joy of knowing that his achievements would last forever. He was freed from prison in 1794 and continued as Inspector of Quarries and as Director of the Gobelins Tapestry Works until his death in 1807. Half his adult life had been devoted to the salvation of Paris.

He was buried in the Cimetière Sainte-Catherine, in the east of the city, between the Gobelins and the Rue d'Enfer, but when the remaining cemeteries of Paris were excavated in 1883, Guillaumot's gravestone disappeared. His bones were gathered up with all the others, carried to the ossuary he had built, and incorporated into the walls. Somewhere now in that vast cathedral of calcium and phosphate, Charles-Axel Guillaumot is still helping to prevent Paris from vanishing into the void.

5

THE MAN WHO SAVED Paris died two hundred years ago. It is almost as long since he was mentioned in any history of Paris. Men who demolished or caused the destruction of large parts of the city are commemorated in street names and statues, but there are no memorials to the work of Charles-Axel Guillaumot. A side-street near the Gare de Lyon is called the Rue Guillaumot, but it was named after a local landowner, and has no connection with Charles-Axel.

He might have seen this as ingratitude, or as tacit recognition that the debt could never be repaid. But perhaps it is simply that the City of Paris is reluctant to remind its citizens and visitors of what lies beneath their feet.

The section of the Rue d'Enfer that collapsed in 1777 on Guillaumot's first day at work was incorporated in 1859 into the new Boulevard Saint-Michel. In 1879, the remainder of the street was renamed Rue Denfert-Rochereau, after the colonel who defended Belfort against the Prussians. No doubt the naming committee felt that the railway terminus should bear a less forbidding name than 'Paris-d'Enfer'. Or perhaps the pun, d'Enfer / Denfert, was an attempt to hide the traces of the old Street of Hell without entirely denying the Devil his share.

When the Rue d'Enfer was renamed in 1879, no one had any reason to fear a recurrence of those infernal disasters. The cracks that damaged three houses that year, near the site of the 1774 collapse, were blamed on the railway trains that rumbled in and out of the Denfert terminus. Further down the street, towards the centre of Paris, geologists and mineralogists had shown their confidence in the work of consolidation by moving the École des Mines to the edge of the Jardin du Luxembourg, opposite the site of the 1777 collapse.

One day the following April (1879), at six o'clock in the evening, lecturers and students leaving the School were surprised to see the barber who lived across the boulevard sitting in his dining room, exposed to the passers-by. He was holding his knife and fork, looking down at his dinner, which was perched on a *cloche de fontis* that had just completed its long journey up from the depths. The house-fronts of numbers 77, 79, and 81 Boulevard Saint-Michel had detached themselves from the rest of the block and disappeared. This time, citizens were more inclined to blame the accident on the Highways and Bridges Department than on the Devil.

Such incidents are now comparatively rare. The public streets, and any building that belongs to the City of Paris, have little to fear from subsidence. Only about ten sinkholes appear each year. Most of them are quite small, and few people have died as a result. The larger holes are dealt with according to modern techniques, and the people affected are re-housed at the expense of the city. The vast cavity that appeared under the Gare du Nord in 1975 was promptly filled with two thousand five hundred cubic metres of cement. Practically all of Paris, apart from Montmartre and certain *quartiers* to the east of the Place Denfert-Rochereau, is now officially deemed to be safe.

LOST

'You cannot imagine the intrigues that are being woven all around us, and every day I make strange discoveries in my own house.'

Marie-Antoinette,
letter to Gabrielle de Polignac, Tuesday, 28 July 1789

NOT LONG AGO, in the old days, the place had served her well as a pied-à-terre. When she attended the Opera and the performance finished late, it had been a blessing to spend the night in Paris and to avoid the long ride home on a dusty road. Now that she had been forced to make it her permanent home, its disadvantages were obvious. Even when the tenants had been evicted and their apartments refurbished, it felt cramped and over-complicated. She occupied the ground floor and an entresol on one side of the building; her husband and the children were on the floor above. If things had been different, she and some of the ladies might have been pleased to be lodged in the city, but she rarely came home after dark these days, and had never much enjoyed the thought of her husband enthroned in his geography room, peering down through his telescope as her carriage entered the courtyard.

She was used to the inconvenience: all her homes had been building sites. Sometimes, she found herself envying the peasant who could put up his hovel in a day. There were rooms she had planned that she would never see, except as watercolour sketches and pasteboard models. After the wedding, her first bedroom had been strewn with the confetti of flaking plaster and gold paint. In her impatience to be settled she had ordered a plain white ceiling, but His Highness had insisted on a full restoration, with paintings of corpulent nymphs set in gilded stucco. As she came to know the ins and outs of family history and finance, this regime of endless renovation had at least allowed her to impose her own taste. Parts of the gardens were almost exactly as she had intended. The old labyrinth had been uprooted and replaced with an English grove in which she could almost imagine herself at home. But now, in the new residence, every 'improvement' was dictated by circumstance.

Carpenters had installed sliding doors behind the shelves in some of the wardrobes. A section of wood panelling behind a tapestry disguised another secret door that opened onto a small staircase. The false floors that had been added for forgotten purposes made it hard to form an impression of the building as a whole. Her home had been turned into a maze. To reach the courtyard, she would have to slip out of her apartments at the rear, walk along a corridor past an empty apartment, then descend another staircase. Nothing would ever have been straightforward in such a place, and she was not entirely unhappy to be leaving it behind.

Her apartments looked away from the courtyard, onto the gardens and the river to the left. When the wind blew from that direction and threw rain against the glass, she saw nothing but dim avenues of trees marching towards the Place de Louis XV. The gardens had been noisier in the daytime since soldiers, servants and poorly dressed people had been allowed in. At night, they were closed to the public and, presumably, empty, but there were sounds to which she had recently become attuned, a vast and blurry soundscape formed by distant walls and embankments that seemed to catch the whispers of the city.

Beyond the railings and the line of trees that were treated as though the terrace were the back-lane in a village, Parisians learned to swim in their river under wooden sheds, and engaged in other incomprehensible activities that involved shouting and waving long poles about. On the far bank, there was nothing much to see. She knew from some of her friends and her husband's confessor that the people there enjoyed a finer prospect (her home was part of the vista), though they were disturbed by the wood yards that spoiled the appearance of the riverbank. If the piles of wood caught fire, her friends would be forced to flee by the servants' quarters into the web of streets behind the grand facades of what was now the Quai Voltaire. Some of them, she knew, would be forced to flee in any case.

THOUGH ELABORATE on paper, the plan would apparently be straightforward in the execution. She had organized the journey herself as far as Châlons, but her husband had shown a lively interest in the smallest details. After the horrendous exodus from Versailles, when the guardsmen's heads were wigged and powdered and held aloft on pikes, it had been a consoling hobby. He was a man who liked to fiddle with simple but intricate mechanisms. More than once, he had been found kneeling at doors in various parts of the building, trying to pick the lock. He was thrilled by the thought of a modern house crammed with curious contraptions. A certain M. Guillaumot, a relative of her friend, M. de Fersen, who was to drive the coach, had been commissioned to design an underground fortress for the new home, which, she supposed, would hardly allow for much decorative fancy.

While she sat in her drawing room discussing the contents of the trunk (the diamonds, a warming pan, a silver basin, etc.), the King was talking to a group of men who were about to set off on a great expedition through France, from the Channel coast to the Mediterranean Sea. Their mission was to determine the exact line of the Paris meridian, which ran a few yards from where she sat, across the Place du Palais-Royal and the maze of alleyways that huddled between the Tuileries and the Louvre. Mathematical exactitude would force them to pass through wild regions south of the Loire that were untouched by civilization, and whose inhabitants had never heard of Paris. But once they had finished, they would be able to create maps of unprecedented accuracy, which, among other things, would keep His Highness happily engrossed for weeks on end.

Their own expedition called for a similar degree of precision, but it would be considerably more dangerous. M. de Fersen had ordered a special long-distance coach that was to wait outside the city at the Barrière Saint-Martin. Meanwhile, General de Bouillé was positioning loyal troops at various key points along the route to the eastern frontier. Nothing had been left to chance. The coach contained a well-stocked larder, a cooker, and a false floor that could be turned into a dining table. Apart from this, and its great size, it was unremarkable. The King himself had selected the three guards who were to assist in the departure. He had been advised to employ men who were used to finding their way in difficult circumstances – a gendarme, a soldier, and a retired postmaster who was said to know 'every road in the kingdom' – but His Majesty had wanted to demonstrate the high regard in which he held his *gardes du corps*, and had asked the commanding officer to provide three men, without revealing the nature of their mission.

To avoid arousing suspicion, they were to leave in four separate groups. The governess would take the dauphin and his sister to the nearby Rue de l'Échelle, where M. de Fersen would be waiting outside a busy hotel, disguised as a cab driver. Three-quarters of an hour later, they would be joined by the King's sister Mme Élisabeth, and, when the ceremony of the Coucher du Roi was over and the King had been put to bed, by the King himself, dressed as a *valet de chambre*. (Every night for the last two weeks, a valet whose height and orb-like corporation gave him a remarkable resemblance to the King had left by the main door, and the sentries were used to seeing him pass.) The Queen would leave the palace last of all, with one of the trusted bodyguards, M. de Malden.

The route from her apartments to the corner of the Rue de l'Échelle was short enough to present no obvious difficulties. The Tuileries Palace formed what would have been the western edge of a great rectangle if the Louvre had ever been completed. It was separated from the Place du Carrousel and the warren of medieval slums that occupied most of the rectangle by three walled courtyards. The courtyard closest to the river and her apartments, and furthest from the Rue de l'Échelle, was the Cour des Princes. Once beyond the courtyards, one might be said to have left the palace. Then there was just the Place du Carrousel, a corner of the King's stables, and the lozenge-shaped remnant of a square before the Rue de l'Échelle. The total distance was less than five hundred yards.

The courtyards were always busy with lawyers, ambassadors, servants and, recently, rough-looking men whose business was known only to themselves. Cabs and carriages waited in line for their passengers to emerge from the palace and the neighbouring hotels. Few people believed the rumours spread by some hysterical journalists that the royal family was intending to escape, but M. de La Fayette had doubled the guard just in case, and ordered the palace to be lit as though for a grand occasion. The Queen was to wear a broad-brimmed hat to hide her face – a needless precaution, she thought, since some of her own friends had failed to recognize her after her hair had turned white. In the unlikely event that she was stopped by a sentry, she was to identify herself as Mme Bonnet, a governess. One day, the people of Paris, who had been led astray by ruffians, would say that their Queen had been well suited to the role.

As a foreigner in Paris, like herself, M. de Fersen, a Swedish nobleman, was probably better equipped for the task than a native. A French aristocrat would not have been able to sustain a casual conversation, as M. de Fersen did, in cab-drivers' slang, nor would he have had the wit to provide himself with a cheap snuff-box from which to offer his bothersome interlocutor a pinch. Thanks to his skilful impersonation, he was able to stand his ground in front of the lodging inn, until Mme de Tourzel arrived with the King's daughter and the sleeping dauphin dressed as a little girl. Without waiting for the King's sister, Fersen set off with his precious cargo, drove along the quays, turned right across the Place de Louis XV and returned along the Rue Saint-Honoré to rejoin the line of cabs in the Rue de l'Échelle.

While they waited in fearful silence, a woman circled the cab. The door opened, and Mme Élisabeth clambered in, stepping on the little dauphin, who was hidden under Mme de Tourzel's skirts. She explained in flustered tones that she had passed within a whisker of M. de La Fayette's coach, which was taking him to attend the Coucher du Roi. Then they settled down to wait for Their Majesties to emerge from the palace.

From the corner of the Rue de l'Échelle, it was possible to see some of the upper windows of the palace, brilliantly lit from the outside, as though a great spectacle were about to begin. The bells of neighbouring churches began to strike midnight, but there was still no sign of the King. It was not until the dignitaries had departed – somewhat later than expected – and the *valet de chambre* had seen His Majesty washed, disrobed and laid between the sheets, that a portly servant who would have answered to the name Durand walked calmly down the steps of the main entrance and passed through the sentry-box of the Cour des Tuileries. As the servant began to cross the Place du Carrousel, the sentry's attention was drawn by the sound of a brass shoe-buckle clattering across the cobbles. He saw the servant retrieve his buckle, kneel down and deftly make the necessary repair, before setting off again in the direction of the Rue de l'Échelle.

Though the unforeseen delay had made the occupants of the cab almost sick with apprehension, the King, as he settled into his seat opposite the ladies, expressed the view that these small setbacks were just the sort of contretemps that proved the soundness of the plot. Even a clockwork mechanism contained imperfect pieces, which, by compensating for one another's failings, in a well-regulated system of balances and escapements, coaxed the whole machine into a satisfactory semblance of accuracy. He was not, therefore, unduly troubled by the non-appearance of the Queen.

BY THEN, AS PLANNED, the Queen had left the palace on foot with M. de Malden. They had passed, unchallenged, through the guard-post of the Cour des Princes, and were about to cross the Place du Carrousel when a blaze of light approached from the side. Just in time, they squeezed into the narrow *guichet* that led out of the square, and, as the carriage thundered by, she saw quite distinctly, framed by its window, the features of M. de La Fayette. An impulse stronger than the instinct for survival made her try to hit the carriage with her stick. According to one of the other bodyguards, M. de Malden tried to reassure the Queen, though it seems more likely that the Queen had to reassure her escort, and that she tried to instil in him the courage that comes with a sense of destiny and duty. In a few moments, they would be sitting safely in M. de Fersen's cab, well on their way to meeting the coach at the Barrière Saint-Martin.

It was then that something apparently extraordinary but in fact quite normal occurred. It was described in the years to come by several of the people involved, including General de Bouillé. The most detailed account, and the closest in time to the incident itself, was written by her chaplain, M. de Fontanges, who recorded his later conversations with the Queen. Some modern historians have doubted that such a thing could ever have happened, but they live in an age when cities are filled with aids to navigation, when there are enough signposts to obliterate the sights they indicate, and when the streets of Paris could be carpeted several times over with street-maps of Paris.

As the coach disappeared into the night, the Queen and her bodyguard left the Tuileries through the *guichet* in which they had taken cover. They knew, from the King's instructions, that they were to turn left on leaving the palace. They also knew that it was impossible to go wrong, and that despite the momentary confusion caused by the appearance of La Fayette's coach, they were only a few hundred yards from the meeting point.

In front of them, beyond the parapet, was the river, and, a little to the right, clearly delineated by the reflector lamps, the Pont Royal, which led to the Left Bank. A few lights were burning in the tall houses on the opposite bank, but the quays were deserted, and so, without wasting any more time, they crossed the Pont Royal, and hurried into the street that opened on the far side of the bridge.

No one knows for certain whether it was M. de Malden who led the way, or whether, out of deference to the Queen, he simply followed in her wake. The other two guards left personal accounts of the night's adventure: François-Melchior de Moustier remembered only that the Queen had been frightened by the sight of La Fayette and became separated from her guide; François de Valory wrote a more detailed account, but his notes were lost, and when he came to retell the story in 1815, he found that his memories had faded. However, he did recall being told that the Queen 'at once left the arm of her guide and began to flee in the opposite direction, with the guide following her as closely as he could'. The third bodyguard, who might have settled the matter, never wrote his memoirs, for a reason that might be guessed. The Queen herself, in conversations with her chaplain, graciously shared the blame: 'Her guide knew Paris even less than she ... They turned right instead of left, and crossed the Pont Royal.'

In ideal circumstances, a rational person might have paused to consider the situation, and realized that, if the chosen route were correct, the Tuileries Palace must lie on an island ... But circumstances were not conducive to calm reflection, and since the street in question lay on approximately the same line as the palace and the Rue de l'Échelle – though in the opposite direction – the route was sufficiently plausible to allow wishful thinking to lead the way.

The street they had entered was the Rue du Bac, named after the ferry that had been used to carry the stones that built the Tuileries. But street signs were still a rarity: it was not until 1805 that the Prefect of Paris made sense of the muddle by inscribing the names of streets on yellow porcelain plaques – red letters for those that ran parallel to the Seine, and black for those that ran away from it.

They passed one street and then another, expecting at any moment to see M. de Fersen's cab standing on a corner. The road bent slightly to the right, and ran between the high walls of grand *hôtels*, and then between a convent and a chapel. They might have been in the aristocratic *faubourg* of a provincial town. Calculating their position from the probable delays and the known itinerary, and assuming a speed of four miles an hour, they must have advanced along the Rue du Bac until all hope of finding the Rue de l'Échelle was lost, to the point where the sounds of wailing and an occasional scream might lead a stranger to imagine that he had stumbled on a secret purgatory on the edge of the city: the Rue du Bac ended in an area once reserved for lepers, between the Hospice des Incurables and the Petites Maisons, where lunatics were locked away.

Only now did they turn back towards the river. But instead of retracing their steps, they chose a different route, as though, in addition to being lost, they had still not realized that their principal mistake lay in crossing the river.

AT THIS POINT, attention inevitably turns to M. de Malden. There is no question of his deliberately misleading the Queen. He was simply a man who was used to following orders, who found himself in an unknown street at night with a woman who lashed out at passing carriages, and who had a surprising ability to get lost a few yards from her own home; a woman, moreover, who, in view of her rank, might not take kindly to contradiction.

The Queen may well have reproached her escort with incompetence. She may even have suggested ways in which he might have prepared himself better for a journey of less than five hundred yards. Not only her own life but also those of her children and her husband were at stake, not to mention the future of civilized Europe.

M. de Malden's failure to equip himself with a map, or to study one in advance, is perhaps not quite as reprehensible as it seemed to General de Bouillé when he wrote his memoirs and exclaimed at the 'inconceivable ignorance' of the Queen's escort. (He was too polite to criticize the Queen herself.) But to explain exactly how M. de Malden was able to lose his way so completely would require a long detour in a story which is itself a long digression. Suffice it to say (since a brief digression is after all unavoidable) that M. de Malden was a man of his time: he might follow the dictates of Reason, but he could look for enlightenment only where Reason had cast its light.

In 1791, Paris was effectively uncharted. There were one or two beautifully engraved maps of the city that showed the streets in the proper proportions. These maps were known to army officers, librarians, kings and rich collectors, few of whom had any practical use for them. Strangers were commonly advised to climb a monument if they wished to form an impression of the city as a whole. Crude plans sold by stationers showed the approximate location of the principal sights and avenues, but little else. A map was supposed to be a compliment to the city, not a brutal exposure of its medieval meanderings and cul-de-sacs. Cointeraux's map of 'Paris As It Is Today' (1798) painstakingly omitted all the minor streets, 'for otherwise the map would have presented nothing but a veritable chaos'.

The inhabitants of Paris had managed quite well since the days when the city was confined to an island. Most people never left their *quartier*, and for those who went further afield, there were cabs. 'Parisians', said Louis-Sébastien Mercier, 'take cabs for even the shortest journey'. This may have been good sense as much as laziness: 'Not even the inhabitants of the capital may flatter themselves on knowing its streets', the Larousse encyclopedia observed in 1874. The topographical knowledge of cab drivers themselves is something of a mystery. In all the centuries of regulations pertaining to hired carriages, there is not a single mention of the need to be familiar with the streets. There are hundreds of rules concerning speed and sobriety, suspension and interior padding, the proper feeding of horses, the undesirability of blocking pavements, driving through processions, insulting pedestrians, mistreating female passengers and removing one's clothes in warm weather, but nothing that required a driver to know the shortest way to get from one place to another. But since cabs eventually displayed lanterns of different colours to show which part of Paris they would serve, it might be assumed that the drivers' knowledge had always been limited in any case, and that the exact route was often left to the whim of the cab horse.

Half a century after Marie-Antoinette was lost on the Left Bank, the benefits of a city map were still far from obvious, even to the people who printed them. In 1853, a guide for typesetters 'who do not know the capital', but who wished to find work there, listed sixty printing-works in an extraordinarily long piece of prose that was intended to serve as an itinerary. The unemployed typesetter was to have himself delivered to a print-shop on the Rue de Rivoli ('formerly no. 14 of the Rue des Fossés-Saint-Germain, the staircase on the right after the first courtyard'), and then,

> On leaving this establishment, turn left along the Rue de Rivoli as far as the Rue Saint-Denis, where you should turn right and go down to the very end of this street, cross the Place du Châtelet and the Pont-au-Change, and into the Rue de la Barillerie, which is facing you, to the first street on the right, which is the Rue de la Sainte-Chapelle, where, at no. 5, is M. Boucquin.

The complete tour, 'supposing that one spend two minutes in each workshop, will occupy seven and a half hours' – after which the unfortunate typesetter could make a start on the list of 'all print-shops within a 100-kilometre radius of Paris'.

It so happens that, on that Monday night, perhaps not far from the Rue du Bac, the man best able to direct the Queen was working on one of the great masterpieces of modern cartography. Somewhere in that vast, confusing city, Edme Verniquet was squinting through a spyglass, measuring the angle of a street corner while a servant held up a torch. (He and his team of sixty geometers always took their measurements at night, when they could work without being jostled by the crowd, pestered by dogs, or crushed by carriages.) His dream was to create the first completely reliable map of Paris on a scale that would show every buckling wall and crooked niche: he had started work on it, at his own expense, fifteen years before, and it was still several years from completion. The King had given his blessing to the project, but the new government proved less enthusiastic. When it was asked to fund the expedition, a *député* demanded that the matter be sent to committee for discussion, 'in order to determine whether or not this map is really of any use'.

I F   T H E   Q U E E N and her escort had shared Edme Verniquet's bird's-eye view of Paris, they would have seen that the street whose course they had followed formed the outer edge of a spider's web of lanes centred on the Croix Rouge crossroads. Some of those lanes were reassuringly straight, but they bisected other streets at odd angles, creating squares that were parallelograms, and trapezoids that seemed to rearrange themselves from one day to the next. Time in those asymmetrical streets passed at some indeterminable speed. It might have been five minutes or half an hour since they crossed the bridge to the Left Bank.

By chance or by smell, they found their way back, via the Rue des Saints-Pères or some other adjacent artery, to the river, and re-emerged on the *quai*, but further upstream from the Pont Royal. The walls of the Louvre faced them from the opposite bank. The *quais* were still deserted, but a sentinel had resumed his post on the far side of the bridge. To the left, the Queen could see, as though in memory, her wing of the Tuileries Palace, and perhaps for the first time surmised its place in the larger scheme of the city. A short distance beyond it, her husband and children were sitting in the cab, counting the minutes, wondering when the King's absence would be discovered, and whether or not the Queen had been arrested as a traitor.

Perhaps it was the calm that comes with desperation, or perhaps just the impatience of someone who, having wrapped up for a long journey, is forced to take vigorous exercise: as though the whole adventure had been a masquerade, and there was no further need for dissimulation, the Queen and her escort now walked up to the sentinel on the bridge, and asked for directions to the Hôtel du Gaillardbois on the Rue de l'Échelle.

Assuming that he knew the way, the sentinel could hardly have directed two citizens on foot to take a short-cut through the palace, and they could hardly be seen to ignore his directions – which would explain why the Queen's involuntary exploration of Paris led her into the labyrinth of slums that had survived for centuries on the very doorstep of the royal palace.

The Quartier du Doyenné was a relic of the medieval city. Coiled within that small space were almost three miles of malodorous alleyways, some of which were barely distinguishable from drains. There were slums that might once have been abbeys, and curious dips and mounds that were the uninscribed memorials of the vaults and streets of earlier ages. Some of the cul-de-sacs led to patches of wasteground cluttered with stones intended for the Louvre. At night, it looked as though the Louvre itself were being demolished, while the ancient hovels in its midst were preserved in a state of permanent decay.

As they picked their way through the unlit lanes, a church bell struck a quarter or a half of the hour. In a small town, they might now have taken their bearings, but in Paris, a peculiar situation had arisen. The oldest churches, like Notre-Dame, pointed east-south-east along the river, following Christian tradition, with the rising sun illuminating the window behind the altar. But such was the demand for space that other churches had had to fit themselves in as best they could. Saint-Sulpice, founded in 1646, was probably the last church in Paris to be 'oriented'; now, they pointed in all directions. Of the four churches within two hundred yards of the Queen and her escort, only one pointed east. Seen from the air, the great fleet of churches would appear to have moored itself in a busy harbour full of smaller vessels each going about its own business. By the end of the eighteenth century, it was only a man with the science of Edme Verniquet who could look to the churches of Paris for guidance, by climbing their steeples and using them as triangulation points.

Since the several accounts of the escape disagree in the details, it is impossible to say exactly how much of that labyrinth they explored, or how much time had elapsed when they came upon the Rue Saint-Honoré and walked along its lighted pavements for a hundred yards to find the other members of the royal family beside themselves with anguish. The King – according to the governess's account – displayed the affection that had often struggled to express itself in the years of pomp and protocol. He threw his arms around his Queen, kissed her quite passionately, and exclaimed, several times, 'How happy I am to see you!'

M. de Fersen, knowing the tricks that streets can play, instead of trying to reach the north-eastern perimeter by passing through Paris at its widest point, drove east along the Rue Saint-Honoré and the meandering Faubourg Saint-Antoine, all the way to the Bastille, where he turned left and followed the boulevards until, at long last, after a journey of more than three miles, he took what might be called the exit at the Barrière Saint-Martin. He could, of course, have turned left much earlier at the church of Saint-Merri, and pursued the conveniently straight hypotenuse provided by the Rue Saint-Martin. But it is easy to give directions after the event. The expedition, all told, went off much better than it might have done. As the custom-built carriage raced through the Forest of Bondy and set out across the plains of Brie and Champagne, passing the point at which the news from Paris could have overtaken them, the King declared himself extremely satisfied. He imagined the effect that his address to 'Frenchmen, and above all Parisians' would have on the National Assembly, and he announced to the other occupants of the coach with undisguised delight,

> So, here I am out of that city of Paris, where I've had to swallow so much bile. I can tell you all that, once I've got my arse back in the saddle, you'll see a very different man from the one you've seen until now!

His optimism at this point in the journey was fully justified. In fact, had it not been for the long delays in Paris, they would have reached Pont-de-Sommevesle, a hundred and ten miles to the east, before the royalist troops were forced to decamp by a suspicious populace; and they would not have been exposed to the curiosity of the citizens of Sainte-Menehould, one of whom, a postmaster's son, recognized the King from the face on a coin. This was at eight o'clock in the evening of 21 June 1791: the journey had lasted barely six-and-a-half hours. At about the same time, one of those tireless Parisian wits, who seemed to thrive in even the darkest times, attached a piece of paper to the walls of the Tuileries Palace:

> Citizens are advised that a fat pig has fled the Tuileries. Whoever encounters him is requested – in exchange for a modest reward – to bring him home.

*   *   *

16 October 1793

The view from the Place de la Révolution (formerly Place de Louis XV) was one of the finest in Paris. The afternoon sun shone through the trees on the Champs-Élysées and bathed the square in deep shadows and pink light – which is why the face of Charlotte Corday appeared to blush when her head was shown to the crowd. The phenomenon, observed by several thousand people, gave rise to an official scientific enquiry into the question of sensory survival, and, since Mlle Corday had dressed herself nicely in the manner of her native Caen, it started a fashion for lacy Norman bonnets.

The men and women who were taken to the square in open carts showed astounding calm. For all the ferocious, gloating rhetoric of the sans-culottes, there is scarcely a single account of an aristocrat disgracing herself with a cowardly display. The words of those who stood ten feet above the square and looked about them at the scene of chaos contained by uniformed soldiers and by the very architecture of the city are almost universally impressive:

> 'O Liberty! What crimes are committed in thy name!'
> (To the plaster statue erected in the square.)
>
> 'May my blood cement the happiness of the French.'
>
> 'Monsieur, I beg your pardon. I did not do it on purpose.'
> (To the executioner, after stepping on his foot.)

They came in tumbrels from the Conciergerie, across the river, and along the Rue Saint-Honoré. It was a journey of about two miles. Some of them, as they descended from the cart and climbed the wooden steps, knew for the first time in their lives exactly where they were, and how they had got there. At the end of her ride through Paris, Mme Roland asked for pen and ink so as to record the last moments of her journey, and 'to consign to paper the discoveries she had made on the way from the Conciergerie to the Place de la Révolution'.

Though she seemed to commune silently with herself and to concentrate on her courage, the Queen at times appeared to become observant of her surroundings. Several witnesses saw her studying the revolutionary inscriptions on the walls, and the tricolour flags that flew from windows. She would have heard the noonday cannon in the Palais-Royal. As the cart turned off the Rue Saint-Honoré and into the square, she was seen to look across the gardens towards the Tuileries Palace. 'Signs of deep emotion' were noted on her face by the official reporter.

From that vantage point, the city had an almost providential air. Several of Verniquet's principal triangulation points were visible from the Place de la Révolution, and several more if the observer was on a platform: the dome of the Tuileries, the north tower of Saint-Sulpice and the summit of Montmartre. By some inexplicable design, the curve of the Seine appeared to have been straightened, so that the eye might have traced an uninterrupted line along the palace walls and the river to the hills beyond the city. The colonnades of the Tuileries, the tall houses that ran away to the east and the billowing architecture of clouds that rested on the rooftops made it possible to imagine that what had seemed a chaos created by the centuries was in fact a model of the heavenly city. From the centre of the square, one could see a long way and be seen from a great distance. A man who was standing that day in front of the Tuileries Palace, and who, hearing the noise of the crowd, climbed onto the pedestal of a statue, quite distinctly saw the blade of the guillotine fall, at a distance of almost half a mile.

RESTORATION

IT ENDED SOMEWHERE IN England in 1828. An elderly man lay in bed, dying of an illness that left his mind clear enough to feel the weight of sin that clung to his immortal soul. Beside the bed, a French Catholic priest sat at a writing desk with a sheaf of paper. A scene like this suggests Soho, where most French exiles and expatriates lived. The abbé P ... (only his initial is known) would have heard dozens of death-bed confessions in which the recent history of France was twisted up in personal tales of loss and betrayal, but this man's tale was long and twisted even by the standards of exile. Fortunately, the story had told itself in his head so many times that the dictation was quite straightforward.

He reached the end of his tale – his flight from Paris and arrival in England. Then the abbé handed him the confession and held the candle while the dying man scratched his signature on every page. A few days later, he died and the abbé P ... kept his promise: he sent the signed confession to the Prefect of Police in Paris. In the accompanying letter, he explained that he and his parishioner thought that 'the police should be apprised of the series of abominable events of which this wretch was both the agent and the victim'.

There might have been a brief investigation and some tying-up of loose ends, but the events in question dated back more than a decade, and the Paris police had more pressing concerns. A new Prefect of Police had just been appointed and was busy cleaning up the city: M. Debelleyme had instituted regular sweeping and sprinkling of the streets; he obtained government funding for sanitary inspections of prostitutes; he poisoned unclaimed dogs and silenced hurdy-gurdy men who sang obscene songs; he also arranged for all the beggars who were not from Paris to be given passports and money and sent back to their towns and villages. Following the example of Sir Robert Peel, he was equipping his previously invisible policemen with bright-blue uniforms, cocked hats and shiny buttons bearing the arms of the City of Paris.

The confession was sent to the archives, where it would have disappeared forever were it not for the man who should really be the hero of this story. When the confession arrived in the vaults of the Préfecture, it was immediately devoured by one of the hungriest minds ever let loose in an archive. Until recently, Jacques Peuchet had been the head archivist of the Paris police. It was the job he had dreamed of, a reward for the courage and duplicity he had shown in the dark days of the Revolution. In his early thirties, Peuchet had been elected as a representative of the Commune of Paris but had grown disgusted with the violence of the mob. He became a secret royalist overnight. By posing as a blood-red revolutionary, he secured the job of dealing with fleeing émigrés, refractory priests and royalist conspirators. In this way, he claimed, he was able to save many people from the guillotine. 'Running with the wolves', he later told his friends, 'does not mean having to share their meals.' Of course, to keep his job in such terrible times, he must have sacrificed a few to save the many. Even so, he was never out of danger. The infamous Billaud-Varenne, who demanded the execution of the King 'within twenty-four hours', warned Peuchet: 'Friend, take care. You have the face of a fanatical moderate.'

Somehow, the fanatical moderate survived. Jacques Peuchet pops up in so many places that it is hard to believe that he was a single human being. A search for him at any time between the fall of the Bastille and the fall of Napoleon might have found him hiding in the countryside north of Paris, running a town four miles to the east (and sending only a few of its citizens to the guillotine), languishing in prison, being released by a friend, editing two official newspapers and, later, censoring the press. He also compiled two encyclopedias and a statistical survey of the provinces of France.

At last, he came to rest in the archives of the Préfecture de Police. After years of looking at the world through the peephole of politics, he saw it in all its bulging reality. Those wooden shelves and boxes in the vaults of the Préfecture were the streets and dwellings of a megalopolis of secret information. Everyone who had ever lived in Paris could be found there – the rich and the poor, the innocent and the guilty. This, he thought, was the single source from which a complete picture of human nature could be deduced. In classifying the archives, he would organize 'the unfathomable chaos' of human history. In that seething mass of detail, he would discover 'the mysterious *tableau* of private life' and reveal it to the world in a work of many volumes.

Every morning for eleven years, Peuchet crossed the bridge by Notre-Dame and disappeared from the light of day to rummage through the chaos. Every evening, he emerged, his mind filled with conspiracies and crimes, and a growing sense of enlightenment. But a man with a murky past and a passion for the truth inevitably has enemies. Someone – a jealous colleague, a policeman whose misdemeanours were recorded in the archives, a forgotten survivor from the difficult days of compromise – spread a rumour that Peuchet was an unreformed revolutionary. Could such a man be trusted with the nation's dirty secrets? Obviously not, especially since more dirty secrets were being created all the time. As Peuchet himself would reveal in his book, the Prefect of Police, M. Delavau, was allowing his officers to run protection rackets, gambling dens and brothels.

Peuchet was removed from his post. In a city of twenty-six thousand civil servants who read about each other's promotions and demotions in the daily paper, it was a very public humiliation. In his memoirs, Peuchet lied and said that he gave his beloved job to someone else. In private, he described his dismissal as 'a fatal blow'. A mysterious illness crept up on him. He sensed its progress and blamed it on his enemies. For three years, he grovelled and cajoled, cashed in old favours, traded on his reputation, and when the new Prefect, Debelleyme, took office in 1828, he was given a job in the archives, but lower down the hierarchy. After serving the state for forty years, he found himself, at the age of sixty-eight, in the position of a junior clerk.

It was then that the confession arrived from England. With his encyclopedic eye, Peuchet saw in those sheets of paper a priceless gem. The confession showed what could happen when a population was not properly policed. It also contained certain details that reminded him of his own predicament. He took copious and precise notes and added them to the enormous pile of documents at his home.

By now, he was working night and day, converting the raw material into prose. But his enemies, too, were hard at work. Peuchet was rumoured to be suffering from a mental illness. He was a threat to national security. He should be sent away to die a harmless death.

With each attack on his reputation, he felt his illness gain in strength. He began to use the book he was writing as a diary, which is not a good sign in a historian, unless perhaps he felt that his own truth was part of the bigger picture. The last pages of his manuscript contained some terrible notes:

Today I am in so much pain that I thought I might throw myself into the Seine, if I had the strength.

Today, 5th March 1830, the eve of my birthday, I feel so sick and disheartened that I am setting down my pen to start again later, if ever I can clamber out of this abyss.

A few months later, death released him from physical pain, but it came with the gloating face of his enemies. At least he had the consolation of knowing that his work was practically complete – which was just as well, because, forty years later, the Préfecture de Police went up in flames, torched by the anarchists of the Paris Commune. In the space of a few hours, the archival evidence of five hundred years of Parisian history – including the signed confession – disappeared into the skies above the Île de la Cité.

PEUCHET HAD left his wife with a civil servant's pension and an embryonic *magnum opus* that was crying out for publication. Publishers came a-courting with their contracts. After several years of indecision, Peuchet's widow sold the manuscript to Alphonse Levavasseur, who had published Balzac's first book.

Peuchet's style was a little dry for modern tastes but his tales of conspiracy and murder, despite apparently being true, were highly marketable. Levavasseur assured the widow that her husband's memory would be well served and did what any reasonable publisher would have done: he hired a fluent processor of texts who could turn the swathes of documentation into tidy tales. Since retiring from the civil service, Baron Lamothe-Langon had specialized in writing the memoirs of people who never wrote their memoirs. His publications included the six–volume *Memoirs of the Comtesse du Barry, Written by Herself*, the *Recollections of Leonard, Hairdresser of Marie-Antoinette*, and several multi–volume novels such as *The Vampire, or the Virgin of Hungary* and *The Hermit of the Mysterious Tomb*. The Baron's memorable description of epic witch-burnings in fourteenth-century France (in his well-received *History of the Inquisition in France*) gave historians a seriously skewed impression of the period until it was shown, in 1972, to be a complete fabrication.

The Baron left most of Peuchet's writing intact but went to town on some of the tales, especially the confession. He added dialogues and saucy details to please the novel-reading public. The confession finally saw print ten years after it was dictated to the priest in England, tarted up and travestied, and reeking of implausibility. It can be found in the fifth volume of *Mémoires Tirés des Archives de la Police de Paris*, by J. Peuchet, Police Archivist (1838). The Baron's name does not appear on the title page, which is why Jacques Peuchet is often described by historians, who are forced to use the *Mémoires* instead of the incinerated archives, as a hack writer, a fantasist and a forger.

Extracts from the book were reprinted in magazines and miscellanies. In 1848, Karl Marx read the chapter on suicide and abortion and misquoted it to make Peuchet sound like a Marxist. The confession, titled 'The Diamond of Vengeance', was read by a popular novelist, who found it 'ridiculous' but captivating. 'In that oyster', he wrote, 'I saw a pearl – a rough pearl, without shape or value, but a pearl that merely required the hand of a jeweller'. He took the plot and turned it into a magnificent, rambling and fantastic tale in a hundred and seventeen chapters. That pearl was *The Count of Monte-Cristo*.

The pearl, of course, was the work of Alexandre Dumas. He used the basic elements of the plot and threw away the oyster, which has lain ever since on the rubbish-heap of literary history. But perhaps, if that remnant of a lost confession could be purged of the Baron's elaborations, and subjected to a test of historical plausibility, it might yet reveal a corner of that 'mysterious *tableau*' to which Peuchet devoted the last years of his life.

1

IN 1807, A BLIND MAN tapping his way through the muddle of streets between the Seine and Les Halles might briefly have imagined himself hundreds of miles away in the South of France. Migrant workers always settled in certain districts where they could speak their own language and eat the food of their region. The Sainte-Opportune *quartier* near the central markets had a thriving colony of Catholic migrants from Nîmes. In Nîmes, all the best jobs went to Protestants, but in Paris, a man could make a living regardless of his religion. If he fell on hard times, the network of relatives and compatriots would ensure that he never starved. Naturally, those crowded urban villages were not the cosy havens outsiders imagined them to be: they magnified the petty rivalries of provincial towns, where one family's gain was another's loss. But it was better for a man to know his neighbours than to cast himself blindly into that ocean of humanity.

Each migrant community had its café, which served as a meeting place. As such, they were well known to the police, and any café owner who cared about his profits made sure that he was on good terms with the local *commissaire*. The café of the Nîmois community stood in a street near the Place Sainte-Opportune, close to the central markets. On the day in question (Sunday, 15 February 1807), the owner of the café, Mathieu Loupian, was listening to the gossip even more attentively than usual.

A cobbler from Nîmes called François Picaud, a handsome and hard-working young man, had come to share his good news with the café regulars. He had just become engaged to a local girl, Marguerite de Vigoroux, who was, according to the *Mémoires*, 'fresh as a daisy, comely and alluring' and in any case endowed with the kind of beauty that comes from having a large dowry. Picaud's compatriots concealed their envy and congratulated him on his astounding good fortune. With twenty thousand cobblers in Paris competing for one-and-a-half million feet, it was not often that a simple cobbler made such a good marriage. When Picaud left the café, Loupian and the regulars did what a bridegroom's acquaintances were supposed to do: they tried to think of a way to make the lucky man's last days as a bachelor as uncomfortable as could be.

Apart from Loupian, there were three men in the café that Sunday. Their names (unknown to the cobbler at the time) were Antoine Allut, Gervais Chaubard and Guilhem Solari. None of these men can be identified with certainty, but the names are worth mentioning as a mark of the tale's authenticity. All of them were found in the region of Nîmes, but not so frequently as to be glaringly typical.

It was Loupian himself who came up with the best idea. He called it 'a little prank'. They would tell the *commissaire de police* that Picaud was an English spy, then chortle merrily while Picaud tried to talk his way out of a police cell in time for his wedding. This struck Chaubard and Solari as an excellent scheme, but Antoine Allut refused to have anything to do with it. It seems his motives were sensible rather than honourable. He must have known the danger of toying with the police and was afraid that Picaud would fail to share the joke. He also suspected the café owner of having designs on Marguerite: Loupian had lost his first wife and was looking for another; the comely Marguerite would make a splendid *dame de comptoir*, enthroned on a red velvet chair in front of a gilded mirror, arranging sugar-lumps on the saucers, giving orders to the *garçons* and flirting with the customers. A girl like that was worth several thousand francs a year.

Allut was right to be wary. Yet he did nothing to warn Picaud. He left the café and went home to mind his own business. At least *his* conscience was clear.

IN THOSE DAYS, police *commissaires* were professional writers. They concocted dramas and novelettes, the success of which was determined, not by happy audiences and good reviews, but by a prison sentence or an execution. That afternoon, the *commissaire* of the 13th *quartier* closed the door to his waiting room and cleared a space among the licences and passports and confiscated song-sheets. He sat down with just a few details – cobbler, Catholic, Nîmois, possible English spy, a name sufficiently unremarkable to be an alias – and by the time the sun set over the city, he had in front of him the masterful revelation of a plot to overthrow the Empire. Even if Loupian was wrong about the English spy, cobblers were a notoriously trouble-some breed. They suffered from liver complaints (too much sitting), which gave them melancholia, and from constipation (same cause), which made them disgruntled and politically active. As anyone who had lived through the Revolution knew, cobblers were always looking for trouble.

The *commissaire* sent his report to the Minister of Police, who was mulling over the news from the west of France. Since 1804, there had been fresh stirrings in the Vendée. British ships were occasionally seen off the coast. Spies had reported links between the rebels of the West and the royalists of the South. In the Minister's clockwork mind, the details slotted into the grander scheme. In Nîmes, noble Catholic émigrés had returned from English exile to find the Prot-estants still in power. They were dangerously disillusioned with Napoleon. Now, while the Emperor was away fighting in Prussia, a web of sedition was being stretched from the Mediterranean to the Atlantic coast.

It mattered little whether the *commissaire*'s intelligence was reliable and true in every detail. There was either a doubt or there was none. In this case, there was a doubt. Even if he was innocent, Picaud was guilty of having been denounced. And there were sufficient similari-ties between François Picaud and a previously untraceable suspect by the name of Joseph Lucher to warrant immediate action.

That night, men came for the cobbler and took him away without disturbing the neighbours. For the next two months, Marguerite de Vigoroux made frantic enquiries, but no one knew or no one could tell her what had happened to her fiancé. Like so many people in those turbulent times, Picaud had vanished without rhyme or reason. Loupian, who was one of the last to have seen him, consoled Marguerite as best he could. Given the slightly unexpected turn of events, it would have been madness to confess to the *commissaire*. Only a lunatic would try to save a falling man by jumping off the cliff after him. And perhaps, after all, the police had known something about Picaud?

Two years passed with neither news nor rumour. Then, one day, Marguerite dried her tears and married Loupian. With her dowry and the profits from the café, they were able to leave the old neighbourhood with its sad memories and its thrifty customers. In a bright new *quartier*, life could begin again. All those faces and carriages passing on the boulevard, the officers playing cards and the ladies sipping lemonade, the daily panorama of a great city, would make it easy to forget the past.

2

BEYOND THE PEAKS that mark the border of France and Italy, in one of the most desolate valleys of the Cottian Alps, the fortress-complex of Fenestrelle clings like a parasite to an almost vertical crag. Its bastions once blocked the road that led to France – if a trackless, rubble-strewn ravine could be called a road. According to scholars of the time, the name Fenestrelle means either 'little windows' (*finestrelle*) or 'end of the earth' (*finis terrae*). Both interpretations are appropriate. From the courtyard of the lower fort, a prisoner could watch the eagles soar over the snowy wastes and trace with his eye the Great Wall of the Alps that climbs for two miles along Mount Orsiera. Inside, with the hangings pulled across the window, he could hear the howling of the wind and the wolves. This Siberia of Italy was a wretched place to live and die, and it would have been hard to explain, other than by insanity or deep religious conviction, why the old man who was preparing for his final journey that day in January 1814 had a gleam of satisfaction in his eyes.

Fenestrelle was one of the strongest links in Napoleon's chain of prisons. Instead of rebuilding the Bastille, 'that palace of vengeance', as Voltaire had called it, 'where crime and innocence alike are locked away', he used the fortresses that had survived the Revolution: Ham in the north, Saumur on the Loire, the Château d'If in the Bay of Marseille. These were the Bastilles of the new age: capacious, impregnable and a long way from Paris. Fenestrelle itself was like a human anthology of the last ten years of empire. Napoleon occasionally wrote to his brother Joseph, King of Naples: 'You may send to Fenestrelle all whom you find troublesome' (February 1806); 'None but abbés or Englishmen are to be sent thither' (March 1806); 'I have given orders to arrest all Corsicans in the pay of England. I have already sent many to Fenestrelle' (October 1807). In Fenestrelle, hired thugs from the slums of Naples rubbed shoulders with Roman nobility; bishops and cardinals who had refused to take the oath to the French Republic held clandestine masses with spies and assassins as the altar boys.

Even in Fenestrelle, social distinctions survived. The prisoner who was about to escape into death that winter was a Milanese noble who had once held high office in the Church. His cell, we may suppose, was not completely bare: some pieces of furniture rented in the village of Fenestrelle, a few unreliable chairs, a flimsy curtain, a rough wooden table that was little better than a cobbler's bench. (This is how one prisoner, Cardinal Bartolomeo Pacca, secretary of Pope Pius VII, described the comforts of his cell.) Some cardinals had contrived to have their own valets incarcerated with them; others found a servant among the common prisoners. For most of those men, the outside world had ceased to exist: the disaster of the Grande Armée on the Retreat from Moscow was just a rumour, and the only reliable bulletins that reached their ears were the rumblings of the mountains: the thunder of the avalanche, the earthquake that drew a crack across the wall like a road on a map. Yet with so many wealthy and powerful men imprisoned in its walls, it is not surprising that Fenestrelle had proved to be permeable after all. Even in that Alpine cul-de-sac, money, like water, could find its way through stone.

One of the immediate effects of Napoleon's invasions had been to send huge sums coursing through the financial veins of Europe. Fleeing princes entrusted their millions to men like Mayer Rothschild of Frankfurt. After the French invasion of Italy, the Treaty of Tolentino raised fifteen million livres in currency and another fifteen million in diamonds, which lined a few pockets on the way from Rome to Paris. Paintings and works of art were squirrelled away or sold before they could be transported to the Louvre. One of the cardinals who were expelled with the Pope – Braschi-Onesti, nephew of Pius VI and Grand Prior of the Order of Malta – returned to Rome after the fall of Napoleon and 'had the good fortune to find intact the treasure he had secreted before his departure'.

There was, in short, nothing extraordinary in the fact that the ecclesiastical Milanese nobleman of Fenestrelle had deposited large sums of money in banks in Hamburg and London, that he had sold most of his estates and invested the proceeds in a bank in Amsterdam, nor in the fact that, somewhere in or near Milan, he possessed 'a treasure' that was prudently divided into diamonds and the currency of various nations. His motives were not quite so ordinary. He was dying in the belief that his children had abandoned him and were looking forward to spending his fortune. A prison guard or a servant from the village had smuggled out a message for his lawyer in which he arranged to have every member of his worthless family dis-inherited.

Perhaps this had been his intention all along, but during his long imprisonment in Fenestrelle, he had found the perfect tool of his revenge. He had taken as his servant a young French Catholic, a simple but passionate man in whom he saw an image of his own distress. He, too, had been abandoned and betrayed, and there was something inspired and terrible about his suffering. He had learned the awful truth that torture has its subtleties of which the torturer is unaware. His persecutors had not simply made him wretched; they had robbed him of the capacity to feel happiness.

Those two men of very different age and background formed an attachment more lasting than the bond between a father and his son. A man of the Church might have been expected to instruct his servant in Christian virtues; instead, he taught him about loans and interest rates, shares and consols, and the art of gambling with complete certainty of success. He made his servant the sole heir to his wealth and treasure, and, that winter, as the storms lashed the walls of Fenestrelle and the Continent prepared for another great upheaval, he died in his cell as happy as an abandoned man could be.

TWO MONTHS LATER, in the spring of 1814, the defeated Emperor signed his abdication and sailed for Elba, which lies thirty miles north of Montecristo Island in the Tuscan Archipelago. All over Europe, men and women emerged from prisons and hiding places, blinking in the light of a new dawn. Kings returned to palaces and tourists returned to Paris. In the Alps of north-western Italy, a wraithlike man of thirty-six, bearing a passport that identified him as Joseph Lucher, left the fort of Fenestrelle.

It was almost seven years – or, to be precise, two thousand five hundred and thirteen days – since he had arrived at Fenestrelle in a windowless carriage. In the village below the fort, he entered the tavern and saw a stranger staring at him from a mirror. On passing through the gates of Fenestrelle, he had felt the shock of liberation, the sudden shattering of certainty and habit. Now, as he contemplated those emaciated features, he felt something else besides: the uncanny freedom of a man who was no longer himself. Whoever he might have been before, 'Joseph Lucher' was now a ghost, but a ghost who had, as if by some absurd error of the universe, retained the ability to act on the material world.

He followed the valley of the Chisone river, which was swollen by torrents of melting snow, and reached the broad, green plain of the Po. At Pinerolo, he took the road to Turin, from where the icy battlements of the Alps looked like a distant dream.

A man in rags walking into a banking house in April 1814 was not necessarily a sight to bring the constables running. A vagrant whose papers were in order, and who was legally entitled to sums too large to be the fruit of common theft, was probably an exile or an émigré. As far as the banking house was concerned, he was robed in splendour.

For reasons that will become apparent, the next few months are a blank. Lucher must have travelled to Milan, where he probably visited a lawyer and signed some papers. Perhaps he made a brief excursion to a country estate or a lonely wood. Whatever the instructions he had received in Fenestrelle, they were obviously accurate and effective. Before long, he was able to take stock of the situation and to study the new hand that fate had dealt him.

The money that was held in Hamburg and London, added to the income from the bank in Amsterdam, amounted to seven million francs. The treasure itself consisted of over three million francs in currency and one million two hundred thousand francs in diamonds and other small objects – jewel-studded ornaments and cameos that would have graced the Louvre. Applying the lessons he had learned in Fenestrelle, he set aside the diamonds and one million francs and invested the remainder in the banks of four different countries. With an interest rate of six per cent, this gave him an annual income of six hundred thousand francs. It was enough to satisfy almost any habit or desire. By comparison, the deposed Napoleon landed on Elba with four million francs, which enabled him to build a regal residence, several new roads and a sewer-system, and to organize his return to France. Lucher's total fortune – something in excess of eleven million two hundred thousand francs – was approximately equal to the combined annual income of every cobbler in Paris.

To anyone else, it might have seemed an astounding stroke of luck. With a fortune so colossal, a man could do anything he liked. But how could mere wealth rewrite the story that had told itself in his head a million times? His benefactor and companion in betrayal had taught him to know and hate his enemies. But there was something beyond hatred – the desire for some absolute consolation, a hunger for justice so complete that the events that had led to his living death could never have happened.

No hint of this would have been visible to the proprietor of the *maison de santé* to which Lucher admitted himself in February 1815, and he would have been amazed to learn that his patient was one of the richest men in France. Lucher had himself delivered to the quiet Paris suburb with very little luggage and no servants of his own. He paid for his board and lodging and settled in to convalesce and regain his strength after what he described as a long illness. The more salubrious nursing homes were built on slopes around the city, with verandas and small gardens. Before regulations were introduced in 1838, a private *maison de santé* would accept almost anyone who could pay, which meant that the residents were usually a mixed bunch of people: invalids recovering from surgical operations, pregnant women, the old and decrepit, harmless lunatics and wealthy hypochondriacs. The resident of a respectable *maison de santé* could expect more privacy and discretion than someone who lived in a street with a concierge and neighbours.

At first, M. Lucher appeared to be making a good recovery. But then, at about the time Napoleon, having escaped from Elba, returned to Paris and marshalled his troops, his condition seemed to worsen. During the hundred days when Paris was once again the capital of an empire, M. Lucher remained in bed, with just enough strength to eat his meals and to read the newspaper. It was not until Napoleon had been defeated at Waterloo and banished to Saint Helena that he felt well enough to venture out and visit some of the sights of Paris.

3

THE THOUSANDS OF émigrés who returned to Paris that summer and saw the arcades of the arrow-straight Rue de Rivoli marching in perfect order towards a distant Arc de Triomphe, and stone embankments corseting the curves of the Seine, might have wondered whether the character of a city could be transformed in a matter of years by a few architects and masons. Paris had changed more in a decade of war than in half a century of peace. There were new bridges and canals, new markets and fountains, warehouses and granaries, better street-lighting and huge, hygienic cemeteries on the northern and eastern perimeter of the city. There was an unfinished Stock Exchange that resembled a Greek temple and a column in the Place Vendôme that would not have looked out of place in the forum in Rome. Napoleon had turned Paris into the backdrop of his imperial drama. Now, the stage was occupied by a new troupe of actors. The Restoration avenged itself on the Corsican dictator by settling into his palaces and enjoying his public promenades – which is, after all, the meaning of 'revenge': asserting a legal right or laying claim to something that was taken away.

The biggest change was not immediately apparent. The Sainte-Opportune district near Les Halles was still the puzzle of streets and cul-de-sacs it had been since the Middle Ages. But the people who gave the *quartier* its life were not the same. Thousands from that district alone had moved away or died in distant wars. Even without the drastic alteration of his face and bearing, Lucher would have been a total stranger.

There was a shop where a young man with a knife in his hand was cutting leather and fitting it to a last. There was a café with an unknown name painted above the door … Perhaps some tiny spark of hope had survived those years of darkness. If so, it was extinguished that morning. Lucher found out that the previous owner of the café, M. Loupian of Nîmes, had bought a new business on the boulevards, and that the woman who had shared his good fortune and his bed these last six years was Marguerite de Vigoroux. No one could tell him the names of Loupian's cronies, which was a shame, he explained, because he owed one of those men some money. Fortunately, a neighbour eventually recalled the name of Antoine Allut. But as far as he knew, Allut had returned to the south of France many years before and no one had heard of him since. Lucher went back to the *maison de santé* and paid his bill.

The terminus of the Messageries Royales lay a few streets away in the Rue Notre-Dame-des-Victoires. There was a daily long-distance service to Lyon and the south, advertised as a hundred-hour journey, which sounded less forbidding than four days. Though it carried only eight passengers, it always brought a crowd of porters, anxious families, sightseers, pickpockets and policemen. In all the bustle, no one would have paid much attention to the elderly priest who boarded the coach to Lyon. The abbé's name, we happen to know, was Baldini, which means 'audacious'. The name is common in Italy and the south of France.

The coach left Paris by the Barrière des Gobelins and followed the paved road to Fontainebleau. At Villejuif, at the top of the hill, passengers often alighted near the pyramid that marked the Paris meridian to look back along the road, which was precisely aligned with the towers of Notre-Dame. A traveller's guide described the view:

> From this height, the eye embraces Paris, which is to say an immense and greyish mound of towers and irregular-shaped buildings which compose this city and which stretch away to left and right almost as far as the eye can see.

Travellers on those epic journeys came to know each other extremely well, but it is unlikely that any passenger on that particular coach was much the wiser about the abbé Baldini when he left it at Lyon. He boarded the riverboat that descended the fast-flowing Rhône to Pont-Saint-Esprit, and then the coach that plied the dusty post-road through the foothills of the Cévennes and the hot scrubland of the Gard. He reached the Roman city of Nîmes a week after leaving Paris, checked in at the best hotel (which means that he must have held a passport in the name of Baldini) and spent several days making enquiries. At last, in a seedy part of town, he found himself in a sparsely furnished room, staring at one of the last faces he had seen in his previous life.

The tale the abbé Baldini had to tell – a tale we know in greater detail than parts of the true story of Joseph Lucher – would have seemed incredible to anyone but Antoine Allut. The abbé had been a prisoner in the Castel dell'Ovo in Naples, where he had heard the dying confession of a Frenchman called Picaud. At this, a strangled cry escaped Allut and the abbé raised his eyes to heaven. By some mysterious means (he described it as 'the voice of God'), Picaud had learned, or dredged up from his deepest memory, the name of a man, Allut, who would know the identity of his betrayers. Being a devout Catholic of almost superhuman moral strength, Picaud had forgiven the men who had destroyed his life. His only wish – the slightly odd but understandable wish of a dying man – was to have the names of his assassins inscribed on a plaque of lead that would be placed in his tomb. In order to reward Allut, or to encourage him to divulge the names, the abbé was to offer him a token that Picaud had received from a fellow prisoner by the name of Sir Herbert Newton.

If Allut or his wife had been readers of serial novels, they might at this point have smelled a rat, but the abbé then produced a large and sparkly diamond which, as far as Allut's wife was concerned, provided complete and incontrovertible proof of the abbé's good faith. Momentarily forgetting herself, she flung her arms around the skeletal frame of the abbé Baldini. Why her husband hesitated to accept the diamond was beyond her. Torn between greed and fear, and egged on by his wife, Allut overcame his doubts, and the abbé inscribed in a small notebook the names of Mathieu Loupian, Gervais Chaubard and Guilhem Solari.

A few hours later, the abbé Baldini boarded the north-bound coach from Nîmes.

He left behind him a soul in torment. Antoine Allut had suffered what seemed to him a terrible injustice. He had lived with the fear, confirmed by the abbé, that he had allowed an innocent man to be taken to his death. Now, he had been forced to betray his former friends. Worse still, the local jeweller sold the diamond for twice what he paid the Alluts. Such was Allut's state of mind that he felt a perverse kind of relief when he finally committed a tangible crime and murdered the jeweller.

It was not a well-planned crime. The gendarmes shaved his head and gave him a green bonnet with a tin plaque on which his matriculation number was engraved. The green bonnet signified a life sentence. As he stood with his ball and chain weaving rope in the factory at Toulon, and when he lay awake on a wooden bench without a blanket, it must have seemed to him that François Picaud had taken revenge from beyond the grave.

4

MATHIEU LOUPIAN had prospered, not quite beyond his wildest dreams, but enough to be able to offer his compatriots an occasional drink at the bar. (They could scarcely afford his prices now.) Applying the business stratagem known as blind luck, he had acquired the new café at exactly the right moment. Restoration Paris was awash with money. The Allied troops who occupied the city had been followed by hordes of eager tourists. The reassuringly sober and expensive Café Anglais was not the only establishment to thrive on the river of foreign currency that flowed along the boulevards.

Loupian was the sort of man who, though rich and successful, was never too proud to bend down and pick up a coin that had been dropped in the gutter. And so, when the unexpected offer was made, he was quick to seize the opportunity. An impeccably dressed old lady, who had never been seen before in the *quartier*, had asked to speak to the proprietor. Her family, she explained, had been saved from an awful calamity – perhaps a scandal had been averted or a wayward son had been helped to escape from the police. Their saviour was a man who had since lost all his savings but who was so honourable in his indigence that he refused to be helped. M. Prosper's only wish was to find work as a *garçon* in a reputable café.

Desperate to pay back their benefactor, the grateful family had decided to play a little trick on him. Without telling Prosper, they would pay the café-owner one hundred francs a month if he agreed to employ him and to overlook the fact that he was no longer in the first flush of youth. A man of fifty was not ideally suited to the athletic life of a Paris *garçon*. But since a hundred francs was the equivalent of two *garçons'* monthly wages or the retail cost of two hundred and fifty *demi-tasses* with sugar and a glass of cognac, Loupian agreed to help.

Prosper turned out to be quite a find. He was not exactly prepossessing, and there was something about him that troubled Mme Loupian. In fact, his true character was a mystery, but then this was often the mark of a good servant, who was always self-effacing and could mould himself to a customer's desires. He was quite unflappable and dealt well with all the little accidents of café life. He also had a good eye for detail. It was Prosper who gave the *commissaire de police* a full description of the customer who was seen feeding biscuits to Loupian's hunting dog on the day that it suffered a fatal heart attack. It was Prosper, too, who discovered the pile of bitter almonds and parsley when Mme Loupian's parrot died a horrible death.

Those were difficult times for honest people, when even a domestic parrot could not sleep peacefully in its cage. A king was on the throne again, but thirty years of war, tyranny and unrest could not be wiped out by a few decrees and executions. Napoleon's marauding armies had not simply vanished into the gun smoke at Waterloo. On the pavement outside the café, mutilated beggars sat in their tattered uniforms, bothering the customers. Gangs of ruffians who had burned and pillaged their way across Europe in the name of the glorious Empire were making the streets unsafe, and the new Prefect of Police was too busy with anarchist provocateurs and royalist counter-terrorists to do much about them. The newspapers that were placed in the rack at the entrance of the café were full of grisly tales of violence and crime.

One morning, when Prosper was laying out the papers to fold them neatly into place, Loupian happened to notice a familiar name: Gervais Chaubard, his compatriot from Nîmes. The day before, Guilhem Solari had visited the café. For once, Chaubard had not been with him, and his concierge had not seen him return the previous evening. The newspaper supplied the explanation. Just before dawn, on the new iron pedestrian bridge by the Louvre, Gervais Chaubard had been found with a fatal stab-wound to the heart. A curious detail recommended this murder to the newspaper readers' attention: the knife had been left in the wound, and on the handle someone had glued a small piece of paper bearing these printed characters:

Nº. 1.

THOUGH NO OFFICIAL RECORD of it survives, the murder on the Pont des Arts must have tested the wits of the new Sûreté brigade. Suspicion probably fell on typesetters, who, as literate members of the lower orders, had always been a threat to public stability – though, of course, the murderer could simply have cut the characters from the title page of a gazette. The only likely motive was theft. The fact that the dead man's pockets contained some coins presumably meant that the murderer had been disturbed and had run away without retrieving his knife.

On learning of Chaubard's murder, Loupian felt something like the first inkling of an illness, but he was too busy and distracted to worry about other people's misfortunes. The man who had risen from provincial obscurity to become the owner of one of the finest cafés in Paris was now contemplating the kind of advancement of which his fellow Nîmois could only dream.

Loupian had a sixteen-year-old daughter from his first marriage. She was a tasty little creature, besotted with her nascent charms and excited by the possibilities she saw in men's eyes. Her parents' money had dressed her almost to perfection. Mlle Loupian was the special dish awaiting the special customer. In those changing days, even the daughter of a Loupian could dream of marrying a lord.

So much money had been lavished on her that it seemed only right and proper when a man of superior manners and appearance declared his interest in an unmistakeable fashion. He tipped the *garçons* like an English tourist and bribed the girl's governess with a fabulous sum. Mlle Loupian received the homage of his purse and, in exchange, allowed him a taste of future happiness. It was not until the dish had been not only sampled but devoured that she confessed to her parents. Too late, they saw their mistake. They should never have trusted a man who overpaid the *garçons*.

There was enormous relief, therefore, in the Loupian household when the gentleman – who turned out to be a marquis – announced his honourable intentions, offered proof of his lineage and fortune, and ordered a wedding feast for one hundred and fifty guests at the Cadran Bleu, which was the most expensive restaurant in Paris.

The fairy-tale came true. The marquis married Loupian's daughter and caused quite a thrill at the banquet when he sent a messenger to apologize for his late arrival: the King had asked to see him, but the marquis expected to be free by ten o'clock that evening; meanwhile, the Loupians and their guests should proceed with the meal. The wine flowed as swiftly, but not as cheaply, as it does at harvest-time in Provence, and although the bride was not in the best of moods, the banquet was a great success. Several courses passed before dessert. Fresh plates were placed on the tables, and then, on each plate, a letter in which the bridegroom was revealed to be an escaped convict. By the time the guests read the letter, the groom would have left the country.

A financier who sees his chief investment suddenly lose its value could not have been more distraught than Mathieu Loupian. Luckily, Prosper was on hand to offer advice: at his suggestion, the Loupians spent the following Sunday in the country, to erase the painful memory and to count their blessings. The café was still a successful business, the bill from the Cadran Bleu would be paid off within the year, and Mlle Loupian, though irreparably spoiled, was still young and might yet be served up to a foreign gentleman or a wealthy customer who was unfamiliar with the *quartier*.

While the Loupians breathed the country air and planned a rosy future, a column of smoke was rising from the city somewhere north of Notre-Dame. Fire had broken out in several different rooms above the café. Long before the *sapeurs-pompiers* came galloping down the boulevard with their brass helmets and canvas buckets, the fire had spread to the café below, and as the plaster mouldings dropped from the ceiling and the paintings shrivelled up, a gang of ragged paupers, as though forewarned, came rushing in to help. They carted out the chairs and tables and everything of value, and in so doing broke the mirrors, gouged the polished counter and smashed every single piece of glass and porcelain. When the Loupians returned from their picnic, they found in place of their home and business a smouldering, empty space.

Insurance companies usually refused to cover damage caused by 'popular riots' – which appeared to be the cause of the inferno. The man who owned the building had no choice but to turn them out. All their true friends rallied round, which is to say, no one, except the faithful Prosper, who not only stayed at their side but also refused to accept his wages. It was a comfort to know that there was still some good in the world. When, a few weeks later, Loupian's wife died of cerebral congestion and nervous exhaustion, Prosper arranged the funeral as conscientiously as if it had been his own wedding.

THE LONG STREET that snakes into the heart of the Faubourg Saint-Antoine towards the Place de la Bastille is the continuation of the rectilinear Rue de Rivoli. A person who could read the configuration of streets as a chiromancer reads the lines on a hand might have interpreted its sly meandering as a sign that, in that surly suburb where workers and revolutionaries plotted their coups, no course would ever run true.

At about the time of Loupian's disaster, a young writer called Honoré Balzac moved into a small room in the Faubourg Saint-Antoine. He described the view from his side-street window:

Sometimes the pale glow of the street-lamps cast yellowish reflections up through the fog, showing the roofs in faint outline along the streets, packed together like the waves of a great motionless sea. The fleeting, poetic effects of daylight, the mournful mists, the sudden shimmering of the sun, the silence and magic of night, the mysteries of dawn, the smoke rising from every chimney, each detail of that strange world became familiar to me and entertained me. I loved my prison, for I had chosen it myself.

Without the imagination of a novelist, the *quartier* seemed drab and unpromising. Loupian had been forced by the terms of the marriage contract drawn up by his parents-in-law to pay back his wife's dowry. With the remnants of his fortune, he had rented a café in the Faubourg Saint-Antoine that was little more than a drinking-shop: it had a smoky oil-lamp, a wrinkled rug, the smell of cheap tobacco and customers who made cleaning seem a waste of time. His handsome *dame de comptoir* was dead, and Mlle Loupian's unrefreshed ringlets hung down like the tendrils of the weeds that grew from the gutters. Only Guilhem Solari seemed pleased. This was more like the café of the old days, where he could talk in Provençal without being treated like a country bumpkin.

Sitting alone with his everlasting beer and lemonade, Solari was not good for business – especially not when it became known that, after a visit to Loupian's bar, he had suffered convulsions and died after several hours of intense, untreatable pain. Nevertheless, Loupian's customers might not have made the connection with the earlier murder if the newspapers had not reported a peculiar detail. Before the funeral, as was customary, Solari's coffin was displayed just inside the entrance of his building. It had lain there for a while when someone noticed a small piece of paper on the black cloth covering the coffin. It bore these printed characters:

Nº. 2.

News of this grisly sequel to the murder on the Pont des Arts spread quickly through the *quartier*. From one day to the next, Loupian found himself without a single customer. The two straw chairs outside the door were permanently empty and used only by the neighbourhood dogs. Perhaps he was beginning to suspect that all these horrible events were in some way connected, but he could find no reason for his ruin, and though murder no. 2 had filled him with foreboding, he had only the faintest inkling of a motive.

Without the faithful Prosper, Loupian and his daughter would have found themselves on the street. Prosper offered them his meagre savings, which would at least allow them to avoid the beggars' hospital. However, even this small mercy came at a price. Prosper attached to his offer a condition so humiliating and foul that Mathieu Loupian was surprised to find himself capable of accepting: Mlle Loupian was to live with Prosper as his concubine, to warm his bed and to satisfy his aged longings.

The arrangements were made. A double bed was installed, and the girl who was to have been the instrument of her family's social rise became a prostitute in her father's house.

As Loupian lay on his thin mattress at night, listening to the muffled howl of the city and trying to let the sound of that restless ocean drown out the noises that came through the partition wall, he knew that Prosper, though old in face and body, was filled with savage energy.

5

ON SUNNY DAYS, the avenues of the Tuileries Gardens were thronged with children and nurses, shop assistants and office workers on their lunch break, dog-walkers and dandies, and elegant women who filled the air with perfume and colour like the flowers in front of the Tuileries Palace. At dusk, the gardens took on a more reflective air. A few lonely figures wandered along the terrace by the river and among the trees, where white statues seemed to beckon from the gloom.

One evening, a burly man in a dark coat slipped into the gardens shortly before the iron gates along the Rue de Rivoli were closed. Just then, Mathieu Loupian was walking back along one of the shadier avenues, delaying the moment when he would have to return, past the shops and the busy cafés, to the scene of his misery and shame.

A figure appeared in front of him. As he moved to let it pass, Loupian heard the name 'Picaud'. Even before his mind had attached the name to a memory, his body froze. The face was close enough for him to see it clearly; yet its features were not, it seemed to him, those of the cobbler Picaud; it was the sneering mask of the man who feasted on his daughter every night.

The brief conversation in the Tuileries Gardens is not recorded in the confession. Loupian would certainly have learned that he was looking at the man who had stabbed Chaubard, poisoned the parrot, the dog and Solari, married his daughter to a convict, arranged for the café to be looted and destroyed, caused the death of his wife and turned his daughter into an adulteress and a whore. He would also have learned that Picaud – also known as Lucher and, more recently, Prosper – had spent seven years in hell. And he probably had just enough time to feel his eyes burn with fear and hatred before the knife marked No. 3 was pushed into his heart.

LOUPIAN'S BLOOD was still forming a dark pool on the gravel when a powerful arm seized his murderer from behind. In less time than it takes to truss a pig, Picaud was gagged, bound with rope, wrapped in a blanket and hoisted onto a man's shoulders. It may have occurred to him that the police had finally traced the murders to Prosper. But a gendarme would not have acted alone nor taken such extraordinary precautions. Though he could see nothing under the blanket, the smell of the river, the sudden chill and the sounds of the city coming from a wider vista would have told Picaud that his abductor had left the gardens by the riverside gate and was crossing to the Left Bank.

The confession states only that Picaud was carried on the man's back for about half an hour and that, when the blanket was removed, he found himself, still bound, on a folding bed in an underground room. Apart from the bed, the room contained a dim lamp and a Prussian stove, the pipe of which disappeared into the ceiling. The walls seemed to be the rough limestone sections of an abandoned quarry. If the Paris police had conducted an investigation when they received the confession several years later, these details would have enabled them to identify the location with some precision. Walking at about two miles an hour, along the Quai Voltaire and across the Place de l'Odéon, Picaud's abductor could, within thirty minutes, have reached the area where charts show a zone of ancient quarries rising up towards the river. This would put the room in which Picaud was held captive somewhere along the northern end of the Rue d'Enfer.

Many months, perhaps years, had passed since the abbé Baldini's visit to Nîmes, and many things had happened to Picaud's abductor since he escaped from the hulks of Toulon. He, too, had changed almost beyond recognition. He had to introduce himself as the man whose life had been ruined by Picaud's mad campaign, the man who – though less guilty than the others – had been singled out for an especially subtle form of punishment. Whether or not Picaud had known that the diamond would be the ruin of Antoine Allut was irrelevant; Allut was bent on revenge. Unfortunately for him, he made the mistake of trying to satisfy two passions at the same time.

In prison, Allut had seen something that should have been obvious to him from the start: the abbé Baldini's tale was a fabrication. Allut was a God-fearing man, but could he really believe that 'the voice of God' had whispered his name in Picaud's ear? After making his escape, he could easily have discovered that there was no such person as Sir Herbert Newton, and that the Castel dell'Ovo in Naples had not been used as a state prison since the days of Emperor Romulus Augustus. It would not then have taken a genius to guess the abbé's true identity and to suspect that the famous numbered murders were the result of the information that he had extracted from Allut.

The abbé Baldini was a fake, but the diamond was unquestionably genuine, and it was safe to assume that a man who could treat a diamond as loose change must be extremely rich. It is more than likely – for a reason that would become ever clearer to Allut in the years to come – that Picaud confirmed his assumption: he was indeed fabulously wealthy and owned a treasure almost too big to be imagined.

Allut now put into effect a plan that must have struck him as fiendishly clever when he first thought of it: he would starve Picaud until he was forced to reveal the location of the treasure. By this simple device, he would not only become a millionaire, he would also avenge himself on Picaud and rid the world of a rampaging maniac. He might even escape with a clear conscience.

The account of what happened next in the room beneath the Rue d'Enfer unfortunately bears the bloody fingerprints of the novel-writing Baron, who liked to reward his readers with an occasional shower of gore, and it leaves several questions unanswered. But since Peuchet's record of the confession has disappeared along with the confession itself, this is the only evidence from which the facts can be deduced.

To Allut's surprise, Picaud declined to pay several million francs for a crust of bread and a glass of water. Even after forty-eight hours without food or drink, the former prisoner of Fenestrelle seemed to consider his own existence a matter of small concern. It gradually dawned on Allut that his scheme had a serious flaw: if he starved Picaud to death, the treasure would be lost forever.

Picaud's refusal to divulge the whereabouts of his treasure was – according to the confession – inspired by simple avarice. But the confession itself contains a detail that contradicts this. As Allut paced about the room in a frenzy of greed and disappointment, he suddenly noticed a diabolical smile on Picaud's face. Enraged to see his enemy triumphant, Allut *'pounced on him like a wild animal, bit him, pierced his eyes with a knife, disembowelled him and fled the premises, leaving behind him nothing but a corpse.'*

There are no further details on the fate of Picaud's mortal remains. A shrivelled, eviscerated body strapped to a bed in an underground room would surely have been mentioned in the newspapers, and although rats could dispose of a corpse and its clothing in a matter of days, the landlord would surely have noticed the smell. Yet no other record of such a murder has so far come to light.

The end of the story, as we know, is relatively uneventful: Allut fled to England, where he lived, manacled to his own conscience, until a French Catholic priest known only as the abbé P ... 'helped him to see the error of his ways and to loathe his sins'. (These are the words that the abbé himself used in his letter to the Prefect of Police.) Allut dictated his confession to the abbé, received his sacred blessing and died in the knowledge that he had been absolved of his sins.

When the abbé P ... sent the confession to Paris with an accompanying letter, he drew the obvious conclusion. Now that the horrors of the Revolution and the Empire were over and Paris was once again the capital of a Catholic monarchy, it was important to make sure that the Prefect of Police understood the moral:

> Men in their arrogance try to outdo God. They pursue vengeance and are crushed by their revenge. Let us worship Him and submit humbly to His will.
>
> Yours faithfully, etc., etc.

* * *

THIS IS THE STORY that was dictated to the abbé P ..., recorded by Jacques Peuchet, and embellished by the Baron. Even in its novelized form, it contains several gaps and inconsistencies – which might be taken as a mark of its authenticity. The moral – vengeance destroys the avenger – scarcely matches the events described in the confession. That 'diabolical smile' on Picaud's face suggests that, for a man who considered himself in some way posthumous, there was indeed such a thing as complete and happy vengeance. And there are other problems, too. How, for instance, did Allut know so much about Picaud's life in Fenestrelle, the exact composition of his treasure, his hiding place in Paris, the orchestration of his crimes and a hundred other details? How did such a clueless man become so well informed? And why, if he knew so much, was he never able to locate the treasure?

The Baron – or perhaps it was the abbé P ... – noticed the inconsistency and found a gratifying solution: Allut had been visited by the ghost of François Picaud. 'No man's faith can be stronger than mine', Allut is supposed to have said, 'for I have seen and heard a soul detached from its body.' After the restoration of the monarchy, devout, mystical fantasies were in fashion, and few readers of the *Mémoires Tirés des Archives de la Police de Paris* would have felt cheated by the novelistic device of a garrulous ghost. Many would have been perfectly willing to accept it as the literal truth.

One day, some of the incidents described in the confession may be authenticated by the chance discovery of a letter or a police report that escaped the conflagration of the archives, but it is too much to hope that this particular detail will ever be confirmed. Information supplied by disembodied souls is of little use to historians. From a rational point of view, there was only one person who could have known the whole story, and that person had either been disembowelled or left to die twenty feet below the Rue d'Enfer.

There is every reason to believe that Picaud's death was indeed described in the original confession and duly registered by the Paris police. It is also quite likely that the blinding and disembowelling occurred only in the Baron's Gothic brain, and that, in reality, Allut left the half-starved remnant of François Picaud to die a miserable death. So much of the story is missing that no definite conclusions can be reached. Birth, marriage and death certificates went up in flames in 1871 on the same day as the police archives. It is a sad irony that a story that was rescued from obscurity and destruction by an archivist with a passion for the hidden truth should be so full of unconfirmable facts. It is even more ironic that the abbé P ... who provided the Paris police with all this information, who taught Allut to loathe his sins, recorded his confession and sent him to the next world with the absolution that only an ordained priest can confer, is, for some reason, the only person in the story whose full name is unknown.

FILES OF THE SÛRETÉ

1. The Case of the Crayfish

New Year's Day, 1813, Rue des Grésillons

AT SOME POINT in the night, while the snow was falling thickly, the pile of rubbish had crossed the street, and was now positioned a few doors down from no. 13, Rue des Grésillons. This street, which was later swept away by the Gare Saint-Lazare, ran along the edge of the grim and grimy *quartier* known as Little Poland. It was the kind of area where a pile of rubbish might expect to pass unnoticed, even if it did occasionally put forth a gnarled head that swivelled and disappeared.

The Rue des Grésillons was the haunt of mysteriously industrious people who considered themselves lucky to be tenants, because no landlord or bailiff ever dared set foot there. It was Paris, but it had nothing that anyone would have recognized as Paris. Once, it had marked the point beyond which no building was allowed. On one side – the old perimeter of the city – were half-empty scrap-iron yards, smutty laundries, windowless brothels and nameless hostels. Most of its inhabitants came from distant parts of France, and some of its teetering tenements housed the entire adult male population of an Alpine valley. On the opposite side of the street – the side further from Paris – were the desolate slopes and gullies of the city's northern waste dump.

In any other street, the pile of rubbish would have been dismantled in a trice by a licensed rag-picker, a municipal cleaner or by one of the unregistered scavengers who darted about like shadows, poking at piles of waste and filling a leather bag with objects of unidentifiable desire; but by the time they reached the Rue des Grésillons, the sweepings of Paris had attained a state of refinement that placed them almost beyond the digestive aspirations of a rat. Every cabbage-stalk and bone, every nail, splinter, scrap and thread, every bandage and poultice from the hospitals of Paris had been gathered or eaten, leaving only a gravelly coagulation of mud, soot, hair, faeces, and whatever else ten thousand brooms had mustered in the street before nine o'clock in the evening. There was just enough compostable matter in that residue of seven hundred thousand human lives to start the process of fermentation – which was fortunate, because the night was bitterly cold, and the occupant of the pile of rubbish was dressed only in the thin felt jacket of a messenger.

As he crouched in the steaming filth, the bogus messenger felt the warm glow of satisfaction that always seemed to presage a successful operation. The others had succumbed, hours before, to the lure of an all-night wine shop, but he knew that, however long it took, the wait would be worth his while. To the man known as 'Sans-Gêne' ('Have-A-Go') – the man who had tricked, chiselled, sawn and bludgeoned his way out of every prison in France – a night of cramp, frostbite and stench was nothing. As everyone knew, Eugène-François Vidocq was impervious to pain. He also possessed the curious faculty of lessening his height by four or five inches, and in this contracted form could walk about and jump. He could carry on a normal conversation with a metal file in his mouth. He had thought nothing of staining his face with walnut juice and clogging up his nostrils with coffee and gum arabic in order to imitate the skin colour and chronic nasal discharge of a criminal known as Tête-de-Melon. At last, his hard work and persistence were about to pay off. The case that had brought him that New Year's Night to the Rue des Grésillons would, he was certain, be the last nail in the coffin of his enemies at police headquarters.

Twenty-two members of the gang had already fallen into his net – including the Pissard twins, and the fiendish criminal who, until he was tortured, was known only as 'The Apothecary'. They had carried out their thefts with such elaborate cunning and such minute knowledge of the premises (including the apartment above the *commissariat* of the eighth district), that it was obvious they must have been employees of the victims. In bringing these men to justice, Vidocq had, almost single-handedly, destroyed the centuries-old reputation of Savoyard immigrants for honesty and reliability. No one would ever trust a chimney-sweep, floor-polisher or errand-boy again, which, in a city where people habitually left their key in the door and invited strangers into their home, could only be construed as an act of public philanthropy.

The one remaining member of the gang was the notorious 'Crayfish', whose whereabouts had remained as mysterious as his nickname. (Perhaps he owed it to his grasping claws or a bright-red complexion, or perhaps he had achieved proficiency in the potentially useful art of walking backwards.) Though the Crayfish had eluded capture, his girlfriend, a laundress, had been traced to the Rue des Grésillons, and it was reasonable to suppose that the Crayfish would attempt to deliver her New Year's gift in person.

Dawn's chill fingers were already stretching over the eastern suburbs when a shadow passed along the house-fronts. The door of no. 13 opened, and the figure scuttled in, looking up and down the street as it backed into the courtyard. A minute later, the frozen heap of filth was standing in the hallway, beneath the stairs, whistling in the manner of a Savoyard coachman. On hearing the signal, the Crayfish emerged on the landing two floors up, and the following conversation took place:

'Is that you?'

'Yes.'

'I'll be down in a minute.'

'It's too cold to wait here. Meet me at the bar on the corner – and look sharp.'

It was not until he was holding up his trousers with one hand and, with the other, presenting his braces to a smelly man with a pistol in his hand, that the Crayfish realized what had happened. An hour or so later, his ankles tied with napkins to the legs of his chair, he was helping Vidocq to celebrate his capture in a private room at the Cadran Bleu restaurant, divulging all sorts of information about his criminal colleagues, in the mistaken belief that this would ensure his release.

THAT MORNING, Commissioner Henry arrived for work as usual, turning off the Quai des Orfèvres, and passing along a glass-covered arcade that led from the river to the courtyard of the Sainte-Chapelle. It was there, under the shadow of the medieval basilica, in a frequently fumigated office at no. 6 Petite Rue Sainte-Anne, that M. Henry conducted his never-ending war on crime.

As a man who had passed many a delightful Sunday fishing in the Seine, M. Henry knew the pleasure of outwitting a slippery creature. It was a pleasure that was denied to him as head of the Second Division of the Préfecture. Criminals, who were supposed to live by their wits, were desperately stupid. Their slang was a secret code that gave them away as surely as a bag marked 'swag'. Recently, a thief called Mme Bailly, having learned that there was money to be made as an informer, had provided the police with details of all the burglaries she had committed herself, and was surprised when they came knocking at her door.

The Commissioner's own modest powers had earned him a reputation for supernatural percipience. He was known to the criminal underworld of Paris as 'the Bad Angel', and it was said that no one ever left his office without accidentally confessing his crime or giving some vital clue that led to his conviction. Unfortunately, M. Henry was forced to work with a team of skivers and incompetents. His constables had been known to lie in wait in a burglar's cupboard for seventy-two hours, only to be locked in by the burglar and almost starved to death. And so, when Vidocq had offered his services as a thief-catcher, and proposed the creation of a special Brigade de la Sûreté staffed by ex-convicts, Commissioner Henry – to the envious indignation of his regular officers – had promptly organized Vidocq's 'escape' from La Force prison, and given him his own office, with a monthly salary of one hundred francs and the promise of a bonus for each arrest.

Vidocq returned the compliment by following M. Henry's orders with almost sheepish devotion. There was something in Vidocq's ability to grind a man's face to an unidentifiable pulp that filled him with devoted tenderness towards anyone who earned his respect.

The Commissioner was briefing his officers when a powerful smell filled the room, followed by a visibly intoxicated Vidocq, holding his latest catch by the collar. Seeing the line of policemen, the Crayfish squirmed with loathing and spat out a stream of abuse. Vidocq bowed to his colleagues, and said,

'Allow me and my illustrious companion to wish you a Happy New Year!'

The Commissioner looked at his man with pride. Then, turning to his officers, he said, frostily,

'Now that's what I call a New Year's gift! Would that each of you, Messieurs, had come bearing a similar gift.'

The Crayfish was led away to the cells, and, from that day on, Vidocq's position as Head of the Sûreté appeared to be unassailable.

2. The Case of the Yellow Curtains

New Year's Day, 1814, Rue Poissonnière

THANKS TO Vidocq, Paris now had a centralized criminal bureau, instead of forty-eight competing *commissaires* who gave up the chase as soon as a felon turned a street corner and left the *quartier.* The ex-convict not only made police work more professional, he also conferred a rough sort of glamour on what had previously been seen as a rather squalid branch of government administration.

To M. Henry, Vidocq was simply the most effectual of all the two-faced opportunists who went back and forth between police head-quarters and the underworld. To criminals, he was something weird and unnerving, a will-o'-the-wisp with fists of steel. His prestige and power were rooted in superstition: the edges of Paris were still half-dissolved in their rural hinterland, where werewolves and witches were as much a part of daily life as rabid dogs and concierges. Once, Vidocq was told by an unsuspecting policeman's daughter that the great Vidocq could turn himself into 'a truss of hay'.

'A truss of hay! How?'

'Yes, Monsieur. One day my father followed him, and just as he was going to put his hand on his collar, he grasped only a wisp of hay. That's not all talk, the whole brigade saw the hay, which was burned.'

There was, however, nothing magical about Vidocq's methods,

and they deserve a purely rational investigation. It would be hard in any case to imagine a better guide to the devious streets of Paris than the human bloodhound who sniffed out their secrets with such ruthless delight.

OF ALL THE MYSTERIES that Vidocq solved – or rendered irrelevant by brute force – few were as revealing as the Case of the Yellow Curtains.

It was almost a year since the Crayfish had been netted, and M. Henry was hoping to present the Minister with another New Year's gift. Unfortunately, the case that lay in front of him that Christmas Eve seemed too risky for Vidocq. A convict called Fossard, who specialized in making keys from wax impressions and in jumping out of upper-storey windows without hurting himself, had escaped from Bicêtre prison. (Bicêtre, two miles south of Paris, was a clearing-house for convicts: from there, they left in chains for the hulks of Brest, Rochefort and Toulon.) Apparently, Fossard was 'armed to the teeth', and had vowed to kill any policeman who tried to arrest him.

The problem was that Fossard had known Vidocq in prison and would certainly recognize his former cell-mate. M. Henry therefore entrusted the job to his regular officers, who, giving due consideration to the words 'armed to the teeth', busied themselves with paperwork and harmless enquiries which showed that Fossard was indeed still forging keys and jumping out of upper-storey windows. Faced with craven incompetence, the Commissioner reluctantly gave the job to Vidocq and presented him with the latest piece of intelligence. It took the form of a detailed but inconclusive report:

> The said Fossard is now in Paris. He is lodged in a street that runs between the market and the boulevard, from the Rue Comtesse-d'Artois to the Rue Poissonnière, via the Rue Montorgueil and the Rue du Petit-Carreau. It is not known on which floor he resides, but his windows may be recognized by yellow silk curtains. In the same house, there is a little hunchback seamstress, who is a friend of Fossard's concubine.

With this shred of information, Vidocq set off in search of the escaped convict.

The four streets in question formed a single, serpentine stretch of road that twisted and turned so often that it seemed to be heading nowhere in particular. In fact, it ran north from the central markets, bisecting the boulevard and the 'Great Drain' that girdled Paris. The main segment was the Rue Poissonnière – so called because this was the route by which fresh fish reached the capital from the ports of the Pas-de-Calais. In the festive season, the road was even busier than usual, and no one paid much attention to the elderly man with a three-cornered hat, a pigtail, and wrinkles painted on his face; nor did anyone stop to ask him why he was gazing up at windows and scribbling in a little book.

The task was daunting. Yellow was a popular colour for curtains – and many others had yellowed with age – and there were enough seamstresses in northern Paris to populate a small town. Assuming young men to be representative of the whole population, medical reports on army conscripts would suggest that there were something in the region of 6,135 hunchbacks in Paris. The streets of Paris had a total length of 425 kilometres, and the fish-route along which Fossard lurked behind yellow curtains was 900 metres long. Allowing for variations in population density in the different *quartiers*, this would give the streets in question a total hunchback population of thirteen.

A fictional sleuth might have interviewed the local haberdasher, interrogated the informant as a possible source of red herrings or examined the muddy street for the tell-tale prints of a female hunch-back. But since this was real life, where the tediously simple and the impossibly confused left little room for tidy puzzles, Vidocq recorded over one hundred and fifty pairs of yellow curtains in his notebook, then trudged up and down the same number of staircases, knocking at doors. The result was a handy address list of 'ravishing' seam-stresses, but no hunchback and no Fossard.

It transpired that the yellow curtains must have gone to the cleaners, and that Fossard no longer lived along the Rue Poissonnière. However, so dense and intertwined were the threads of mutual acquaintance, daily routines and knowledge of neighbours' doings, and so tirelessly did Vidocq wear out his shoe-leather on the cobbles, that even if the report had falsely specified green curtains and a one-armed seamstress, he would still have found his man.

He eventually caught Fossard – just in time for the New Year – by asking hundreds of questions, spending a small taxpayers' fortune in bribes, disguising himself as a coalman and, finally, by pouncing on Fossard 'with the speed of a lion'. Fossard went back to Bicêtre, and from there to the hulks of Brest. No doubt, like most convicts, he managed to escape, but the coal-blackened face of the colossal Vidocq had put the fear of Satan in him, and the Sûreté Brigade was never troubled by Fossard again.

THE ULTIMATELY disappointing case of the yellow curtains is a good example of what might be termed the early Vidocq method of investigation. Ever since his boyhood in Arras, he had been paring down his modus operandi to a few infallible devices. His first theft had involved the use of a glue-coated feather, fed through the crack of the cash-box in his parents' bakery – a crime as difficult to explain as it was tedious to commit. Since the feather extracted only the smallest of small change, he resorted to a false key, and when the key was confiscated by his father, he used a pair of pliers, wrecked the box, grabbed the cash and walked 'very quickly' to the next town.

These simple means were well suited to the urban villages that made up early-nineteenth-century Paris. But the city was growing by the day: in some *quartiers*, even a concierge or a police spy could barely keep abreast of the influx of strangers. In the sixteen years during which Vidocq ran the Sûreté Brigade (1811–27), the population of Paris increased by over one hundred thousand. The drainage system grew by ten kilometres, the hills of rubbish turned into mountains, and streets that had never wandered far from their medieval origins reached out into the countryside like the veins of a gigantic parasite. Soon, it would take something more than mere persistence to stretch the net of public safety over the whole crime-ridden metropolis.

3. The Case of the Six Thousand Missing Criminals

20 June 1827, 6 Petite Rue Sainte-Anne

ONLY A BUREAUCRAT with a heart of stone would have felt no pity for the fifty-two-year-old man who sat alone in his office that Wednesday in June, hunched over a large desk on which a single sheet of paper remained. That musky suite of rooms under the shadow of the Sainte-Chapelle had been his home for the last sixteen years, and the little platoon of twenty-eight men and women – scribes, spies and half-reformed convicts – had been the only family he had known since he left his parents' bakery as a boy. He had grown to love the accommodating file cabinets, the capacious ward-robe that would have been the envy of a boulevard theatre and the little galley where, at any hour of the day or night, a convict's mistress cooked the meals that kept them on the trail of criminals.

Commissioner Henry, who had been like a father to him, had retired to devote himself to fishing, and his departure had caused a flurry of administrative manoeuvrings. In his place, the Minister had appointed a neat and tidy young man with a heart of stone, who had begun to investigate Vidocq's distant and not-so-distant past. Rather than await the outcome of the investigations, Vidocq had decided to tender his resignation. He signed the sheet of paper, and left the office for what seemed likely to be the last time. As he passed along the glass-covered arcade, lugging a trunk full of documents, he wondered how his suc-cessor as Head of the Sûreté – an ex-convict known as Coco Lacour – would manage to match his impressive record of arrests.

Vidocq had brought to justice enough criminals to sink a prison ship. His name was a household word, and he was somewhat incon-veniently famous as a master of disguise from Cherbourg to Marseille. He had solved so many cases that to the tradesmen, cab drivers, clerks and, for that matter, criminals, who read about his exploits in the newspapers, nothing seemed quite as innocent as before. That feeble old woman might be a secret agent on a case, and that loaf of bread she was carrying might be an improvised valise containing a loaded pistol and a pair of handcuffs.

It is a tribute to Vidocq's efficiency that when he left the Sûreté, most of the mysteries that remained unsolved concerned Vidocq himself. Why, for instance, were his hands covered with blood when his former mistress Francine was found with five stab-wounds inflicted by his knife – a knife, admittedly, that she later claimed in a signed statement to have borrowed for a suicide attempt? Why was an ex-convict, who was known to be a habitual gambler, put in charge of the Police des Jeux, which supervised casinos? And how did he manage to retire from the Sûreté in June 1827, with almost half a million francs, when his annual salary was only five thousand francs?

One case was so mysterious that it seems to have escaped attention altogether, and it is especially unfortunate that the lack of evidence makes it the shortest case of all.

The mystery is this: the number of people Vidocq arrested each year far exceeds the annual number of convictions for crimes against the person or against property in the entire Seine *département*. In one year, the Sûreté Brigade arrested seven hundred and seventy-two murderers, thieves, forgers, conmen, escaped convicts and miscellaneous miscreants. Even subtracting the forty-six unexplained arrests made 'by special warrant', and the two hundred and twenty-nine 'vagabonds and thieves' who were expelled from Paris, this leaves a very large number of criminals who do not appear in the official statistics. Even at a conservative estimate, in the sixteen years of Vidocq's reign, the number of criminals arrested by the Sûreté, but unaccounted for in the official statistics, is approximately 6,350. At this rate, it would have taken fewer than fifteen Vidocqs to arrest every criminal in the country.

If Commissioner Henry had devoted his well-earned retirement to writing his memoirs instead of fishing in the Seine, he might have explained that Vidocq was more dangerous as a detective than he ever was as a crook, and that, by casting the eerie light of crime over the whole city, he created a demand for people like himself: legalized avengers who would give the taxpayers their money's worth by cleaning up the streets. He might have granted Vidocq his proper place in history, and hailed him as the man who reinvented crime-fighting as a means of controlling the innocent population ... But, as Vidocq may have reflected that June morning, as he set down his trunk on the Quai des Orfèvres to take a swig from his brandy-flask, a true genius is never recognized by his contemporaries.

4. The Case of the Mysterious Unpleasantness

17 October 1840, 13 Galerie Vivienne

SOME TIME AFTER Vidocq's departure from the Sûreté, that characteristically Parisian breed known as *badauds* ('gawkers'), who had nothing better to do than stand and stare, as though any object, whether living or lifeless, might become interesting if stared at long enough, began to notice Xs – sometimes accompanied by Os – marked in white chalk on the walls of certain houses. If a particularly patient *badaud* had lingered within sight of one of the single Xs, he might eventually have seen a man or a woman take a piece of white chalk and inscribe an O beside the X before disappearing down the street or behind the brick column of a public urinal; and, if he followed the mysterious defacer of public property, he might in due course have found himself in one of the plusher parts of Paris, under a glassy arcade thronged with people who, like himself, had nothing better to do than stand and stare.

The Galerie Vivienne had been built in 1823 as a speculative venture. It quickly became one of the busiest arcades on the Right Bank. On a summer evening, Parisians out for a stroll would leave the dazzling sun on the boulevard and plunge into its gleaming shadows to feast their eyes on chocolates and pralines and miniature armies of petits-fours, or to gaze at the frills and ornaments that were displayed like holy relics under the nymphs and goddesses of the rotunda. A man could smoke a cigarette there on a rainy day while examining the curves and unexpected vistas of the marble galleries and the pretty women who came to shop for lingerie and the latest fashions. Like an elegant marquise, the Galerie Vivienne had a sort of indestructible frivolity, and its fame as the centre of Paris fashions spread far beyond the city. The words 'Galerie Vivienne' appeared like a sacred motif on beautifully wrapped bandboxes that were delivered to ladies in provincial towns when their husbands were away. It was, in short, the sort of place a woman could safely visit on her own without arousing suspicion.

That Saturday afternoon, a young woman, who will have to remain nameless, entered the Galerie Vivienne and passed through the monumentally respectable entrance of no. 13. She climbed the magnificent, swirling staircase where windows set high in the marbled wall made it possible to look onto the stairs without being seen. She knocked at a door and was ushered into the comfortable office of the man who was described on the metal plaque, the headed notepaper and in countless advertisements as 'Ex-chief of the special Sûreté police, which he directed for 20 years with undisputed success'.

The Bureau of Universal Intelligence at 13 Galerie Vivienne was the world's first private detective agency, founded two decades before Allan Pinkerton, 'the Vidocq of the West', launched his National Detective Agency in Chicago. It offered a range of discreet services: 'Prosecutions and debt-collection, intelligence of every sort, surveillance, and investigations in the interests of business and families.' Other agencies had sprung up in imitation, but none of them had prospered, as the Bureau's prospectus cheerfully explained:

> All those who tried to imitate me have come to grief, and were bound to fail. 'The Alarm-Bell' was melted down in the prisons of Mézières. 'The Lighthouse of Commerce' was snuffed out in the cells of Bicêtre. 'The Illuminator' shed so much light on its own shady dealings that it went to jail for several months. Their successors will inevitably fail in their turn.

To some minds, there was a touch of menace in the Bureau's advertising. It was almost as if a blackmailer had extended his operation to the entire commercial world of Paris ...

> Certain businessmen who subscribed to my Bureau for several years, and then saw fit to discontinue their subscription, found that, no sooner had they dispensed with my experience and advice, than they fell prey to rogues.

But since the Bureau performed such useful services, and since a more liberal government was preventing the police from interfering in family affairs, it enjoyed some powerful protection. It had a huge database of file-cards on every known criminal – and several thousand law-abiding citizens too – and a team of specialized sleuths: 'the Cyclops', 'the Faun', 'the Man-about-Town', and a very tall detective who could peer through first-floor windows without using a ladder. Even when the Bureau was raided, and more than two thousand old Sûreté files relating to the years 1811–27 were confiscated, its filing-system was feared by politicians as much as Vidocq's fists were feared by criminals.

The Bureau's 'undisputed success' had not come easily. The house rules, which were prominently displayed in the director's office, gave some idea of how difficult it was to work with agents who had acquired their skills and manners in prison-cells and slums:

> Employees must always be dressed in a clean and respectable fashion, and especially not have muddy shoes.
>
> Employees must be equipped at all times with necessary items such as knives, rulers, pens, etc., and must always leave their desk tidy.
>
> Drunkenness and gambling, those two shameful vices, will be severely repressed. Eating and drinking, smoking and chewing tobacco are forbidden in the offices, as is anything unconnected with the service.
>
> Any employee who writes on the walls, notice-boards, windows, etc., will be punished with a fine three times the cost of the damage.
>
> Documents and notes are to be turned face down in the office so that prying eyes cannot read them. Anyone who can prove that his comrade has divulged the details of a case to him will be rewarded with the day's pay of the one who blabbed.

The final rule would have been of particular interest to a *badaud*. It pertained to 'external operations'. When a house was under surveillance, the agent was to mark the nearest street corner with an X. 'To this effect, white chalk will always be at his disposal.' When he left the house to follow a subject or to 'satisfy a need', he was to mark the wall with an O. In this way, the director could monitor his agents' activities and take punitive action where necessary.

It is fortunate, in a sense, that the Bureau was closed down in 1843 and its files dispersed. Some of the paperwork found its way to government offices and, from there, eventually, to second-hand bookshops and archival collections. One of the salvaged records appears to be the office copy of a letter that the young woman in the Galerie Vivienne had received that Saturday. (In 1840, there were six deliveries a day, so that a letter posted in Paris to an address in the city before 9 a.m. would arrive before noon.)

The letter was sufficiently disconcerting to bring the addressee to Vidocq's office. It was written on the usual headed paper, with the Bureau's motto beneath the address:

20 FRANCS A YEAR
Give protection from the wiles of the wiliest rogues.

Mademoiselle,

Having a matter to discuss that concerns you and that might cause you some unpleasantness and expense, please take the trouble to drop by my office on receipt of this letter.

Respectful regards,

It would be too much to hope that a case requiring such discretion should be transparent in all its details after so much time. The envelope has not survived, and the woman's address is unknown. There is as much chance of identifying Vidocq's client as there is of seeing Vidocq himself emerge from the offices of the historical preservation society that now occupies no. 13 Galerie Vivienne. However, the Bureau's copy of the letter at least makes it possible to follow the progress of the case over the following week.

Several notes were scrawled across it. The first, in thick, clumsy characters suggesting a quill gripped by a fist, says: 'She won't pay more than 2 francs a month.' Then, in another hand, 'Wrote on 19 Feb. 1841 to pay'. Another note, in the first hand, says, 'A note to find out the lady's possition [*sic*].' The final note says, 'Made note on 23 February'.

No further information is available. The precise nature of the 'unpleasantness' to which the young woman was exposed must remain a mystery, and we shall never know whether or not her two francs a month were considered sufficient payment, nor in what manner the Bureau of Universal Intelligence intended to offer her protection from 'the wiles of the wiliest rogues' ...

5. The Case of the Bogus Revolution

6 June 1832, Île de la Cité, to 11 May 1857, Rue Saint-Pierre-Popincourt

ONLY A MAN who had hidden himself in piles of rubbish and watched the same door or alleyway for days on end would have known how many obscure dramas were wiped from the history of Paris by demolition and urban renewal. Street corners and crossroads were the synapses of a gigantic, convoluted brain, and when, in 1838, Prefect Rambuteau began to cut through the living tissue of ancient lanes to create the broad, hygienic street that bears his name, large parts of the city's memory were lost without trace.

Since Vidocq was occasionally employed on special missions, even after the demise of his detective agency, he could certainly have written something more revealing than his 'pocketbook for decent people', *Thieves: A Physiology of Thievish Behaviour and Language* (1837). He might, for instance, have written a practical manual for army officers and would-be heads of state. He might have shown that anyone who wished to conquer France should first control the capital, and that, in order to control the capital, he should assemble at certain key points in the city the following items: two carts, some tables, chairs, bed-frames and doors, several mattresses, and some well-chosen rubbish untouched by rag-pickers. Since few streets were more than seven metres wide, a collection of such materials could quickly reach a first or a second floor. In this way, a whole battalion could be held at bay.

In a later chapter, he might have shown that in order to confirm the change of regime, and to damp down the fires that had forged the new administration, the head of state should provoke another revolution, and then repress it.

On 5 June 1832, one of the last victims of the cholera epidemic, the popular republican orator General Lamarque was being taken to his final resting-place by one of the largest funeral processions ever seen in Paris. Rumours had been spreading since the morning that the funeral would be the occasion of a royalist revolt. The liberal monarchy, which had been established by a three-day Revolution in July 1830, was threatened by discontented royalists on one side and disgruntled republicans on the other. Strangely, though, despite its fear of a further republican uprising or a royalist counter-revolution, the government did nothing to prevent the crowds from assembling, and when a colossal man appeared on a horse, waving a red flag and a Phrygian bonnet, no soldier or policeman intervened until panic had begun to spread.

Three hours later, half of Paris was choked with barricades, and a handful of intrepid men, dressed in the style of blood-red revolutionaries, were calling on citizens to resist the royalist revolt.

A cynic might have said that this chaotic revolt was a stroke of luck for the new regime. By dawn, many of the rioters had been killed or captured, and the rebellion was concentrated in the narrow streets around the church of Saint-Merri. It was there, as readers of Victor Hugo's *Les Misérables* know, that the final scenes of that bloody drama were acted out. Order was restored by government troops, who fired cannon at the bulwarks of mattresses, and smashed their way through partition walls to fire on the barricades from upper windows. Any general would have realized that a battle concentrated in such a small area would not eradicate the threat for good. Many of the troublemakers slipped through the cordon and escaped across the rooftops. But there was no doubt that, after the events of 5–6 June 1832, Paris was safer for the monarchy than before.

SURVEYING PARIS that morning from the Île de la Cité, a keen observer would have seen the clouds of gun-smoke and pulverized rubble rise over the impenetrable mass of roofs to the north. But he might also have heard sounds of fighting closer to hand. While the massacre was taking place across the river at Saint-Merri, barricades had appeared in the narrow lanes of the island, behind the Quai des

Orfèvres. They were first noticed at about ten o'clock that morning, by which time, according to every history of the 1832 revolt, all resistance was confined to the Right Bank.

As they retreated from the massacre and fled across the river, several bands of rioters were alerted to the presence of barricades on the Île de la Cité by men who seemed to have a precise knowledge of the ebb and flow of the battle. Since the barricades occupied a position of clear strategic importance between the government buildings on the Right Bank and the army of starving workers and seditious students in the Latin Quarter, the insurrection was quickly reignited in the heart of the old city.

If any of the men and women who rushed to defend those barricades had paused to examine them, they might have noticed something odd about their architecture and composition. The barricades had firm foundations, as though the builders had manoeuvred the carts into position according to some unwritten principle of barricade construction. There was an unusual preponderance of desks and file cabinets forming neat courses with bridged joins and buttresses, and, running along the top, a row of cartwheels and chairs that served as coping-stones and battlements. If the battle had been long in coming, the insurgents might have realized that a barricade in a maze of alleyways could be attacked from several directions at once, or isolated from the neighbouring barricades by a handful of troops. They might have flushed out the occupants of the houses that looked down on the barricades, and picked off any snipers who squatted behind the chimneys and the mansards. Any such precautions would, of course, have been futile if some of the rebels defending the barricades had turned out to be soldiers or policemen in disguise.

In the absence of detailed records, it is hard to say exactly what happened that morning under the shadow of the Sainte-Chapelle. The most explicit document is a letter drafted by an unknown hand and signed by two hundred and fifty inhabitants of the neighbouring streets (Rue de la Licorne, Rue de la Calandre and Rue de la Juiverie). This testimonial, which was later produced by Vidocq in support of his application for a government pension, praised 'the zeal and courage of M. Vidocq', who, though no longer officially employed by the Sûreté, had somehow managed to capture the 'malefactors', and 'cleaned up' the *quartier* by 'sweeping away the rabble'.

The notion that the barricades on the Île de la Cité had been constructed under Vidocq's direction and manned by his agents provocateurs was expressed, long after the events, by some of the revolutionaries who were captured that day on the barricades, and then tortured and imprisoned. Some of the survivors later made attempts on Vidocq's life, and their testimony has always been considered unreliable.

* * *

SO MANY MURKY TALES are attached to Vidocq's name that he seems to hover over nineteenth-century Paris like a phantom. Governments that were increasingly sensitive to public opinion, and inclined to farm their policing out to criminals, were bound to find a man like Vidocq indispensable. There were probably few political pies in which he did not have a finger. In 1846, Louis-Napoléon Bonaparte (the future Napoleon III), who had been imprisoned after bungling a coup d'état, escaped from the fortress of Ham with the benefit of Vidocq's advice. He fled to London, where Vidocq was sent to spy on him, and where Vidocq also took the opportunity to advise him on his next coup d'état. After the Revolution of 1848, and before Louis-Napoléon's successful coup d'état of 1851, he served Lamartine as a secret agent. Lamartine himself paid tribute to the ex-convict, saying that he would have 'mastered the situation with only Vidocq to help'.

The exact truth of these and other tales is almost impossible to separate from the mass of rumour and misinformation. In a city as large and as volatile as Paris, where ministries came and went like commuter trains, and whole *quartiers* disappeared from one year to the next, a historian is reduced to sifting through piles of suspect evidence like a rag-picker. Most of the documents have long since vanished, and many were probably destroyed. Within minutes of Vidocq's death in 1857, a squad of policemen rushed to his house in the Marais and removed his files, leaving not a single clue by which to solve the penultimate mystery: when news of his death reached the newspapers, eleven women turned up at his home, each carrying a signed will that made her the sole heir to his fortune.

The old convict had remained slippery to the end. Some of the people who attended his quiet funeral at Saint-Denys-du-Saint-Sacrement in the Marais might have been forgiven for wondering whose body was in the coffin. The grave in Saint-Mandé cemetery, marked with the half-erased inscription, 'Vidocq, 18--', is now known to contain the body of a woman. It is most unlikely that Vidocq's final resting-place will ever be known, and there will probably never be a monument or even a street name to commemorate the part he played in making Paris safe.

A PROPERTY
IN BOHEMIA

I

Théâtre des Variétés, Thursday, 22 November 1849

THE SHADOWS DREW IN, until only her lily-white hands and her pale face could be seen. Figures dressed in black stood around her: they might have been angelic undertakers, waiting to bear her flimsy body to the grave. The silence was almost complete. The only sounds were the hissing of the gas-jets and the murmur of a thousand people barely breathing. Then a voice cried out, '*O my youth! It is you they are burying!*'

Darkness engulfed the scene, and furious applause cascaded down from the upper circle and the *amphithéâtre*. As the shabby section of the audience rose to its feet, waving its hats and food-wrappers, a rich, stale smell wafted through the auditorium. It had something of the fog on the boulevard outside, where the pavements were sticky with rain, but also something more intimate: it suggested old stew and coarse tobacco, the coat-racks and bookshelves of a pawnshop, and damp straw mattresses impregnated with urine and patchouli. It was – as though the set-designer had intended some ironical epilogue – the smell of the real Latin Quarter.

A denizen of that world walked stiffly onto the stage to shouts of 'Author!' He went to stand between the lovely white creature, now back from the dead like a sheet from the laundress, and his ideal alter ego, the elegantly disconsolate Rodolphe. A few smiles broke out among the *parterre*, which was still savouring the novelty of seeing garret-room revolutionaries portrayed as considerate young men. Liberties had obviously been taken with the truth ... Someone must have kidnapped M. Murger and delivered him to a tailor. His body was still making the acquaintance of a perfectly black jacket and an unventilated pair of shoes; the handkerchief he clutched was unmis-takeably white. His 'knee', as he called his balding brow, looked almost distinguished, and a fearless barber had ventured into the virgin forest of his beard and turned it into a tidy hedge. No one would see the fear and the sarcasm in those big, gloomy eyes, but the footlights might catch the tear that ran endlessly down his cheek – for the master of pathos was blessed with a defective lachrymal gland.

Beyond the footlights, he could make out the faces of famous critics who were about to crown him King of Bohemia. They had shown him their reviews of *La Vie de Bohème* before the performance and implicated him in the conspiracy of praise: '*It positively rains witticisms.*' '*Never has the public been so moved . . . those penniless young men and women have won our hearts.*' '*One can tell that this work was lived before it was written.*'

He saw the new President, Louis-Napoléon, smiling approval from his box, the living assurance that the revolutions of 1848 – in which Henry Murger himself had played a small and only slightly shameful part – now belonged to history. The dishevelled originals of the stage Bohemians were hard to distinguish beyond the chandelier and the red velvet of the upper circle: they were a dark mass of heads and caps, just below the rotunda and the gilt cherubs made grubby by the gas-light. But he knew them well enough – the lank hair, the old men's teeth, the humorous foibles that had hardened into vices. It should have been obvious to everyone that *La Vie de Bohème* was a highly selective version of the truth.

The actress who had incarnated Mimi placed her hand in his and curtsied to the critics; then his collaborator, the professional play-wright, joined him on stage and the applause grew louder. He had imagined his moment of triumph a thousand times and was surprised to find himself thinking about furniture – a pair of matching chairs, a mattress with springs, and a full-length mirror. He thought of doors that filled the doorway and windowpanes that would not be shattered by a gust of wind. He pictured an apartment that would not have been out of place on the stage of the Variétés, with a boudoir in which to hide a beautiful new admirer and an antechamber in which to detain her beautiful predecessor.

It was an understandable distraction. Henry Murger, the tailor's son and penniless scribbler, was about to leave that suffering land of debts and dreams where 'bold adventurers hunt from dawn to dusk that savage beast known as the five-franc piece'. The success of *La Vie de Bohème* was his passport to the Right Bank. Most of his friends had forgiven him his sentimental depiction of Bohemia. Some of them had even begged him to expunge that last, calculatedly selfish line, '*O my youth! It is you they are burying!*' But the professional playwright had already turned his little tales into a sugary fantasy. Something had to remain of the bitterness and the wasted time. If 'they' had not buried his youth, he would have butchered it himself and danced on its grave.

As they left the stage, he squeezed Mimi's tiny hand and looked forward to the sequel.

II

The Latin Quarter, 1843–46

IN THOSE DAYS, long before, a view over the rooftops of Paris was an unaffordable luxury. The apartment he had shared with a mousy young writer from Laon had a view of the Jardin du Luxembourg – if he stuck his head out of the window as far as it would go and twisted it to the left, a smudge of green foliage appeared in the corner of one eye. That had been his best apartment to date. They had decorated it in the 'Bohemian' style of the 1830s: a few volumes of Shakespeare and Victor Hugo, a Phrygian cap, an Algerian hookah, a skull on a broomstick handle (from the brother of a friend, Charles Toubin, who was an intern at one of the big hospitals) and, of course, a window box of geraniums, which was not only pretty but also illegal. (Death by falling window box was always high up the official list of fatalities.) For a proper view of Paris, they visited Henry's painter friends who lived in a warren of attic rooms near the Barrière d'Enfer and called themselves the Water-Drinkers. When the weather was fine and the smell of their own squalor became unbearable, they clambered onto the roof and sat on the gutters and ridges, sketching chimneyscapes, and sending up more smoke from their pipes than the fireplaces below.

Three of the Water-Drinkers had since died of various illnesses known collectively as 'lack of money'. When the last of the three was buried, in the spring of 1844, Henry and the others had found themselves at the graveside without a sou to give the gravedigger. 'Never mind,' said he, 'you can pay me next time,' and then, to his colleague: 'It's all right – these gentlemen are regular customers.'

Four times a year, when leases expired, half the population of Paris took to the streets in a mass, short-distance migration. Few people owned more furniture than would fit on a hand-cart, and few were so enamoured of their dwelling that they wanted to stay for more than a year. Henry's migrations had left him almost as far down the residential ladder as it was possible to go. After his latest move, he was living in the Hôtel Merciol near Saint-Sulpice, in a dingy little room on the third floor ('for the excellent reason that there isn't a fourth').

The Hôtel Merciol was one of those grudgingly furnished hotels where so many people came and went – hiding from creditors, borrowing a bed, staying drunk as long as their friends' generosity allowed – that it could hardly be called home. Working girls in search of more congenial employment sometimes brightened the place with their chatter and their imitation of domestic respectability, until the police raided the hotel in the name of public morality and sent the girls to be hygienically inspected and registered as prostitutes.

Despite the boredom, the discomfort and the constant anxiety, Henry had decided to live by his pen. Since his mother's death, his father had behaved like a typical bourgeois, which was particularly irritating in a man who earned his living as a tailor and a concierge. He refused to subsidize his son's career as France's future greatest poet. He scoffed at Henry's ragged clothes and suggested that he find work as a domestic servant. Henry was forced, as he put it, to 'prostitute his muse'. He wrote for a bath-house journal that was printed on waterproof paper, and for two children's magazines, whose editors found his sentimental style well suited to the junior reader.

He wrote verse for *Le Palamède*, which printed chess problems and gave the solutions in rhyming couplets. As 'Viscountess X', he wrote a fashion column for *Le Moniteur de la Mode*. ('Everyone this season is wearing periwinkle blue', he wrote, dressed in his mouse-brown overcoat.) He had even penned a few sarcastic editorials for the organ of his father's trade, *Le Coupeur*:

> *The Tailor's Art* – that deplorable expression! Does a man who improves his stitching technique thereby acquire the right to stand proudly beside our artists and to claim, when he hears the names David, Girodet or Horace Vernet, 'I, too, am an artist! . . .' No, a thousand times no. He should say no such thing, or run the risk of bringing a smile to every lip.

At the age of twenty-three, he saw his dreams of poetic glory turn to dust. His longest poem had been written for Mr Rogers, whose name appeared on walls and buses all over Paris. Mr Rogers liked to advertise his product in Romantic verse and paid one franc per couplet. Henry's ode was supposedly written by a countess to her friend, who could now face the world again thanks to a mouthful of hippopotamus ivory. It was by far his most widely read publication:

> A dire calamity had come about –
> There is none worse: – my teeth had fallen out.
> ROGERS! My husband's love I owe to thee,
> Thou hast restor'd domestic harmony.
> (Men love not the woman but the idol.)
> Touch'd by thy hand, of Nature's the rival,
> By no gold thread, nor hook, nor tie oppress'd,
> Our tender jaws become a treasure-chest!
>
> I'd bade adieu to Youth's sweet adventures,
> When, my dear, you told me of His dentures.
> May HIS name ever in my heart reside,
> ROGERS! without thy skill I should have died,
> Or ever lived a prisoner of my house,
> The toothless widow of a living spouse!

Since the muse was beginning to lose her appetite for doggerel like this, it was just as well that her poet had another source of income. A certain Count Tolstoy employed him as a secretary on a small but regular wage. Though the young man was often ill and lying idle in a hospital bed, Count Tolstoy found that with his intimate knowledge of political clubs and underground journalism in the Latin Quarter, Henry Murger made an excellent informant for the Tsarist spy network.

AT THE TIME the great event occurred, Henry's personal life was in a similarly wretched state. The Danish 'sylph-in-velvet' who had spent two nights sleeping in his chair had flown away, complaining to a mutual friend that he was physically unambitious ('which only goes to show that I'm a fool'). The overweight *soubrette* ('two hundred pounds, not including petticoats') had frightened him off with talk of weddings and babies. The search for a 'legitimate mistress' who would marry him 'in the thirteenth *arrondissement*' – as they said when there were only twelve of them in Paris – had been long and fruitless. Even his most ingenious plan had come to naught: the principal of the girls' orphanage at Saint-Étienne-du-Mont had not received his application for a wife with undisguised delight.

It was, therefore, with a mixture of ecstasy and relief that, in the spring of 1846, he discovered a creature sent from heaven via the Faubourg Saint-Denis who seemed destined to fill his heart with joy and his pockets with money.

III

A newspaper office, 1846 ·

ON TUESDAY 5 MAY, slightly later than he had intended, Henry Murger crossed the river to the Right Bank and turned into a busy street between the Passage des Panoramas and the Stock Exchange. At no. 36, Rue Vivienne, the index finger of a disembodied hand pointed up a staircase to something called '*Le Corsaire-Satan*'.

His heart was pounding even before he began to climb the stairs. That Sunday, he had returned to Paris on a cloud, accompanied by his friends, who travelled more mundanely on the number 9 bus. They had been taking the air at Bougival by the Seine, where shop-girls and factory workers went to remind themselves of the sun, and where the riverbanks bristled with painters' easels.

Champfleury – the mousy young writer with a cat's-whiskers moustache – had brought along his girlfriend, Mariette. Their fellow Bohemian, Alexandre Schanne, who was known to a handful of fellow artists and several hundred exasperated neighbours as the composer of a symphony 'On the Influence of Blue in the Arts', had brought his mistress, Louisette. She was, according to Henry, a typical *grisette* (the name given to working girls because of the cheap grey cloth they wore). She got about the city by hanging on to the back of carriages and supplemented her wages as a flower-girl by attaching herself to cheerful young men until their money ran out. She was known to have seduced her married landlord in lieu of a month's rent, and then to have blackmailed him for a further month. Like most girls at her factory, she had green hands – from the arsenic dye that was used on the artificial petals. It was monotonous work and poorly paid. Each girl performed a single task and never saw the finished flowers that adorned the tables and ball-gowns of the ladies whose husbands flirted with the flower-girls.

They were lying on the grass, discussing the delicate art of paying one's debts without spending any money, when Louisette's friend from the factory arrived on the arm of a young architect called Crampon. Henry removed the pipe from his mouth and turned to look.

She was wearing a blue polka-dot muslin dress, tied at the waist with a ribbon that matched her blue eyes. Her boots were laced tightly over white stockings. Her puff sleeves and white collar had been carefully stitched by candlelight in the few hours that remained after work. Like all flower-girls, she was deathly pale, but not pale enough to hide her scars. Her face had been ravaged by smallpox. A friend of Henry's later compared it to a honey cake, because it was sweet and had a pitted surface.

Her chaperone that day, M. Crampon, had met her in the street by chance – so he thought – when she was trying to find the key to her apartment. In fact, at the time, Lucile Louvet had no permanent address. Five years before, she had left her father's tripe shop in the Rue Saint-Denis, and married a cobbler in the same *quartier*, a

M. Paulgaire, who beat her and bored her to tears. Since then, she had lived in garrets in the Latin Quarter, in hospitals for indigent women and sometimes in houses in the back streets where the charms of even the plainest flower-girl were appreciated to the full.

She never smiled. If she had ever had a sense of humour, she had lost it – or, as Henry might have said, had mislaid it or taken it to the pawnshop, hoping one day to redeem it. But at Bougival, the shadows of the leaves and the darting sun painted expressions on her face that would have charmed an artist. Henry's eye, being bolder than the rest of him, explored her from top to toe, loosened the ribbon around her waist and entered the chestnut forest of her hair. Without saying a word, she made it obvious that the exploration did not offend her.

That evening, on the journey back to Paris, M. Crampon had somehow become detached from the rest of the party, and Henry had found himself alone with Lucile.

Now, two days later, as he climbed the stairs of no. 36 clutching a roll of paper, he was still in what he described as 'a state of wild intoxication'. He passed the old soldier on the landing who repelled irate readers and welcomed actresses and politicians bearing bribes. He walked along a corridor where men in overalls were reading proofs and eating fried potatoes, and entered a large office that looked like a schoolroom several days after a pupils' coup d'état. About twenty young men in varying states of dilapidation and dandification sat and sprawled around a table covered in green baize. On the far side was a bookcase devoid of books, and an illustrated wall-chart of world history on which all the cartouches bearing names and dates had been patiently obliterated with sealing-wax. A tall, elderly man wearing green-tinted spectacles was marching from one group to the next, shouting like an actor in a boulevard theatre and snatching up sheets of paper.

'Let me see that ... *"My word!"*, *an actress with close ties to the Ministry was heard to say the other day* ... Rubbish! Into the basket. . . . What's that? Say that again. *Creditors are like women?* ...'

'You can't love them enough.'

'That's good. Write it down. It's two o'clock. There's nothing at the printers! ... Oh, I forgot ... *Monsieur* Baudelaire is a genius – we can't expect *him* to soil his hands with ink ...'

The chief-editor of the *Corsaire-Satan* was the man who, as he never tired of saying, had 'discovered' Balzac in 1821 and shown him how to write pornographic novels for money. Since then, Auguste Lepoitevin Saint-Alme had steered at least half a dozen newspapers to ruin but still harboured dreams of dominating the Parisian press. His latest venture – a scandal sheet called *Satan* – had taken over the old daily arts paper, *Le Corsaire*. He had sacked the salaried journalists and replaced them with the freelance geniuses who walked every morning from the Latin Quarter in the hope of seeing their names in print and to spend the day in a heated room. He paid them a niggardly six centimes a line ('so they won't get lazy'). But once they had produced ten articles that caused irreparable damage to the reputation of a public figure, they were allowed to puff each other's books and praise the performances of any actress they happened to fancy. Saint-Alme called them his 'little cretins'. ('The future of literature, sir!' he told his rivals.)

Until then, most of Henry's work for the *Corsaire-Satan* had consisted of anecdotes of life in the Latin Quarter – that far-fetched world where mildly deranged young men discussed 'hyperphysical philosophy' until dawn, joked about squalor and starvation and paid the rent by immortalizing the landlord in oil. Saint-Alme took the paper from Henry's hand, and read aloud to the assembled cretins.

It was a description of Henry's meeting with Lucile. He had called the girl Louise and himself Rodolphe, and transposed their encounter to the Prado dance-hall on the Île de la Cité. Then, without changing any other detail, he recounted their return to Paris from Bougival on Sunday evening:

> They stopped in front of a shop in the Rue Saint-Denis.
> 'This is where I live,' she said.
> 'When shall I see you again, Louise, and where?'
> 'Your place, tomorrow, eight o'clock.'
> 'Really and truly?'
> 'Here's my promise,' she said, offering her fresh cheeks to Rodolphe, who took a bite of those beautiful ripe fruits of youth and health.
> He returned home, as they say, 'in a state of wild intoxication'.
> 'Oh!' he exclaimed, striding about his room. 'It can't go on like this. I must write some poetry.'

Saint-Alme guffawed his approval: Murger's tale was just the sort of thing to titillate the middle-aged subscribers. The 'little cretins' listened as Saint-Alme read on:

> After tidying up the temple that was to receive his idol, Rodolphe dressed for the occasion, bitterly regretting the absence of anything white from his wardrobe.
> The 'holy hour' struck, and with it came two timid knocks at the door. He opened it. It was Louise.
> 'You see, I kept my word.'
> Rodolphe pulled the curtain across the window and lit a fresh candle.
> The girl removed her bonnet and shawl, and placed them on the bed. She saw the dazzling whiteness of the sheets, and smiled. In fact, she almost blushed.
> When she complained that her boots were rather tight, he knelt down and obligingly helped her to unlace them.
> Suddenly, the light went out.
> 'Oh!' said Rodolphe. 'Who can have blown out the candle? . . .'

The rest of the evening was left to the fertile imaginations of the little cretins, who congratulated Henry on his new acquisition and his literary style.

IV

The Latin Quarter, 1846–47

NEXT DAY, Henry left his female protagonist in bed and went to read the *Corsaire-Satan* at the café. His tale had been given the honours of the '*rez-de-chaussée*'. (The 'ground floor' was the bottom half of the front page, where the serial usually appeared.) More importantly, it ran to two hunded and seventy-four lines. At six centimes a line, it would pay the rent for two weeks. If he could keep up that tone of ironical gaiety, he and Lucile might even enjoy the luxury of a daily meal.

From that brief period of happiness – as it later seemed to Henry – only two letters have survived, both written by Lucile. They can hardly be counted among the great love letters of the nineteenth century, but at least they have the flavour of reality:

> Since you're not back, I'm going out to see my aunt.
> I'm taking the money so I can take a cab.
>
> Louise

('Aunt' was a euphemism for the pawnshop.)

> I'm going to have some boots made. You'll have to find some money so I can pick them up the day after tomorrow.

(A pair of boots cost twenty francs, or, in the circumstances, three hundred and thirty-three lines of prose.)

Henry liked the letters so much that he quoted them in his next 'Scene of Bohemian Life': the hero's friend, seeing a shiny new pair of women's boots at his door, assumes that he has come to the wrong address. Afterwards, the Bohemians eat a lobster and drink a few bottles of wine to celebrate Rodolphe and Mimi's 'honeymoon'. (He had decided to rename his character 'Mimi'.) The friend discourses on the origins of coffee ('discovered in Arabia by a goat'), while Mimi goes off to fetch the pipes and to serve the coffee, saying to herself, 'Good heavens! What a lot of things that gentleman knows!'

It was only after a month of blissful moments to treasure in his memory – the faint smile on her lips when he brought her back a blue scarf from the fashion magazine, or the morning when he kissed her hair a hundred times while she slept – that he began to notice certain things. Lucile spent ages dressing and arranging her hair, just to go to the market. She talked to the women who sat on the street corner. She spread out her second-hand tarot cards on his desk, examining them like a scholar of ancient languages, and on the days that were supposed to be lucky she was gone for hours. When he asked what she was doing, she said, 'getting to know the neighbours'.

Henry sat at his desk, trying to be witty. Lucile was useless as a housewife, and since she had given up her job at the flower-factory, it was hard to satisfy her extravagant desire for cooked food and an occasional outing to the dance-hall. But at least, with Lucile as his mistress, there was no shortage of material. Without exactly spying on her, he found out about the gentleman from Brittany, and the precocious schoolboy who promised her a cashmere shawl and some mahogany furniture. From Lucile herself, he knew that Alexandre Schanne, who was probably envious, had called her 'a little slut'. Another friend had been looking rather bashful, and Henry wondered how far the 'neighbourhood' extended. Sometimes, when she rested her head on his shoulder, he thought he could smell the men on her clothes. It was not surprising, after all, and the readers who were enjoying his 'Scenes' in the *Corsaire-Satan* would understand that this was quite normal in Bohemia – 'those flighty birds of passage', he had written, 'who, out of a whim or more often out of need, one day (or rather, one night) make their nest in the garrets of the Latin Quarter and agree to stay for a few days if they can be lured with a caprice, or with ribbons.'

The little household had to live, and M. Saint-Alme was pestering him for copy. Henry served up ever more intimate slices of his life, still warm and *saignant*. He sold Lucile's infidelities to the *Corsaire-Satan*, and became, in effect, her literary pimp. If 'Mimi' had stayed at home and darned his socks, the stories would have dried up. They would have been poor but happy, or, more likely, dying at the hospital. It had a curious effect on his writing. Behind the jolly scenes of garret life, he began to sketch that other world that was never mentioned in print – the world of disillusioned 'artists' with small, hungry imaginations, the provincial businessmen who sat alone in dance-halls, and the students who came to Paris armed with their parents' money, wanting to while away the months of academic idleness with a housewife-prostitute-companion before returning home to impregnate the chosen virgin. He used Lucile's 'adventures' to give some tactful, fleeting notion of a darker Latin Quarter, in which illegal pamphlets such as *Bachelor Life in Furnished Rooms* advertised cheap clinics where midwives learned their trade, 'mechanical corsets' guaranteed to flatten the evidence and, as a cheap alternative to infanticide, '*breuvages avortifs*'.

Of course, he could only hint at this in the newspaper, and some of the details had to be changed in the name of romantic fiction. In one of the Scenes, Mimi, having grown tired of starving in a garret, disappeared with a viscount, at about the time that the real Henry wrote to a friend, 'My wife has gone off to get married to a big soldier who wants to slit my throat – something to which I am opposed.' To his own surprise, he saw his flimsy heroine turning into a character of substance: 'Her features were not without a certain delicacy and seemed to be lit gently by her clear blue eyes, but at certain moments of boredom or ill humour, they wore an expression of almost savage brutality, in which a physiognomist might have recognized the signs of deep egotism or great insensitivity.' Rodolphe, too, was becoming alarmingly true to life: he hit his mistress when she left him and when she returned like an alley cat, purring and striking poses. In the absence of opium, violence was the drug that induced the tearful reconciliations and the long, greedy nights when Lucile was as eloquent in bed as Henry was on the page. In muted forms, he described their fights and his jealous agonies; he wrote about the rosy fingernails that lacerated his heart, and he wondered why Mimi kept returning to Rodolphe, and why he allowed her to return.

After eight months of hell, he drew up the balance sheet: six 'Scenes of Bohemian Life' amounting to one hundred francs, some broken ornaments and a smashed chair, a pawnshop pledge on the shelf where his poetry books had been, and a feeling that anger and jealousy were all that remained of his passionate youth.

They had said goodbye so many times that he could never remember who decided to end it once and for all. They discussed it for a day in a strange state of calm. Henry was to keep the ornaments and the chair, and Lucile would keep the 'antique' statuette of Homer that she had bought one day to prove that she was not entirely insensitive to literature.

They spent a last night together in bed. He turned away from her and bit his pillow. She heard him sobbing in his sleep. In the morning, she waited until he was awake. She told him that she had no plans, which he found hard to believe. When they parted, he kissed her hand and moistened it with tears. She might have let him kiss her properly if he had tried. Then she opened the door and walked down the stairs.

That evening, Champfleury took him to a restaurant, and he drank a bottle of her favourite wine. As he stared at the sweet red liquid through tear-filled eyes, he found to his surprise that her face was already beginning to merge with all the other faces he had loved.

ONE DAY AT THE end of November, sitting at the wooden table of a *cabinet de lecture* between a flea-ridden scholar and a concierge engrossed in a novel, she opened the *Corsaire-Satan* and saw the poem he had inserted in his latest 'Scene of Bohemian Life'. He must have written it, she supposed, on the day they parted. (In fact, the poem was three years old and had been written for another woman, but it suited the occasion quite well.) By the time she left the *cabinet de lecture*, she knew the poem by heart.

> I've run out of money, which means, my dear,
> That we're legally obliged to forget.
> I'm so *démodé*, you won't shed a tear,
> Mimi, you'll forget that we ever met.
>
> Ah well, we had our days of happiness –
> Never mind the nights. My darling, it's true,
> They didn't last long, but that's how it is:
> The most beautiful days are the shortest too.
>
> Let those whom God hath joined together part;
> Ring down the curtain on our song and dance.
> In no time at all, you'll learn a new part,
> And raise the curtain on a new romance.

THERE WAS NO new romance. Lucile would soon be turning twenty-five: it was the age at which a woman was thought to be past her prime. She posed in unheated studios for painters who needed a breast or a lower torso. She sat with her friends on the street corner; she shared their wine and sometimes their customers. She grew so desperate, she went back to the old *quartier*, to the smell of boiled tripe and the tapping of the cobbler's hammer. At the flower factory, she pushed against the rubber pad that made the petals soft and lifelike. She drank a bottle of detergent and waited for the time to pass. But like a landlord with a bill for overdue rent, life refused to let her go.

Sometimes, she thought of the attic where they had sat and

shivered over a last meal of bread and sardines. She remembered his jealous questions and his hand across her face. She thought of the gloves she had left in his drawer on purpose. Once, she ran into Alexandre Schanne in the street, and he told her about the new girl. Her name was Juliette: Henry apparently liked to kiss her hair, one strand at a time, until each one had been kissed. She thought that if she ever went back and found the new girl there, she'd lie down on the bed and loosen her hair, and that would be that. She pushed a hand through her thick brown mane, and said, 'It's lucky for him he didn't try doing that with me or we'd have had to stay together for the rest of our lives.'

V

A garret and a hospital, 1848

EVEN IN SUMMER, the Rue Mazarine was dark and damp; in winter, it was like a crypt. Daylight was blotted out by the tenements and the dome of the Institut, which guarded the exit to the river. Henry's new room, in the boarding house at no. 70, suited his increasingly venerable appearance: it had a straw chair that was going bald and a mirror that was going blind. The bed was not much wider than a bookshelf.

Juliette had left to find another Romeo. The price of bread was rising, and hungry peasants were trudging in from the countryside. As usual when people were queuing outside the pawnshops, there was talk of revolution. Henry's neighbour at the boarding house, M. Proudhon, was visited at all hours by serious men with long beards and elegant, threadbare coats.

He was lying – or rather, balancing – on the bed, wondering how to spend the five hundred francs he had unexpectedly received from the benevolent fund of the Académie Française, when there was a knock at the door.

It was not quite the Lucile he had known. He moved aside to let her pass. In her post-suicidal state, she looked tremendously appealing, as though purified by the disinfectant. Her pockmarked face had a smooth, waxy complexion. Tuberculosis had widened her blue eyes and given them an expression of childish candour.

'I'm disturbing you,' she said.

She told him how to arrange the bed and sent him out to buy some food. When he returned with a loaf of bread, a bottle of wine and some firewood that was still recovering from its long journey down the river, she was fast asleep and snoring.

This time, there were no arguments. Death was a third person in the room, imposing a certain false courtesy and restraint. She lay in bed, coughing into a basin, while Henry busied himself with his column for the fashion magazine and then – while workers and Bohemians fought their revolution in the name of liberty, vanity and sloth – with his reports for Count Tolstoy. He sent copies of the anarchist paper that his friends, Baudelaire, Toubin and Champfleury, had been selling nearby on the Place Saint-André-des-Arts. He supplied some 'unofficial information' on those 'conceited brutes', the proletariat, who thought that hunger was a virtue and other people's wealth a sin. Meanwhile, Lucile was becoming smaller and more angelic by the day.

It was Charles Toubin who arranged for the hospital bed. His brother, the intern, had obtained an admission card. Henry was out when he knocked at the door. Lucile saw the card in his hand and understood.

Later, when he came to write the 'Epilogue of the Loves of Rodolphe and Mademoiselle Mimi', Henry would describe the painful, jolting journey in a taxi, two miles along the *quais* to the hospital of La Pitié. 'Amidst her sufferings, her fondness for pretty clothes – which is the last thing to die in women – survived. Two or three times she had the cab stopped in front of drapers' shops to look at the window displays.'

The hospital register shows that 'Lucile Louvet, florist, wife of François Paulgaire, native of Paris, aged about 24', was admitted to La Pitié on Monday, 6 March 1848. It was the second anniversary of Mimi's first appearance in the *Corsaire-Satan*. Unfortunately for Henry's reputation as a historian, the bus drivers and cabbies were all on strike on Monday, 6 March. Lucile cannot possibly have taken a taxi; she must have reached the hospital on foot.

Henry did not go with her. Toubin assured her that her lover would visit the following Sunday, which was the normal visiting day, but she waited in vain. He knew the leprous walls, the steely nurses, the nightly concerto of coughs and groans. Before long, he would be back in hospital himself. And so he stayed at home, he told himself, out of fidelity to the past. He would preserve the precious memory of their love on paper.

TOUBIN WENT TO the hospital every day and found the girl delirious and in pain. He urged his friend to go and see her.

'I haven't even got two sous to buy her a little bouquet,' he told Toubin. 'But I know of some bushes down Vaugirard way that one day soon will be covered in violets.'

'Just take her your heart,' said Toubin, 'but get a move on.'

He was sitting in the café when he heard the news from Toubin's brother. Passing through the ward, Dr Toubin had found her bed empty and was told by the nurse that 'Number 8 is dead'. Henry went and stood by the window, mopping his eye. Strangely, he felt nothing, as though his love had died with the woman who inspired it. Later that day, he went out to buy a mourner's black felt hat.

In a hospital as large and busy as La Pitié, mistakes were inevitable. Lucile had been moved to another bed. She was calling out for Henry and disturbing the other patients. It took a while to find him and tell him the news. This time, he set off for the hospital without waiting for the violets to bloom.

Dr Toubin met him at the entrance and took his hand. Lucile had died – this time for real – on 8 April, and no one had claimed the body. Henry asked to see her, but the doctor simply pointed to a large wagon standing in front of a building marked 'AMPHITHÉÂTRE'.

In his writer's mind, he saw the students ranged in tiers, writing notes to their mistresses, telling jokes and peering down at the lifeless body of the flower-girl lying in a pool of light while the surgeon exposed the course of a nerve, galvanized a limb or laid bare the heart. A man climbed onto the seat, and the wagon trundled off with another load for the common grave. There would be no funeral. The hat would have to wait for another occasion.

The doctor offered to walk with him, but he felt a sudden craving for solitude. He turned away and retraced his steps along the river towards the forest of chimneys on the Montagne-Sainte-Geneviève. Ill-matched emotions swirled in his mind. The epilogue was already half-written; he wondered who might provide him with the sequel … A coal barge was moving slowly towards the Île de la Cité and the grey dome of the Panthéon. He turned up his collar against the fog. As he walked along, something welled up inside him like the swollen waters of the Seine and the Marne depositing their silt along the *quais*.

VI

Théâtre des Variétés, Thursday, 22 November 1849

THE AUDIENCE FLOWED through the marble foyer, spilling out through the iron gates of the Théâtre des Variétés and into the clutter of cab-horses and umbrellas. It was nine o'clock in the evening. Despite the rain, the pavements were crowded and the cafés were coming to life. The carriage lanterns and street-lamps sent strings of pearls dancing along the boulevard.

The King of Bohemia left the theatre with the young actress on his arm. 'Mimi' was wrapped in a dark cloak. As far as he could tell, she had removed her face paint, though she still looked to him like a coloured engraving in a keepsake. She seemed frail but full of life, like a convalescent leaving the house for the first time after a long illness. As she climbed into the cab, he heard the rustle of her petticoats. He smiled at her through his beard, crying with one eye, and wondered whether he might address her as Mimi. It was not beyond the bounds of possibility that an old theatrical tradition entitled the author to enjoy the favours of the leading lady on the first night …

As it turned the corner of the Rue Drouot, the carriage swayed and he felt her warmth against him. 'Mimi' shifted delicately towards her corner of the coach … It would take some time to find himself in this new world, and to acquire the necessary accoutrements. Mlle

Thuillier's heart was a fortress that would not be conquered without a long, expensive siege. He lit a cigar and savoured the moment. Lowering his window to blow out the smoke, he saw two lovers standing by the glow of a chestnut-seller's brazier, and the pickpockets circling the crowd.

The actress said goodnight while Henry was paying the driver. He walked back past the theatre and the offices of the *Corsaire-Satan*, then across the river to a tiny room under the leaking roof of no. 9, Rue Touraine-Saint-Germain. The tingle of Mlle Thuillier's gloved hand was still on his lips. He sat down at the worm-eaten desk on which he had immortalized Lucile and wrote to a friend: 'You cannot imagine what it's like to find yourself for the first time in your life sitting next to a woman who smells nice.'

A few days later, when *La Vie de Bohème* was still filling the Variétés, Henry Murger gathered up the mementos of his love affairs and 'crossed the bridges' to a plush apartment at no. 48, Rue Notre-Dame de Lorette. It was a new street with no history and a smooth asphalt surface, built on wasteground at the point where the Right Bank rises up towards Montmartre. Funeral processions used it as a quiet short-cut to the cemetery. It was particularly favoured by the deceptively elegant women known as *demi-mondaines*, whose carriages came and went at odd hours, and by wealthy artists who liked to think that they, too, had once lived the Bohemian life.

MARVILLE

I

THE PHOTOGRAPH shows the back end of a Paris square, early on a summer morning, when the noises and smells of the city are still gathering their strength. The time of day can be deduced from the light, which falls from the east, the shadow of the building behind the camera, which has already cleared half the square, and the cleanness of the cobbles. The sun is up, but no one is about, except of course the photographer and his assistant.

The picture was taken in 1865, which is hard to believe, given the glassy clarity of the shot. There is more detail per square inch than seems possible for the period. Here at the dawn of the visible past, the buildings look almost radiant in their grime, as though they haven't yet learned how to pose for a camera.

This is a real neighbourhood, scoured and crannied with habits and ambitions. Two or three splats of horse manure are visible on the cobbles, like blobs of paint on a canvas. A zoologist could probably identify the animal's diet, estimate its speed across the square and even guess its breed and colour, if the droppings are consistent with the small grey horses that are waiting in front of a low building, hitched to removal carts, patiently enough for their heads to be only slightly blurred. Otherwise, the square is clean. The crossing sweepers have come and gone. In a poem written four years before this photograph was taken, Baudelaire remembered walking across a deserted square

> . . . at the hour when the cleaning crews
> Send their dark storms swirling into the silent air.

On the corner of one of the two narrow streets that run away to the west, a grey blur might be a dust-devil raised by the sweepers, or perhaps just the albumen-and-collodion ghost of someone hurrying from the scene into the Rue Saint-André-des-Arts.

The odd shape of the square commemorates something that no longer exists. The church of Saint-André was one of only two churches in Paris that were entirely separate from the surrounding buildings. It was sold during the Revolution and removed like an unwanted growth, leaving only the space it had occupied for six hundred years. Somewhere near the spot where the photographer has set up his tripod, a crying infant was held over a font and baptized François-Marie Arouet (he later rechristened himself Voltaire). The masonry remains like some ancient volcanic surge when the softer stone has been eroded.

Now, the walls that used to see nothing but other walls are festooned with letters from every page of a typesetter's sample book, as numerous as the cartouches in an Egyptian tomb. Fifty feet in the air, a giant invalid lies on a mechanical bed that can be hired or purchased at 28 Rue Serpente. The forty-centime baths around the corner in the Rue Larrey are in competition with the more distant but sophisticated steam baths at 27 Rue Monsieur-le-Prince.

Even if the date of the photograph were unknown, it could still be deduced from the addresses on the advertisements: the greater the distance, the later in time. In 1865, no one is expected to go shopping in streets across the river. A person could stand where the photographer stood and compose a comprehensive shopping list. She could buy some glass for a broken window, some wallpaper and furniture – or a piece of leather for the armchair – and hire a removal cart (from M. Mondet) to take away the items that were damaged by the rain. M. Robbe (5 Rue Gît-le-Cœur) could repair the window frame, and M. Geliot at no. 24 could check the lead flashing and the zinc roofing. She could buy a print engraving (a Notre-Dame is displayed in the furniture-shop window), and a new piece of porcelain or crystal from A. Desvignes. She could order some coal and some wine (also from M. Mondet), buy a cheese at the *crémerie* and a book to read by the fire. She need never leave the *quartier*.

So much information is contained in that split-second burst of photons that if the glass plate survived a holocaust and lay buried under rubble for centuries in a leather satchel, there would be enough to compile a small, speculative encyclopedia of Paris in the late second millennium. It might even contain some pieces of information that were missing from encyclopedias published while the city still existed. If the middle section of M. Robbe's advertisement for firewood had not come adrift, we might never have known that some of those words were not painted on the walls but printed on rainproof cloth and hung up like backdrops.

Few writers even mention this ubiquitous plague of advertising. A single phrase in Baudelaire's notebook is almost the only surviving evidence of its impact: '*Immense nausée des affiches*' – an overdose of advertising, or a bad case of publicity sickness. Imagine a poet testing words in his mind, measuring rhythms with his feet, bombarded with verbless phrases. As a teenager, he walked the streets of his native city,

> . . . stumbling upon words as on the paving-stones,
> Sometimes bumping into lines I'd dreamt of long before.

Now, there are pavements, like the one in front of the glassware depository, with proper kerbs and gutters. There is no longer any excuse for stumbling. Baudelaire has taken to writing poems in prose. The art lover who grew up with the smell of his father's oil paints has begun to look at photographs, and even to savour their 'cruel and surprising charm'. He probably knows the photographer, and he certainly knows his work, but Charles Marville usually sends an associate to exhibitions. He keeps his techniques and his friendships to himself. He feels quite at home in a city devoid of people, at the hour when the sun shines for no one but himself and his assistant.

By the time the removal carts have trundled off, and the chairs outside the wine-shop are occupied, the photographer and his assistant will be back in the Faubourg Saint-Germain, on the aerial terrace at 27 Rue Saint-Dominique, photographing the vast pageant of clouds, the airborne battalions that are several times wider than a city, bound for some indefinable realm beyond the suburbs.

WITH THE SKIES' rippling explosion still developing on his retina, Marville leaves the terrace and retreats into the studio where the light is purple and umber. There are stained-glass windows and dark oak cupboards. The wallpaper is embossed with sombre vegetation. The assistant carefully removes the pane of collodion-coated glass from the wooden frame. At this stage of the process, the glass appears quite blank. Then he pours on the solution of pyrogallic acid and ferrous sulphate, and, by some chemical trick for which science has no explanation, the light from the morning square turns the silver into reality.

This alchemy-in-reverse always amazes him. It looks like a pristine, miniature city from which the inhabitants have fled, a neighbourhood after the plague or a chemical bomb dropped from a balloon. There are traces of human life but no people. His assistant plunges the plate into the gold chloride to darken the tones. Marville watches the young man's dark hair fall across his cheek-bone as he bends over the porcelain basin. The assistant washes the negative and fixes the image with cyanide of potassium. Words appear as though they were printed on the plate before it was exposed to the light: BAINS d'EAU; LITS & FAUTEUILS; *COMMERCE DE VINS*.

He sees the *quartier* caught unawares. This is the square *en déshabillé*, in its own private time zone, a section of abandoned city with all its interiors intact. He is pleased by the evident chaos of misaligned walls, the stain-trails of rainwater, the patched-up render, the slump of the house-fronts, the dislocated cobbles and the absence of people. The only vehicles are the removal carts: perhaps, behind one of the windows, someone is gathering together her belongings.

The image joins the other prints that are waiting to be framed for the exhibition: four hundred and twenty-five pictures of a magical, vacant metropolis called Marville. The Emperor will see the dingy peristyles and the crumbling pylons, and be reminded of his uncle's expedition to Egypt, the monuments to vanished gods, frozen in the desert. He might wonder how much of Paris he has really seen, and how anyone can be said to govern a city so full of secrets.

IN THE STUDIO, the light grows darker as the sun grows more insistent. The assistant tightens the latch on the shutters, and makes certain that the curtains overlap.

When photography was still a sideshow on the boulevard, Marville set up his easel in the Forest of Fontainebleau. He drew empty landscapes for magazines and illustrated storybooks – *Paul et Virginie*, *The Banks of the Seine, The Arabian Nights* – and left his colleague to insert the human figures. His own figures were always clumsy and incongruous. Now, he finds his solitude in Paris, on expeditions with his assistant. Certain times of day are more suitable than others, but the time of day can be lengthened indefinitely, divided up into fractions of seconds.

Fresh coffee helps to neutralize the smell of ammonium and varnish; it concentrates the mind. These days, only an old-fashioned artist with a paint-spattered smock would use alcohol to stimulate his brain and to steady his hand. The silken slip of albumen paper is laid on the proof. The slightest defect will be visible – a mote of dust, a speck of tripoli stone, a furtive sunbeam.

The scene glows red (an effect of the albumen) until the final washing. The print is rinsed, dried and pressed. A light coat of wax and mastic is applied. The assistant places the print on the table and stands back like a painter from his easel.

Marville takes a magnifying-glass: his eye wanders from window to window, looking for the familiar pattern of smudges. It takes a long time to explore the scene … At last, he sees them: they might be mistaken for imperfections on the plate, and even at this level of precision, it is hard to be sure. A slightly stooping form in a long, grey coat is entering the *crémerie*. At the window between the Bains d'Eau and the Bains de Vapeur, a pale circle bisected by the railing, and a patch of light beneath, might be someone holding a bowl of coffee, looking out at the two photographers in the square below. There is so much clutter in the scene that these wan blotches are barely noticeable.

He sits up now and surveys the whole picture. This time, he realizes that it has an unexpected focal point – the little balcony on wooden struts, high above the wine shop, level with the invalid on the orthopedic bed. A shed with six windows and a stovepipe – it might almost have been transplanted from some outlying village – leans against a whitewashed wall that might almost be a cottage. A long pole is propped on the railings to keep open a skylight in the tiled roof. Six box shrubs have been arrayed in pots, and there, to the left of the little hedge, a figure bends over a piece of work. It might just be a rag that looks like a head of grey hair, but it has a certain distracting poignancy.

The figure could be removed with a paintbrush dipped in India ink and a gum solution. This is how some photographers eradicate splotches on a face or a sleeve. But he likes the way in which the camera turns a human form into something small and fleeting, like a puddle on the cobbles or a reflection on a windowpane.

The varnished print is left to dry. Marville spends the afternoon indoors with his assistant. He photographs him from behind, poring over prints in the studio. He photographs him with his shock of black hair, reclining on the terrace with chimney-pots in the background, like a Nubian lion or a Paris alley-cat. He photographs him in close-up, as delicately as though his face were a row of buildings, with his marble forehead and the slender balconies of his eyebrows under the stormy sky of his hair. It might be the portrait of a poet, with almond eyes and cruel lips, lit beautifully like the square in the morning sun.

II

IN HIS OFFICIAL OFFICE above the Seine – not the private study next to his bedroom, but the state room with three large windows looking onto the Place de l'Hôtel de Ville – the model inhabitant of New Paris sits at a large desk. It is, without a shadow of a doubt, a glorious morning. His shoes are spotless; he is breathing easily. No one has arrived late for work. A statistic can be brought to him within minutes. A garden of Mediterranean shrubs and sub-tropical flowers separates his building from the river.

Georges-Eugène Haussmann almost dwarfs his desk, which occupies the centre of the room. When he wears his medals, as he does today, his chest looks like an expensive apartment block. He can imagine – he has seen enough caricatures of Baron Haussmann the demolition man, the trowel-wielding beaver, the monumental hench-man of Napoleon III – his forehead supported by caryatids. When the Emperor arrives, he will have to stoop to compensate for the difference in height.

Behind him, mounted on rolling frames, the specially engraved 1:5000 map of Paris (not sold in shops) stands ready to be wheeled into the light. It forms his backdrop when he sits at the desk. He often turns around and becomes absorbed in it. Notre-Dame, which is now exposed and visible across the river, precisely where it ought to be in relation to everything else, is the size of his thumbprint; the rectangle of the Louvre and the Tuileries is contained within the compass of his index finger and his pinkie.

He looks down at the Place de l'Hôtel de Ville and sees the accelerated movement of carriages across the square. He understands the flow of traffic, the vents and flumes of intersections, the multiple valves of his radiating, starry squares, of which there are now twenty-one in Paris.

Thanks to him, parts of Paris have seen the sky for the first time since the city was a swamp. Twenty per cent of the city now consists of roads and open spaces; thirty per cent if one includes the Bois de Boulogne and the Bois de Vincennes. For every square metre of land there are six square metres of floor space. The outer suburbs have been incorporated into the city, which is now fifty per cent larger than it was before 1860.

Recently, he has been asked to redesign Rome. The irony is not lost on him, Georges-Eugène Haussmann, the son of Alsatian Protestants. The Archbishop of Paris paid him a compliment that is engraved in his memory and that he would like to see engraved on a plinth:

> Your mission supports mine. In broad, straight streets that are bathed in light, people do not behave in the same slovenly fashion as in streets that are narrow, twisted and dark. To bring air, light and water to the pauper's hovel not only restores physical health, it promotes good housekeeping and cleanliness, and thus improves morality.

It also allows a busy man like Baron Haussmann to reach any part of Paris within the hour and in a presentable condition. It means that he can dovetail his duties as a father and a husband with official functions, and with the performances of Mlle Cellier at the Opéra – the actress he dresses like his daughter – and Marie Roze at the Opéra-Comique. He has created a city for lovers who also have families and jobs.

He was brought in as a steam-roller, as a man of experience and grit. He knows that a regime founders, not on barricades, but on committee tables. The Emperor would rather not disband the Conseil Municipal, but he would like to see it behave with one mind (his

1. From the 'Plan Turgot', by Louis Bretez (map commissioned by Michel-Étienne Turgot), 1734–39.

2. Louis-Léopold Boilly, *The Galleries of the Palais Royal* (1809; the original version, now lost, was shown at the 1804 Paris Salon). Some of the gentlemen may be British visitors, taking advantage of the Peace of Amiens (1802–03).

3. *View taken from under the Arch of Givry* (1807), by John Claude Nattes, engraved by John Hill: Pont au Change, Conciergerie and Tour de l'Horloge. The arcades, flooded at high tide, ran under the Quai de Gesvres and later formed part of a tunnel in the Métro.

4. 'Monsieur, someone has robbed me of a thousand-franc note':
Honoré Daumier's view of Vidocq's Bureau des Renseignements.
Le Charivari, 6 November 1836.

5. Gustave Le Gray, *Paris, View of Montmartre*
(a montage: cityscape, c. 1849–50; sky, c. 1855–56).

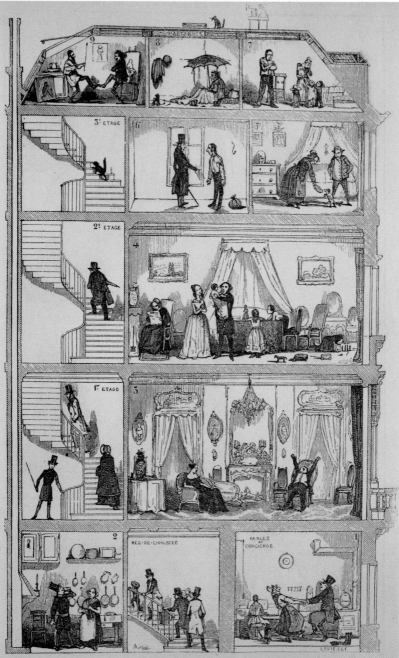

COUPE D'UNE MAISON PARISIENNE LE 1ᵉʳ JANVIER 1845.

— CINQ ÉTAGES DU MONDE PARISIEN —

6. *Opposite.* 'Cross-section of a
Parisian house on 1 January 1845',
by Bertall (Albert d'Arnoux).
Le Diable à Paris, vol. II (1846).

7. 'Le Stryge' at Notre-Dame
(1853), by Charles Nègre. The man
is the photographer Henri Le Secq.
The streets below were demolished
to make way for the new
Hôtel-Dieu hospital.

8. *Above*. The Siege of Paris, 1870, by R. Briant: the Prussian army to the south of Paris, and Thiers's fortifications, on the line of the present Boulevards des Maréchaux, just inside the Périphérique.

9. *Left*. The Hôtel de Ville, torched by Communards. June 1871.

10. *Opposite*. Gustave Caillebotte, *Young Man at His Window* (1875): the artist's brother at the corner of Rue de Miromesnil and Rue de Lisbonne, with Boulevard Malesherbes in the background.

11. Camille Pissarro, *Avenue de l'Opéra, Sun, Winter Morning* (1898), from the Grand Hôtel du Louvre.

12. Universal Exhibition of 1900: Champ de Mars station, Celestial Globe and Maréorama (an attraction simulating a sea voyage from Paris to Yokohama).

own). Baron Haussmann has no intention of running budgets like a petit bourgeois. The days of cautious, paternalistic Préfets are over. A great city like Paris must be allowed her whims and extravagance. Paris is a courtesan who demands a tribute of millions and a fully coordinated residence: flower-beds, kiosks, litter-bins, advertising columns, street furniture, *chalets de nécessité*. She will not be satisfied with small-scale improvements.

Later that month, his childhood home will be demolished.

He is often asked (though not as often as he would like) how he manages to run the city and to rebuild it at the same time. He tells them what he told his accountants and his engineers when he took over as Préfet de la Seine, thirteen years ago:

There is more time than most people think in twenty-four hours. Many things can be fitted in between six in the morning and midnight when one has an active body, an alert and open mind, an excellent memory, and especially when one needs only a modicum of sleep. Remember, too, that there are also Sundays, of which a year contains fifty-two.

Since he grasped the reins of power in 1853, three Heads of Accounting have died of exhaustion.

He looks down at the square and sees a row of taxi-cabs and a small detachment of cavalry. The Emperor is due to arrive, to view the commissioned photographs. His carriage will encounter a stretch of unrepaired tarmacadam where the Avenue Victoria meets the Rue Saint-Martin, and he will arrive approximately three minutes late.

Seventeen years ago, Louis-Napoléon arrived at the Gare du Nord with a map of Paris in his pocket, on which non-existent avenues were marked in blue, red, yellow and green pencil, according to the degree of urgency. Nearly all of those avenues have now been built or scheduled, and many of the Baron's own ideas have enhanced the original plan. The Île de la Cité, where twenty thousand people lived like rats, is now an island of administrative buildings with the Morgue at its tip. The waters of the River Dhuys have been brought sixty miles by aqueduct, and Parisians are no longer forced to drink their own filth, pumped from the Seine or filtered through the corpses of their ancestors.

Haussmann told the Emperor about the conversation that took place after the council meeting – because the Emperor likes to hear about his steam-roller getting the better of ministers and civil servants:

'You should have been a duke by now, Haussmann.'
'Duke of what?'
'Oh, I don't know, Duc de la Dhuys.'
'In that case, *duc* would not suffice.'
'Is that so? What should it be, then? Prince? ...'
'No, I should have to be made an *aqueduc*, and that title is not to be found in the list of nobiliary titles!'

Some people say that the Emperor never laughs, but he laughed when he heard about the aqueduke.

Anything that binds him to the Emperor is good for Paris. That year, his daughter gave birth to the Emperor's child, three days before her marriage, to which the Emperor gave his blessing. His Majesty even offered to pay for a dowry, which the Baron refused, because no one must be able to accuse him of corruption.

HE STANDS WHERE the mirror shows him in his entirety, from bald head to polished boot. At times like this, when a few extra minutes have been built into the schedule, he allows himself the luxury of remembering. He remembers the boy with the body of a man and an incongruous susceptibility to asthma. He remembers – in this order – his home in the quiet Quartier Beaujon, the boots that stood waiting for him every morning, the walk to lectures in the Latin Quarter, the depressing view that faced him like an insult from the arch of the old Pont Saint-Michel, and the state of his boots after the square where the drains of the Latin Quarter had their muddy confluence.

All that ugliness will vanish from one edition of the map to the next. The Boulevard Saint-Michel has smashed through the warren of streets, and the new Boulevard Saint-André will erase the Place Saint-André-des-Arts. The ends of the buildings exposed by the Boulevard Saint-Michel have been cauterized with a fountain on which a snarling Satan (too small for the Baron's liking) is trampled by a Saint Michael with wings as beautiful as a waterproof cloak. He calls this his revenge on the past.

When he took the Emperor to see this new gateway to the Latin Quarter, the Emperor looked along the parallel lines of house-fronts, and his eye fell, as planned, on the spire of the Sainte-Chapelle across the river. Then he turned to the Baron and said, with a smile, 'Now I can see why you were so keen on your symmetrical arrangement. You did it for the view!'

He hears the clatter of horses and guardsmen's sabres on the square below. The Emperor will see the photographs and perhaps, this time, won't tease him about his 'weakness' for symmetry. He always talks about London, where traffic and troop movements were the essential point. But, as Haussmann reminds him, 'Parisians are more demanding than Londoners.' He has been known to triple the width of an avenue for effect, and also, he would admit, to sabotage the paltry designs of the Emperor's favourite architect, Hittorff. He may be a steam-roller but he understands the principles of beauty. A painting must always have a focal point and a frame, which is why it is now possible to stand in the middle of the Boulevard de Sébastopol and to see the Gare de l'Est at one end and the dome of the Tribunal de Commerce like a full stop at the other – except when the mists are rising from the Seine, filling the avenues and blurring perspectives, turning carriages and pedestrians into a procession of grey ghosts.

THE DOUBLE DOORS are opened to admit His Imperial Majesty Napoleon III.

The man still has the dimensions of the prison cell about him. He lives in palaces but looks as though he could fit into a tiny space at a moment's notice. There is something about his smallness that commands respect. Baron Haussmann will not be asked to die for his Emperor, but he is prepared to sacrifice his reputation, which is besmirched almost every day – by liberals and socialists, who forget that the poor now have more hospital beds and proper graves; by nostalgic bohemians, who forget everything; and even by his own social equals, who find the inconvenience of moving house too heavy a price to pay for the most beautiful city in the world.

The framed photographs have been arrayed on the table in geographical order.

This makes a nice change from the usual squabbles with architects. (The Emperor speaks in short sentences, like an oracle.) He has sat for many photographers, but this Marville is unknown to him.

The Baron explains – it is unclear whether it was his idea or the Historical Committee's: Marville is the official photographer of the Louvre. He takes photographs of emperors and pharaohs, Etruscan vases, and medieval cathedrals that are being demolished and rebuilt; he records artefacts that have been disinterred and rescued from the past. Marville was commissioned to photograph the sections of Paris that are about to be buried and forgotten. It might be seen as archaeology in reverse: first the ruins, then the city that covers them up. A copy of the Plan was given to M. Marville, who then set off to erect his tripod at every designated site.

At this, the Emperor turns his head towards the Baron with what could be a quizzical smile: knowledge of the Plan (as their enemies point out) would allow a speculator to buy up properties before the City expropriates them and pays a handsome compensation. But Marville is an artist, not a businessman – so much is clear from the photographs.

They stand at the table and survey the scenes that are about to disappear. They see the wasted space, the lack of uniformity, the corners where rubbish collects and thieves lurk. They sense the provincial hush and the age-old habits. Sometimes, there are flecks that might be bullet-holes in the walls, and scratches on the plate that look like scraps of cloud above a battlefield, but mostly the images are sharp and clean.

They pause over one print in particular, though it has nothing of obvious interest. It shows the back end of a square that looks overpopulated and deserted at the same time. The Baron identifies the tenements on the right as the handiwork of one of his predecessors, Prefect Rambuteau, and makes a rumbling sound of satisfied disapproval. He points to the tenements wedged into the corner of the square and the Rue Saint-André-des-Arts. The photographer has captured the anaemic radiance that fills the Latin Quarter in the early morning. The light that bathes the facade of no. 22 only intensifies the gloom. Its shielded windows suggest some secret life behind.

The building has wooden blinds instead of shutters, hung out over the window railings, which means that the day is warm but not windy. This is the economical style that was used by Prefect Rambuteau in the 1840s, with grooves scored in the plaster to imitate expensive freestone, and, instead of a continuous balcony, iron railings at the foot of each window and a ledge no wider than a kerb. Baron Haussmann remembers the scene from his student days: the area of no particular shape, veering off from the Place Saint-Michel; the bookshop at no. 22 with the puddle in front of it. The image is so vivid that, without thinking, he glances down at his boots.

Only a man who had walked there a thousand times would know that the neighbourhood is bulging with books. No. 22 alone contains one hundred thousand volumes, advertised as *dépareillés*, which means they belong to broken sets. This is a bookshop that can make a mystery of any life. It once shared the building with the publisher of 'la Bibliothèque Populaire', a series devoted to antiquities: Chardin's history of the East Indies; Chanut's *Campagne de Bonaparte en Égypte et en Syrie*. This is where Champollion-Figeac, brother of the decipherer of hieroglyphics, published his famous treatise on archaeology.

The *quartier* has barely changed. From one of those windows at no. 22, Baudelaire looked out on his first Parisian landscape. He was seven years old. His father was dead, and his mother was still in mourning. He wrote to his mother in 1861 and reminded her of their time together in the Place Saint-André-des-Arts: 'Long walks and never-ending kindness! I remember the banks of the Seine that were so melancholy in the evening. For me, those were the good old days . . . I had you all to myself.'

By chance, no. 22 appears on another of the photographs, further along the table, at the foot of an advertisement for kitchen stoves and garden furniture: 'The Special Billposting and Sign Company is still at 22, Rue Saint-André-des-Arts.' Some of those advertisements that upset the poet's mind must have come from his childhood home at no. 22. Coincidences like this are unremarkable in a set of four hundred and twenty-five photographs. If Baron Haussmann notices any of those words on the walls on Paris, it is only because wall space is a source of revenue for the city, and because some of the words are the visible portents of his power: 'VENTE DE MOBILIER', 'FERMETURE POUR CAUSE D'EXPROPRIATION', 'BUREAU DE DÉMOLITION'.

THEY SPEND much longer than they mean to, staring at the glassy image. The Emperor has no intention of inspecting all four hundred and twenty-five photographs, but he lingers over this one, as though trying to dissolve some difficult thought into the image. The Baron adjusts his position once or twice. He pictures the gaping space that will open up where the masonry blocks the view. He briefly imagines himself standing on the demolition site, recognizing the twisted metal remnant of that balcony in the centre of the picture – if such a cluttered mess can be said to have a centre. He imagines the Emperor's compliment when he notices the columns of the Odéon Theatre neatly framed at the far end of the new Boulevard Saint-André.

As he wedges a finger under the photograph to turn to the next one, the Emperor raises his hand. Something has occurred to him ... He sometimes asks odd questions, perhaps on principle or simply out of distraction, it is hard to tell. He wants to know where the people are. (Marville is not there in person to explain; he has sent a messenger with the photographs.) Why are those daylit streets so empty? Is the *quartier* already half-abandoned?

The answer is obvious. The streets are empty because anything that moves, disappears – the smoke from a pipe, a cart-wheel turning a corner, a bird fluttering down to the cobbles. All movement is lost in long exposures. But this is one of those false gems of historical wisdom (photography has made such rapid progress): the thought of a sitter forced to resist an itch, smile frozen, head clamped ...

The first photographic image of a human being in the open air is the scarecrow figure of a man on Daguerre's photograph of the Boulevard du Temple, taken from the roof of his studio in 1838. This lone pioneer in the photographic past seems to have stopped at the last tree before the corner of the Rue du Temple to have his shoes shined. Everyone else has vanished, along with all the traffic. But in 1838, the shortest exposure time for a daguerreotype was fifteen minutes. Unless the bootblack was unusually conscientious, rubbing and buffing until a faint image of his face appeared on the leather, the man must have been sent down by the photographer to stand still for as long as he could in the river of vanishing pedestrians, to give some human life to the scene.

In 1865, exposure times have been reduced to the blink of an eye. In 1850, Gustave Le Gray was photographing summer landscapes in forty seconds. In 1853, the Emperor's photographer, Disdéri, removed and replaced the cotton pad in front of the lens as quickly as a conjurer waving his wand: 'If I count to two, the print is over-exposed.' He took razor-sharp pictures of children, horses, ducks and a peacock displaying its tail, though, for some reason, he could never make the Emperor's eyes look focused. Twelve years later, some of Marville's photographs show dogs going about their business, stuck to the pavement in perfect, four-legged focus.

The streets are empty because this is early morning. But even in the heart of Paris, despite Baron Haussmann's thirty-two thousand gas lamps, the working day is still regulated by the sun. The horses are standing on their shadows, and the hour is later than it seems. There is still just one 'business district' – around the new Opéra, where only bank managers and courtesans have nested in the expensive new apartments financed by men with close ties to Baron Haussmann's son-in-law. Everyone else comes in from leafy *quartiers* in the west. Most Parisians commute to work from round the corner, from one room of the apartment to the next, or from the entresol to the shop below.

Baron Haussmann's secretaries could produce the statistic in an instant: every minute, on the biggest and busiest boulevards – Capucines, Italiens, Poissonnière, Saint-Denis – at the busiest times of day, fewer than seven vehicles go past in both directions. On the Rue de Rivoli and the Champs-Élysées, one vehicle passes every twenty seconds. Just behind the photographer's right shoulder, on the new Pont Saint-Michel, only the blind, the deaf, the lame, the distracted and the dithering are in danger from the traffic. Baudelaire was already suffering from premature old age when he wrote 'To a Passer-By' in 1860:

> The deafening street was roaring all around me ...

The woman whose eye he catches is 'agile' and 'fleeting', 'lifting and swaying the hem and scallop of her dress'. She is dressed in formal mourning but still able to cross the road with dignity.

> A flash ... then darkness! ... Shall I never see you again
> Until eternity begins?

A century later, the passer-by and the poet might have had time to start a conversation while they waited for the lights to change. They might have sat down at the pavement café, or stood still in the rushing crowd. A photographer with a high-speed camera might have caught them kissing ...

Baron Haussmann leaves the Emperor's question unanswered. The Emperor is probably thinking of London – the last place where he deigned to notice the life of the streets, and where he acquired his irksome predilection for 'squares' and tarmacadam, which is expensive and difficult to maintain.

'Give me another year,' says the Baron, 'and I'll turn that square into Piccadilly Circus.'

The Emperor has to leave for Compiègne, where the Empress goes riding in a forest filled with signposts. Before he leaves, he mentions the stretch of unrepaired tarmacadam on the Avenue Victoria. The Baron takes the opportunity to mention asphalt coating, wood-block paving, granite and porphyry slabs. He is investigating a new adhesive paste and leather soles for horses ... The Emperor, as ever, appreciates the Baron's sense of humour. He looks forward to seeing the later photographs, when the streets have been cleansed of their festering tenements and exposed to the full light of day.

III

IN A CITY that changes almost from one blink of an eye to the next, urban planners and photographers must resign themselves to the knowledge that some of their time will be wasted and their efforts in vain.

Under the soaring minarets of the Trocadéro Palace, which was constructed for the Universal Exhibition of 1878 by the architect who designed the fountain in the Place Saint-Michel, three rooms have been assigned to the City of Paris. One thousand wooden frames containing photographs are hinged to wooden columns and can be turned like the pages of a newspaper. The display is listed in the catalogue as '*Modification of streets – photographs of streets old and new.*' The prints, which are so vivid that the viewer seems to be examining the scenes through a flawless lens, are paired with other photographs, of wide avenues, endless iron balconies and isolated monuments that retreat into the mist.

Charles Marville is not at the exhibition, and his name is not mentioned in the official report on the exhibits, which confines itself to generalities: 'In the various branches of its immense administration, the City of Paris has continual recourse to photography.' The report regrets the use of silver salts and gold-tone in the reproduction of prints 'that will sooner or later disappear', and it notes that the photographs have proved useful as forensic evidence 'in questions of expropriation'.

The picture of the Place Saint-André-des-Arts is missing from the exhibition. Baron Haussmann is no longer at the Hôtel de Ville (he was forced to resign in 1870 to placate the liberal opposition), the Emperor has returned to exile in England and some of the avenues that were traced on the map in coloured pencil are in perpetual abeyance. The Boulevard Saint-André will never be completed. Marville himself has disappeared and his business has been sold. The last evidence of his activity is an invoice sent to the Committee of Historical Works for photographs of the new streets that replaced the old. A photographer with the name of his assistant died in 1878, and Marville is thought to have died at about the same time. The place of his death is unknown.

Though some of Marville's techniques can be deduced from the surviving plates, his own opinions remain obscure. Nostalgia has coated his scenes with its tenacious patina, and in the absence of letters and reported conversations, no one knows what Marville himself thought about the modernization of Paris. His photographs might be portraits painted by a lover, or municipal documents in which the only trace of passion is the photographer's love of light and shade and unsuspected detail.

THERE IS NOTHING to compare with the photograph of the Place Saint-André-des-Arts until 1898, when another photographer sets up his tripod on the same spot. He was once a cabin boy and then an actor. Now, Eugène Atget lugs his heavy bellows camera and his glass plates about the city, taking photographs which he sells to painters as '*documents pour artistes*'.

Thirty-three years have passed. The glassware depository has disappeared – demolished to make way for the street that never became a boulevard – but Mondet is still a big name in the *quartier*. The family came from the Hautes-Alpes, and its 'Commerce de Vins' now has a picturesque name: Café des Alpes. A removal cart and a dray loaded with barrels stand in front of the café, where a customer can eat the 'Plat du jour', screened from the square by the horse's rump. The horse is at least two hands taller than the horses in Marville's photograph. The invalid on his orthopedic bed has been replaced by an advertisement for a piano salesroom, two miles away across the river on the Boulevard Poissonnière. The balcony is still clinging to the masonry, with what appears to be the same railing, but the shed and its windows have gone. The light is murkier, either in reality or on the print, and there is no sign of the balcony's inhabitant.

As time passes, it becomes harder to resolve the details. On a postcard that must have been printed in 1907, the scene is almost totally eclipsed by the black girders of a circular caisson being lowered into the square: this will be one of the entrances to the Saint-Michel Métro station. The wall above the café can be glimpsed through the girders: it carries an advertisement for the Dufayel chain of department stores, where everything can be bought for cash or on credit 'at the same price in more than 700 shops in Paris and the provinces'. A postcard picture of the floods of January 1910, when the square lay under six inches of Seine water, is just sharp enough to show a new name on the café awning: 'Au Rendez-Vous du Métro'.

In 1949, the little balcony makes a fleeting appearance in Burgess Meredith's adaptation of a Simenon novel, *The Man on the Eiffel Tower*. Maigret's sidekick pursues the mad villain (played by Franchot Tone), skipping impossibly across the chimneys all the way from

Montmartre to the Place Saint-André-des-Arts. Tone drops down onto the balcony, opens the door and disappears.

In a book on Baudelaire's Paris homes, published in 1967, a black-and-white photograph shows the café beneath the balcony (now called La Gentilhommière) half-obscured by a Citroën DS, but instantly recognizable from Marville's photograph of a century before. It must have been taken at about the time when La Gentilhommière was frequented by Jack Kerouac, who came in search of ancestors, love and alcoholic illumination. The wall above the café is white and bare. Soon, it will be covered with graffiti, which appears in the early 1970s and changes faster than the advertisements ever did.

The balcony can still be seen on some images on the Internet: it seems to be one of those secret places that inspire a fleeting desire in anyone who happens to notice them. Some of the images show the building to the right of the café, on the corner of the Rue Saint-André-des-Arts. In the days of Baron Haussmann, when whole neighbourhoods were being reduced to rubble, and houses shook to the vibrations of demolition carts, no one would have guessed that Baudelaire's childhood home would be standing after a century and a half. It still has blinds instead of shutters, perhaps because the windows of pre-Haussmann buildings are too close together to allow wooden shutters to be fully opened, or because buildings, like people, have ingrained habits, and there is little point in changing one's ways when demolition is imminent.

REGRESSION

7

As far as anyone knew, the head had last been seen in the attics of the École de Médecine. It was an unusual item, not the sort of thing that would have been easily mislaid or confused with something else. Unlike its neighbours – most of whom were prehistoric bipeds, chimpanzees, murderers and lunatics – it was fully fleshed. Its owner had not been dug out of a neglected graveyard or eaten by his enemies. He had been a great leader, who had forged tiny nations into a powerful and righteous alliance, and dealt a mighty blow to French national pride and interests.

This much was known for certain: the head had been shipped to the Ministère de la Marine in Paris. From there, it had been sent across the Seine to M. Broca's little museum at the École de Médecine, where it might have proved useful to scholars as they stumbled towards a better understanding of the advance and occasional regression of the human race.

What was done with heads when they decayed or were no longer required by science, no one could say, and so there was quite a flurry of paperwork and rummaging in old storerooms when Prime Minister Rocard acceded to the request of independence movements to have the head of their historic leader returned to the home of his ancestors.

That was in 1988. A century and a decade had passed since the head had arrived in Paris, and the science that had looked to skulls for a measure of its own state of civilization had long since been discarded as jiggery-pokery. A few objects bearing some relation to the head had appeared at the Universal Exhibitions of 1878 and 1889, but not the head itself, which would have been considered too precious a specimen to be exposed to the rough and tumble of such an event. There were mummified remains, a few tools and musical instruments, a crude bust of Victor Hugo and some weapons – stone axes, spears and stolen rifles – that were described by the *Bulletin* of the Geographical Society as 'the last efforts of a doomed race, which, far from setting it free, serve only to tighten its bonds and hasten the hour of its complete extinction'.

Unfortunately, no record could be found of the head, and the negotiators from the overseas territory had to return home with nothing but diplomatic documents and promises. A Parisian newspaper, being less than sensitive to the political aspirations of the former colony, joked that, once again, the administration of Prime Minister Rocard had 'lost its head'.

6

NEWS OF THE INSURRECTION had reached Paris with an even longer delay than usual. The telegraph wires had been cut, and the postal service to Sydney (five days in fair weather) had been interrupted. The first detailed list of victims appeared in the *Figaro* before the government received the news. A *Figaro* reader who had sailed from Nouméa after the first troubles had sent it on the packet from the Sandwich Islands. The list was divided into settlers, civil servants, gendarmes, freed prisoners, deportees and domesticated natives. In all, there were one hundred and thirty-six names. The brief descriptions gave readers in Paris the impression of a peaceful colony that had been struck by a terrible disaster: there were soldiers and policemen, but also a telegrapher, a gardener, a road engineer, a deportee who served at the hotel and two families whose little children had been murdered by the savages.

Though the report explicitly denied that this had ever been the case, Nouméa itself had been threatened. The capital of New Caledonia covered approximately the same area as Paris, but it counted barely four thousand inhabitants, almost all of whom were European. By normal standards, its fortifications were primitive. They had been constructed by French and Algerian deportees from the penal colony on the Ducos peninsula, which formed the northern shore of the harbour. The harbour was protected by gun batteries and by the white coral reefs that placed a ring of silver around the island, as well as by a mariner's nightmare of little coves and marshy creeks. But an attack from the interior was hard to repel. The bare hills that looked down on the wooden town were surrounded by forests. When the man who kept watch from the semaphore tower was butchered and eaten, his Kanak murderers could only be driven back into the hinterland, where a dry haze hung over the Humboldt Massif. At the time the troubles began, only a band of soldiers and a Basque shepherd with a flock of two hundred sheep had safely traversed the southern part of the island, though several explorers had reported helpful and inquisitive natives who indulged their cannibalistic instincts only on special occasions.

It had been obvious from the outset that, despite their willingness to defend their farmsteads to the death, the colonists would provide insufficient reinforcements for the garrison. And so the decision had been taken, with some misgivings on the part of the Governor, to arm the convicts and the political prisoners. On 19 June, a settler called M. Chêne had refused to return a native woman to her tribe and had been brutally murdered. This first hint of a tribal uprising gave everyone a keen sense of their frailty and common purpose. Hardened criminals who had been shipped to Nouméa in irons, anarchists who had plotted the downfall of France and Algerian freedom fighters who had tried to repel the French invader, all served with distinction – though a small number of anarchists lived up to their reputation. Louise Michel, known as the Red Virgin, showed Kanak tribesmen how to cut telegraph wires, and when their forests were set on fire, some of the savages who hoped to escape by setting out across the Pacific Ocean in canoes came to bid her farewell and were given the famous red scarf she had worn on the barricades in Paris.

Apart from this predictable reversion to type, the deportees behaved with discipline and courage. The skills they had acquired in fighting the French were put to good use, and the people of Nouméa, seeing the columns of smoke that rose above the forests becoming ever more distant, felt reassured. The confederation of troops and deportees marched against the slings and spears of the Kanak tribesmen, hunted them down like wild boar and sterilized their fields with salt. Some tribes surrendered and were deported to the islands that lay just beyond the northern horizon. Their wives were given to enemy tribes. Between June and September 1878, fifteen hundred Kanaks were shot, burned and starved to death. At least some good had come of the insurrection. The *Figaro* of 17 November published a copy of the Governor's letter to the Ministère de la Marine:

> The attitude of the deportees was excellent, and, by their knowledge of the country, they rendered valuable service to the expeditionary columns. In view of their particular devotion, I would ask that the following be granted a complete pardon. [There followed the names of three deportees.]

From an objective point of view, this boded well for the future of the colony. Before long, settlers would be more preoccupied by the price of gold and nickel on the international markets than by movements in the dark interior. The convicts and political prisoners who had survived the first four years of exile would eventually be absorbed by the rest of the population. The new quarter of Nouméa, known as 'the Latin Quarter', would be a thriving community in some ways more civilized than its namesake.

Even so, the uprising had come as a shock. The native population had been carefully studied and incorporated into a growing body of scientific knowledge. Nature had divided the islanders into geographical zones and assigned a colour to each group: black (the primitive race) in the mountains, bronze in the valleys and plains, yellow in the centre, reddish-brown on the coast and half-castes in the town. A live Kanak had been taken to Paris, and although the ethnological findings were called into question when he was shown to be mentally retarded, there was no doubting the inferiority of a race that was unable to count beyond its ten fingers. Consequently, when the insurrection had broken out in several different places at once, and when previously antagonistic tribes had banded together under the leadership of Ataï, who was black, this had been profoundly

unsettling. Ataï had effectively created a national liberation movement, and some of his reported sayings sounded remarkably like the
self-righteous sarcasm of a sans-culotte. He had promised to fence
off his property and to respect the settlers' land rights 'on the day he
saw his yams rise out of the ground to go and eat the settlers' cattle'.

The blade of the guillotine that was shipped to Nouméa was the
same that had been used almost a century before to decapitate
Louis XVI and Marie-Antoinette. In the event, it was not required.
A price of two hundred francs was placed on the head of Ataï. He
was betrayed by a neighbouring tribe, and his encampment was
surrounded. After a ferocious battle in which he showed the courage
of a wild animal, he was killed with a spear, then beheaded with a
knife. Such had been the savagery of the rebellion that few regretted
his grisly end. Settlers were demanding the complete eradication of
the native race. In view of the atmosphere that prevailed, it is hard to
say whether the head was shipped to the Ministère de la Marine as an
anthropological specimen or as a trophy of war.

5

THE MASSACRES IN New Caledonia were reported on the inside
pages of the *Figaro*, after domestic politics and society gossip, 'News
from the Exhibition', the serial, the list of commonly misused words
and the day's weather. The violent doings of savages on the other
side of the world were of little concern to Parisians. The main local
interest lay in the behaviour of the deportees. Letters had been
appearing in the London *Times*, accusing the French government
of cruelty to its own citizens. Political prisoners who had escaped
from the island by rowing out beyond the coral reefs to a British
schooner had published bitter accounts of their torture and captivity.
The successful repression of the Kanak revolt showed that, on the
contrary, the colonial experiment had been justified.

The idea behind the experiment was simple but inspired: the
terrorists who had turned the City of Light into a beacon of
barbarism should be sent to populate the new colony. Removed from
the cobbled canyons of Paris, and forced to till the soil of a tropical

paradise, they would be civilized by their contact with Nature. Then, in their newly civilized state, they would help to civilize the natives.

It had been a long and difficult process. To the exiles themselves, it had often seemed that it was designed to achieve the exact reverse. They were held for many months in the hulks of Brest and the Île d'Oléron, and given a communal trough of beans, but no cutlery. On the dilapidated frigates that took them to Nouméa, they were locked in metal cages on the gun deck – each deportee and his hammock took up less than one cubic metre – and allowed out for half an hour each day. The Arab deportees were given pork and wine, and lost the ability to walk. Four months after bidding farewell to the coasts of Europe, they saw the bleak, green mountains of New Caledonia, which look grey at a distance.

Fifteen hundred deportees had been delivered to the penal settlements of the Ducos peninsula and the Île Nou, where sadists avenged themselves for the hell of boredom to which greed and exotic fantasies had led them. Three thousand others – those who had been deported for life – were each given a thatched hut and a tiny plot. They were forbidden from making or acquiring any tools. Instead, they used their nails, and harvested radishes that were little more than filaments. If they sang songs, cut firewood or tried to give lessons to each other, their huts were flattened and their gardens destroyed. Forced into idleness, they exchanged their socialist ideals for other, more practical aspirations. A man might improve his lot if he gave away a conspiracy or reported a careless comment. He might spend a blessed day with a bottle of absinthe, oblivious to the sun that fell like a stone, dozing peacefully under the muddled stars in a pool of his own vomit.

This is why the Kanak insurrection of 1878 was such a vital event for the young colony, and why, in spite of the loss of European life, it brought fresh hope for the future.

4

THE *FIGARO* NEWSPAPER, whose offices had been vandalized by some of those reluctant colonists seven years before ('they were half drunk, because it was only noon'), had taken the same line throughout the whole affair – from the panic that followed the Battle of Sedan, to the Prussian siege of Paris and then the occupation of the city by terrorists. The editor, who had been forced to sit out the troubles on the Côte d'Azur, had called for the complete eradication of the socialist menace, but also for the application of science to 'the gangrene that has been eating away at Paris for the last twenty years'.

The Communard insurrection in Paris and its aftermath had provided irrefutable evidence of atavism. Among the 'wild animals' that had been marched to the reception centres at Versailles, there were a fair few hunchbacks and cripples. There were flattened brows, prognathous jaws and brutish faces etched with loathing. The females who stood, stripped to the waist, within spitting distance of the crowd, were swarthy and gave off a peculiar odour. Never before had the phenomenon of degeneration been so clearly displayed. Roused from the sleep of countless centuries by alcoholism and political hysteria, primitive traits had reasserted themselves in the modern world.

Those who had been deported to New Caledonia were not the worst. Justice had disposed of many others before the trials of the Communards had begun. The Parc Monceau, where nurses sat with prams under the leafy parasol of plane trees, had been closed for several days. Passers-by heard the syncopated rattle of shots. In the Jardin du Luxembourg, the soldiers had dumped bodies in the shrubberies and the ornamental lake. There had been long queues of captives outside the railway stations and the barracks. A man leaning over the Pont de la Concorde had seen a red streak flowing under the second arch. When the wind blew from the north-east, the smoke from the Parc des Buttes-Chaumont could be smelled in the city.

On a crowded boulevard, a man with dirty hands was hoisted on the bayonet of a soldier, to the delight of a group of well-dressed women, who urged the soldier to 'cut the rat's head off'. One in every six Parisians sat down to write a letter to the Ministry, giving names and addresses and details of subversive acts. The 'cull', as it was called, reduced the population of Paris by about twenty-five thousand, but it returned to its earlier level when the bourgeoisie came back from the country.

It was all very well for *The Times* to accuse the French of barbarism. No rational person could have been expected to behave with moderation after what had happened. In the late spring of 1871, Paris was a stage set for a scene of madness. There was a Gothic cathedral on the Boulevard de Sébastopol, where a department store was buttressed with enormous wooden beams. Tiles clung to the rafters of the Tuileries Palace – whose central clock had stopped at ten minutes to nine – like fish caught in nets. A hundred feet in the air, a porcelain vase stood on a mantelpiece, and the reflections of birds flashed across a mirror.

Special guidebooks were published for foreign tourists, and there were postcards of the most impressive monuments: the wrought-iron creepers that covered the Ministry of Finance; the empty metal tube of the Vendôme Column; the headless statue of the City of Lille sitting on her own remains. At the Hôtel de Ville, the anarchists' fire had dipped its flames in a palette of ink and molten metal. Seen from the square, it was a foundering ship with shattered masts and gaping portholes, while the side that faced the river had been painted a range of shades from lilac to grey, reminiscent of the latest developments in modern art.

The *Guide à travers les ruines* (June 1871) particularly recommended a tour of the Père-Lachaise cemetery. The hill on which it stood had been occupied by the anarchists during the last days of the Commune, to hinder the advance of government troops from the east. The emaciated pyramid that rose above the other tombs contained some chicken bones and bottles of wine. An anarchist evening paper called *Paris Libre* lay on the ground as though it had been left there after a picnic. Unused petrol bombs were scattered all about. Shells had been fired by government troops from the summit of Montmartre, and had inflicted poignant damage on the homes of the dead.

Though the cemetery was a maze of paths and the gravestones had served as shields, few had escaped. They had been encircled, then ignored while government troops reoccupied the city, then slowly hunted to extinction. Lower down, in a quiet part of the cemetery, a long, drab wall was pocked with holes. Soft soil was heaped up where hundreds of bodies had been dumped. Arms and legs were seen jutting out of the soil, and a bullet-ridden head had either been pushed up from below or deliberately placed on the mound as a vindictive memorial.

3

IN THE 'WEEK OF BLOOD' when Paris was recaptured from the anarchists by the French army – watched from the surrounding heights by the Prussian army – it was already becoming difficult to form a clear memory of those distant days of early spring, when Paris was no longer the capital of anything but itself.

There had been no *Figaro* to report events and to transmit the government's view. Instead, there were dozens of hysterical little newssheets written in an obscene and barbarous form of French. Paris seemed to have been overrun by journalists who took revenge for two decades of imperial censorship by filling their columns with *foutres* and *merdes*.

Oddly, though, in those two months of psychopathic democracy, there was often a dearth of news. Nothing extraordinary appeared to be happening: the buses were running again, the streets were being swept, dogs were chasing pigeons and pedestrians were running into long-lost friends, as usual, on the Pont Neuf. In the autonomous urban enclave that had once been the capital of France, the year 1871 had ceased to exist. It was 79 in the revolutionary calendar, and the clock was running backwards towards a new dawn. After the defeat by Prussia, and the siege of Paris, normal life was an amazing novelty, and complete nonentities suddenly found themselves the centre of attention.

One such nonentity was a man called Léon Bigot. On 10 Floréal 79 (Saturday, 29 April 1871), when the streets appeared to be safe, he left his apartment on the Boulevard Beaumarchais and set off towards the Place de la Bastille. He had every reason to feel hopeful. He had not been blown to pieces by a Prussian shell, nor had he been starved to death by the besieging army. Until recently, he had worked as an interpreter at the Grand Hôtel du Louvre. As a luxury hotel with a telegraph office, steam-powered lifts and a reputation for culinary excellence, the Grand Hôtel had been requisitioned by the Commune's Chief Director of Barricade Construction. But one day soon, M. Bigot would be back at work. Tourists would want to see the bombed city, to sketch the ruins, to hear tales of mad anarchists, and so M. Bigot kept abreast of events.

He bought a paper at the newsstand. It was called *Paris Libre* – a single sheet, twenty-four inches by eighteen, with six columns on either side. He stopped in the middle of the pavement, urinating involuntarily: he saw his name in an alphabetical list, BIGOT, LÉON, between the names of a carpenter and a schoolteacher, his job ('interpreter attached to the Hôtel du Louvre'), the date of his application (June 1868), and his address (89 Boulevard Beaumarchais).

The series had just begun, and it was already proving a great success. The editor – a short man with a very large hump, who sat on the Commune's Public Services Committee – had been the secretary of the serial novelist Eugène Sue. His own literary effort, based on documents that had been liberated from the Ministry of Police, promised to be just as popular as *Les Mystères de Paris*.

We shall publish the names and addresses of all individuals who asked for employment as spies under the empire.

A daily list of names and addresses lacked the narrative complexity of an Eugène Sue serial, but it had its own suspense and energy, and there were occasional examples of application letters to add some colour to the list:

'I know people of all classes and opinions, and am well placed to keep an eye out in all directions at once, in addition to which I am endowed with manly vigour, matchless courage and passive obedience.'

A guard employed by the Northern Railway Company, 8 Rue de la Nation, Montmartre.

The volunteer spies had come from all walks of life: grocers, bakers, office clerks, retired soldiers and seamen, students, writers and artists. There was a house painter, a photographer's assistant, a solicitor and a clown. There were insurance salesmen, a seamstress and a former Mayor of Chassenon near Limoges. According to *Paris Libre*, those *mouchards* were all alike, driven to acts of sly brutality by hunger and hatred. 'They deserve no mercy.'

Naturally, the dénouements had to be left to the reader's imagination or initiative. Did M. Léon Bigot, for instance, return to his apartment at 89 Boulevard Beaumarchais after seeing his name in the paper? Did he try to leave the city, or did he spend a fortune buying multiple copies of *Paris Libre* from every newsstand in his *quartier*? Did he, like other readers – especially those whose names came later in the alphabet – visit the offices of *Paris Libre* bearing a high-denomination banknote?

> Those scoundrels thought they were immune from exposure …
> We shall continue until the letter Z is exhausted.

Only one visitor to the offices of *Paris Libre* seemed to find the editor inclined to take pity on him:

> One man appeared deserving of consideration. So great and so obvious was his remorse that we are convinced of his sincere repentance. His name is Fouché, and he lives at 20 Grande-Rue, Saint-Mandé.

The last issue of *Paris Libre* (24 May 1871) was a 'Call to Arms'. It urged all its readers to defend the Commune by whatever means, and to prevent the nation from sliding back into the bad old days of imperialist dictatorship.

2

LOOKING BACK THROUGH the layers of history to the origins of the disaster becomes increasingly difficult. So many documents disappeared when the Communards set fire to Paris, and so many educated people who might have left reliable accounts of the Commune abandoned the city when it surrendered to Prussia and the siege was lifted. Even if the death of certain individuals on the alphabetized lists could be inferred from their subsequent absence, it would be impossible to say whether they died in the fire, were shot by soldiers or lynched by their neighbours.

Two million Parisians had been dreaming the same convoluted dream. They had gone to the ballot box, and voted for a government of idealists who might prevent them from waking up. Meanwhile, beyond the gates, on the hills that surrounded the enchanted enclave, the Prussians had been assessing their new domain. Prussian cartographers had been creating relief maps more accurate than any the natives had ever seen. They took aerial photographs, and collated data from different sources. They itemized the estates and chattels of the region's inhabitants, paying particular attention to the homes of the rich.

The Commune had been doomed from the start. With more effective barricades and better luck, it might have defended the labyrinth of streets until some diplomatic compromise was reached, but it was fatally handicapped by its simple state of mind, its futile hopes and above all by the fact that the rude awakening had come before the dream.

Parisians had seen their conquerors march along the avenues that had, after all, been designed for triumphal parades. Despite what the *Figaro* called their 'wounded patriotism' and 'popular resentment', they had allowed the Prussians to spend two days sightseeing in Paris without a single shot being fired. But the Prussians had taken the sensible precaution of dressing up. They brought out the silvery trumpets and the blue-and-white flags; they burnished the harnesses and the weaponry. The Battle of Paris was won with flattery and polish. The indigenous population saw tall young men in freshly laundered uniforms, riding sleek and confident horses. They saw the sun of Paris dance on the gleaming guns, and were mightily impressed.

The decisive engagement had taken place, not on the battlefields above Sedan on 4 September 1870, but on the Place de la Concorde on 1 March 1871.

The triumphal parade had descended the Champs-Élysées and reached the statue of Strasbourg, which was draped in black crêpe. The square was already filling up, and the eddies caused by the motion of horses through the crowd had begun to scatter the procession into separate groups. Some grim-looking men gathered around Bismarck and his horse. They had come in from the eastern suburbs, to see, and perhaps to act. The German Chancellor looked down from his horse and seemed to smile under his moustache. A hiss came from one of the men, and for a moment, the crowd fell silent. Bismarck signalled to the man with his gloved hand, bent over his holster and asked if Monsieur would have the kindness to light his cigar. The match was reluctantly struck, a cloud of smoke rose into the sky and the procession moved on into the Rue de Rivoli. A little later, a café that had unpatriotically stayed open was ransacked by an angry mob.

1

PARISIANS HAD NO DOUBT exhausted their courage and their ingenuity in the siege. One hundred and thirty-two days of dog food had not been good for the rational faculties. They had reverted to the simplest aspirations: eating and staying alive. They had reduced the size of their stomachs and their brains. (There were medical studies to prove it.) When buildings suddenly disappeared in a cloud of dust, they showed remarkably little interest. The men in the bar on the Rue d'Enfer, the girl walking home from school by the Jardin du Luxembourg, the horses at the Grenelle bus depot knew nothing – a rush of air, a roof falling in. (All the shells fell on the Left Bank.) Everyone else was a spectator and a collector of Prussian bomb casings and pieces of carved stone.

Faced with starvation and superior technology, the city succumbed to an epidemic of credulity: Mme Bismarck had been arrested while out shopping and was being held hostage; the Prussians were going home for Christmas; thousands of sheep were pouring into the city through secret tunnels that connected Paris to the provinces.

Men in top hats dreamt of annihilating human beings in numbers too large to be counted: a battalion of prostitutes would go traipsing out across the Plaine Saint-Denis to infect the Prussian army with syphilis and smallpox; an airborne platform carrying scientists and cauldrons would float over the Prussian lines and dissolve their respiratory tracts with chemicals; a machine-gun disguised as a music box playing Wagner would be offered as a token of peace; a sledge-hammer three miles wide would be dropped from the sky.

Even before the beginning of the siege, when the news from Sedan was printed in the *Figaro* – *'People of France! A great misfortune has befallen the fatherland. After three days of heroic struggles, forty thousand men have been taken prisoner. Paris is in a state of defence!'* – many of the sixty thousand Prussians domiciled in Paris were hunted down. The catacombs were prepared for long-term human habitation, and scientists were summoned to the Ministry.

We are under attack from intelligent barbarians; civilized science must defend us!

Paintings from the Louvre were evacuated, and precious archaeological specimens were carried from the Cluny museum to the crypt of the Panthéon. An employee of the Paris Gas Company was found to be a Prussian officer. The quarries of Montmartre were searched for explosives. Then the Prussian army was reported to have reached Reims, then Épernay, then Troyes. Towns in Picardy and the Ardennes were reported to have been wiped off the map.

The *Figaro* urged Parisians to remember the Breton guerrillas of 1793 who had lived in impenetrable forests, festooned with vegetation, and who had attacked the soldiers of the French Revolution with axes and spears.

National defence requires nothing more of every town and village that is exposed to enemy incursions!

The Government of National Defence ordered every forest, wood and copse in the environs of Paris to be set on fire, 'to prevent the enemy from reaching the fortifications under cover'.

The fortifications consisted of a road, a line of trees and then a bank of earth leading up to the rampart, with bastions at regular intervals. Then came the parapet and the walkway, protected by a curtain-wall, looking down into a ditch forty metres wide. A narrow path cut into the upward slope allowed troops to move along under cover. A man could walk all the way around Paris without being seen from either side. Beyond the ditch, a grassy bank sloped down to the unprotected zone.

On 15 September, lookouts on the parapet noticed the first signs of an approaching army. Columns of smoke were rising from the region of Drancy, Le Bourget and the Forest of Bondy. Farmers had set fire to their haystacks to prevent the harvest from falling into the hands of the enemy. But the vast crop of cabbages, beets, potatoes and radishes that would normally have fed the all-consuming city was not so easily destroyed. Then someone had the idea of sending out word to all the remote villages, where peasants lived in a state of medieval poverty as though the great city were a thousand miles away. The supply zone of Paris had always been the first to suffer in times of need. Its development had been stunted by the proximity of the capital. Recently, anthropologists had explored that neglected hinterland beyond the outer suburbs, and had recognized in certain facial features 'the living remnants of a separate race that predates the Cimmerian invasions with which our historical era began'.

Despite the primitive state of the roads and the lack of modern communications, word spread through the countryside with astonishing speed. They came from the forgotten hamlets with wheelbarrows and baskets, mattocks and forks, with their children, old people and cripples in ancient carts. The sun-baked horde was let loose on the fertile fields, and that vast tribe of famished peasants grubbed up in a single day a harvest that would have kept Paris eating for a season. They worked until their thin shadows stretched out across the fields, whimpering with delight – according to the *Figaro*'s eye-witness account – 'and with a delirious enthusiasm that is hard to describe'. 'Poor, benighted creatures, for whom a day of such calamity is a day of feasting and celebration!'

MADAME ZOLA

PART ONE

1

THEY TOOK THE ELEVATORS on the way up, because none of them were as young as they used to be, and there was a long evening ahead. The Otis elevator, which was more like a mountain railway than an elevator, took them to the first platform, where they paid another franc each and stepped into the cage of the hydraulic lift. Alexandrine felt a tug at her stomach, and saw the crowds on the esplanade turn into a scene from one of her husband's novels – a swarming ant-hill, and then, as details disappeared, a smear of black and grey. The sky was heavy with cloud. She thought of the reports, which had troubled Émile, that the Eiffel Tower would alter the weather and bring thunderstorms flocking to Paris.

They looked out over the *quartiers* in the north and east where they lived and worked. A windowpane two miles distant caught the sunlight and seemed to be signalling to the Tower. To the left of it, the Gare Saint-Lazare was a giant greenhouse, and the patch of vivid green in front must be the copper roof of La Madeleine. The men – Émile, his publisher and the publisher's son-in-law, Edmond de Goncourt, and an art critic – tried to identify the monuments and to find their homes. The biggest surprise was that Paris had a mountain in the north-east with a big square Buddha on top of it. Beneath it, the tenements of Montmartre and the Goutte d'Or, which she knew to be filthy, were bright white cubes, like the houses of a Muhammadan city, cascading down the slopes as though they expected to find the Bosphorus at the bottom.

It was hard to trace a route along the crevices that ran here and there through the mass of roofs. The city seemed to have been designed by a race of architects who worked in only two dimensions. The importance of everything had changed, as though years had passed with every yard of the ascent. Notre-Dame was a small toy lost in wasteground, while the pepper-pot towers of Saint-Sulpice had become a major landmark. Vast shadows swept across the scene, plunging the Batignolles into darkness, turning the Seine into a livid streak. The men at last fell silent. As the countryside beyond Paris came into view, they all felt – it seemed to her – a kind of fascinated disappointment. There was a mortal sadness in the spectacle. A great lake seemed to have welled up, spread itself across the land, and solidified into a grey mass.

The cage juddered and came to a stop. They got out and walked over to the railing. From that height, there were no signs of life. Nothing below seemed to move and no sound reached them on the platform. She had expected to see the city where she was born and where she had lived for fifty years spread out beneath her like the floor-plan of a familiar house, but now it seemed that all along she had been living in a strange place.

They took the lift back down to the first platform, from where Paris looked more recognizable than it had a few moments before. A table had been booked at the Russian restaurant, which was already noted for its wine cellar under the north-eastern foot of the Tower. They ordered from the menu and looked out at the panorama. She chose enough dishes to encourage Émile to order at least as much as she was intending to eat. He had surprised her recently by keeping to his diet and by refusing all alcohol – except when he had been bicycling – for three months. He had lost fourteen kilograms, while she, for a reason that escaped her, had gained six. She ordered caviar, *batvinia*, the boiled sucking-pig, and she would probably join them in the vodka and the Chambertin and then a Château d'Yquem with whatever came after.

They talked about the Javanese dancers they had seen performing in the little thatched palace on the Esplanade des Invalides. Goncourt had found their 'chubby yellow flesh' 'somewhat repulsive'. ('Repulsive' was one of his favourite words.) Nine years before, she had ridiculed his unnaturalistic brothel scenes in *La Fille Élisa* (the gentlemen had found her observations highly amusing), and ever since, Goncourt had taken every opportunity to prove that he was a connoisseur of women. Of course, he was jealous of her husband because Émile Zola stood head and shoulders above his contemporaries, and he was frightened of her because she had once been a laundress. She looked at Émile as if to prompt him. 'There is a certain softness in their fat,' he said, 'that one doesn't find in European flesh.' Then he squeezed his nose between his fingers and moved it about as though it were made of india rubber. He was always more scientific about such things than Goncourt.

Darkness gathered while they ate. Now, when they looked out, they saw only their own reflections. After the *gélinottes* – which she had wanted to compare with hers – the bear's paw (out of curiosity), the Polish waffles, the *napoleonka*, the tea from the samovar, which Émile could have emptied on his own, and the gold-tipped cigarettes, they picked their way down the three hundred and forty-five wooden steps, which were already showing signs of wear. Goncourt said that he felt like an ant descending the rigging of a metal ship. She seemed to remember the image from one of Émile's novels.

The crowds on the Champ de Mars were even noisier and smellier than in the daytime. The sightseers filled the streets and doorways like a flood. They managed to stay together and found their way to the Rue du Caire which, with its minarets and musharabiya designed by a French architect, was said to be more authentic than any street in modern Cairo. They stared at the Africans, who stared back, and entered the Egyptian café to observe the *danse du ventre* that had supposedly scandalized the thousands of Parisians who went to see it.

She sat next to Marguerite Charpentier, the wife of Émile's publisher, and discussed the dancer's costume – the lilac bodice, the low belt and the tight skirt, the panel of yellow gauze that revealed the extraordinary mobility of her navel. There had been some difficult moments with Marguerite in the past. Mme Charpentier had grown up in the Place Vendôme, was always elegant, knew three languages and had never had to work, but somehow her husband's philandering, which Alexandrine had known about before Marguerite, had brought the two women closer together. Émile had always been faithful, but for the other wives, a husband's fidelity meant only that he didn't keep a mistress, and she had overheard Julia Daudet's husband say that if only Julia would allow him to do the things that any barmaid in the Brasserie des Martyrs would be glad to have done to her, he would be 'the most faithful of Fidos'.

'What I can't understand,' Goncourt was saying, as they watched the Syrian dancer who danced with a jug of water on her head, 'is that when one sleeps with a Moorish woman, there's only the most imperceptible swaying, and if you ask them to spice it up with some pitching and tossing in the fashion of our European women, they complain that you're asking them to make love like dogs!' The men agreed that the dance would be more interesting if the woman were completely naked, because then they would be able to observe the arrangement and displacement of organs in the female body.

After the sabre dance and the whirling dervish, they walked along the artificial street and bought some of the sticky sweetmeats that everyone was eating. They talked to the cafetiers and sat down at one of the Tunisian cafés to drink a glass of date brandy. Even this late in the evening, the Rue du Caire was full of people. The Egyptian donkey-drivers seemed to be having the time of their lives. The faces of the crowd were lit by red lanterns, and everyone looked slightly drunk. At the end of the street, women queued for the water-closets and talked in loud voices. A group of men stared up at the finely wrought windows of a harem. The Exhibition was an immense department store where all the world came to indulge its pleasures and to find out what it wanted.

The Chemin de Fer Intérieur that had been built for the Exhibition had a little station by the Galerie des Machines. They would take it all the way to Les Invalides, where they were more likely to find a cab. As they waited under a wooden pagoda for the next train, Émile took out his notebook and jotted down some observations. Charpentier asked Alexandrine if the train would appear in his new novel about railways, *La Bête humaine*, but she didn't know, because she had been less involved with the research than usual.

The locomotive pulled into the station and sent up a cloud of steam. Before they boarded the train, they looked back across the Champ de Mars and saw what could only be seen from a distance. At the very top of the huge metallic structure, in the gallery that was closed to the public, two projectors were sweeping their powerful electric beams over the city. The idol of the Exhibition seemed to be looking for something in the sea of roofs, searching for the secrets that only a novelist could discover.

2

THE MAIN RAILWAY LINE from Paris to Le Havre ran past the foot of their garden. Médan was less than two hours from the centre of Paris – a train from Saint-Lazare, then a short walk along the Seine. They had bought the little house, which Émile called 'a rabbit hutch', for nine thousand francs in 1878, when only one other Parisian owned property in the district. Of course, they had kept the apartment in Paris, because of his work, and because she had always been a city girl. Two hundred thousand francs later, the rabbit hutch was a residence fit for a genius. The original cottage with its little shuttered windows was squeezed between two tall towers like a victim of mistaken identity being marched to the commissariat by two hefty gendarmes.

The big square tower had risen while he was writing his novel about the daughter of a laundress who became a courtesan. It was called, in her honour, the Tour Nana. The hexagonal tower, which had been completed in 1886, was the Tour Germinal. It was there, above the billiards room, that she had her spacious *lingerie*. She sat among the piles of linen, sewing and embroidering, looking out at the misty trees along the river, calculating the wages of the servants and the builders, while Émile sat writing on the other side of the house.

His mother had lived with them for the first two years, which might have been even worse than it was without the silent games of dominoes in the evening. Since her death in the autumn of 1880, they had been busier than ever. They had acquired some adjoining plots and the island in the river, on which they erected the Norwegian chalet that had been part of the 1878 Exhibition. They went shopping for all the things they had never owned as children and had never dreamed of wanting. In the original part of the house, she had a kitchen with blue porcelain tiles and copper pans of every size and a white wooden table in the middle with sliding compartments. Émile had some specially made stained-glass windows and a collection of antiques that Victor Hugo would have envied, including a sarcophagus and a medieval bed that had sent Gustave Flaubert into raptures. He had a gas lamp disguised as a candle, and the latest kind of orguemélodium with foot-pumped bellows and a stop for 'celestial voices'. He played chords on it at dusk, which either alleviated or exacerbated his hypochondria, she wasn't sure. They had a horse, a cow, rabbits, doves, chickens, dogs and cats, all of whom had names. Their friends – when the house was finally ready to receive them – were amazed.

She had hoped that Marguerite, Julia and the others would stop feeling sorry for her because she had no children. She and Émile had abandoned the idea of a family long before. As Émile said, his novels were their children, and all his creative energy went into *Les Rougon-Macquart*, which was now only four novels from completion. Sometimes, she remembered the foundling hospital in the Rue d'Enfer, when she was practically an orphan herself, a flower girl, twenty years old, with a baby whose father she had almost forgotten. She had seen them attach a piece of white paper (white for girls) to the baby's bonnet, with her name, Caroline, her number and her date of birth, and watched them carry her into the big dormitory with the inscription above the door, 'My Father and Mother Have Abandoned Me, But The Lord Will Take Care Of Me.' In the year when Caroline would have turned eighteen, Alexandrine had told Émile about her long-lost daughter, and they had gone to consult the register, in which it was recorded that the baby had died in 1859, twelve days after being left at the hospital.

When they moved to Médan, she had thought that she would miss the city. She did miss their research expeditions – the sweatshops in the northern suburbs, the dressing-rooms of the boulevard theatres, their nocturnal exploration of Les Halles and the delicious cabbage soup that was served on a street-corner at dawn, for which she still had the recipe. She thought of their tiny apartment by the Odéon on the Rue de Vaugirard, the long nights of literary discussions and their enormous appetites. She was looking forward to equipping the new apartment in the Rue de Bruxelles, which was a short walk from the Gare Saint-Lazare. But in the end, though she was often dissatisfied, she told herself that Médan had been a wholesome break with the past. She had discovered her talent for organization, her love of the countryside and boating on the river, and she liked the fact that his friends from the old days felt ill at ease there, especially Cézanne, who was making a career out of failure and who always seemed to have mud on his boots even after a week without rain.

She had even relished the responsibility of managing staff. Having worked long hours herself, as a flower-girl and a laundress, she knew what to expect of servants. She knew how to train them and when to dismiss them. Her chambermaid and seamstress, Jeanne Rozerot, had been a particular success. As soon as she saw the tall girl – timid but elegant, dressed in a modern, practical skirt and a high collar – she had known that she would enjoy the task of teaching her the trade. Jeanne had lost her mother when she was still a baby and been sent to a convent school. She might almost have been Alexandrine's daughter. Though she looked quite frail, she was lively at work and always cheerful, even when her mistress was being bossy.

Alexandrine had explained Jeanne's qualities to Émile, and he had not objected when she declared her intention to take the girl with them to Royan, where she had coped well with all the turmoil of a summer vacation. (He could hardly have objected, since Royan was his idea.) That had been barely nine months before the dinner on the Eiffel Tower. She was still disappointed that, after the holiday, Jeanne Rozerot had handed in her notice for 'personal reasons', which she had tactfully not enquired after. With all the important visitors and two rather moody employers, she must have found life at Médan somewhat bewildering. It was vexing, all the same, to spend so much time training a servant only for someone else to have the benefit.

3

THEY SET OFF for the Pyrenees on 9 September 1891, which was rather late in the year, but he was determined to leave, saying that he

needed a holiday after the battle of writing *La Débâcle*. She stopped
in the middle of packing to write to her cousin:

> Where are we going? You can probably guess. Where I least want to
> go, of course. It's the story of my life – never having what I want, or
> getting it only when I no longer want it.

They took the train to Lourdes and saw cripples throwing away
their crutches and falling over in the crowd, and consumptives being
plunged into water that even the sloppiest laundress would have
poured away. They saw the chilly spa towns and the jagged curtain of
the Pyrenees. When they crossed the border to San-Sebastián, it
poured with rain, and all the time they both felt that they should
have been somewhere else.

On the beach at Biarritz, where they stayed at the Grand Hôtel,
she realized that they looked like an ill-matched couple, which
was normal at their age, but it made her feel sad, and also faintly
apprehensive, but mostly sad. Émile was beginning to resemble the
portrait that Manet had painted of him twenty years before. The
defiant curl of his mouth was almost mischievous. He wore white
flannel suits and struck jaunty poses. All that developing of photographs – an art that she herself had never quite mastered – was
making him behave as though he was always about to be photographed. He looked like a man who knew how to take a holiday, even
in late September. He might almost be described as thin. The bicycle
had something to do with it, of course, but this was also his reward
for spurning their shared indulgences.

He folded the newspaper and pushed himself out of the deckchair.
He was going to take an energetic walk. She saw that his face was
slightly flushed. She might ask him later on, and he would probably
say that it was a symptom of his '*malaises nerveux*', which he attributed
to his relentless work.

When he had gone, she picked up the newspaper. There was a
long editorial on the Jews. It was the centenary of their emancipation
by the Revolution, but now, said the writer, 'things have gone too far
the other way'. Several articles were devoted to 'the future war' with
Germany, and to the fact that French citizens were to be allowed to
enter Alsace-Lorraine without a passport. Footmen and printers were

on strike, and the union of café *garçons* had asserted its right to wear facial hair: every *garçon* in Paris was now growing a moustache in a show of solidarity. A penniless Austrian tailor who had had himself delivered to the Exhibition in a crate had become a 'café-concert phenomenon' and was touring Europe as 'the Human Parcel'.

None of this was likely to have altered Émile's mood or to have brought a flush to his face. There was nothing in the paper about Émile Zola, and nothing about any of his literary rivals. In fact, the news was as uninteresting as it usually was in the holidays. The movements of grand duchesses and princes were assiduously reported. A courtesan wrote to deny the malicious rumours of marriage that had been printed in the gossip column, and blamed them on 'feminine vengeance'. Various violent crimes had been committed in the provinces, and the new tramlines in the Avenue de la Grande Armée were causing accidents. There was rain over the Channel, and cloud over Paris.

Page three and the back page were always the same. Even sitting in a deckchair, with the gulls wheeling overhead and the bunting flapping in the Atlantic breeze, it was easy to imagine oneself in Paris. *Lohengrin* was at the Opéra, *Cinderella* at the Châtelet, 'eccentric clowns' at the Folies-Bergères, and *La Demoiselle du téléphone* at the Nouveautés. The Eiffel Tower would be closing for the winter on 2 November, but there were still concerts every evening in the restaurant on the first platform.

She read on, through the advertisements for false teeth, hair-restorer and soap – soap was everywhere, even among the serious news, disguised as editorial comment. '*The exquisite, persistent perfume of Savon Ixora makes the skin silky, white and delicate.*' Mme Baldini of 3 Rue de la Banque gave daily lessons on the art of remaining forever young. Émile had no need of such lessons, even if they had been offered to gentlemen. Perhaps something in the 'Correspondances personnelles' had given him an idea for a novel.

She was not a storyteller – she could never have pieced together the million details that went to make a novel – but she found those telegrammatic messages as evocative as the first page of a serial. Some of them suggested the happy continuation of a normal life. Some of them were sad, though it was hard to say why. She wondered whether the people to whom they were addressed would see the messages, and she thought it ironic that things that had to be kept secret from a husband or a wife were printed where everyone could see them.

Diane. Écriv. proj. fer. t. m. pos. . . . Dés. v. voir. Amit.

2^{43} imp vs vr vs svz pquoi att avc imp esp btot att depuis merc ts ls jrs mme hre écvz.

C^{21}. Gw xoaowg qsg zwubsg hcapsbh gcig hsg msil goqvs eis xs h'owas sh h'owasfow hcixcifg.*

A. B. 70. Faisan bien arrivé superbe 25. Duval.

The Duval household would be celebrating the arrival of the 'superb' pheasant by eating it, she imagined, with oysters and a nice bouillon. It was the meal that she and Émile had always shared when they returned to Médan, though with a partridge instead of a pheasant. It reminded her that they would soon be home. She scanned the advertisements on the back page, which, apart from the 'very fetching and curious photographs' from a Dutch publisher, were all addressed to women. There was a carpet sale at the Grands Magasins du Louvre, and the new winter collection was about to be unveiled at the Samaritaine. That, too, had been one of their shared pleasures – the orgies of shopping in the big department stores, and all the research for *Au Bonheur des Dames*, the ravenous accumulation of facts, the desire to know everything that went on in the basements and the attics. He had been like a little boy, wallowing in the lingerie, blushing at the buxom dummies, 'turning pink with pleasure' like the man in his novel. She preferred to make her own jackets and dresses, but there might be something to buy for the new maid that she couldn't have worn herself.

When he returned from his walk, Émile still felt slightly out of sorts, and suggested that they bring the holiday to an end. While Alexandrine organized the packing, he wrote some letters. He seemed pleased to be returning, but also reluctant to leave. It was the first time that either of them had been abroad. Perhaps he was sorry that

---

* 'Si jamais ces lignes tombent sous tes yeux, sache que je t'aime et t'aimerai toujours.'

the adventure was over. Soon, when his sequence of novels was complete, there would be more time for holidays and more time to enjoy the house.

4

THE LETTER ARRIVED on Tuesday 10 November, forty days after their return. Her own post was usually quite humdrum: family correspondence, begging letters, bills for food, clothes and work on the house. But she also read his correspondence and told him how to reply to people who wanted articles or translation rights. She wrote to editors of supposedly impecunious magazines who owed him money. Sometimes she felt that the person least able to defend the fortune and reputation of Émile Zola was her husband. There was the time, for instance, when he gave away the manuscript of *Nana* to a journalist, who promptly sold it to an American collector for twelve thousand francs!

This letter was addressed to her, Madame Émile Zola. She did not recognize the hand, and the letter was unsigned. It was as short and orderly as an invoice. She read it in an instant: 'Mlle Jeanne Rozerot . . . 66, Rue Saint-Lazare . . . has had two children by your husband.'

LATER THAT DAY, the clerk at the telegraph office was presented with a terrific piece of gossip, a nugget of scandal in the bland stream of greetings and condolences. M. Émile Zola wished to send an urgent message to his friend in Paris, M. Henry Céard – or, as he was sometimes known, for the purposes of private communication, M. Duval:

> My wife is going absolutely mad. I fear a calamity. Could you go to the Rue Saint-Lazare and take the necessary steps? Forgive me.

IN THE TWENTY-SIX YEARS they had lived together, she had often been able to follow a plot as it developed in his mind. A story, she knew, could begin almost anywhere. It might start with a short railway journey and a woman in a compartment, clutching a small package. The window, in which her face is reflected, shows scenes from the past and the present, like slides from a magic lantern: a house by the railway, a sail on the river, the telegraph poles ticking past, the coal smoke over the northern suburbs.

Next, a slate-grey autumn evening in the city: the crowd, cowering under the drizzle in the Rue Saint-Lazare, between the station and the fish-food restaurants; the endless funeral procession of black suits and umbrellas.

A woman in a dark dress stops on the pavement and stares up at a soot-streaked window. Behind the window, a tableau in the style of Mary Cassatt: a young mother putting her child and her baby to bed. The woman in the dark dress climbs the stairs with the steady trudge of a rent collector. Outside, the evening sky above the Gare Saint-Lazare floods the street with red. Over the traffic, the shunting engines can be heard shrieking and bellowing like great beasts in their wrought-iron cage.

The Rue Saint-Lazare met the Rue Blanche a few yards from the south-eastern corner of the station. It was the opening scene of *La Bête humaine* – the fifth-floor room with the view of the railway lines disappearing into the Batignolles tunnel, and a piano banging away downstairs. It was curious how often her spirit seemed to inhabit one of his male characters.

'Admit that you slept with her or, by God, I'll cut you open!'

He would have killed her. She could see it clearly in his eyes. As she fell, she noticed the knife, which lay open on the table. . . . She was overcome with a feeling of cowardice, an abandonment of herself and everything, a need to get it all over with . . .

'All right, it's true. Now let me go.'

What happened next was abominable. The confession he had wrung from her with such force struck him in the face like something monstrous and impossible. He could never have imagined such infamy. He grabbed her head and banged it against a foot of the table. As she struggled, he pulled her across the room by her hair, knocking over the chairs. Each time she tried to get up, he punched her again and sent her sprawling back onto the floor. The table was pushed and nearly knocked over the stove. Some hair and some blood clung to a corner of the dresser . . .

The music continued downstairs, with loud laughter and the sounds of young people.

A FEW DAYS AFTER the letter arrived, an upholsterer came to Médan. The walls and door of the bedroom were to be padded in case the servants, who were so hard to replace, were frightened away by the shouting and screaming.

5

SHE HAD GONE TO number 66 and broken the lock and found the apartment empty. She had found a room full of someone else's life: homemade curtains, flowers in a vase, some plates and cutlery, the sweetish smell of breast-milk. She found two cots that must have come from the Samaritaine. There were framed photographs – riding his bicycle in the Bois de Boulogne, standing on a beach somewhere. She did not know who had taken the photographs. There was a writing desk, which she easily broke open, and enough letters inside to make a novel, which she began to read and then burned to ashes.

She might have stayed in the room for a few minutes or for more than an hour. She walked back past the house at number 16 where she was born. Because of the station, the area was always crowded. It was the best place to buy fresh seafood. She passed the fishmongers' stalls across from the station but the smell of the apartment stayed with her.

Until she decided what to do, they would both stay indoors. She went to the kitchen, which she had practically abandoned those last few years. The recipe called for a fire that could roast a sheep in a few minutes, though the only meat was fish. A bottle of oil, one tomato, garlic, a fistful of pepper. Everyone must have known – the men, of course, and probably Marguerite Charpentier and Julia Daudet, who each had three children of their own.

Every afternoon at four o'clock, tea was served with a plate of pastries, which had to be finished.

NINE MONTHS LATER, in 1892, they went on holiday together, just the two of them, to Provence and Italy, for seven weeks. He published the last novel of his great sequence, which had taken twenty-five years to complete. The main character was a man, Dr Pascal, who, having 'forgotten to live', tries to make up for lost time by falling in love with his niece: 'All that solitary passion had given birth to nothing but books.' He dedicated it to the memory of his Mother and his dear Wife. Since his wife no longer had herself placed next to journalists at dinners and told them what to write, the novel was not well reviewed.

She did, however, attend the celebration lunch on the island in the Bois de Boulogne. Two hundred people were rowed across the lake and sat under a marquee, eating *truite saumonée*, *noix de veau aux pointes d'asperge*, *galantine truffée de perdreaux* and *bombe panachée*, to mark the completion of *Les Rougon-Macquart* and the Master's imminent promotion to the rank of officer in the Légion d'Honneur. According to the newspaper, when Charpentier mentioned Mme Émile Zola in his speech, 'she had to fight back her tears'.

Six weeks later, she attended one of those intimate dinners whose principal purpose had always been to allow everyone to see how much older everyone looked. They dined at Goncourt's house in Auteuil with the Daudets and some other friends. The men talked about their difficult profession, and asked each other how much they were paid by newspapers. Alexandrine sat in the corner with Julia Daudet, and told her all about her life at Médan. Émile, on the other side of the room, looked nervous and tried to hear what she was saying. Now and then, he asked, 'Is everything all right, *ma petite chérie*?'

'. . . Then he walks about the garden, waiting for two o'clock, which is when the papers are delivered. He hardly says anything, except that I ought to go and do something about the cow, which I know absolutely nothing about. That's a job for the gardening woman. Then he goes up to read the papers and has his snooze . . .'

They ate dinner by the windows and saw a dark cloud in the sky. It was certain to rain. She brightened the conversation by telling them how terrified Émile had been of lightning when he was a little boy. His mother had had to take him down to the cellar and wrap him in blankets. Even now, when there was a thunderstorm, they had to sit in the billiards room beneath the laundry with the curtains drawn and all the lights on, so that she had to wear dark glasses, and he would take out his handkerchief and use it as a blindfold, which was especially funny because of all the scientific rationalism in his novels – the thought of Émile Zola quivering at electrical discharges like some biblical sinner under an angry sky…

She knew that, when they had gone home, Goncourt would write it all down in his diary, and when future generations came to study the works of the great novelist, his life would have no secrets.

PART TWO

6

THE AUTUMN OF 1895 was miserable in Paris. When the drizzle finally stopped, raindrops sprang from the trees along the boulevards. The pavements were always slippery, and the top of the Eiffel Tower was lost in cloud.

In Italy, the sun lingered late into the season. The sky was an intense blue, like some impossibly perfect memory of childhood. Every day, she wore summer dresses, and organized her afternoons around the sites where she might find some shade and a cool drink.

She wrote to him every day – from the Royal Hotel in Naples and the Grand Hotel in Rome – because he had been unsettled by her departure. In thirty years, they had never spent more than a day or two apart. She told her sister's child, Elina, that she had fallen in love with Italy: 'There are so many things that one knows only from history books – but how much more interesting they are when one can walk about in these historic places!' She learned enough Italian for shopping; she even wrote some thank-you letters in Italian; but everyone was so welcoming that she was able to speak French whenever she liked.

She was fêted by the French ambassador at the Vatican, and her movements were reported in the society column of the *Figaro*, along with those of princes and duchesses. Count Edoardo Bertolelli, who had published some of Émile's novels in *La Tribuna*, insisted on seeing her every day. She was fourteen years older than the count, but he called her his 'ray of sunshine'. When she dressed for dinner, she tied a bunch of violets to her belt. He took her fox-hunting, and she saw the Sistine Chapel, the Villa Borghese, the Villa Medici, the Forum and the Catacombs. She felt the earthquake that shook Rome one night in mid-November. The count was so charming that he ordered her portrait from a painter, for which she wore a silk dress and some feathers in her hair, and in one hand she held the bouquet the count had given her.

Sometimes, when she was alone at the hotel, she remembered the foundling hospital and the baby with the white paper attached to its bonnet. She thought of the young woman alone with two small children, and the father who was hardly ever there, and terrified that his wife would leave him. As ever, she had faced up to the inevitable. He was allowed to take tea with them every afternoon, but it was a strange life for Denise, who was six, and Jacques, who was four. She saw them only occasionally, like a visiting grandmother, but she already knew them better than Émile. She would have to tell him how to treat the children, and how different they were from each other. In Rome, she bought them presents and looked forward to their next walk together in the Tuileries. If Denise asked for news of 'the Lady' while she was away, he was to say that 'the Lady' sent kisses to them both.

'Devote yourself to the ones who are near you,' she told him. 'Show them a smiling face as much as you can.' (Some things were more easily explained in a letter.)

> You say that you would like to see me happy. You know me better than anyone else, but you still don't know me very well if you hope to see me happy. I know that the happiness I had dreamt of for our old age has gone for good. My only pleasure now is to be useful to you and to help the ones I love. That is the task I have set myself, and I shall persevere for as long as I can.

7

SHE RETURNED TO Italy the following year, and again in 1897. But that year, the holiday was cut short. He needed her at his side in Paris, because how could he face the storm alone? Kitchen slops and excrement were tipped over the garden wall; some soldiers had thrown stones at the house; a bucket of dirty water was poured over the children when they were riding their bicycles. Six months after his open letter to the President of the French Republic on the Dreyfus Affair, when every wall in Paris was covered with the words, 'J'Accuse!', he was sentenced to jail for criminal libel and forced to flee to England.

She went with him to the Gare du Nord, with his nightshirt wrapped in a newspaper. He was in a terrible state of agitation, but she insisted on staying behind. Someone had to talk to the journalists, the lawyers and the politicians. At least there would always be something interesting to report. When he had gone, she wrote to her friend, Mme Bruneau, whose husband had accompanied Émile to the court house every day:

There are secret police agents at our door, and some more in the hotel across the road, and also some at Médan, with reporters from the gutter press to help them with their spying. If I blow my nose or cough, it's reported next day in the newspapers.

They know when the servants go to bed, and when I go to bed. People write shameful things on the walls, and they send threatening letters to me and the servants. But I'm as hard as iron, and no one who sees me would guess that I'm under attack.

She read all his letters and sorted them into separate piles – the messages of support and the death threats, which he did not need to see. Exile was arduous enough as it was, and so she spared him unnecessary details.

Some of the anonymous letters were addressed to her:

Madame,
If you haven't buggered off a week from now we'll find a way past your servants and fuck you in your fat belly until you die. Since your

filthy husband has gone into hiding, we'll attack his family instead and show no mercy.

Death to the Jews and all them that support them.

After reading each letter, she made a note of the date of reception, and filed it away for posterity.

She worried about him, sitting there without a word of English at the Queen's Hotel in Upper Norwood. She told him to be brave, and that he would have to finish what he had started. 'His latest letters saddened me,' she told Mme Bruneau, 'not because of his health, but because he seems disheartened. So I got on my big warhorse and terrorized my hero, which did him a lot of good, because today I can tell that his mental barometer is getting back to normal.'

She finally joined him in England in the autumn of 1898, but she stayed for only five weeks. There was little she could do for him while she was away from Paris. Captain Dreyfus was still on Devil's Island, and Émile was still a fugitive from what the government called 'justice'.

Upper Norwood was no substitute for Rome. Everything was served with potatoes. The fish, which was cooked without butter or salt, tasted waterlogged, and the pastries in the bakers' windows were so stodgy that it made one ill just to look at them. She returned to Paris in time to buy Christmas presents for the children, to see the doctor about her emphysema and to catch up with his work. There were so many letters to write and so many people to visit. 'I have to be you and myself at the same time', she told him.

WHEN AT LAST the tide was turning and the hero was able to return, their half-marriage resumed. She settled in to her sadness as though arranging their possessions in a house that was too small or too dark. The days of literary battles and endless research were over, but he seemed happier now that he could indulge his hobby. He liked to say that only when one had taken a photograph of something could one claim to have truly seen it, because a photograph showed details that would otherwise have escaped attention. He invented a release mechanism that allowed him to take photographs of himself, and she saw them all sitting together, taking tea in the garden of the rented house near Médan – Émile pouring the tea – and the mother of his children, who had once been so pretty and who now looked so glum, as though she were contemplating the life that could never be hers.

Since he owned at least eight cameras and various pieces of equipment in heavy boxes, he needed Alexandrine to help carry them about the Champ de Mars. Day after day, they went to the Exhibition. He wanted to record everything. For the first time since 1889, they climbed to the second platform of the Eiffel Tower and looked down over the city. The sun was shining. A new century had begun, and Paris was dressed for a new beginning.

He photographed the roofscape, moving around the platform, until he had a complete panorama of the city, from the industrial *quartiers* in the east to the avenues and gardens in the west. When they viewed the assembled panorama, they saw a world as grandiose and coherent as his great sequence of novels. This was not the shrouded mass of roofs she had seen the first time; it was the vast, collective work of the nineteenth century, the man-made ocean in which her husband had been one of the brightest beacons.

8

THEY WOKE IN the night with headaches and stomach pains, and thought it must have been something they had eaten. He said to her, 'We'll be better in the morning.' Then they had fallen asleep again, and it seemed to her that she could see him lying there and could do nothing to help him.

She woke in the clinic at Neuilly. It was three days before she was strong enough to be taken to the house. She went straight to the room on the first floor and fell on her knees, sobbing, and embracing the body, and stayed with him for an hour. Even in her weakness, when she was still at the clinic, she had thought of Jeanne and asked the publisher to go to Mlle Rozerot and tell her the terrible news, so that she and the children could bid him their last farewell.

No culprit was ever found. The death was described as a dreadful accident and a national calamity, but both women knew that someone must have crept across the rooftops, while the unseeing searchlights swept over the city, and blocked up the chimney, then cleared it again in the early morning.

His enemies had not prevailed. A huge, silent crowd followed the hearse from the Rue de Bruxelles to the Montmartre cemetery. Soldiers presented arms as the procession passed. She had planned every detail of the ceremony herself. It was the greatest public event in Paris since the funeral of Victor Hugo. She was too frail to attend the burial, but she knew that somewhere in the crowd that stood at the graveside were two children and a young woman who might be mistaken for a widow, and that their photographs would join hers in the coffin.

SHE SOLD some of the paintings and antiques, and the land at Médan between the railway and the Seine. She made certain that Jeanne had everything she needed – because he had not made all the necessary financial arrangements – that Denise and Jacques worked hard and did not try to take advantage of their mother's kindness. They discussed clothes and furniture and the flowers that were placed on the tomb where the children's father had been laid to rest.

She still went to Italy every year, but her true place was in Paris, and at the house in Médan, which became a site of pilgrimage. Every year, on the first Sunday in October, the leading lights of the literary world arrived at the station and walked up to the house to pay homage to the Master. Two years after his death, in 1904, hundreds of people attended the commemoration. It was a shame that the children had been unable to witness their father's glory. Little Jacques was suffering from tuberculosis and was being treated at the clinic in Normandy that Alexandrine had investigated herself. She reminded Jacques's mother that he was to eat as much as he could and that he should be given plenty of milk and eggs between meals. A few days later, when all the disciples had gone home, she wrote to her again:

The demonstrations of homage to our dear great hero were truly magnificent. The future bodes well for the father of our dear children. One day, they will want to find out all they can about the labours to which he devoted his life before it was cut short. I hope that they will understand that by the manner in which they comport themselves they will help to preserve the glory of the name Zola. You will be there to direct them and to teach them many things – unfortunately far fewer than I might have taught them, for you did not know him as well as I, who lived at his side for thirty-eight years.

His violent death has struck us both a cruel blow, and in our suffering, the affection of his children has been a great happiness to me. I feel as though their affection comes from him, and this makes me cherish them even more than I would have thought possible.

MARCEL IN THE MÉTRO

* THE MAGNIFICENT MÉTROPOLITAIN *

IN THE STIFLING HEAT of the early afternoon of Thursday, 19 July 1900, a hundred people of all ages, shapes and sizes were standing in front of the little kiosk that had recently appeared on the pavement of the Avenue de la Grande Armée. Some, acutely aware of their place in history, were looking at their watches. Others were there simply because they happened to be passing and had joined the crowd on principle or because they wanted to find out why so many people were all waiting to use the same toilet.

At exactly one o'clock, the glazed doors swung open and a heady smell of pine forest escaped into the Paris air. The crowd passed under the glass umbrella and clattered down the wooden steps to an illuminated newsstand where banknotes could be changed, and a counter where a pretty face was waiting with a ticket and a smile. They were delighted to find the underworld pleasantly cool. Someone exclaimed, 'I could spend my holidays down here!', and everyone agreed.

They bought their tickets – rectangles of pink or cream card, with a background design that might have been a cathedral or a power station – then they hurried down another flight of steps, and a blast of Arctic air had them clutching at their throats. Despite the cold, the stench of creosote was overpowering. As their pupils dilated, they were able to distinguish, by the aquarium light of the electric lamps, an asphalt pavement stretching away into the darkness. On either side of the pavement were two cement-lined trenches and, at the bottom of each trench, an elevated bar of shiny metal. Men in black sweaters with red piping and the letter 'M' embroidered on the collar emerged from the gloom, announcing that anyone who touched the shiny rail would die in an instant. Impressed, the crowd drew back, and three wooden crates the colour of ceramic bricks, scintillant in the electric light, positioned themselves in front of the passengers.

Second-class passengers shared the front carriage with the Westinghouse motors; then came first class with red leather seats; then first and second class together. Everything looked neat and clean. On the outside, the varnished coat-of-arms of Paris in blue and red adorned the painted panels. At the front of the train, two men standing behind glass windows looked like animated statues in a museum: one had his hand on the regulator, the other held the brake. Another train would come along in five minutes, but the crowd was in no mood to wait and surged into the carriages. The women admired the fluted wood furniture and the polished wooden decking. The men quickly occupied the seats in order to have the pleasure of giving them up to ladies.

In the front carriage, one of the employees tried to make himself heard above the hubbub. '*One hundred and twenty-five horsepower – times two, equals two hundred and fifty horsepower! Direct current of six hundred volts! Three-phase current of five thousand volts! Supplied by the factory on the Quai de la Rapée!*' The train began to move, and, as it entered the tunnel, the passengers saw huge blue sparks leaping through the darkness like ghostly dolphins escorting a ship.

'The cold is relative to the heat above ground,' said the employee. 'Mademoiselle has nothing to fear for her chest!' A dozen pairs of eyes fastened themselves on the object of concern. 'We shall shortly be pursuing the audacious curve that will place us on the line of the Champs-Élysées!' With that, the employee opened a door and vanished into the next carriage.

It was hard to tell how fast the train was moving until a dimly lit cavern appeared and disappeared in a flash. One of the passengers began to read from a folded piece of paper as though he were reciting a prayer: 'PORTE MAILLOT – OBLIGADO – ÉTOILE – ALMA – MARBEUF. The first station should be Obligado . . .' Two minutes later, another illuminated cavern passed the windows, and the train seemed to be gathering speed. A young man claimed to have caught sight of a word on a tiny plaque, too short to be 'Obligado', but possibly 'Alma' or 'Étoile'. 'It's too soon for Obligado,' someone said, 'we won't be there for a while.'

A multi-coloured blur clattered past in the opposite direction. The train slowed down and stopped in a glittering nave full of people rushing about. A voice outside shouted the name of the station and the girl in the low-cut dress screamed, '*Champs-Élysées!*' 'Eight minutes from Porte Maillot,' said her neighbour. 'That's no time at all!' said the young woman. 'It's so *fast!*' The man on the other side of her leaned over and said, mysteriously, 'Nothing in life is ever fast enough, Mademoiselle.'

Twenty people boarded the carriage, which was already full, but no one alighted, and the temperature rose to a comfortable level. The employee reappeared. 'We're missing out all the stations!' said the man with the paper. 'Eighteen stations,' said the employee. 'Eight already open. Ten to open before the first of September. Next stop: PALAIS-ROYAL!'

Now that they could visualize the route – down the Champs-Élysées, across the Place de la Concorde and along the Tuileries Gardens – it seemed all the more miraculous. At Palais-Royal, the passengers on the platform had to wait for the next train. Then came Louvre – which was hard to imagine – Châtelet and Hôtel-de-Ville, where they stopped for half a minute. A darkened station that must have been Saint-Paul flicked past, then the wheels gave a horrible screech, daylight flooded the carriage and, blinking as though at some amazing novelty, they saw the snail-like traffic on the Place de la Bastille.

A respectable-looking woman began to shake with helpless laughter as the train gave a jolt and plunged back into the tunnel. GARE DE LYON – REUILLY – NATION – PORTE DE VINCENNES. '*Tout le monde descend!*'

The crowd spilled out, their faces radiant with satisfaction. They placed their tickets, marked '*À la sortie jeter dans la Boîte*', in a wooden collection box, while the empty train slid away behind a large rotunda. They climbed the steps, passed under the glass umbrella, and found themselves in a suburban landscape of dirty little houses and dusty grey trees blasted by a scorching wind. They stopped on the edge of the street, looked at one another, and said, in a single voice, '*Let's go back to the Métropolitain!*'

By the time they had bought their tickets from the smiling face behind the counter, the train had completed the return loop and was standing at the other platform, waiting to take them back to the other side of Paris in twenty-seven minutes. Everyone agreed that, from now on, they would take the Métropolitain whenever they could.

* THE ADMIRABLE CONVENIENCE *

MARCEL PROUST, former man-about-town, writer of occasional elegant articles in the newspapers and collector of rare aesthetic sensations, often sat for a long time in the iris-scented room like a sphinx, with the door (in case someone rang) and the window left open, despite the smell of laundry and the pollen of the chestnut trees on the boulevard, remembering the views from other *cabinets* – the ruined tower of Roussainville-le-Pin, the glistening white walls of the trellised pavilion on the Champs-Élysées, the skylight in his mother's toilet, which, seen in the mirror, might have been a cloud-reflecting pool. The days of perilous journeys from kitchen to *cabinet*, with all the risks of tripping up and spilling, were long past. In well-appointed apartments, the water was already waiting in the bowl: a smart tug on a nickel-plated bronze and ivory handle emptied it in a flash and filled it with two fresh litres of water from a reservoir mounted on the wall.

It was the only room in the apartment in which the outside world was audible. Anywhere else, the noise would have been a distraction, but here, it plunged him into a pleasant state of half-conscious meditation. The parping of automobiles was a simple melody for which his mind automatically supplied the words: '*Get up! Go to the country! Take a picnic!*' Petrol fumes gusting up from the street suggested the shade of willows and a brook singing duets with the softly puttering Panhard-Levassor.

The room was arranged, like his table at the Ritz, for special, daily occasions. He ate once every twenty-four hours, the same meal whenever possible: one roast chicken wing, two *œufs à la crème*, three croissants (always from the same *boulangerie*), a plate of fried potatoes, some grapes, a cup of coffee and a bottle of beer, followed, nine or ten hours later, by an almost empty glass of Vichy water. He rarely visited the *cabinet* for anything else. When the convoluted journey was over, the rest was taken care of by English engineering. (These days, nearly all the household gods spoke English: Maple & Co. on the Place de l'Opéra and Liberty on the Boulevard des Capucines for modern-style furniture, the Société Française du Vacuum Cleaner – *'nettoyage par le vide'* – for the fitted carpets, Remington for the typewriter, the Aeolian Company for the pianola.)

On the day the Paris Métro had opened, he had found himself in Venice, lying in a gondola on the Grand Canal, from which he waved to his mother as she stood in the window of the Hotel Danieli. He returned to his parents' new apartment at 45, Rue de Courcelles, which, even after the opening of the Étoile–Anvers segment in October 1902, was as far as one could be in central Paris from a Métro station. In August 1903, when eighty-four passengers were held up at Couronnes station by a smouldering train in the tunnel, and refused to leave until their fifteen centimes were refunded, and were asphyxiated and trampled to death, thus becoming the first consumer martyrs, he was preparing to join his mother at Évian and, daringly for him, to take the funicular to the Mer de Glace. In 1906, when both his father and his mother were dead, he moved to an apartment at 102, Boulevard Haussmann, which was noisy, dusty and new, but the only apartment on the market that his mother had seen. 'I could not bring myself to move to a house that *maman* never knew.' This placed him less than three hundred yards from the Saint-Lazare Métro station, which had opened only two years before.

Without the hammering of his neighbours' electricians, plumbers and carpet-fitters, he would have heard the excavations on the boulevard for lines A and B, which were managed by a separate company called Nord-Sud.

The Nord-Sud was to the Compagnie du Chemin de Fer Métropolitain de Paris what Maple's was to Au Bon Marché, or the Ritz to a shelter for the homeless. It used Thomson motors, fed by a pantograph that continually caressed an aerial wire. First-class carriages were bright yellow and red; second class were aquamarine and electric blue. In the connecting corridors of Saint-Lazare, a customer of the CMP passed into an enchanted world in which transportation was a pretext and every decorative detail a compliment to good taste: the mosaic lettering of the station's name, the delicately lavatorial entrances of wrought-iron and ceramics. Saint-Lazare's famous ticket-hall of multi-coloured columns and tiled, ventricular vaults bore a remarkable resemblance to the abbey of Fontevrault, and made it possible to imagine that Eleanor of Aquitaine, Richard the Lion-heart and the other sepulchral effigies had risen up and assumed the garb of modern Parisians, and were setting off for a monastic herb garden or a Saracen stronghold on the other side of Paris.

In 1906, at the age of thirty-five, when his literary baggage was extremely light, he was already acquainted with the law of modern life according to which one's immediate surroundings remain a mystery while distant places seen in guidebooks and paintings are as familiar as old friends whose material presence is no longer required to maintain the friendship. The Métropolitain, whose rumble was perceptible to the spiders on the ceiling, might as well have been a fantasy of H. G. Wells. This, combined with an inability to leave his apartment, explains why, when very few Parisians had never taken the Métro, and when more kilometres were travelled every day in Paris than on the entire rail network, Marcel Proust had yet to descend to the Métropolitain. He had never, as far as we know, even written the word; nor had any of his friends ever mentioned it. In August, he had tried to reach the Père-Lachaise cemetery in order to attend his uncle's funeral, but had spent two hours wheezing in the Saint-Lazare railway station, galvanizing his asthmatic lungs with coffee before returning to his apartment. In September, imagining the marvels that might correspond to the exotic syllables 'Perros-Guirec' and 'Ploërmel', he had left for Brittany. The journey had ended at Versailles, where he took a room at the Hôtel des Réservoirs. He was still there in December when he wrote to an old friend:

> I have been at Versailles for four months, but am I really at Versailles? I often wonder whether the place in which I am living – hermetically sealed and electrically lit – is somewhere other than Versailles, of which I have seen not a single dead leaf fluttering over a single solitary fountain.

That year, he had planned a trip to Normandy. He had pored over guide books and gazetteers, and pestered his correspondents for information on rented accommodation. He had promised himself a quiet holiday somewhere near Trouville, if the ideal house could be found, with varied relaxations and occasional tours in a covered automobile.

> Nice and dry, *not in the trees* . . . electricity if possible, reasonably new, neither dusty (*modern style* is exactly what I need for easy breathing) nor damp. I need only my master bedroom, two servants' rooms, a dining-room and a kitchen. A bathroom is not indispensable though very agreeable. Drawing-room pointless. As many WCs as possible.

But Trouville had fallen through, leaving only the near-perfect memory of something that had never taken place.

* THE MIRACULOUS TELEPHONE *

THE FOLLOWING SUMMER (1907), he surprised himself and his servants, who were accustomed to working in artificial light and sleeping in the daytime, by reaching the Channel resort of Cabourg. He chose Cabourg because he had spent some long and unforgotten holidays there with his mother, and because the Grand Hôtel was responsive to his needs. He wrote to a friend from his suite on the top floor: 'I have just spent an entire year in bed.' Then, after a brief calculation, he corrected himself: 'This year, I have left my bed five times.'

This was slightly inaccurate. In March, he had visited a friend in Paris who had been poisoned by oysters. In April, whilst enjoying a respite from the cacophonous installation of his neighbour's toilet ('she keeps having the seat changed – widening it, I expect'), he had gone to the balcony and taken the air. He had attended three *soirées* and visited a newspaper office to discuss an article. Including his departure for Cabourg, he had left his bed seven times in all.

For longer trips across Paris, he had only to descend to the street, where, summoned by telephone, his chauffeur would be waiting. But there was always the possibility of getting lost at either end.

Two years before – when his mother was alive, listening out for the creaking floorboard that announced the return of her son – he had left the taxi and stepped into the *'ascenceur'* (which he always misspelled), and nearly committed a criminal offence against the General Secretary of the mortgage-lending bank, Crédit Foncier, who lived on the floor above:

> I absent-mindedly took the lift to the fourth floor. Then I tried to go back down, but it was impossible to reach the first floor. All I could do then was to take the lift back up to the fourth floor, from where I walked down, but to the wrong floor, where I tried to force the lock of M. Touchard's door.

Once, he took the *ascenseur* to the street, turned right towards the Byzantine dome of Saint-Augustin, then right and right again towards the cupola of the Printemps department store, and then, after completing a triangular itinerary of one kilometre, found himself so close to his starting point that, despite being unable to identify his own front door, he located it at the third attempt.

The telephone made everything much simpler. Connections with Cabourg were not always reliable, because provincial exchanges often closed at nine o'clock in the evening. But in Paris, his friends could ask for the magic number – 29205 – and find themselves speaking to his concierge (who would send a messenger up the stairs), or even to Marcel himself, as if in person, provided that the telephone had been connected and that he had heard, from his bed or from the *cabinet*, the spinning-top sound that he preferred to the jangling bell. A telephone conversation was a little play for two or three voices. Sometimes, he transcribed the dialogue for the pleasure of his friends:

> Someone comes hurrying up from the concierge: you want to talk to me. I rush to the telephone. 'Hello, hello?' (Nobody there.) I call back ... nothing. I ask for number 56565. They ring: it's engaged. – I insist. They ring again: it's engaged. Just then, there's a call from you: 'M. de Croisset would like to know whether this evening ...'. I expect that, at that exact moment, you signalled to your secretary to indicate that some more agreeable invitation had caused you to change your mind. Whatever the case, silence ensues, and the person hangs up. I ring again; they give me a wrong number. And so it goes on.

On that occasion, the unseen *demoiselle*, who placed distant souls in touch with one another, and whose utterances were always short and sibylline (because she was paid by the number of connections she made), finally delivered an unusually long burst of oracular wisdom: 'In my opinion, M. de Croisset has disconnected his telephone so that he won't be disturbed. Monsieur could telephone until two in the morning and would still be wasting his time.'

THOUGH HE HAD yet to descend to the underworld in person, his words, transmitted by copper wires, had crossed subterranean Paris many times; his written messages had traversed all four hundred and fifty kilometres of the pneumatic tube network. The telephone was no less miraculous for having a scientific explanation. Had he been writing a novel, he would certainly have devoted long passages to it – the misunderstandings, the jocular friends who pretended to be somebody else, the total strangers whose voices suddenly entered his apartment. Without the distraction of a face, certain inflections and even aspects of a personality were instantly revealed. He himself had once been mistaken for a woman. Because of the telephone, his letters had become longer, more frequent and less trivial. 'You only ever send me messages that could have been telephoned,' he complained to a friend.

The maid, too, was often forced to resort to pen and paper:

Having been asked by Monsieur Proust to place a telephone call to Madame la Princesse which I was unable to do successfully because no one answered me I am taking the liberty of writing down this telephone message because Monsieur Proust was extremely anxious to learn whether the mouthful of soufflé had indisposed Madame la Princesse.

Exasperated subscribers wrote to the newspapers, complaining about the inefficiency of the miracle. Unlike them, Marcel was always respectful of the mystery, and patient with wrong numbers and delays. He wrote an article on the subject for the *Figaro*:

We fill the columns of the *Figaro* with our complaints, finding the magic transformations still not fast enough, because sometimes minutes pass before we see at our side, invisible but present, the friend to whom we wished to speak. . . . We are like the character of a fairy-tale who, his wish having been granted by a wizard, sees his fiancée, lit by the vivid light of enchantment, leafing through the pages of a book, shedding a tear or gathering flowers, close enough to touch, yet in the place where she then finds herself, very far away.

Every conversation with a disembodied voice seemed to him a foreshadowing of eternal separation. The lovely expression that had entered daily speech – 'It was nice to hear your voice' – filled him with poignant anxiety. Years before, his mother had chided him for his reluctance to use the telephone. He sometimes heard her voice, crackling but distinct, rising from his memory as though it came to him through the labyrinth of wires:

The apologies you owe the telephone for your blasphemies in the past! The remorse you should feel for having despised, scorned and rejected such a benefactor! Oh, to hear the voice of my poor little wolf, and the poor little wolf hearing mine!

⋆ THE INDISPENSABLE CHEMIST ⋆

EVERY MODERN CONVENIENCE implied its ideal form – the electric switch that was always within reach, the automobile that never broke down, the telephone that never cut short a conversation. Yet when the invention malfunctioned, it could conjure up an unexpected variety of perfection that would never have existed if the convenience had worked as advertised.

The Theatre in the Comfort of One's Own Home!
Opéra, Opéra-Comique, Variétés, Nouveautés, etc. Apply to
THÉÂTROPHONE, 23, Rue Louis-le-Grand. Tel. 101–03. For sixty
francs a month, three people can hear performances daily.
Trial audition on request.

The théâtrophone had disappointed him at first. A live performance of *Pelléas et Mélisande* reached him like something precious that had been smashed and sullied by the post. The *Pastoral Symphony* was almost as inaudible as it had been to Beethoven. *Die Meistersinger* was full of interruptions, like an over-literal demonstration of Baudelaire's dictum, in his essay on Wagner: 'In music, as in the written word,

there is always a gap that is completed by the listener's imagination.'
Yet without that intermittency, the remote performance would have
lost its power: his memory would not have been forced to rush
about the orchestra pit, playing every instrument, until the musicians
returned from nowhere.

The mind, too, could be made to behave like a faulty contraption.
Several chemists in his *quartier* stayed open into the night – the
coloured jars gleaming in the gas light, a courteous magician presid-
ing in a white coat – to dispense the precisely measured solace that
only science could provide. Drugs helped him to sleep (Veronal,
valerian, Trional and heroin, which he had once recommended to his
mother), and to stay awake (caffeine, amyl nitrate and pure adrenalin).
In certain states of drug-induced half-sleep, when the clatter of
tramcars and the street-cries that had survived the advent of department stores reached his ears, muffled and distorted, the telephone
operators in his brain started pushing plugs into sockets at random,
rousing old memories, giving voice to the creaking floorboards and
the ticking clock, initiating party-line conversations in which dozens
of people spoke at once, repeating themselves endlessly or whispering
things that could never quite be heard.

Certain drugs were best avoided. Of cocaine, he said, contrasting
its visible effects with those of a healthy diet and a recent haircut,
that 'time has special express trains bound for premature old age,
while return trains run on a parallel line and are almost as fast'. But
other drugs, dispensed by a chemist, could send him on circular
journeys from one end of his life to the other, after which, when the
doors and the furniture had resumed their habitual positions, he was
surprised to find himself still in bed on the second floor of an
apartment block in the ninth *arrondissement* of Paris.

IN THE GLOOM of his soundproofed apartment, he had seen the
years slip by. He sat in his nest of pillows and pullovers, writing long
letters to friends and elaborate notes to the maid. In the time it had
taken him to compose a few articles and reviews, the Métropolitain
had become a world in its own right.

By the time he started work on his 'Parisian novel' in 1908 –
fearing that he had left it too late – there were sixty kilometres of

tunnels and ninety-six stations. The spread of the Métropolitain was such a normal part of life that newspapers no longer bothered to report the opening of a new line. The original Métro was already a quaint memory. Its sleepers of creosoted beech, which were blamed for breathing difficulties, had been replaced by solid oak. In 1909, the moving staircase at Père-Lachaise, which covered thirty centimetres a second, made the old kind of staircase seem intolerably uncooperative. Hundreds of other escalators followed. The climb out of the depths was now no more arduous than the descent. Lighting was improved, and it became possible to read in the underground. Travellers who were offended by the smell of their fellow passengers could place ten centimes in a slot, hold a handkerchief under a tap, pull the handle and collect a dash of sweet myrrh or ylang-ylang. There were weighing machines, inscribed 'Know Your Weight – Know Yourself', and a continually refreshed museum of cheerful pictures: a cow giving milk to a *chocolatier*, a cod offering its liver to a person with anaemia, a mongrel listening to a gramophone.

Fears that Parisians would turn into a mindless herd obsessed with time had proved unfounded. Workers and businessmen in every part of Paris were delighted to be able to spend a few extra minutes in bed every morning. The Métro oiled their social activities and lent itself to their desires with unquestioning efficiency. At the music hall – which he sometimes attended in a box, sitting above the thickest layers of tobacco smoke – it was celebrated in songs: Landry's 'La Petite Dame du Métro', Dranem's 'Le Trou de mon quai'. Less than ten years after the opening of Line 1, it was impossible to imagine Paris without the Métro. For tourists and returning natives, it was an inexhaustible source of what would one day be called 'Proustian moments'.

A patient chemist might have concocted the magic potion: old perspiration reactivated by new; a hint of stagnant water; various industrial lubricants and detergents; cheap scents from a dispensing machine; a selection of hydrocarbons and carboxyls, and, dominating the other smells, pentanoic acid, from brakes and human warmth, which occurs naturally in valerian. It would have surprised him to learn that the infusions of valerian that sent him into the echoing realms of somnolence filled his apartment with an odour that had some of his visitors involuntarily rushing back to the Métropolitain.

* THE CELESTIAL MACHINE *

ANOTHER DECADE PASSED, and the great novel was finally nearing completion. The world described in *À la recherche du temps perdu* was disappearing in the cratered fields of northern France, but the novel, with its gleaming inscrutability, the flawless circuitry of its sentences and its bewildering modes of efficiency, belonged to the new world as much as passenger aeroplanes and the Theory of Relativity.

The author, meanwhile, inhabited a dimension where time moved as imperceptibly as an hour-hand. When he dined at the Ritz, he wore the same stiff white collar; his shoes came from Old England and his dinner jacket from Carnaval de Venise. The thin moustache, waxed by the man who had cut his father's hair, was the kind of impeccable anachronism that inspired devotion in the waiters. The car waiting outside the hotel was the old Renault, which he had refused to allow the chauffeur to replace with a more modern machine. Apart from a few uniforms at the tables and talk about the lack of coal, the war had barely intruded on the Ritz.

In July 1917, when the sirens had sounded, he had climbed to the balcony with some of the other diners to see the first German planes over Paris since January 1916. The searchlights from Le Bourget had lit up the celestial dogfight, and he had watched the constellations of stars and planes rise and disintegrate, replicating with breathtaking accuracy the apocalyptic firmament in El Greco's *Burial of Count Orgaz*. He had walked home blissfully in the dark while the Gothas dropped their bombs. One night, the maid had found little splinters of metal in the brim of his hat, and exclaimed, 'Ah, Monsieur, you didn't come home in the car!', and he said, 'No. Why? It was much too beautiful for that.'

On 30 January 1918, feeling the urge to hear some music unmediated by the théâtrophone, he accepted an invitation from the Comtesse de La Rochefoucauld to attend a private performance at her home in the Rue Murillo of Borodin's Second String Quartet. At the end of the evening, he was leaving the house when the sirens began their mournful warning. It was half-past eleven. A squadron of Gothas, taking advantage of the unusually clear skies, had flown high over the French defences north of Compiègne and were dropping their bombs on the north-eastern suburbs. His usual chauffeur had been unavailable, and the old man who had replaced him was unable to start the Renault. Since Borodin's poignant and stately *notturno* was still playing in his mind, and since he did not wish to repeat the farewell ceremony, he stood by the car while the chauffeur fiddled with the engine. Now and then, people rushed past, heading for the nearest Métro station, which was less than four hundred metres away.

Having hit their targets in the suburbs, the Gothas were now flying over Paris. Some of the explosions were clearly audible, and it was possible to tell on which *quartiers* the bombs were falling. At last, the engine coughed and rattled. Marcel climbed into the seat, and they set off slowly down the Rue Murillo.

They had crossed the Rue de Monceau and were heading along the Avenue de Messine when the engine stuttered and the car lurched to a halt. They were still close enough to take shelter in the Métropolitain, at Courcelles or at Miromesnil, but the chauffeur was busy with the engine, and Marcel himself had never felt the slightest fear during air-raids, and had never once even visited the basement of his building – and wouldn't have known how to get there – because of the damp air and the dust.

Fire engines rattled along the boulevard. He thought of Parisians crowded together in the darkness, like Christians in the Catacombs, and of things that certain friends of his had said: that, in the black night of the Métropolitain, when the bombs were falling, men and women satisfied their desires without the preliminaries of etiquette. He had written a passage on the subject for the last volume of his novel:

Some of those Pompeians, as the fire of heaven rained down on them, descended into the corridors of the Métro, knowing that they would not be alone there; and the darkness that irradiates everything like a new element abolishes the first phase of pleasure and offers direct access to a domain of caresses that is normally attained only after a certain length of time.

He had promised himself that, one night or day, he would witness those 'secret rites' for himself.

Six or seven streets away, towards Saint-Lazare, he heard the screeching glissando, then the sound of windows imploding and a building rushing to the ground. He waited by the car. The chauffeur turned the crank in vain. A squeak of metal, imitating the interval of E and A sharp, and he might have heard the beautiful *notturno* as though it had been playing all along and he had only to be silent to hear it. Borodin had composed his second movement as though in anticipation of the telephone, with interruptions and expectant pauses, and the cello that seemed to fade like a distant voice, but then continued on its way. It was the sound of regret and its remedy, a slightly faltering serenity, like that of someone unexpectedly able to breathe in a place of danger and confinement. The bombs were a symphonic accompaniment, a reminder of tribulations overcome. They were a celebration of the knowledge that his life's work would be completed in time.

The engine roared into life. A few moments later, they were parked in front of his home at 102, Boulevard Haussmann. He climbed out of the car. A bomb exploded barely five hundred yards away in the Rue d'Athènes. He tried to usher the chauffeur into the hall and offered him a bed for the night in the drawing room. But the man, it seemed, was hard of hearing. 'I'm off back to Grenelle,' he said. 'It was just a false alarm. Nothing fell on Paris.'

Next day, in bed, he read in the newspaper that when the sirens had sounded, hundreds of people had rushed out to take shelter in the Métro, but had found the doors closed. The Prefect of Police had decreed that, from now on, during air raids, every station of the Métro would remain open throughout the night.

THE LAST VOLUME of the novel to appear in his lifetime – *Sodome et Gomorrhe II* – was published in the spring of 1922. He knew that it would take time for his readers to become accustomed to the new idiom: at first, the novel would leave them feeling frayed and disoriented. He had once said that he did not write novels that could be read 'between one station and the next'. Yet his readers had evidently kept up with modern developments and were eager for innovations. He was more pleased than he would have thought when he learned that from the very day of publication, Parisians were reading *À la recherche du temps perdu* in buses and trams, and even in the Métro, oblivious to their neighbours and so engrossed in the novel that when they reached the end of a sentence, the station had passed, and they had to cross to the other platform to wait for the train that would take them back to their destination.

THE NOTRE-DAME EQUATION

△

To the small number of questing spirits whose daily perambulation in Paris was a divinatory walk through a sacred labyrinth, and whose indoor activities – despite fumes in the hallway and strange lights under the door – were a complete mystery to their neighbours, the change, which was both subtle and profound, appeared to have occurred at about the time of the First World War.

Their ancient science expressed only its most basic precepts in words, and so they would not have been able to offer much in the way of evidence. If they had been willing or able to convert their knowledge into the simple currency of fact, they might have adduced some apparently insignificant phenomena: an alteration of the light that fell on certain buildings at certain times of day, a modification in the nesting habits of birds or an imperceptible shift in the anatomical geometry of Parisians as they walked along a street or looked to the sky to see what the weather was going to do. They might have hinted at something more devastating than the annihilation of a million soldiers and civilians. But no one would have believed them anyway, and it was only when modern science had progressed to a point where the insights of the two disciplines became mutually comprehensible that one of those questing spirits (the subject of this story) tried to warn his contemporaries. By then, the world was once again on the brink of catastrophe, and although the ancient science proved its practical worth in unexpected ways, few people had any use for its wisdom.

As for the rest of the population, only those who had emerged alive from the horrific crucible of war had any inkling of the change. Paris had sat out the conflagration like a medieval citadel, suffering little more than a chipped turret and a dented portcullis. It was this near-total preservation of the city that alerted some people to the fact that the capital of France had disappeared, along with the old world, and been replaced by an almost perfect copy of itself.

If any single event had the power to reveal the change to ordinary eyes, it was the great Peace Conference, which, from January 1919 to January 1920, turned Paris into a gaudy bazaar of foreign dignitaries. Delegates came from east and west to redraw the map of the world and to share the spoils of war. Many saw their hopes squashed and smeared across marble floors by the patent-leather boot of international diplomacy. While Georges Clemenceau, Woodrow Wilson, David Lloyd George and Vittorio Orlando held stately discussions in sumptuous hotels, 'flooded after sundown with dazzling light, and filled by day with the buzz of idle chatter, the shuffling of feet, the banging of doors, and the ringing of bells',* other emissaries, from countries whose names were known only to scholars, envied the waiters and chambermaids who had access to the tables and beds of the mighty, and as they laid their glittering robes of state on the dusty coverlets of cheap hotels, felt themselves shrivel up into illegible footnotes in the history of Europe.

Little attempt was made to sustain the illusion of lasting peace. Recently installed dictators sought to confirm the advantages they had gained by the massacre of neighbouring populations. Others, whose star was in the descendant, blew vigorously on the embers of their ambitions, and quietly pondered future policies of assassination and deceit. Mortified to be assigned to the depressing Hôtel des Réservoirs and to be forced to carry their own luggage, the German mission observed how much influence attached to the House of Rothschild, and was struck by the bitter conviction that the war had been staged by Jews and Freemasons, and that the United States of America had intended all along to play the role of deus ex machina.

Though their fortunes varied enormously, victors and vanquished alike took part in the same unconscious conspiracy to revive the

---

* E. J. Dillon, *The Inside Story of the Peace Conference* (New York and London, 1920).

glories of the past, and to behave as though the capital of Europe had never seen her luxury grow dim. In the ballroom of the Hôtel Majestic, while the pavements outside were rutted with frozen snow as sharp as steel, the British delegation held an extravagant party at which 'the latest forms of dancing were to be seen, including the jazz and the hesitation waltz'. At such events were policies discussed that would decide the destinies of millions. Men who were called upon to exercise the power of rational thought with purity and precision pored over dinner menus as long as treaties. They whirled their unidentified foreign partners across the floor and fell prey to the collective madness. Many of those who observed these spectacles of wild dissipation as they passed in the street, begging for relief from cold and hunger, gave voice to the sentiment expressed by Cicero: 'Quam parva sapientia regitur mundus!'*

Yet even the conquerors were strangely muted in their exultations. As Dr E. J. Dillon, an eye-witness and participant, observed, 'the smile of youth and beauty was cold like the sheen of winter ice. The shadow of death hung over the institutions and survivals of the various civilizations and epochs which were being dissolved in the common melting-pot.' Less than two hours away by motor car, black hordes, whose limbs stuck out of shell-ploughed fields, were a ghastly scene from a medieval tarot, convincing those who made the journey from Paris out of curiosity that nothing would ever change, that dominions would continue to flourish and decay, and that the means would always be found, in spite of everything, to prevent any conspicuous diminution in the sum total of human misery.

WHEN THE DELEGATES of the Peace Conference had returned to their homelands and places of exile, they left behind them an atmosphere of half-reality in which preposterous things were strangely plausible. It rose like a miasma from the Seine, drifted past the fluted columns of the Assemblée Nationale, and crept along the corridors

---

* 'With how little wisdom is the world governed!'

of power. Parliamentary debates went on as before, but now Truth wore a garb that made her fiendishly difficult to identify. Thus it was that a group of republican *députés*, moved by the pleas of the exploited people of Poldavia, took up their cause against the capitalist oppressor and were about to petition the Foreign Ministry when the true status of Poldavia was revealed, and the letters signed by Lineczi Stantoff and Lamidaëff of the Poldavian Defence Committee were found to have been written by a member of the extreme-right Action Française movement. Only then was the name Lamidaëff seen to be *L'Ami d'A.F.* and the exotic syllables of 'Lineczi Stantoff' to contain the words *'l'inexistant'*.

Radiant particles of wisdom were always surrounded by clouds of ignorance. A few men, such as the enigmatic figure whose intervention in the affairs of the world is the basis of this true story, realized that the Great War and its political consequences were a distraction. Or rather, he saw that the ruination of Europe, perpetrated in the name of a cause that remained obscure, was merely a side effect of the confusion that had entered men's minds. The war to end all wars was just the most recent of the 'violent storms and tempests that attend the collision of the volatile and the incombustible, the Universal Solvent and the lifeless body', when, in layman's terms, the material composition of reality itself evolves new configurations that elude the control of the civilized mind.

There was surely some cruel significance in the fact that the change had manifested itself in a city that had been the refuge of wisdom since the end of the Dark Ages. Even before the war, the humming hive of laboratories and lecture rooms had also been a magical place where people came in search of non-existent treasures. More than a century after its disappearance from the Sainte-Chapelle, when the sans-culottes had waged their mindless war on gullibility, there were sightings of the Holy Sponge of the Passion, which Louis IX had purchased for an exorbitant sum from Baudouin II, Emperor of Constantinople, in 1241. According to some lovers of the city who claimed to remember this as a golden age, Paris was a treasure house where manuscripts of unknown ancient texts, maps of vanished continents and authentic sacred relics could be bought at flea markets for next to nothing. They were remembering a time when everything had been at once believable and incredible. Every day at Les Invalides, veterans with wooden arms and legs persuaded visitors to wait, sometimes for hours, to see the invalid with the wooden head, who had been there just a moment before and had probably gone for his shave but would be back directly. At the Bibliothèque Nationale, librarians were often importuned by bogus readers poking about in the flower-beds, looking for Cleopatra's mummy, which, having been deposited in the archives by Napoleon Bonaparte, was said to have been removed from the cellars when her fragrance began to spread through the stacks, and to have been buried in the inner courtyard one rainy evening in 1870.

Most troubling of all, the very embodiment of mortal beauty had been veiled with suspicion and was no longer the object of unquestioning devotion. In August 1911, Da Vinci's masterpiece, *La Joconde*, disappeared from the Louvre. An exhaustive search turned up the frame but not the painting, which had gone home on the bus with the Italian carpenter who had made the glass case that was supposed to protect her from anarchists and vandals. She spent more than two years in a garret, smiling enigmatically at her abductor and sharing the warmth of his stove, and was only recovered when the carpenter tried to sell her to the Uffizi. But in the meantime, rumours had spread of an American collector who commissioned perfect copies of stolen paintings and then pretended to restore the originals to the grateful museums. The new science of fingerprinting proved its worth, and photographs were presented that showed every crack and wrinkle of the original painting, yet no one could quite summon up the conviction that the recovered Mona Lisa was the real one. The more means there were of determining authenticity, it seemed, the more doubt was cast on the artefact. And even if it *was* the original Mona Lisa, how was one to judge her timeless beauty, since even men with long experience of such things had recently admired, at the Salon des Indépendants, an *Adriatic Sunset* painted by Lolo the donkey from the Lapin Agile in Montmartre?

Reality itself fell into decay, and in that darkness, luminous spirits such as Marie Curie and Henri Poincaré, who alone appeared to understand the muddled workings of the universe, became the objects of religious veneration. Others, to whom mathematical equations were meaningless hieroglyphs, longed for the old-fashioned certainty of a sacred miracle. Every day, hundreds of pilgrims queued at the Chapelle de la Médaille Miraculeuse in the Rue du Bac, where the Virgin Mary had commanded a young novice to have a medallion struck – the medallion, bearing the Virgin's image, to be reproduced as many times as required, and each one to be as genuine as the next. Unfortunately, the market in fake medallions flourished as never before, and even those glinting, tangible icons of cosmic truth were contaminated with doubt.

Sceptics might have sneered at what they called 'superstition', but how could anyone be expected to distinguish fantasy from reality when things that happened in broad daylight in front of large crowds were called into question? The Tour de France – the great sporting symbol of national unity that began and ended in Paris – should have been immune from the corrosive effects of incredulity. It seemed to represent a simple application of human will and elementary mechanics. Yet even those who witnessed it could not trust the evidence of their eyes. Some of the riders were known to have boarded trains and to have pedalled away from quiet stations in the night. Others were thought to have shared the impossible burden with identical twins. In 1904, the first four riders to finish – who ever after asserted their innocence – were disqualified for cheating, and the victory went to Henri Cornet, who was only twenty years old and who, for a reason that has been lost to history, was known as 'Rigolo' ('the Joker'). Some of those who had actually seen the riders struggle into Paris on flat tyres or on foot, with a mangled bicycle frame around their neck, firmly believed that the Tour de France was a lucrative fiction, cooked up every July by the journalists of *L'Auto*, who had been seen drinking in the back room of a café at Montgeron, writing Homeric reports of fantastic exploits in the Alps.

IN THAT AGE OF rampant unreality, when the supposedly deranged Surrealists of Montmartre and Montparnasse were simply the faithful chroniclers of what remained of reality, it might be thought that the sleepless seekers after truth who studied the ancient science of Hermes were suffering a crisis of confidence. Yet even one of the more conservative estimates puts the number of practising alchemists in post-war Paris at about ten thousand. Since so much trade and manufacture had moved out to the suburbs, this would make alchemy one of the city's leading industries between the wars.

The alchemists themselves could be found in poky 'esoteric' book-shops with names from Egyptian mythology and shy but hostile owners huddled over huge bronze ashtrays, and in university labora-tories, where they worked as assistants or attended public seminars. Most of them were thin, bearded and anxious, and remarkably slow of speech. Old-fashioned alchemists still spent long evenings at the Bibliothèque Nationale or the Bibliothèque Sainte-Geneviève, deci-phering unreliable editions of medieval texts with a pocket French–Latin dictionary. They had the doleful, watery eyes of the mad. Without the occasional gas explosion or spilling of toxic chemicals, they might have been described as 'harmless'. One luckless adept, well known to his younger colleagues, had chanced upon a convinc-ingly antiquated edition of a work attributed to Paracelsus, in which a mistranslated passage advised the student to refine his base metal in a small oven for forty years (instead of 'days'). The next stage was to have been the distillation of the Universal Panacea or elixir of long life, but as he contemplated the charred nugget that had been the focus of his yearnings since adolescence, he saw with the bitter clarity of a true philosopher that the process of acquiring immortality was too lengthy to be contained within the span of a human life.

Such men were increasingly rare. Alchemy had entered a thrilling new age, and there was as much difference now between the old and new type of alchemist as there is between a shopkeeper totting up the day's takings and a mathematician calculating the proof of a theorem. To anyone unfamiliar with the science, it might seem ironic that such a far-fetched discipline should have enjoyed a renaissance in the twentieth century, but to those who took a scholarly interest in the subject, alchemy's achievements were evident and substantial. For centuries, alchemy had kept alive the spirit of experimentation, and it was only recently that it had been overtaken by chemistry. Alchemists had produced the first descriptions of several elements; they had established the existence of gases, and developed molecular theories of matter; they had discovered antimony, zinc, sulphuric acid, caustic soda, various compounds used in medicine, eau de vie and the secret of porcelain. And it was while searching for the philosopher's stone in his urine that an alchemist discovered phosphorus, which means 'bringer of light'. Many other discoveries had certainly been lost or had disappeared with the knowledge of the hieroglyphic languages in which they were recorded.

On the evening on which this story begins, an alchemist known only by a florid pseudonym, which was probably invented by his publisher, was deciphering one of those cryptic texts that are often misconstrued as primitive ornamentation. A tall, elderly man of aristocratic appearance, he stood in silent contemplation at the west front of Notre-Dame. From the three great portals, graven figures looked down on him with the mysterious serenity of their sightless eyes. Without his air of analytical inspection, he might have been mistaken for one of the old brotherhood of obsessed insomniacs. Throughout the Middle Ages, the alchemists of Paris had gathered every Saturn's Day afternoon at the cathedral dedicated to Our Lady of Paris. The square on which they met had been sacred long before the cathedral was built. It was there, in 464, that Arthur, son of Uther Pendragon, had invoked the Virgin Mary, who offered him the protection of her ermine cloak, and thus enabled him to defeat the Roman tribune called Flollo. That was a relatively recent event in the history of the site. Archaeological excavations had uncovered pagan altars beneath the square, and the early Gallo-Roman temple on the island had certainly replaced an even earlier building sacred to gods whose very names had perished.

The crowd of tourists was growing thin, and the late sun etched deep shadows into the carvings of the west front. Details that were usually invisible were emblazoned with the sun's dazzling gold, and it was possible to imagine the sight when the wooden scaffolding was first removed and the heavenly host shone forth in all the mesmerizing colours that medieval alchemists had purified in their crucibles.

The man who gazed on this glorious spectacle from another age was one of the very few who knew what they were seeing. He knew not only the harmonious confusion of antagonistic beliefs that had formed the great cathedral, but also its modern history, which lovers of the past thought too recent to be of interest. Ninety years before, the architect Viollet-le-Duc had immersed himself in the mysteries of early Gothic art. He had questioned archaeologists, and sent librarians deep into their archives in search of manuscripts that showed the cathedral in its original state. He had tracked down the statues that had been stolen in the Revolution or spirited away to Versailles. The Perpetual Secretary of the French Academy had mocked him for trying to revive an art that predated the Renaissance, but to Viollet-le-Duc, the thirteenth century was not an age of fumbling infants; it was a forgotten world whose peculiar wisdom had been lost.

He had noticed, for example, like the alchemist, that the towers and portals of the great cathedral were not symmetrical, and that its solid structure was a subtle configuration of forces and imbalances. Instead of seeing those anomalies as marks of barbarism, he realized that he was faced with something foreign and unexplained. He saw that Gothic architecture was a language with its own vocabulary and grammar. In an act of faith rarely found in conjunction with precise scholarship, he 'humbly submitted' to the incomprehensible beauty of the vanished age. And because he was inspired by love, the sneering of the Perpetual Secretary only spurred him on. He ridiculed the man's ignorance with the cheerfulness of a true believer: 'It is tempting to suppose', he wrote in *Du style gothique au XIX* *siècle*, 'that the only stained-glass windows the Perpetual Secretary has seen are those that one finds in the kiosks and public toilets of Paris'.

As a connoisseur of Gothic arcana, Viollet-le-Duc refused to allow any genuine relics of the early cathedral to be 'improved': he preferred mutilated sculptures to 'an appearance of restoration'. Though many of the riddles would remain unsolved, he would at least restore the pieces of the puzzle. The result of his labours was almost too strange and pristine in appearance to be appreciated by anyone who had known the cathedral in its muddled, palimpsestic state. Viollet-le-Duc had allowed Notre-Dame to find her way back to the thirteenth century, accompanied, it is true, by several of his own petrified fantasies. To the man who stood there that evening, reading the portals like the pages of a giant book, it was as though the architect had been tinkering with a machine abandoned to time by an earlier civilization, and, by accident or design, had supplied the missing parts that would bring it back to life.

IN ORDER TO UNDERSTAND what set this man apart from other admirers of Notre-Dame, and why he himself was under observation, it is necessary to say something of the more common forms of esoteric curiosity inspired by the great cathedral. More than a decade after the Peace Conference, Paris was still the centre of the world's attention. Every year, despite the Great Depression, more than one hundred thousand tourists came from the United States alone to feast their eyes on Paris and to wonder how such an obstreperous race could have created such a beautiful city. Almost all of them, if they only spent a day in Paris, went to gaze at Notre-Dame.

Many of those secular pilgrims were fans of Victor Hugo's bestselling novel, *Notre-Dame de Paris*. Having enjoyed what they took to be the true adventures of Quasimodo the hunchback, Esmeralda the gypsy-girl and Frollo the mad archdeacon, they pored over the runic stones and looked for gnostic clues in the stained-glass windows. They discovered pagan riddles in Latin funerary inscriptions and pieces of ecclesiastical furniture that were not much older than themselves. When they climbed the towers, they saw with a thrill the enigmatic graffito, ΑΝΑΓΚΗ,* with which the novel begins, and noticed with disappointment that mischievous hands had scratched the same puzzling characters in every nook and cranny.

Some who had made a special study of the matter felt quietly superior to their fellow tourists who failed to realize that the nave and chevet of the cathedral formed the ancient Egyptian symbol of the Ankh. Since the demonic priest of Victor Hugo's novel had – correctly, as it happened – identified Notre-Dame as 'a summary of hermetic science', they followed the priest's example and searched for the crow on the left-hand portal of the west front, 'in order to calculate the angle of vision of the crow, which looks at a mysterious

* 'Fate'.

point in the church where the philosopher's stone is certainly hidden'.* The legend had been recorded in Gobineau de Montluisant's work of 1640: *Explication très-curieuse des énigmes et figures hiéroglyphiques au grand portail de l'église cathédrale et métropolitaine de Notre-Dame de Paris*. If the tourist-pilgrims had pursued their studies a little further, they might have discovered that the alchemical crow symbolized putrefaction and the *caput mortuum* of the Magnum Opus – a stage in the purification of the metal and of the alchemist's soul – and that the crow was in fact a death's-head. (The location of the skull and the object of its gaze are best left to individual curiosity since the present occupants of the site in question would not welcome the attention, and because they have the means to make their displeasure lastingly apparent.)

Strange to say, apart from a few alchemists, no one seems to have pursued the most obvious clue of all. On the gallery of the south tower, two hundred feet above the square, a human figure stands among the gargoyles and chimaeras. It leans on the balustrade, gazing over the roof of the nave towards the Marais or – since the gaze of such figures is often oblique, like that of a bird – through the corner of its eye over some dog-ravaged flower-beds at a point of no apparent significance. The figure's long hair and beard, its Phrygian cap, its long laboratory coat and above all its knitted brows, show this to be the Alchemist of Notre-Dame. The expression on the stone face is one of astonishment bordering on horror and dismay, as though he were about to be consumed by something emerging from his crucible.

The apparent aimlessness of the figure's gaze is misleading. In 1831, just before the publication of Victor Hugo's novel, the archbishop's palace that used to stand between the cathedral and the river was destroyed in a riot. The much older medieval chapel around which the palace had been built, and which predated most of Notre-Dame, was also destroyed, and its treasures were thrown into the Seine. Later, the rubble was cleared away, leaving the space now occupied by flower-beds. If the ancient chapel once contained the philosopher's stone, it must now lie somewhere under the Pont de

* *Notre-Dame de Paris*, IV, 5.

l'Archevêché or, more likely, under some northern field or landfill site along the Seine. Meanwhile, the Alchemist of Notre-Dame still ponders with knitted brows the priceless, vanished treasure.

These things, and many more besides, were known to the mysterious viewer. He knew that the anonymous architect of Notre-Dame, and the craftsmen of the powerful Masonic guild that built the cathedral, had inscribed the procedures of the hermetic science where none would expect to find them – which is to say, in full view – and that, furthermore, they had encoded and engraved their knowledge in buildings that would outlive tapestries and manuscripts, and whose ecclesiastical owners would want to keep their pagan significance a secret. If a literal-minded scholar had objected that many of those stone figures had been placed there, or recarved, by Viollet-le-Duc, he would have retorted that no modern architect, consulting his imagination alone, could have produced that mysterious combination of scientific accuracy and simple faith.

Though there was no other sign of agitation in the elderly gentleman, anyone who happened to notice him as they left the cathedral might have seen an expression similar to that on the face of the stone Alchemist. But if they searched for the cause of his consternation, they would have seen nothing in particular, and might have assumed that he was one of those melancholy lost souls who haunt the religious sites of Paris. While the few tourists who remained on the square scanned the gallery of the Kings of Judah and Israel, and, guide book at the ready, identified the signs of the Zodiac and the labours of the months on the pillars of the left-hand portal, the gentleman stared almost straight ahead of him at a row of square medallions. The medallions were sheltered by little arches at the feet of the saints and angels. They depicted a series of rather murky scenes in low relief. Compared with the larger statues above them, they were unremarkable, and few people spared them a glance.

The sun was sinking behind the Préfecture de Police, and dark shadows moved across the cadaverous face of the cathedral. The gentleman turned away and walked slowly across the square. A bell in the north tower tolled the hour, and some pigeons clattered away from the black louvres that are like the lowered lashes of the cathedral's eyes. Without looking back, he turned towards the river and disappeared in the direction of the Right Bank.

As he left the square, a man who had been waiting a short distance away came and occupied the spot where the gentleman had just been standing. The superior quality of his suitcase, his Kodak camera and his travelling cloak – and the interest he aroused in the beggars – marked him out as a wealthy tourist. He placed his suitcase on the ground and set his camera on a tripod. He adjusted the screw, raised the lens almost to the height of the medallions and proceeded to photograph each one in turn. A group of people stopped to watch, and, following the angle of the lens, were struck by all the unsuspected details that suddenly burst into blinding clarity as each flash-bulb exploded.

The scenes had no apparent connection with the Bible. In one, a man armed with a shield and a lance was protecting a citadel from a savage-looking sheath of flames protruding from the top-left-hand corner of the frame. Next to it, a man in a long robe was rushing into a sanctuary that already contained a huddled form. On the other side of the central portal known as 'The Judgment Portal', a group of well-preserved figures appeared to sympathize in advance with the future effects of time and vandalism on a mournful seated figure with a mutilated, three-fingered hand and flaking flesh.

The medallion that seemed to have been a particular object of scrutiny was such a peculiar composition that it was hard to believe it belonged to the original cathedral; yet there was no sign of any modern restoration. On the far left of the doorway known as 'The Virgin's Portal', it showed a winged figure with its right arm raised in a gesture of aggression. Most of the panel was filled with a cloud that rose from the earth in a funnel or from an oddly shaped gourd. A small creature with a human torso and a reptilian head – perhaps a salamander – was falling headlong out of the cloud. The cloud itself was filled with six-pointed stars as though it contained a universe, though no constellation was recognizable in the arrangement of stars.

After photographing the last of the scenes, the photographer dismantled his tripod and placed the camera in his suitcase. Then he walked across the square in the same direction as the elderly gentleman. The sun was now eclipsed by the buildings on the far side of the square. Its gorgeous radiance gave way to the wan glow of street-lights along the *quai*, and the details of the medallions shrank back into darkness. A few stars glimmered in the gas-lit skies above the Île de la Cité.

THE ORIGINS OF NOTRE-DAME might have been 'lost in the night of ages', as the tour guides liked to say, but most of its history is easier to trace than the comings and goings of certain individuals who lived in its shadow.

Paris was no longer the biggest city in continental Europe, and it was less than half the size of London. Its eighty *quartiers* – even Montparnasse, where almost every vacant building was being converted into an American bar – were like villages in which everyone knew everyone else's business. There was a buoyant and extrovert bureaucracy that would have delighted Napoleon. Names were listed at the entrances of apartment blocks, and there were increasingly comprehensive telephone directories. Hundreds of thousands of *fiches* filled in by hotel guests were periodically scanned by the unhappy squad of policemen known as '*les garnos*' (from *hôtels garnis*). Despite all this, a man who wished to remain anonymous could pass through that teeming mass of information like a ghost through a hail of bullets.

It has, not surprisingly, proved impossible to determine exactly when a foreign agent first picked up the trail of the gentleman who was observed at Notre-Dame. Nor is it known how long the search continued. By 1937, the Nazis' secret intelligence agency, the Abwehr, was on the case, and the gentleman's addresses and regular haunts – but not his identity – were certainly known. Later, the trail went cold, and spying operations became more difficult as the European powers prepared for war. It was several years later, when the German armies were in retreat, that urgent attempts were made by the American Office of Strategic Services to revive the search. At about the same time, Paris booksellers and auctioneers noticed a surge in the demand for alchemical manuscripts, which anonymous collectors were buying '*à prix d'or*' in American dollars.

Given the fantastic nature of certain espionage operations undertaken by the Nazis, and in view of their farcical attempt in 1925 to fill the party coffers with alchemically-produced gold, the base of Paris operations for the Abwehr agent is likely to have been the Hôtel Helvétia at 51, Rue de Montmorency. It was recommended to German tourists, and it occupied the oldest stone building in Paris, which was known as 'The House of Nicolas Flamel'. A wealthy dealer in manuscripts, Flamel had built the house in 1407 as a hostel for the poor. He himself never lived there, and, despite his later reputation, was never an alchemist. This had not prevented seekers of the philosopher's stone from demolishing half the building in their futile search for gold. Blinded by greed, they ignored the most basic precept of alchemy – that the scientist himself must be pure of heart. Evidently, they also ignored the inscription on the wall that said,

> Chacun soit content de ses biens,
> Qui n'a souffisance il n'a riens . . .*

It was there, one might imagine, that the man with the camera pondered the scraps of information he had been able to obtain. What follows is not necessarily a complete list of these gleanings, but it gives a fair idea of his line of enquiry:

- Some undeveloped rolls of film, including photographs of the west front of Notre-Dame.
- A copy of a book on Gothic architecture called *Le Mystère des Cathédrales*, published in 1925, and a modern reprint of the *Livre des figures hiéroglyphiques*, misattributed to Nicolas Flamel.
- An illustrated *Pilgrims' Guide* to Notre-Dame, with a fold-out map of the cathedral.
- A notebook containing some addresses, including those of an institution called the Sacré-Cœur (59, Rue Rochechouart), the offices of the Paris Gas Company (28, Place Saint-Georges) and various academic and pharmaceutical laboratories on both banks of the Seine.

---

* 'Let each man be content with what he has. / The dissatisfied man has nothing.'

– Baedeker's guide to south-western France, 'from the Loire to the Spanish frontier'.

There was also an old cutting, with underlinings in pencil, from a popular magazine called *Je Sais Tout*, bound sets of which could easily be found in book-boxes along the quais.

The article, dated September 1905, was more intimately connected with the case than might appear, and it merits a careful reading. It was an interview with a Dr Alphonse Jobert, who claimed to be an alchemist. There was a picture of a late-middle-aged man sitting by a stove. The caption said, 'Dr Jobert continually conducts new experiments in his alchemist's laboratory'. Other pictures showed 'the transmutation of metals performed under the supervision of a chemist', and something that looked like a gigantic pile of guano threatening to engulf the Paris Stock Exchange: this was supposed to show the total volume of 'all the gold currently in circulation throughout the world'. The doctor bore some resemblance to the gentleman at Notre-Dame, but since the picture was at least thirty-two years old in 1937, and the doctor was already getting on in years when it was taken in 1905, the resemblance was no doubt fortuitous.

Dr Jobert had evidently enjoyed a healthy sense of humour, and one senses that the interviewer was less sceptical after the interview than before. (The foreign agent's opinion can only be guessed, though the underlinings indicate his interest.) Much of the interview was devoted to one of the doctor's friends, who, having produced a certain quantity of gold by the alchemical method, had taken it to the Paris Mint. (It was strongly suggested that the 'friend' was the doctor himself.)

> 'At the Mint, they asked him how he had come into possession of such a quantity of gold, and he told them – in his naivety – that he'd made it himself . . . And do you know what they said?'
> 'No.'
> 'They said – I'm quoting their actual words – "You ought not to know how to do that."'

It is worth pointing out that Dr Jobert was not the first alchemist to visit the imposing *palazzo* on the Quai de Conti with a sample of home-made gold. In 1854 – seventy years before the first serious claim to have produced artificial gold in a laboratory* – a former laboratory assistant called Théodore Tiffereau persuaded M. Levol of the Paris Mint, who was responsible for assaying precious metals, to allow him to conduct some experiments on the premises. The first two experiments were inconclusive. Tiffereau believed, however, that when the aqua fortis or nitric acid had reached boiling-point, the gold must have spurted out onto the floor. The third experiment had to be left to simmer overnight, and when Tiffereau arrived at the Mint the next morning, he was told that the test-tube had cracked. Only a few tiny particles of gold were visible on the glass. M. Levol, obviously unimpressed by low-yield miracles, then said, 'You can see that there really isn't any appreciable quantity of gold.'

Much later, the governors of the Mint seem to have taken a more enlightened view of the matter. In the early 1930s, recognizing the enormous changes that had taken place in chemistry, they appointed as their expert a noted French physicist called André Helbronner. This appointment, which seems to have escaped the attention of the Abwehr agent, was not without significance for the future of the civilized world.

The rest of the 1905 article was devoted to the alarming implications of Dr Jobert's alchemical activities. Spurned by the French authorities, he had apparently received offers from Spain, where the gold market was less strictly regulated. But the doctor's main ambitions lay elsewhere. He pointed out that if the secret were revealed to all the world, and it became possible for anyone with a stove and a test-tube to transmute base metals into gold, this would have 'a somewhat unsettling effect on our institutions, the social question would make a great leap forwards, and the old world would crumble and collapse'.

This was enough to convince the interviewer that Dr Jobert was a dangerous socialist. His suspicions were confirmed by Jobert's sympathy with Pierre Curie, who was known to hold subversive views and who, despite the Curies' pioneering studies of magnetism and radioactivity, had never been accepted by the scientific establishment.

None of this would have surprised a true alchemist. Like the elixir

---

* Hantaro Nagaoka, at Tokyo University in 1924.

of long life, the production of gold was merely a stage in the Magnum Opus, and every alchemist knew that a man who was motivated by personal gain would never reach that stage in any case. The article's interest to the foreign spy was presumably the evidence of alchemy's recent modernization. One of Jobert's colleagues, for instance, employed a chemical engineer in his laboratory and had published a book on 'how to become an alchemist' that might easily have served as a chemistry textbook.* In Jobert's view, if alchemists were now the students of modern chemists, the scientists themselves had much to learn from their ancient predecessors. To prove his point, he quoted the fifteenth-century alchemist-monk Basilius Valentinus, implying that the monk's description of the catalyst known as 'universal mercury' had something to say about the mysterious properties of the Curies' discovery, radium. The foreign agent or his controller had marked this passage with thick pencil lines in the margin:

> *Our mercury* is luminous at night . . . It has such dissolvent properties that, in its ambiance, nothing can withstand it, for it destroys all organic matter. *Universal Mercury* has in addition the property of disintegrating all metals that have first been *opened*, and of bringing them to the point of *maturation*.

In view of what is now common knowledge, it seems obvious that if these scraps of information had been properly analysed, they might have encouraged the Nazis to renew their search for the philosopher's stone. But since, in their megalomaniac eyes, alchemy was nothing but an accelerated fund-raising device, they missed the golden opportunity that might have presented them with the most horrific and lasting revenge for the defeat of 1918.

The fact that the meeting to be described in this story took place at the same time as the Abwehr investigation – the early summer of 1937 – suggests that the elderly gentleman knew that he was under observation and that time was running out. He disappeared after the meeting, and the only plausible sighting of him was many years later, in Spain. This had led some to suppose that the elderly gentleman

---

* François Jollivet-Castelot, *Comment on devient alchimiste: traité d'hermétisme et d'art spagyrique* (Paris, 1897).

and Dr Jobert were one and the same, but until further evidence comes to light, this can only be a matter of speculation.

THAT EVENING, Professor Helbronner left the Mint and headed for the Pont Neuf to return to his laboratory at 49, Rue Saint-Georges. As he passed in front of the magnificent view of medieval towers rising over the Île de la Cité, he could not have suspected that there was any meaningful connection between the Gothic cathedral, the alchemists he occasionally met at the Mint and his own work on nucleonics. It *had* occurred to him, however, that several amusing and, he might almost have said, intriguing parallels existed between the art of the alchemist and the latest discoveries in chemistry and physics.

Some of those gold-seekers were clearly insane, and although they were surprisingly well informed about modern science, they were incapable of distinguishing experimental results from wild fantasy. Their methods appeared to involve very little trial and a great deal of error. The particles of gold, for instance, nearly always turned out to have been present in the base metal. They seemed particularly attached to the idea that certain molecular transformations produced in laboratories were somehow tied to the future of the human race, and that certain ill-advised experiments had already altered the nature of reality itself. This was, to say the least, pushing the Theory of Relativity to the limits.

What struck Helbronner was not so much the idea itself as the fact that it was shared by several individuals who knew nothing of the others' work. A well-organized conspiracy of lunatics was obviously out of the question, and so he was forced to conclude that, however shaky its foundations, alchemy was still a living science.

In fact, Helbronner had more sympathy with the inter-disciplinary delusion than a professor of the Collège de France could safely admit. He knew that the Curies had derived some sort of inspiration from alchemy, and that other colleagues had found it a fruitful source of analogies for their work on the atomic structure of matter. He might also have known – though there is no evidence that he did – that the Oxford chemist Frederick Soddy, having previously derided alchemy as 'a mental aberration', had more recently commended it in public as an untapped source of practical insights. Professor Soddy had made a special study of the notion of transmutation. From his careful reading of hermetic texts, he had come to suspect that, some time in the distant past, a vanished civilization had developed a technology based on some poorly understood and probably accidental molecular processes. This technology, in Soddy's view, had left shadowy traces in alchemical allegories. Remarkably, it was only *after* his discovery of alchemy that Soddy and his collaborator, Ernest Rutherford, recognized, to their astonishment, that radioactive thorium was spontaneously converting itself into a different element. Soddy is said to have cried out, 'Rutherford, this is transmutation!' To which Rutherford replied, 'For Mike's sake, Soddy, don't call it transmutation! They'll have our heads off as alchemists!'

When he reached his laboratory that evening, Professor Helbronner was told by the concierge that an elderly gentleman had called to see him. Finding the Professor out, the gentleman had left a message. Helbronner recognized the name as that of an alchemist who had previously introduced himself at the Mint, and who had shown a keen amateur interest in Helbronner's work on polonium. In his message, the alchemist asked Helbronner to meet him in one of the testing laboratories of the Société du Gaz de Paris, which had its headquarters a few doors away in the Place Saint-Georges. Helbronner alerted his young associate, Jacques Bergier, and the two men set off for what they must have thought would be a curious diversion.

Certain details are missing from the next part of the story, largely because, six years later, André Helbronner was arrested as a member of the Resistance and deported to Buchenwald concentration camp, where he died of pneumonia in March 1944. In the last months of his life, he applied his genius to writing cryptic messages on the printed postcards that prisoners were allowed to send to their families. The only echo of the meeting that comes from Helbronner himself consists of some experimental notes that were submitted in sealed envelopes to the Académie des Sciences in the spring of 1940, a few weeks before the Nazis entered Paris. The main source of information, therefore, is the account published by Helbronner's associate in 1960.

According to this account, the alchemist who asked to meet them that evening in June 1937 was the author of *Le Mystère des Cathédrales et l'interprétation ésotérique des symboles hermétiques du Grand Œuvre*. The book had been published in 1926 under the unlikely name 'Fulcanelli'. Only five hundred copies were printed, and they are now almost worth their weight in gold. At the time, the book had sent ripples of excitement through the tremulous world of Parisian alchemy. It was an erudite but by no means flawless account of alchemical symbols in religious and domestic buildings of the Gothic period, with particular reference to Notre-Dame and to the writings of Basilius Valentinus, Gobineau de Montluisant and Victor Hugo. It owed its charm to its elegant prose, its careful description of the carvings of Notre-Dame, which the author had consulted for his own alchemical experiments, and to an unusual mixture of scepticism and faith. While insisting that certain pseudo-alchemists should be read 'not just with a pinch of salt but with the entire salt-shaker', Fulcanelli had also defended the scientific integrity of his discipline:

> Our science is as concrete, real and precise as optics, geometry and mechanics, its results as tangible as those of chemistry. Enthusiasm and faith are stimulants and precious auxiliaries, but they must be subordinate to logic and reasoning, and subjected to practical experiment.

By the time Fulcanelli contacted Professor Helbronner, his book no longer represented his current thinking. In 1926, he had been too easily distracted by the esoteric ramblings of post-medieval alchemists. In 1937, he had returned to his original inspiration, and especially to what he had described in his book as 'a truly curious little quadrangular bas-relief' on the west front of Notre-Dame.

The abiding interest of the book has proved to be the enigma of Fulcanelli's identity, which has kept thousands of occultists and conspiracy theorists fruitlessly amused for the last eighty years.* A

---

* The name 'Fulcanelli' may be a compound of Vulcan, patron deity of alchemy, and Helios, the sun god. The search for anagrams has proved inconclusive: Lucien Fall, fil nucléal, le cul final, etc. The preface to the second edition (1957) was written

more useful question – one that Professor Helbronner must have asked himself – is this: what was an alchemist doing in a gasworks? To judge by the extensive travels mentioned in his book, Fulcanelli was not short of money and had no need of a job. But when Helbronner and his associate walked over to the quiet Place Saint-Georges and looked up at the amazing building that housed the Paris Gas Company, directly above the old entrance to the Nord-Sud Métro, they might have reflected that this was, after all, an appropriate setting for a practitioner of the hermetic science. The Hôtel Païva had been built in 1840 in what was then a *quartier* of expensive curiosity shops, self-employed courtesans and wealthy artistic types pretending to be recluses. A sculptor noted for his allegorical scenes of animals had covered the facade with wonderfully superfluous figures. One of the statues appeared to be Hermes, equipped with his masonic tools. Blackened by a hundred years of smoke, the building was an eerie sight at dusk, and the yellow gleam that came from some of the blinded windows suggested something more interesting than the production of domestic gas.

In fact, Fulcanelli's reasons for taking a job with the Gas Company were probably entirely practical. As the Office of Strategic Services discovered after the war, radioactive thorium was imported into France for use in cigarette lighters and gas mantles, and not, they concluded, to make thorium piles. A gasworks, in other words, was one of the few places where a man with no academic position could unobtrusively obtain some of that mysterious element whose transmutation Professors Soddy and Rutherford had observed.

The meeting took place in one of the laboratories at the back of the building. The two scientists were dressed in everyday clothes; the alchemist wore a lab coat. He had a strange tale to tell – a tale that

---

by the master's young pupil, Eugène Canseliet. Canseliet belonged to a group called 'The Brothers of Heliopolis', two of whom lived in the Pigalle district, near Helbronner's laboratory, at 59, Rue Rochechouart. They included an absinthe-addicted painter called Champagne, a son of Ferdinand de Lesseps (architect of the Suez Canal), and a man who worked for the Rhône-Poulenc pharmaceutical company. This address was listed in *The Foreign Bachelor's Secret Guide to Paris* as the address of a male brothel called the 'Sacré Cœur'. The Abwehr agent was evidently aware of this, and one can only imagine what adventures he had as a result.

would have seemed utterly fantastic without his detailed knowledge of their work on nucleonics, and in particular their detection of radioactive emissions during the volatilization of bismuth in high-pressure liquid deuterium. It turned out that the alchemist had been a friend of Pierre Curie, and had a good grounding in the subject. He spoke in a clear, metallic tone, with the concision of a lecturer addressing intelligent students. There was a hint of impatience in his voice, which contrasted with the old-fashioned courtesy of his diction.

'You are very close to succeeding in your experiments, as indeed are several of your contemporaries. Might I be allowed to utter a word of caution? The work on which you and your colleagues are embarked is fraught with terrible dangers. They threaten not only you but also the entire human race.'

An ironic smile formed on Bergier's face, which the alchemist either ignored or didn't notice.

'It is easier than you think to release the energy of the nucleus, and the artificial radioactivity that would be produced could poison the Earth's atmosphere within a few years. It is, I might add, entirely possible, as alchemists have known for some time, to manufacture atomic explosives from a few grams of metal that could eradicate entire cities.'

Bergier had been a student of Marie Curie and still had much to learn about the unpredictable world of nuclear physics, but perhaps he felt that his days of being lectured were over. He was about to interrupt when the alchemist raised a magisterial finger:

'I know what you are going to say, but it is of no interest. Alchemists knew nothing of atomic structure; they were ignorant of electricity, and they had no means of detecting radioactivity. But I must tell you, though I can offer no proof, that geometrical arrange-ments of extremely pure materials are capable of releasing atomic forces, without the need for electricity or the vacuum technique.'

He paused, as though to allow the concept of a home-made reactor to sink in. There was a strangely indifferent or perhaps mildly psychotic expression on his face. Neither of the scientists said any-thing. Bergier looked at the charlatan in the lab coat and seemed to observe the beautiful, fleeting effects of some unrepeatable exper-iment. The man's words had set off a chain reaction in his mind.

Though it now seems barely credible, until Otto Hahn and Fritz Strassmann discovered nuclear fission in Berlin the following year, almost no one had considered the destructive potential of nuclear energy, and it was not until 1942, when Enrico Fermi's atomic pile went critical under the football stadium of the University of Chicago, that anything remotely corresponding to the alchemist's 'geometrical' bomb existed.

Somewhere in the building, a door closed. Helbronner and Bergier exchanged a glance, as if to reassure themselves that objective reality was still the prevailing force and that nothing unaccounted for was interfering with their perceptions.

'I would ask you to concede', the alchemist went on, as though oblivious to the effect of his words, 'that there might once have existed a civilization that knew about atomic energy and was destroyed by its misuse, and' – his eyes now seemed to sparkle – 'that a few partial techniques survived.'

By now, Bergier was intrigued. It was not impossible that someone whose mind appeared to function like an uncalibrated cyclotron might have stumbled on some interesting permutations of ideas. He asked politely, 'You yourself, Monsieur ... you have undertaken research in this domain?'

The alchemist smiled as though at a distant memory. 'You are asking me to give you a potted history of four thousand years' philosophy and a summary of my life's work ... And', he added, as Bergier shrugged apologetically, 'even if that were possible, you would be asking me to translate into words concepts that do not lend themselves to language.'

'So', said Bergier, 'if I understand correctly, we are talking about the philosopher's stone ...'

'And the production of gold? ... Those are merely particular applications,' said the alchemist with a wave of his hand. 'The essential point is not the transmutation of metals but that of the experimenter himself.' He directed his gaze at the younger of the two scientists. 'There is something that I would ask you to consider: alchemists never dissociated moral and religious concerns from their research, whereas modern physicists such as yourselves are children of the eighteenth century, when science became the pastime of a few aristocrats and wealthy libertines.'

The conversation ended with this sobering homily. No doubt the alchemist felt that he had said enough, and that any attempt to explain how he had reached his conclusions would only baffle the two scientists or leave them completely incredulous. He conducted them to the laboratory door and left them to make their own way out.

When they looked back at the building, no light was shining from any of the windows, and they never saw the alchemist again.

No one, including the British and American agents who searched for 'Fulcanelli' after the Liberation, has ever been able to explain how a Parisian alchemist employed by a gas company, with a scholarly interest in Gothic architecture, managed to acquire a reasonably accurate understanding of nuclear physics at such an early date. It was not until August 1939 that Albert Einstein wrote his famous letter to President Roosevelt, warning him that the creation of a devastating bomb had become feasible 'through the work of Joliot[-Curie] in France as well as Fermi and Szilard in America'.

In 1937, the only other person to have warned of the dangers of atomic research was that self-taught student of alchemy, Frederick Soddy, who had spoken in public lectures of the possible future development of unimaginably powerful weapons. Fulcanelli lacked Professor Soddy's resources and expertise, but he had the advantage of a lifetime's alchemical experience. From his own experiments and observations, he understood the process of 'projection', the role of what medieval alchemists called *eau pesante* or 'heavy water', and the difference between the 'humid way' and the 'dry way', which took days instead of years. Unlike Professor Soddy, he knew that alchemy's secrets could no more be explained in words than mathematical equations could be translated into Romantic prose.

So many obscure and symbolic disasters had been depicted in the superstitious past – plagues, massacres and divine conflagrations – that it had been no simple matter to relate the experimental evidence to the visible record. It had taken time to see that some of the most puzzling allegories were those that displayed the literal truth. The sequence of carvings had survived for seven centuries on the west front of Notre-Dame where thousands of people could (and still can) see it for themselves, but until the threat had become a reality once again, it was just another historical curio that served as a background to countless tourists' snapshots.

DESPITE THE INCREASING polarization of rich and poor in purpose-built suburbs, much of the population of Paris was still arranged vertically by wealth. A seamstress, a poet, a bank manager, a fortune-teller and a nuclear physicist might tread the same stair carpet every day of their lives and sometimes even exchange a few words on the subject of the unseasonable weather, the pigeons in the courtyard or the latest inexplicable rumblings of the plumbing. The apartment blocks of Paris were a gigantic university of trades and disciplines. Remarkable encounters, such as this meeting of two sciences separated by thousands of years, were not uncommon, and there is nothing odd in the fact that the meeting has never before been mentioned in any history of Paris.

Bergier and Helbronner may or may not have heeded the alchemist's strictures on the amorality of modern science, but they certainly pondered his technical hints. The notes that the two scientists submitted to the Académie des Sciences in sealed envelopes in 1940 were opened in 1948 and proved to contain calculations of self-sustaining chain reactions in deuterium and uranium-238.* These notes do not, as some have claimed, show that the laboratory in the Rue Saint-Georges was on the brink of assembling the world's first hydrogen bomb, but they do demonstrate the surprisingly advanced state of French nuclear research.

This only makes Fulcanelli's actions all the more puzzling. He warned of catastrophic forces soon to be unleashed upon the world, and yet, by describing what was in effect an atomic pile, he set Bergier and Helbronner on the shortest path to nuclear fission.

* *Comptes rendus hebdomadaires des séances de l'Académie des Sciences*, 24 May 1948 (CCXXVI, pp. 1655–56).

The Paris Peace Conference had shown that morality was a spent force in international politics. It was hard now to imagine that a chemist had once demonstrated to Louis XV 'an inextinguishable fire' that could destroy a city, and been paid out of the royal purse to eradicate all traces of his horrible invention, or that an engineer had once presented Louis XVI with a crank-action machine-gun that could kill an entire regiment, and been angrily dismissed as 'an enemy of humanity'.

The agents of the OSS who arrived in Europe in the wake of the Allied armies rushed about the Continent like bargain hunters. The official story was that they were looking for missing American soldiers. Their real aim was to track down atomic scientists and to prevent whatever fissionable material the Nazis had produced from falling into the hands of the Soviets. Some of the agents set off for German cities that were about to come under French jurisdiction. Others searched for Fulcanelli and one of Helbronner's former associates, an Indian called Eric Edward Dutt who had dabbled in alchemy and particle accelerators. But Fulcanelli had vanished without trace, and Dutt had been shot by French counter-espionage agents in North Africa.

In Paris, the operation's main focus was the Collège de France and the laboratory of Frédéric Joliot-Curie. The Curies' son-in-law was known to be an ardent communist. He had thrown petrol bombs at German tanks in the battle for the liberation of Paris. He was believed to have obtained several tons of uranium during the war, and there was some surprise and alarm that French scientists working in such primitive conditions had made such spectacular progress. A recently declassified report on 'Atomic Experiments in France' mentioned Joliot-Curie as a possible threat to security:

> A reliable source reports that there has been a rumor circulating to the effect that French scientists have the formula and techniques concerning atomic explosives, and that they are now willing to sell this information. They allegedly do not wish to sell to the Allies or to their own government for political reasons ... They are supposed to be desirous to sell the discovery to one of the smaller nations.*

* Lt.-Col. Selby Skinner to Col. W. R. Shuler, 18 February 1946. National Archives and Records Administration, RG 226, Entry 210, Box 431, Folder 2.

It would be interesting to know whether or not Joliot-Curie ever discussed the matter with the alchemist who had been a friend of his father-in-law. Perhaps Fulcanelli, like Joliot-Curie and other French scientists, realizing that the secret would soon be known to several powerful nations, thought it better to spread the knowledge as widely as possible. By then, of course, the alchemist, wherever he was, would have seen the astonishing images of what might have been a mythical catastrophe from a medieval depiction of Hell. He would have seen, this time in black and white, the shattered sanctuaries, the fleshless faces that resembled badly eroded bas-reliefs and the towering cloud that contained a million suns. Even he might have found it all very hard to believe.

A LITTLE TOUR OF
PARIS

22 June 1940

EVEN IF ANY OF the soldiers in the escort had been willing to divulge his destination, the howl of the engines would have made conversation impossible. He pictured Berlin in the transparent light of a summer morning shrinking to the size of a balsa-wood model, and the pines of the Grunewald dropping into a bottomless gorge. The plane surged and sank, and he thought how fortunate it was that there had been no time for breakfast. A sudden modulation of the scream suggested that the plane had already levelled out. At that altitude, if there had been a window, he might have recognized the Königsallee in the pattern of streets, and even the exact spot where he had left Mimina in tears. The two SS men had worn insignia that would have revealed their rank if he had known how to interpret such things. He had kissed her briefly, as though embarrassed in front of strangers. He could not remember whether he had only thought it as they parted or had actually uttered the words: 'In a dictatorship, anything is possible.'

There were no seats in the plane, just wooden benches along the sides, for paratroopers, he supposed. He looked along the line of faces towards the cockpit. He saw the light that came from the pilot's window, but his view was obstructed by picnic baskets and crates of fruit juice that he had seen being loaded at Staaken airfield. Was there, he wondered, some little-known military tradition of summoning a sculptor to the victory picnic to preserve the moment in stone? A shrill telephone in a silent house at six in the morning was unlikely to announce a glorious commission. Ever since he had been ordered to devote all his future work to Berlin, and to consider himself, with this exception, a free agent, he had grown accustomed to visualizing every sculpture in his studio on a gargantuan scale, with triumphs and catastrophes to match. Speer, the only friend who might have been able to tell him what was going on, was out of town. All he knew was what the voice on the telephone had said: 'Herr Breker. *Geheime Staatspolizei.*' (He was sure that they had said *secret* police ...) 'You are ordered to prepare yourself for a short journey. The car will be at your door in an hour.'

The roar of the engines filled his ears and permeated his limbs. He half-slept for what might have been an hour. By now, they must have crossed the border, if there was still a border. The morning would be bright and sunny, and so the waxen light from the cockpit ruled out an easterly or a southerly direction. There was nothing to deduce from the soldiers' demeanour or equipment, and the few words that punctuated the din told him nothing. He seemed to be invisible to them in his civilian clothes. He knew that this unaccompanied flight was somehow related to events of unimaginable grandeur and consequence. Vast new spaces were to be created for the artistic 'energies' that would be unleashed when the aspirations of the people were no longer frustrated by the obscurantism of modern artists. Somewhere below were human herds and hundred-mile-long traffic jams of cars with mattresses tied to the roof as a defence against the Stukas. (He knew this from talking to friends on the telephone rather than from the unreliable radio.) Hundreds of Parisians had queued for the number 39 bus to Vaugirard and taken it all the way to Bordeaux. There had been bonfires in Ministry courtyards, and barges on the Quai des Orfèvres piled high with police archives passed along a human chain. The Louvre had been surreptitiously evacuated: he imagined the *Venus de Milo* taking the sea air in Brittany or cluttering up the damp hallway of a château in the Auvergne.

More than two hours had passed when the plane began to lurch and lumber down a staircase of clouds and wind. The heat had become intolerable, and it was this that upset him most of all: the ominous discomfort that so clearly contradicted the Führer's promise that his artists would never have to live in garrets or suffer material distress.

Brûly-de-Pesche, Belgium, 21 June 1940, 11.30 a.m.

HE CALLED IT THE Wolfsschlucht, which means the Wolf's Gorge. There were some pleasant walks on the edge of the woods and behind the village whose inhabitants had been removed. It reminded him of the region of Linz in Upper Austria. The makeshift conference room in the parsonage, where maps of north-eastern France and the Low Countries hung on the walls, now smelled of leather and after-shave. The Wolfsschlucht had been his home for almost three weeks. That morning, after what the experts agreed was the most glorious victory of all time, the map of Paris had been unfurled, and, since then, he had talked of nothing else.

He had been looking forward to this for years. He had sent architects and planners to observe and take notes, but his own visit had remained a cherished dream. In the passion of youth, he had pored over street-maps and memorized blueprints of buildings and monuments. He had taught himself more than he could ever have learned from asinine professors who considered a diploma acquired at the age of seventeen to be the highest proof of artistic merit. Every detail had lodged in his memory, and when he came to make the final preparations, he was delighted to find everything still wonderfully fresh and accurate.

He was convinced that he knew Paris better than most of its inhabitants and could probably find his way about without a guide. The Baedeker had nothing to teach him. He himself had specified the composition of the tour group: Giesler, Breker and Speer; his pilot, his driver and his secretary; Frentz the cameraman, Hoffmann the photographer, and the press chief Dietrich; and General Keitel, who had asked to bring along General Bodenschatz, the physician and three adjutants. Speidel the former assistant military attaché would join them at the airport. They would fly in the Condor and take the six-wheeled Benz convertibles. He would lead the tour himself, which would be a useful lesson to them all. He often thought with a shudder of indignation of all those vapid *Reiseführer* and caretakers in blue uniforms who dispensed inane platitudes and cared only about petty restrictions – don't touch the artefacts, don't step on the parquet, stay between the ropes ...

Six weeks before, he had astonished everyone by saying that he would enter Paris with his artists, and that he would do so in six weeks' time. It was a source of tremendous pride and satisfaction to him that he was now in a position to pay this unprecedented compliment to what was after all, despite its foolish belligerence and the large numbers of southerners and Jews, a great *Kulturvolk*.

He knew that Parisians still thought of him as a house-painter and a *garçon-coiffeur*, because they could not yet bring themselves to see him as the defender of Paris. Time would change all that. If Churchill had had his way, there would have been fighting on every street-corner, and one of the world's most beautiful cities would have been wiped off the map simply because a drunken, war-mongering journalist had hatched a plan of inconceivable stupidity from which his government was too cowardly to dissuade him. Baron Haussmann had seen to it – though obviously with something else in mind – that a modern army could enter Paris and occupy key positions within a few hours. Naturally, the two-thousand-year-old city had defects, but any work that had been brought to completion by kings and emperors was valuable as an example: a surgeon could study a cancerous growth and learn something from it, but what could he do with an incinerated corpse?

For the tenth time that morning, Adolf Hitler placed his finger on the map and ran it along the perpendicular avenues. When he looked up at the clock, it was almost time for lunch.

Brûly-de-Pesche, 22 June 1940, 2 p.m.

TO THE UNDISGUISED delight of his so-called friend, Arno Breker was visibly flustered. The pilot had pointed his plane at the ground and pulled up just in time to hit the airstrip like a wounded goose landing on the Teupitzsee. A staff car driven by a non-speaking private had taken him into a landscape of forest and moor whose inhabitants had either fled or been expelled. He had seen a meal on a table in a deserted farmhouse. He had heard cattle screaming and seen a cow choking on a bed-sheet. He had known nothing until the car had passed a crossroads with a recently carved fingerpost pointing to Brûly-de-Pesche, and even then had been none the wiser.

The staff car stopped in front of a small church and some wooden sheds marked 'O.T.' for Organisation Todt. A group of smiling officers came to greet him. Among them he recognized the architect Hermann Giesler and the man he had called his friend. Albert Speer's face was a toothy, schoolboy grin.

'You must have been petrified,' said Speer. (It was an observation rather than a question.)

Breker suddenly felt the weight of his exhaustion. He looked at Speer and remembered how much he had had to enlarge his forehead and stiffen his mouth. 'Why didn't you get someone to tell me? I had to leave Mimina behind. She was in a terrible state ... What's going on?'

Speer paused for effect before replying. 'You're in Belgium, and this is command headquarters! You weren't expecting *that*, were you?'

An orderly came to usher them into the parsonage, and before they had reached the door, Breker saw him standing there in his usual simple uniform, with that curiously balletic torso and the snake-charmer hands. The thought flashed through his mind that Adolf Hitler himself was part of the elaborate joke. He shook Breker's hand and held it like a father welcoming home a son. The blue eyes that could make every man in a crowd of thirty thousand say, 'The Führer looked straight at me,' fastened themselves on Breker's face. Hitler was still shaking his hand, nodding slowly as though confirming an earlier judgement: Herr Breker would be equal to the task. Then he touched his elbow and took him to one side.

'I am sorry that this had to be done in such haste. Everything has gone according to plan and exactly as I expected. A new phase is now beginning.'

He spoke like an actor impersonating camaraderie or some complex form of duplicity. 'Paris has always fascinated me. Now the gates stand open. As you know, it was my intention all along to visit the capital of art with my artists. A triumphal parade might have been arranged, but I did not wish to inflict further pain on the French people after their defeat.'

Breker thought of his friends in Paris and nodded.

'I must think of the future,' the Führer went on. 'Paris is the city by which others are measured. It will inspire us to reconsider our plans for the reconstruction of our major cities. As an old Parisian, you will be able to devise an itinerary that includes all the architectural highpoints of the city.'

Some urgent news was brought to the Führer, and the audience ended. Breker was left to settle in to the guesthouse. He washed and shaved, then went for a short walk in the woods. The thought of seeing Paris again after so many years was thrilling, but he knew that it would be like visiting an old friend in hospital. When he returned from his walk, he was told that since the Führer did not want to be seen touring a captured city with civilians, they would all have to wear a military uniform. Breker chose a garrison cap that belonged to a lieutenant and a trench coat that covered his grey suit. They fitted him quite well but made his body feel small.

He telephoned Mimina, who had been told nothing, then sat at the table in his room and drew up a list of monuments, which he was to submit to the Führer's staff. At six o'clock, he left the guesthouse in his borrowed clothes and walked over to the mess. It was a strange experience to see the soldiers salute him as he passed. When he entered the mess, dressed up as an officer and walking like a civilian, gales of laughter erupted from the Führer's table.

Dinner was served by soldiers in white jackets. There was meat for anyone who did not wish to share the Führer's vegetarian meal, but the only drinks were water and fruit juice. After nightfall, they heard the sound of thunder. Shortly afterwards, they went to bed. The storm had passed, and the only sounds outside were the hum of a generator and the tramp of a guard's boots.

HE WAS STILL WAITING for sleep when an orderly came to wake him at three in the morning. He pulled on his uniform and walked out into the darkness. An hour later, he was back in the air, trying to remember the route he had submitted, and remembering instead his first days in Paris in 1927: his landlady had taken him to the Galeries Barbès to buy a double bed (she had insisted on a double), and at the Bal des Quat'z Arts, a beautiful negress had engaged him in a discussion about Nietzsche. He thought of his little studio at Gentilly, twenty-five minutes by Métro from the cafés of Montparnasse, where vegetable plots and hen-houses were guarded by dogs of mixed race.

The Condor had proper seats with windows. When the light began to colour the fields, he looked down and saw sheep and cattle but no other signs of life. The centipedal lines of refugees with their wheelbarrows and prams had passed away to the south. All around him, he heard cheerful conversations, and wondered why he seemed to be the only one who knew that they were embarked on a dangerous mission.

Paris, Sunday 23 June 1940

5.45 A.M. – THE ENORMOUS CLOUD of smoke that had filled the streets for several days, and that was said to have rained soot over the south coast of England, had finally drifted off. It had come and gone without explanation, and taken with it all the life of Paris. The city seemed to have been prepared for a grand occasion to which no one was invited. Two guardsmen at the tomb of the Unknown Soldier peered through the low, dawn mist along the Champs-Élysées and saw nothing move except the swastika flags and the grey pigeons.

Six miles across the city, at the far end of the Rue La Fayette, a car appeared from the direction of Le Bourget. It was followed by another, and then by three more, forming a little convoy of five sedans. The leather roofs had been rolled back, and as the cars rumbled across the cobbles, the heads bobbed about in perfect synchrony.

It was an interminable suburban street masquerading as an avenue with no particular destination. The buildings on either side amplified the noise of the engines. All of them seemed empty, their windows either shuttered or daubed with blue paint. In one of the cars, a man was standing up, holding a movie camera. Though the morning haze still clung to the ground, and the city showed itself only in outline, the day promised to be ideal for filming.

Orders were shouted out as they passed a concrete road-block.

The Führer sat next to the chauffeur in the second car, with Breker, Giesler and Speer on the jump seats behind. He had been silent since the airport, and when Breker looked round from the fleeing doorways to the man in the passenger seat, he saw the Führer tightly clenched, almost cowering in his grey coat. He seemed depressed by the ghostly spectacle. It was a sign, thought Breker, of his extraordinary sensitivity, and his unerring ability to concentrate on the essential and to consign the rest to oblivion.

The armistice had yet to come into effect. At any moment, from one of a thousand windows, a sniper might have aimed the barrel of a machine-gun. Perhaps the route had been chosen because in no other part of Paris was it possible to travel so far towards the centre without passing anything of interest. Almost two miles of apartment blocks had gone by before the rear pediment of the Opéra rose unexpectedly above the roof tops.

It struck Breker all at once that this was not the route he had planned, and that the Führer must have studied the document he had submitted at Brûly-de-Pesche and cast it aside. They approached the building from behind, between two corner blocks, and drove along its eastern flank, as though to take it by surprise. Swerving into the empty square, they saw two German officers waiting on the steps. The Führer leapt out and ran into the building.

Inside, all the lights were blazing. Golden reflections danced off the marble and the gilt, and made the floor look as treacherous as ice. A white-haired janitor led them up the monumental staircase.

The man who had sat hunched in his car seat a moment before was almost unrecognizable: the Führer was literally shaking with excitement. 'Wonderful, uniquely beautiful proportions!' he shouted, waving his arms like a conductor. 'And such pomp!' The janitor stood silently by with the expressionless rigidity of a man about to suffer a heart attack.

'You must imagine', said the Führer, 'the ladies in their ball-gowns descending the staircase between lines of men in uniform. – We must build something like this in Berlin, Herr Speer!' At the top of the staircase, he turned and addressed the men who were still ascending. 'Ignore that Belle Époque showiness, and the eclectic architecture, and the Baroque excess, and you still have a theatre with its own very distinctive character. Its architectural importance', he explained, 'consists in its beautiful proportions.'

They entered the auditorium and waited while the janitor threw switches and awakened the fairy-tale spectacle. The Führer swivelled on his heel, taking in the whole glorious scene, and cried out to the empty seats, 'This is the most beautiful theatre in the world!'

He led the way, with the busy step that he always appeared to have in newsreels. The janitor followed as best he could. They saw the dressing rooms and the practice room, where, to Breker's surprise, the Führer was reminded of the paintings of Edgar Degas. For several minutes, they occupied the stage, chatting among themselves or listening to the Führer's disquisition. He appeared to know the Opéra in its most intimate details. Breker was asked to tell the janitor that they wished to see the presidential reception room. For some reason, Breker had difficulty formulating the question in French, and when he finally found the words, the janitor looked puzzled and denied that such a thing existed. But the Führer, certain of his knowledge, and exhibiting only the faintest glimmer of impatience, insisted on seeing the hypothetical room, and the man finally remembered that, indeed, there had been an imperial reception room, but that renovations had abolished it.

'Now you see how well I know my way about!' cried the Führer. Then he added, with an infectious laugh, 'Gentlemen, observe democracy in action! The democratic republic does not even grant its president his own reception room!'

As they left the building, the Führer ordered one of the adjutants to give the janitor a fifty-mark note. The janitor politely declined the tip. Then the Führer asked Breker to try, and the man refused once again, saying that he was only doing his job.

Outside, Carpeaux's famous sculpture, *La Danse*, which had scandalized the bourgeois of the Second Empire, retained the Führer's full attention for a moment. Hefty nymphs cavorted around a tambourine-playing Bacchus. Despite the trails of black filth that made them look like laughing victims of an axe-murderer, the figures' pearly stone teeth could be clearly seen. This the Führer proclaimed to be a work of genius: it was an example of the lightness and grace that foreigners found wanting in German architecture.

With that, they returned to the cars and left the Place de l'Opéra, turning right in front of the deserted Café de la Paix.

6.10 A.M. – EVEN THE DUMMIES were absent from the windows of the expensive shops along the Boulevard des Capucines. Next stop was La Madeleine, which they approached from the rear. An adjutant leapt out of the car while it was still moving and opened the door. The Führer was on the pavement before anyone else and was trotting up the steps when he stopped so abruptly to look up at the pediment that the others almost ran into the back of him. They spent barely a minute inside – just long enough to see the Judgement scene that turned Napoleon's monument to the Grande Armée into a Christian temple. The Führer found the building disappointingly pedantic but superbly positioned for the view across the river to the Chambre des Députés. Then they drove down the Rue Royale and into the Place de la Concorde, where the chauffeur was ordered to drive slowly around the obelisk.

The Führer was standing up in the car, resting one hand on the chrome frame of the windscreen, delivering his observations. The obelisk was too small, and the walls of the square too puny to give it its proper prominence in the city. The radiant vistas, however, were magnificent and allowed the eye to travel unimpeded to different sectors of the city. Two gendarmes in their short capes were standing by a kerb, and the camera fastened on this evidence of human life to give the newsreel an air of normality. '*Early in the morning*', the commentary would say, '*the Führer pays a surprise visit to Paris!*' A dark shape was bustling across the road at the entrance to one of the avenues. The Führer glanced in its direction and saw a man in a black hat and robe, his head bent as if on the lookout for pot-holes or – ridiculously in that vast grey expanse – trying to pass unobserved. As the car went by, the camera turned to keep him in the frame. It would be a fleeting tableau of daily life in the French capital – a *curé* scuttling off to mass like a black beetle hurrying back to its hole.

Now, with a symphonic sense of architectural arrangements and the motions of the convoy, and as though anticipating the stately march that would accompany the images on the newsreel, the Führer ordered a halt at the entrance to the famous avenue. Slowly, then, they started up the long incline of the Champs-Élysées towards the Arc de Triomphe. The heads in the cars turned to right and left, along the side avenues, recognizing views they had seen in picture-books and on postcards: the Invaliden Dom with the Alexanderbrücke in the foreground, the Grand Palais and the Petit Palais, the Eiffel-turm in the distance, the fountains of the Rond-Point (but without water), and the terrace of Fouquet's devoid of people. Cinema posters were still advertising two American movies that had not been seen since the exodus had begun: *Going Places* and *You Can't Take It With You*. High up on the avenue ahead, a row of windows suddenly blazed with sunlight and darkened again as they passed. The Arch itself was a giant magnet, pulling them towards the portal through which triumphal parades traditionally passed in the opposite direction.

The cameraman filmed until the Arc de Triomphe was too large to fit into the frame. This was no longer the Paris that Arno Breker had known. It was some as yet imperfect dream-vision of the North–South axis of the future Berlin. The Grosse Torbogen, which the Führer had sketched in 1916 as he lay in his hospital bed, would be large enough for the Arc de Triomphe to fit inside with room to spare. The avenue that led up to it would be seventy feet wider than the Champs-Élysées, and it would not be constricted by the miserly segments of bourgeois habitation into which Hittorff had divided the Place de l'Étoile. Breker tried to see everything through the Führer's eyes – a city whose overpowering glories would exist whether or not there were people there to see them.

They parked on the Place de l'Étoile. Some of the Arch was under scaffolding, but the Führer was able to read the Napoleonic inscrip-tions, which he seemed to know by heart. He stood with his hands behind his back, looking all the way down the Champs-Élysées towards the obelisk and the Louvre. Breker saw an expression on his face that he had noticed when the Führer was examining the master model of Berlin, crouching down to enhance the perspective. It was the look of pure excitement that immobilizes a child's face when it tries to suck the object of its yearning into a mind evacuated of any other thought. When the time came to leave – it was already half-past six – the Führer could barely tear himself away.

6.35 A.M. – SO MANY AVENUES radiated from the Place de l'Étoile that, despite the presence of so many military strategists and connoisseurs of Paris, after circling the Arc de Triomphe a second time, the convoy slowed in confusion, and instead of waiting for the Avenue Victor Hugo or the Avenue Kléber to come around again, took the Avenue Foch and advanced as far as the first junction, where, somewhat indecisively, it turned left into the Avenue Poincaré. The Führer appeared momentarily to have lost interest in the tour: no doubt he was digesting the sights they had seen, assessing (as he had previously explained) the effects of atmosphere and daylight on the monuments he had known only in the abstract.

A few moments later, they were standing on the terrace of the Palais de Chaillot, gazing across the Seine at the Eiffel Tower. The cameraman was kneeling at the Führer's feet, trying to fit his head and the top of the tower into the same shot. Meanwhile, the photographer was taking the picture that would prove to the world that Adolf Hitler had been to Paris: Breker, Speer and the Führer standing on the terrace with a papery Eiffel Tower behind them looking like the backdrop of a trick photograph. '*A view of the Eiffel Tower!*', the newsreel commentator would say, jauntily hinting at holiday photograph-albums. '*To the left of the Führer: Professor Speer.*' Professor Speer appeared to be suppressing a smirk. The round-shouldered mock-lieutenant with the pallid smile and the ill-fitting cap to the right of the Führer was not deemed worthy of a mention.

Nine days before, German soldiers, having found the elevators sabotaged, had raced up the one thousand six hundred and sixty-five steps to fly a swastika from the top of the Tower, but the winds had torn it to shreds and the smaller flag that replaced it was invisible in the haze. In the next frames, the Führer was seen turning away from the Tower with an upward glance in the direction of the gilt inscriptions on the Palais de Chaillot, but too briefly to have deciphered them:

HE WHO PASSES MUST DECIDE WHETHER I BE
TOMB OR TREASURE, WHETHER I SPEAK OR REMAIN SILENT . . .
– FRIEND, ENTER NOT WITHOUT DESIRE.

The sun was beginning to burn through the haze. The emptiness of the esplanade and the *quais* below looked strange and ominous. No barges passed on the river, and no sounds came from the city other than the whispered exhalation of an urban expanse. It was a mark of the Führer's composure in the face of such unreality that he could think about topography and architectural dimensions. He was becoming quite astonishingly garrulous. He talked of the genius of the architects who had so perfectly aligned the Tower with the Palais de Chaillot and the Champ de Mars. He praised the Tower's lightness and its impressive verticality. It was the only monument that gave Paris a character of its own; all the others might have been found in any city. He knew, as Breker told him, that the Tower had been built for the Great Exhibition, but it transcended its original purpose: it was the harbinger of the new age when engineers would work hand in hand with artists, and when technology would create structures on a scale previously undreamt of. It heralded a new Classicism of steel and reinforced concrete.

They crossed the Pont d'Iéna and drove past the foot of the Tower to the other end of the Champ de Mars, where they admired the stern facade of the École Militaire and looked back at the terrace on which they had been standing a moment before. Before climbing back into the car, the Führer cast a final, farewell glance at the Eiffel Tower. The day was becoming warmer, and an orderly took the Führer's trench coat and helped him into a white coat without a belt. It made him look like a chemist or a man in a laboratory.

As the golden dome of Les Invalides approached along the Avenue de Tourville, they were all acutely aware of the fact that this would be the highpoint of the tour, and a moment of profound emotional significance for the Führer. He came as a conqueror, like Blücher and Bismarck before him, but also as an admirer of Napoleon, his equal, and a representative of the spirit of world history. But when the convoy pulled up on the Place Vauban, he happened to notice, standing proudly on its pedestal, the statue of General Mangin. It was Mangin's vindictive army that had occupied the Rhineland in 1919. The Führer's face darkened in an instant, and he was once again the avenger of national humiliation and the defender of German pride. He turned to the soldiers in the car behind and said, 'Have it blown up. We should not burden the future with memories such as this.'

On hearing this, Breker reflected on the sad lot of a great leader: even at this special moment, he was forced to tear his mind away from art and to plunge back into the brutal world of politics and war.

Inside the Church of the Dome, they stood around the gallery of the circular crypt, gazing down on the maroon-coloured porphyry of Napoleon's tomb. For once, the party was reduced almost to silence, entranced by the unearthly atmosphere and by the sombre light, which was dimmer than usual because of the sandbags that had been heaped against the windows before Paris had been declared an open city and spared the Luftwaffe's bombs. The faded flags commemorating Napoleon's most glorious victories hung from the pilasters. The conqueror of Paris gazed on the fifty-ton tomb of his predecessor, his head bowed, his cap held to his heart.

Breker was standing close enough to hear him breathing and had a spine-tingling sense of history in the making. He listened for the words that would mark the timeless meeting of the two great leaders. An audible whisper left the Führer's lips as he turned to Giesler and said, 'You shall build my tomb.' Then, no longer whispering, he elaborated on the project, saying that the painted dome would be replaced by the vaulted heavens, from which, through an oculus similar to that of the Pantheon in Rome, the rain and light of the universe would pour down on the indestructible sarcophagus. The sarcophagus would bear these two words: 'Adolf Hitler'.

The Führer chose this solemn moment to announce his 'gift to France': the remains of Napoleon's son, the Duc de Reichstadt, would be taken from Vienna and placed in Les Invalides beside his father's tomb. It would be another mark of his respect for the people of France and their glorious past.

7.15 A.M. – SUNLIGHT WAS RUSHING along the Seine as they passed the Palais Bourbon and turned to the east. A quarter past seven struck from a tower. Here and there, a concierge had ventured out with rag and broom to begin the daily purging of the doorstep. Dogs liberated from their owners' apartments were going about their morning business. On the Boulevard Saint-Germain, they stopped briefly in front of the German embassy while the Führer gave instructions for the renovation of the building. Then, hurrying through the narrow streets of the Latin Quarter, they passed in front of Saint-Sulpice, the Luxembourg Palace and the Greek columns of the Odéon theatre. Two policemen saw them head along the Boulevard Saint-Michel and turn into the Rue Soufflot. Earlier that morning, a telephone call had woken the Préfet de Police, who was already accustomed to the sudden whims of his new masters. The gendarmerie of the fifth *arrondissement* had told him that the caretaker of the Panthéon had been roused from sleep by German soldiers carrying sub-machine-guns and ordered to have the iron gates open at seven sharp.

At about half-past seven, the Führer was seen marching briskly into the mausoleum and emerging a few moments later with a scowl on his face. He had been disgusted by the sculptures ('cancerous growths', he called them) and by the wretched coldness of the place, which affected him like a personal insult: 'By God!', he snarled, 'It doesn't deserve the name Pantheon, when you think of the one in Rome!' Breker was familiar with the Führer's views on sculpture and architecture, but he found it interesting to hear them applied to actual examples. According to the Führer, a piece of sculpture that deformed the human body was an insult to the Creator. He must have been thinking of the choir of the Panthéon and of Sicard's tumultuous monument to the Convention Nationale, with its craggy, weather-worn soldiers and its defiant motto, 'VIVRE LIBRE OU MOURIR'. A true artist, according to the Führer, did not use art to express his own personality; he took no interest in politics. Unlike the Jew, he felt no need to twist everything out of shape and to make it frivolous and ironic. Art and architecture were the work of human hands, like boots, except that a pair of boots was good for the rubbish heap after a year or two of wear and tear, whereas a work of art endured for centuries.

There was something in this public display of personal sentiment that inspired Arno Breker with feelings of filial gratitude. He realized that, while encouraging 'his artists' to believe that they were his guides to Paris, the Führer was in fact showing *them* the city as it ought to be seen and preparing them for the daunting task ahead. As they drove away from the Panthéon, the Führer turned in his seat and looked 'Lieutenant' Breker up and down with a sly smile on his face. Then he said, as if to console him for his ludicrous appearance, 'No true artist is a soldier …', and expressed a wish to see the *quartier* where the young Breker had begun his heroic struggle with the muse. 'I, too, love Paris, and, like you, I would have studied here if fate had not driven me into politics, for my aspirations before the First World War were entirely artistic.'

Since there was nothing of architectural note in that part of Paris, the Führer's request seemed all the more considerate. They drove along the Boulevard du Montparnasse and saw the famous café called the Closerie des Lilas, and Carpeaux's fountain of 'The Four Continents', which confirmed the Führer's high regard for Carpeaux's work. Then they returned to the Boulevard Saint-Michel and drove swiftly down towards the river. There was still so much to see, but time was running out, and they were now a long way from the point of exit.

On the Place Saint-Michel, the Führer returned the salute of two policemen. They crossed to the island and turned along the lifeless *quai* towards Notre-Dame. Here, at least, Paris still exuded its mysterious charm. The walls of the Préfecture de Police slid away to the left like a curtain and the Gothic towers rose in the grey light like the backdrop of a Romantic drama. They drove past without stopping. They saw the Palais de Justice and the Sainte-Chapelle, which made no impression on the Führer, who noticed instead the dome on the other side of the street and said to Breker, 'Isn't that the dome of the Chambre de Commerce?', at which Breker shook his head and answered, 'No, it's the dome of the Institut, I think.' But when they drew level with the entrance, the Führer jerked his head and said to Breker, in great amusement, 'See what's written there? … *Chambre de Commerce!*'

7.50 A.M. – THEY CROSSED the Pont d'Arcole to the Hôtel de Ville, passed by the Carnavalet museum and the shuttered shop windows of the Jewish quarter to the Place des Vosges. Trees masked the cream and pink facades, and the Führer looked positively bored. The twittering sparrows, the leafy garden for nannies and well-heeled children and the cosy arcades gave off an intolerable air of bourgeois self-satisfaction. He did not become animated again until they were heading back along the Rue de Rivoli. This was the sort of nobility that he had in mind for Berlin: the endless row of identical house-fronts, the unmistakeable evidence of a grand design, and the invincible peace and happiness of a great imperial capital.

To the right were the dingy streets that led to Les Halles. Even here, the city seemed quite dead. There were no earthy vegetables blocking the roads, no traders massacring the French language, no smells of coffee and *caporal*. But then, penetrating the morning stillness, they heard the cry of a newsvendor. It sounded like the stranded relic of an earlier age. The owner of the voice was approaching from a side-street with his sing-song cry, '*Le Matin! Le Matin!*' He saw the column of sedans and came running up, waving a copy of the paper, coming to the car in front and yelling, until the words stuck in his throat, '*Le Matin!*' Staring in mute terror at the blue eyes that stared back at him, he fled, dropping his papers on the pavement. A little further on, a group of market women, slovenly and self-confident like all the women of Les Halles, stood talking in loud voices. The loudest and fattest of them peered at the convoy as it came along the street, and began to wave her arms about, pointing at Hitler and saying, '*C'est lui – oh, c'est lui!*' Then, with a speed that belied their corpulence, they scattered in all directions.

'I have no hesitation', said the Führer, as the monumental facade of the Louvre hove into view, 'in pronouncing this grandiose edifice one of the greatest works of genius in the history of architecture.' A few moments later, he was just as impressed by the Place Vendôme, which, despite the vandalism of anarchists, still proclaimed the undying glory of the Emperor.

Soon, they were back at the Opéra, to see – as the Führer had intended – the gorgeous facade in the full light of day. Without stopping, they accelerated up the Rue de la Chaussée-d'Antin and the Rue de Clichy, veered right on the square and followed the boulevards past the Moulin Rouge, as silent as ever on a Sunday morning, to Place Pigalle, but without seeing any of those Parisian women whose lipstick was said to be made from the grease of the Paris sewers.

Changing gear in rapid succession, the Benz sedans surged up the steep incline, threaded their way through the provincial streets and came out on the Parvis du Sacré-Cœur. They walked to the edge of the square. With their backs to the basilica, they looked out over the city. Church-goers were entering and leaving the building; some of them recognized Hitler but ignored him. He leaned on the balustrade, searching for the lines that would reveal the master plan of Baron Haussmann. At that height, the beauties of Paris were swamped by homes and factories and other utilitarian buildings; almost everything was washed away by the distance and the haze. Paris was an impression, a muddy watercolour, and the sturdy monuments they had seen at close quarters were like little buoys drifting in a grey sea.

Breker sensed the Führer's disappointment. This had been Adolf Hitler's one and only visit to the city he had studied so fervently and had longed to see for so many years. The tour had lasted barely two and a half hours, during which he had neither eaten a meal, nor entered a private house, nor spoken to any Parisian, nor even used a toilet. On the odd moments they had been able to exchange a few words, Speer had been as cynical as usual, calling the Führer '*le Chef*', by way of a joke. But now, as Breker watched Hitler scanning the space bisected by the Seine and bounded by dark hills, he seemed to see his eyes gleam and moisten. 'It was the dream of my life', the Führer was saying, 'to be permitted to see Paris. I am happy beyond words to see that dream fulfilled.' Ever mindful of the purpose of the tour, he addressed his artists – Giesler, Breker and Speer – saying, 'For you, the hard time is now beginning when you must work and strive to create the monuments and cities that are entrusted to you.' Then, to his secretary, he said, 'Nothing must be allowed to hinder their work.'

They stood at the balustrade for what seemed a long time. Finally, turning slowly from the scene, the Führer looked up at the white basilica behind, said, 'Appalling,' and then led the way back to the cars.

THE CONDOR took off from Le Bourget at ten o'clock. The Führer ordered the pilot to circle over the city a few times. They saw the sunlight catch the steel-blue curves of the Seine, which made it possible to work out exactly where everything was in relation to everything else: the islands, Notre-Dame, the Eiffel Tower, Les Invalides.

Paris fell away for the last time into the summer haze. Now, only forests and fields appeared through the windows. The Führer banged his fist on the armrest and said, 'That was an experience!' The satisfaction of having seen the legendary city outweighed the disappointments (he had imagined everything much grander than it was in reality), and its obvious defects in some way enhanced his appreciation and made him look forward to examining the master model of Berlin with a fresh eye. The only sour note came from Hermann Giesler, who told the Führer that he had not really seen Paris at all, because what was a city without its people? He should have visited it during the 1937 Exhibition, when it was alive with people and traffic. The Führer nodded his head in agreement, and said, 'I can well imagine.'

Back at the Wolfsschlucht, the Führer shared his thoughts, during walks in the woods, with Giesler, Breker and Speer. While his impressions were still sharp, he made a decision which showed that, even in the absence of its human population, Paris had a powerful effect on anyone who saw it. He had often considered the possibility that the city would have to be annihilated but had now decided not to destroy it after all – for, as he told Speer that evening in the parsonage, 'When we are finished with Berlin, Paris will be nothing but a shadow, so why should we destroy it?'

When Professor Breker came to record the notable events of his life in 1971, he found his impressions of the little tour even more vivid than memories of his early days in Montparnasse. That vanishing parade of grey monuments, and the newsreel images of himself standing next to the Führer, were more real to him than his own personal experience of the city. As he told his friends, he was grateful to have had the opportunity to witness an aspect of the Führer that few people ever saw – a Hitler who was, for a few hours, released from the cares of war and the mountains of paperwork under which, according to Breker, his enemies tried to bury his ambitions. Even when the monumental statues and bas-reliefs he had produced at the Führer's behest lay in rubble, he remembered how brilliantly the architecture of Paris, when it was liberated from the distractions of people and traffic, had expressed the continuity of European civilization. He clung to his memories like a secret treasure, all through the difficult years when, as Speer smilingly predicted when they said farewell to each other in the ruins of Berlin in 1945, 'even a dog will refuse to take food from your hand'.

OCCUPATION

I

CHILDREN WHO LIVE in cities are said to grow up faster than other children. They see and hear strange things almost every day, and even if they cultivate a spirit of indifference and try to be unobtrusive, their routines and beliefs are always coming under attack. The daily bus-ride can suddenly become a dangerous adventure, and the puzzle of streets between home and school can turn into a haunted labyrinth. A whole *quartier* can be overshadowed by a misanthropic dog, a friendly beggar, a cellar window, a perplexing caricature on a wall or by any of the million objects and creatures of which a child's itinerary is composed. Parents might complain about 'the same old thing, day in, day out', but every child knows that the city changes all the time, and even the things that don't change can look different from one day to the next. Parents are not authorities on the teeming life of the metropolis. There are many things that they don't notice or that they try to ignore, because not even the most sympathetic parent wants to relive the terrors of childhood.

So many strange things kept happening in Paris in those difficult years that Parisian children must have grown up even faster than usual. They grew up, however, in only one sense. Statistics show that the juvenile population as a whole was actually getting shorter and lighter. The pink vitamin pills and protein-rich 'Biscuits Pétain' that were handed out at school had no noticeable effect, and there was little that mothers could do except to disguise the perennial swede as something more enticing, or to serve the bean soup with beans one night and chestnuts the next.

Boys and girls who lived in a constant state of hunger and gastronomic disappointment were more than usually sensitive to the city's tricks and transformations. In normal circumstances, they would soon have shrugged off the little miseries of urban life, but an empty stomach lends its ominous rumblings to every minor inconvenience. The booths on the boulevards that used to sell spinning-tops and bonbons sold dreary things such as phrase books and bicycle-repair kits. Almost overnight, the infant economy collapsed. Postage stamps and model cars quickly reached unaffordable prices, and some toy shops closed down and their owners went away. There were so many upsetting rules and restrictions that it was hard to believe that Maréchal Pétain, who was known to be fond of children, had been told what was going on in Paris. The pond of the Palais-Royal was drained of water, and a boy who had always gone there with his boat of sardine tins and bobbins now had to walk all the way to the Tuileries Gardens, where the lake was too big for a little boat. Other children went to the park and found that their favourite climbing-tree had been cut down for firewood. Rationing affected children's lives in so many ways that no statistic could possibly encapsulate the misery it caused. When shoes wore out, they had to wear uncomfortable wooden soles marked 'Smelflex', or clumpy clogs, which made it impossible to run. Dolls were forced to make do with the clothes they already had, and some big dolls even had their clothes taken away from them.

Children who had never been fussy about their food found that sweet things tasted bitter, as though someone was playing a trick on them. Beautiful cakes and pyramids of fruit in shop windows had notices in front of them saying '*Étalage factice*', which meant that they weren't real. Nothing was what it seemed any more. New signs appeared all over the city with words on them that meant nothing or that seemed to be misspelled or mixed up with real words, like '*Gross Paris*' or '*Soldatenkino*'. Some of the words were too long and had to be written in very small letters to fit on the sign. The signs were put up by the Germans, who were also called the Boches, and it was usually the Boches who were blamed for everything bad, though sometimes it was the English or the Jews. Worst of all, mothers and fathers were nearly always in a bad mood, because they had to queue for everything, or because they kept running out of cigarettes.

Life under the Boches was probably even harder for older brothers and sisters, who remembered what things had been like before the war. Children who had just started school found some of the new things quite exciting. A boy who lived near Les Invalides saw the statue of a general being blown up with dynamite, and some of the pieces of stone went flying over the neighbouring houses. Some children liked to watch the long lights flailing across the night sky and the red lights coming down in the distance, and they also liked to imitate the sound of the sirens. When the clocks were put forward an hour, everyone had to carry a torch to school, and the bright circles that went dancing along the street looked like a procession in a fairy-tale. Birthdays were often disappointing, but many children who had never been allowed to have pets were given guinea-pigs to look after. Some people even kept rabbits in the bathtub which had to be fed with grass from the park. One girl who lived in an apartment block in Belleville knew a woman whose rabbit ate her food coupons when she wasn't looking, and the woman said that at least she wouldn't feel bad when she cut the rabbit's throat and threw it in a pot with the carrots and the swede.

ALTHOUGH MOST PARENTS kept saying that life was getting harder all the time, it was only after two years of this that many children – especially those who lived in certain parts of the city – began to feel that things really *were* getting worse.

One day that spring, in thousands of homes all over Paris, the wireless was unplugged and taken away, along with all the bicycles that were kept on the landing with padlocks on them because there were so many bicycle thieves about. Telephones were disconnected, and since they were not allowed to use a telephone box or to go into a café, the only way to ask relatives in the country to send more food was to use one of the letters on which the words were already printed: 'The ----- family is well'; '----- wounded ---- killed ---- in prison'; '---- need food ---- money', etc. – but then they weren't allowed to buy stamps to put on the envelope. Sundays became quite boring because the families who were singled out in this way were not allowed to go to the park, the playground or the swimming pool, or even to the market or to any of the museums, and they couldn't even visit relatives in hospital (though they still had to go to school). They couldn't go to the theatre or the cinema, which meant that they missed seeing Charles Trenet sing '*C'est la romance de Paris*'.

It became quite hard to think of things to do, except read books, and even that became difficult. A boy called Georges who lived in the third *arrondissement* had to take all his library books back to the town hall. The librarian, whose name was Mlle Boucher, saw him come in with his books, and she said to him,

'You like reading, don't you?'

Georges nodded his head.

'And I expect you'd like to go on reading, wouldn't you?'

'Yes,' said Georges, 'but I'm not allowed to now.'

Then she said to him in a whisper,

'Come back this evening at half-past five and wait for me outside.'

At half-past five, Mlle Boucher wheeled her bicycle through the gates of the town hall and told Georges to get on the back. They went along the Rue de Bretagne and turned down the Rue de Turenne. Ten minutes later, they stopped in front of the Musée Carnavalet, which was where Mlle Boucher lived, because her father was the director of the museum. She took Georges inside and showed him the library and told him that he could come back whenever he wanted and read all the books he liked, and this is what he did until the day when he and his family were forced to leave Paris.

Georges knew that Mlle Boucher was doing him a special favour. He also knew that she was very brave, because when she took him on her bicycle, he was wearing his yellow star. At school, the teachers had told everyone that they were not to treat the children who had to wear the stars any differently, and most of their classmates felt sorry for them, except when they were children that no one had liked anyway. But there were also pictures pasted up on walls and printed in newspapers that were supposed to be pictures of children like himself, and he often looked in the mirror to see if he had the same horrid nose and silly ears as the people in the pictures.

Parents had to use their clothing coupons to buy the stars, and older sisters complained that the star, which was mustard-yellow, didn't match any of the clothes that they had. Some of their neighbours stopped talking to them and even said rude things to them in public. One child's aunt came home in tears, and when she took off her headscarf her head was covered in soap because the woman at the hairdresser whose job it was to rinse the customers' hair had refused to wash it off. And then instead of having nothing nice to eat, they sometimes had nothing at all, because their mothers were only allowed to queue for food between three and four in the afternoon, by which time all the food had gone.

This was in the summer of 1942. For some people, it was the last summer they ever spent in Paris, and those who stayed behind sometimes wondered whether they were still living in the same city.

II

THAT JULY, two days after everyone had celebrated Bastille Day, some children found themselves in a part of the city where they had never been before, at least not on their own.

Nat stood on the street where all the green-and-white buses with what looked like friendly faces were lined up bumper to bumper. In front of him was a short street at the end of which was the Seine. Though he couldn't see it, he knew it was the Seine because there were no houses, just empty space where the buildings would have been. And then he saw a seagull swerve lazily.

He clutched his coat about him like a thief, without stopping to button it, not because he was cold, but to hide his sweater. He could still feel his mother's hand on his back where she had given him a shove, and he began to walk forwards, towards the Seine. At the end of the street, he turned right without noticing. This was the Quai de Grenelle, which was also the name of a Métro station.

The wind blew along the river in gusts and made his eyes feel sore and dry. He put one foot in front of the other and thought about going back inside to where all the others were. Then the wind brought down the rumble of rubber and metal and the elongated screech. He looked up and saw the green carriages heading out towards the seagull. – *Le Métro aérien* . . . It was called that as though, on that section of the line, it was a different kind of train altogether, as though it might leave the tracks with a sudden silence and run off into the sky.

The wooden steps went up from the middle of the street. The street was sheltered by the underside of the tracks like the roof of a basement. He began to climb into the cage of metalwork. He was still extremely thirsty and he could still smell the urine on his trousers. Across the road, a street-sweeper had stopped sweeping and was watching him climb the steps. At the top was a woman in a uniform with no expression on her face. She sat under the sign that said SORTIE and looked like the woman who opened cubicles in a public toilet, only more grubby. Two policemen came from under the sign marked PASSAGE INTERDIT. The woman was called the *poinçonneuse* because she punched a hole in the ticket, which he did not have, and his mother had not put any money in his pockets. He heard the sound of clanking chains and sliding metal that meant a train was coming.

THE WOMEN were shouting, '*On a soif! On a soif! Nos enfants ont soif!*' They pushed away from the concrete wall, holding each other by the arm, bulging out into the street, staring at the eyes half-hidden by visors, each one picking out a pair of eyes like infantrymen advancing on an army. Behind them, inside the great closed space, the hum of humankind sweltering in the smell of shit and antiseptic. Then the cry went out, '*Une épicerie ouverte!*'

Some of the women broke away from the others and were clattering across the street. As they ran, they were digging in their pockets and shoulder-bags. They were thinking of bottles of water, calculating the weight and bulk of fruit or biscuits, or even a tin of Banania as a compromise if they could get some milk. The line of policemen adopted a waiting position: allow them to buy some water; keep the others close to the entrance between the concrete pillars, under the red letters on the dirty glazed arch: VEL' D'HIV.

Anna was standing near the entrance with her mother. Now – as she had been doing since the day before yesterday – she relieved herself standing up with all her clothes on, because this sudden emergence into the open air was too good an opportunity to waste. Her hair had been combed as if she was about to go on an errand. She felt her mother thrust her sideways and then try to pull her back or try to get a better grip to push her away. She clutched at skirts and pushed against bottoms to let the women know she was there behind them, because they were stamping and going backwards and forwards.

Two policemen were standing by the buses. After she had walked past them, there was the street ahead of her, and the air rushed into her lungs and when one of the policemen called out to her to come back, she said, 'I wasn't in there. I only came to find out about my family.'

She did not look back, because the policemen might not believe her, and she did not run, which was obviously the temptation, because her clogs would come off, and she would have to stop to put them on again or leave them lying in the street.

MILLIONS OF HANDS had pressed against the bar every day and polished it until it was shiny, unlike everything else in the Métro. Nat walked through the barrier and crossed to the other platform to get away from the woman in case she called him back. She had looked at him for several seconds, saying nothing, and then she had said, '*Passez!*', but without looking any friendlier.

A train came and not many people got off. Nat did not get into the last carriage, which was where he was supposed to go. He lifted the metal handle and forced the doors apart, like Samson or a lion-tamer. He had to use both his hands, which made his coat come open. Once he was inside, he turned to pull the doors together, standing as close to them as he could, then he clutched his coat and sat down.

He saw the people who had got off the train racing backwards along the platform. Then black girders went by, and there were faces in the window staring back at him or just looking out of the window. He saw his own face and his eyes, which looked like dark holes. No one spoke in the Métro any more. The train sped up but not very much because the next station was not far away. The faces began to vanish, and there was the street just below, with the buses' white roofs and gas tanks, and policemen standing in groups, then lines of trees and the wide river, where the buses couldn't go. He saw the Eiffel Tower turn slowly and begin to walk away to the right.

A man stood up and went towards the door. Windows flew past – a balcony covered in plants, a big room with a chandelier and a table. The windows were close enough for Nat to climb into the room if the train had stopped. At first, when it reached the station, the train kept moving because he was not in the last carriage. Then it screeched to a stop, and he saw 'PASSY' on the wall.

This was the end of the *Métro aérien*. Daylight came from the river, but the roof blotted out the light from the sky. Soon, the train would go back underground. He said to himself, 'Trocadéro, Boissière, Étoile'. He tried not to think too hard 'Étoile', which is what he was wearing on his sweater above his heart.

ANNA did not look back. When she saw the bridge and the red sign, she knew where she was going, and she knew how to use the Métro on her own. Then she did look back.

The man with the sweeping brush and the little sailboat on his cap was staring straight at her. He lowered his chin and made his head point across the street to where the Métro was. She kept her eye on him while she crossed the street to see if he would do anything else, but he just kept pointing with his head at the steps that went up into the Métro.

She still had the five-franc coin with the Maréchal's face on it. She would be safer in the Métro if she did not get into the last carriage. She put the coin on the counter and the woman took it and gave her a ticket and four coins, which she put into her pocket. If anyone asked, she would say she was going shopping for her mother, though she didn't know where she was going because there was no one left at home. But her mother would find her in the Métro. She went under the sign that said DIRECTION ÉTOILE, because that was where all the different lines came together. Her own station was on a line that went to Étoile, but it was a long way away, on the other side of Paris.

UNDER THE GANTRIES, applause broke out and washed about for a while, then stopped. Beyond the galvanized steel lamps, where the words said RIZLA and PHOSCAO, there was just the faintest flickering of hands. Then a loudspeaker rasped out some names and other syllables, which quickly lost their force and joined the felted layers of dust and sound; whoever was speaking into the microphone evidently had no idea of the effect of his voice. The noise and dust were so dense that shouts and screams were either muffled or too much a part of everything else to be noticed. It was like the oceanic clamour of a railway-station concourse, composed of nothing but the shuffling of clothes, limbs being stretched, a gasp, something dropped on concrete. A woman banged her head on the floor for nearly a minute before a policeman came to knock her unconscious.

Some of them were lying on the steeply banked track, which was dangerous because it was at least eighty feet from there to the top of the stands, and people occasionally jumped off. Other families were still arranged in little encampments marked off by bags and coats, which they tried not to move when the latest influx began to filter through. Some had been found at home with the gas-pipe in their mouth. A woman in the fourteenth *arrondissement* had just finished throwing her children out of the window, and then herself. A young man had seen her do it, and they all died, though someone else said it had happened at Belleville, and by the time the woman jumped, firemen were holding the blanket to catch her.

In the buses, the window seats had all been taken by children, who wanted to see where they were going. In the tenth *arrondissement*, the policemen who knocked at Mme Abramzyk's door found her holding her six-year-old son; they told her to get her things ready and they'd be back in an hour ... But when she rushed down to the ground floor, saying thank you God for this great mercy, the concierge came out of her lodge, where she had the Maréchal in a frame on the sideboard with his country suit and his hunting dog, and bolted the door to the street.

They had all been slow to respond to the rumours, and almost no one had seen the leaflet sent out by the communists, which they only heard about later on. Someone had received a *pneumatique*, someone

else a telephone call – because luckily they had not yet been disconnected. They had sat and discussed it the whole night: it would only
be men, or it would only be immigrants; families with little children
or with fathers who were prisoners of war would be left in peace.
Someone's father had been pulled off a train in the Métro by a
complete stranger who said he was delighted to see him again after
so many years and then told him on the platform, before getting back
on the train, that he was a police agent and that he should not sleep
at home that night.

Now, in the grimy colosseum that contained whole *quartiers*
without any dividing walls, rumours caused sudden eddies and movements of people. In an inner courtyard somewhere behind the stands,
bread was being thrown down from the windows of a workshop in
the Rue du Docteur-Finlay where they made gears for Citroën cars,
and the neighbours who had seen the children's faces in the buses
and smelled the rising stench had been going there all day with food.

Anna's mother watched for these wild surges of the crowd and the
drift of bodies towards the exits. Her daughter had escaped and might
be standing in the street waiting for her. She had already spotted a
boy slip out of the same exit and she hadn't seen him since. The
thought that she might miss her only chance was too much to bear.
She picked her way through the bodies, watching the exits, and
sometimes she went right up to a policeman, who must have a mother
himself, but it was only when she gave in to her anger that she made
an impression. The policeman almost screamed at her, 'I'll put you
in solitary if you don't get back in there!' – as if they had cells in the
Vel' d'Hiv. So she shouted back at him,

'Let me go! What difference does it make to you, one victim more
or less?'

The policeman shrugged his shoulders, and said, in a quieter voice,
'Get back in there.' Then he turned away, and she saw the cropped
hair below his cap and his stiff shoulders, and he seemed to be
finished with her, so she walked out into the street.

Some women were standing in a doorway. She went towards them,
and when they realized she was going to talk to them, they seemed
to shrink back into the wall. She said, 'Let me in. I have to hide.'

One of the women, who seemed more frightened than she was, said, 'No, no! Keep going. Don't stay here.'

The wind wafted the smell of her own clothes into her nostrils, and it was only a matter of time, she thought, before she was dragged back inside, and her daughter would be lost. But then she saw in the gutter what looked like an old coat-sleeve lying at right angles to the kerb with something wrapped in it, and the water rushing out of the drain, and a sloppily dressed man with his City of Paris cap, coaxing the rubbishy water along with his broom. She walked up to him, and as she passed, said, 'Follow me!', which he did, and he kept following her until they reached the Métro.

At the foot of the steps, she looked round and thought she saw the man smile at her, and he raised his hand briefly as if to say goodbye and then went back to his sweeping.

Another bus was coming round the corner from the Seine, with suitcases piled high on the rear platform, and children's faces pushed up against the windows.

THIS WAS SOMETHING that happened at Étoile and nowhere else: there was only one line but two platforms. The doors were opened on one side to let everybody out, then the doors on the other side were opened for the people who were waiting. Anyone who left the train was separated from the other passengers by the width of the carriage. As he walked along the platform, Nat looked through the carriage windows and saw some German soldiers waiting to get on with their rifles and gas masks slung over their shoulders so that they could carry all their parcels and shopping, but there were no policemen, which was more important.

He walked to the end of the platform where the metal plate said TUNNEL INTERDIT AU PUBLIC – DANGER, then he walked through the barrier with all the other people. These days, the escalators never worked and the electric lights were always dim. He climbed the stairs as slowly as all the grown-ups around him. There was a pain in his stomach which reminded him that he had not had anything to eat, though he did not feel hungry.

At the top of the escalator, he stopped behind a pillar that someone had used as a urinal and, reaching inside his coat, he tugged at his sweater and pulled off the star, which he crumpled in his fist and put into his pocket. There were men and women everywhere, heading off into tunnels with the look of people who knew where they were going. He stood in front of the Métro map for quite a long time, following the coloured lines with his eye and, to make it look more convincing, he also studied the board that listed all the stations that were closed. On the map, he mostly followed the blue line that went from Étoile to the top-right corner of Paris. He saw BELLEVILLE and COMBAT and PELLEPORT, and then he thought of his friend from school, Elbode, who did not have to wear a star and whose parents had always been very polite to him.

There were so many people in the station now that sometimes they bumped into anyone who was just standing there. Anna's mother had come into the concourse from the Quai de Grenelle platform and thought it miraculous that she had found her daughter there, though Anna had simply got off the train and waited patiently in the part of the station where all the different lines came together. When he turned away from the map of the Métro, Nat saw a little girl being squeezed against her mother's skirt, and he wondered if he should go and speak to them, but instead, he went past them and joined the crowd of people heading for the sign marked NATION.

Later that day, he stood on the landing in front of the door where the Elbodes lived, and it was a moment he often relived after he crossed the demarcation line a few months later on his way to Grenoble and entered the Zone Libre.

ALL OVER PARIS – that day and in the days to come – people were discovering new parts of the city. It was almost as if they had never lived there before. The Rimmler family at 51, Rue Piat discovered that there was a little room above the garage next door to their apartment block where ten people could sleep if they sat with their backs against the wall. At 181, Rue du Faubourg-Saint-Antoine, the Tselnicks' concierge unlocked one of the old maids' rooms on the fifth floor which they had never seen or even thought about before. In the Rue des Rosiers, where people going to work were surprised by the unusual silence, a boy had been placed in the rubbish bin by his mother and was still covered in kitchen waste when he was taken to a neighbour's house and from there to a reception centre in the Rue Lamarck. Some families moved into back staircases and attics, or into curtained cubby-holes in neighbours' apartments, and felt as though they had been transported a great distance, though they were just a few feet from home.

When all those previously unsuspected places were brought into use, it seemed as though the city was revealing some of its secret resources in an attempt to accommodate a new influx of people, though in reality there were thirteen thousand fewer people in Paris than a day or two before.

While the stinking velodrome was emptied out by buses bound for Drancy in the north-eastern suburbs, and then by trains bound for somewhere in the east, the people who were left in Paris waited in their rooms and hiding-holes, never spending more than two nights in the same place. Anna and her mother lived like hunted animals for two years before they were arrested again and sent to the unknown place that children in their games called 'Pitchi Poï'. Since none of the fugitives could venture out, they had to use other people's food coupons and tried to make their neighbours' generosity last as long as possible.

As usual, concierges had to rack their brains looking for solutions to unanticipated problems. They cut off the water and the gas and the electricity, as they were told to do, but the policemen also had orders to leave any domestic animals with the concierge. Some of those snug little lodges on the ground floor of apartment blocks turned into foul and overcrowded menageries overnight. Cats were set free – there had been warnings in the paper about lethal bacilli passing from vermin to cats and from them to human beings – but when it became obvious that their owners would never return, dogs, rabbits, guinea-pigs and even songbirds were used to supplement the meat ration, which, since life showed no sign of becoming any easier, is probably what would have happened to them anyway.

The city returned to what passed for normal, and the strange stories of arrests, suicides, abandoned children living in empty apartments and the stench of the Vel' d'Hiv joined all the other implausible rumours that poisoned the air and filled it with mysteries that nobody wanted to solve.

Some of the children who were left behind saw their parents again when they were tricked into going to a reception centre run by the Union Générale des Israélites de France, and then put on a train to Drancy. Others were given new names and were sent to live with new parents in other parts of France. When things became really frightening, many children behaved in a very grown-up fashion. While their parents relived the horrors of childhood, their children sent them letters telling them not to worry and using secret code: 'The weather has been quite stormy', or 'The sun is beginning to shine'. They tried to think of all the things that their parents would like to hear, but it was not very easy to comfort mothers and fathers when they weren't there any more to be comforted.

LOVERS OF
SAINT-GERMAIN-
DES-PRÉS

Black and white, 35 mm.
Silence; no titles.
Fade in to:

1. PLACE DE LA MADELEINE.

The cobbles on the square.

JULIETTE's point of view:

Drab figures carrying bags, going about their own business. One or two
cars; bicycles everywhere; a vélo-taxi *pedalled by a young woman in*
culottes. If possible, no pigeons.

Medium long-shot: CHARLOTTE *emerges from the thin crowd on*
the Rue Royale and waves at the camera. She begins to cross the
square, moving purposefully, carrying a shoulder-bag. The sunlight
shines through her white skirt; her hair is blown by the breeze; she
looks young and cheerful.

Camera pulls back and zooms in: CHARLOTTE *seems quite close when*
she still has some way to go before reaching the camera.

A black Citroën enters the square behind her to the left. Sound of doors
banging. Three men in gabardines and fedoras grab Charlotte and
bundle her into the car.

CHARLOTTE *screams.*

The car drives off. Juliette runs into shot, racing after the car.

JULIETTE, *banging on the windows*: That's my sister! That's my
sister!

Close up: Charlotte's face stares back from the retreating window in wide-eyed terror. The car brakes and swerves to a halt. The door opens; an arm pulls Juliette into the car.
Zoom back: the black car accelerates away towards the Place de la Concorde.
Close up: cobbles in the foreground.

2. INSIDE THE CAR.

Two men in front; two behind, Charlotte wedged between them. Juliette sitting on the knee of one of the Gestapo officers.
JULIETTE, *giggling*: It's ages since I had a ride in a car!
The officer punches her very hard in the back. Pain and shock on her face.

3. PLACE DE LA MADELEINE.

The black Citroën accelerating away; pedestrians still going about their own business. The car is increasingly hard to pick out from the background.
The solo trumpet begins – one long note, then the melody – brash, almost slapdash, but forlorn; it sounds like an empty room. The title scrolls rapidly across the screen: LOVERS OF SAINT-GERMAIN-DES-PRÉS . . .

4. TITLE SEQUENCE: LEFT BANK
AND SUBURBS.

Fade to: face of JULIETTE, staring out of the car window. Her black fringe and long, straight hair make her look like a child, but her expression is that of an adult.
While the TITLES appear, street scenes are reflected on the window and pass over Juliette's face. The trumpet continues, with bass and cymbal.

NB: this should be the real route, as taken in September 1943 to Fresnes (they were first taken to Avenue Foch, but that route would be too short and familiar). Film practically the whole stretch from Place de la Concorde, across the Seine, down the Boulevard Saint-Germain and Boulevard Raspail to Place Denfert (the car is moving at speed); empty shops and café windows.

Fade twice to increasingly deserted scenes of suburbs – walls; isolated, scraggly trees; vacant lots . . . Bleary sunlight. Children playing among ruins or whatever else happens to appear.

Trumpet stops. Silence.

Black screen for four seconds.

5. AN OFFICE, 84, AVENUE FOCH.

Sound of a typewriter.

The typewriter, with an apple next to it on the table.

WOMAN in uniform, typing; hair in a bun. A SOLDIER standing by the door. JULIETTE sits in the corner. Ornate fireplace, Second Empire mirror; the incongruous paraphernalia of military administration.

Juliette looks down at the bag between her legs (the bag her sister was carrying in the opening scene). She looks up; the typist sees her looking and pushes the apple towards her across the table, and starts typing again.

Juliette steals a glance at the contents of the bag – papers rolled up – and quickly looks up away. She raises her hand, with a meaningful expression.

JULIETTE: Madame? My tummy's hurting . . .

The typist nods to the soldier, and gestures at a wooden door.

TYPIST, *to Juliette*: Don't lock the door, and don't be long.

6. TOILET.

Art deco tiles; stained glass showing a beautiful woman in a garden full of flowers. Two polished wooden steps lead to the toilet seat.

JULIETTE *opens the bag, removes the papers, flushes the toilet, rolls up her sleeve, and begins to stuff the papers into the bowl as far as she can reach. Then she flushes the toilet again. Loud sound of flushing. Close up of papers (a glimpse of handwritten lists of names and addresses) swirling in the water.*

7. OFFICE.

SOLDIER *goes to the door; opens it.* JULIETTE *descends from the toilet and goes to sit in the corner. The woman typist has disappeared. Close up of clock (11.05). Occasional sounds of someone falling, crying out.*
JULIETTE *(sitting) and* SOLDIER *(standing), with an oak-panelled wall between them.*
Close up of the empty bag between Juliette's legs.
Close up of clock (2.30).
Black screen for three seconds.
Sound of heavy boots on metal walkways. Echoing voices.

8. FRESNES.

Echoing, metallic sounds continue.
The brick facades and perimeter fence of Fresnes prison, seen from a slow-moving vehicle.

9. CONSULTATION ROOM.

A hand in a plastic glove with blood on the fingers.
JULIETTE, *from behind, putting on her skirt, then her sweater.*
Female ORDERLY *wearing a white coat over her uniform, removing the glove. She goes to a shelf and hands Juliette a towel, a folded blanket and a face-cloth.*

10. SHOWERS.

JULIETTE under the shower, seen from behind. Her black hair falls down to her waist. The scene is cruelly lit and wholly unerotic. Inarticulate women's voices shouting.
Close up: water, with dark streaks, running down the drain-hole.
Juliette under the shower, out of focus, behind the rain-like curtain of shower water. Loud sounds of gushing water ...

11. PRISON CELL.

JULIETTE, and four slatternly prostitutes pretending not to be frightened. Camp-beds; slop-bucket. Tall windows with frosted glass and iron bars.
WHORE 1: . . . then he called me a filthy fucking bitch and buggered off without paying – and bugger me if he wasn't back a week later with his friends!
WHORE 2, *nods in Juliette's direction, as if to say, 'Hush; she's just a kid.'*
WHORE 1: Bah! She'll find out soon enough – if she hasn't already . . .
WHORE 4, *inspecting Juliette*: Chubby little thing ...
WHORE 3, *singsong voice*: Chubby little thing with a big fat nose.
WHORE 1: Huh! She's not hiding much under all that hair ... If they did to her what they did to me ...
WHORE 4, *greedily*: So what *did* they do, then?
Raucous voices continue. Improvised jazz trumpet, intermittent throughout the following scenes, except the flashbacks.
Close up: Juliette bending over her blanket, which she holds on her lap. Big tears slither down her eyelashes. She begins to tease out loose threads from the hem of the blanket, and places them next to her on the bed.

12. CHILDHOOD HOME: PLUSH APARTMENT IN RUE DE SEINE NEAR SAINT-GERMAIN-DES-PRÉS.

JULIETTE as a little girl: shorts and blouse, tights, plimsolls, pageboy
   haircut. Her mother and father are shouting at one another. M.
   GRÉCO (Corsican, 30 years older than his wife) hits Mme GRÉCO
   across the face. She screams, falls to the floor.
Little JULIETTE watches this in silence. She seems to be invisible to
   her parents.
Mme GRÉCO: Get out! Get out!
Sound of door slamming. Then more banging and echoing shouts, which
   turn out to be noises heard in the cell.

13. PRISON CELL.

Prostitutes lounging about, dozing or engaged in grooming.
JULIETTE drags her camp-bed to one of the windows, stands on the
   bed, cranes her neck and looks through a pane that has lost some of its
   frosting.
Lingering shot – blurry at the edges but clear in the centre – of a white
   GOAT tethered to a post in a scrubby field beyond the perimeter
   fence. The goat seems to raise its head once or twice towards the
   prison. (Film several minutes in daylight and again at dusk.)
   The goat appears to be munching quite happily. Eight seconds.
Cut to: Juliette's blanket, in tatters. She ties the threads together and
   uses them in place of curl papers.
Close up: JULIETTE twisting the threads into her hair.
Tethered GOAT, munching. The light is fading.
JULIETTE lying on the bed, her hair in papers.
Black screen.

14. CHILDHOOD HOME, RUE DE SEINE.

The tall window of a drawing-room opens. Sounds of the city as heard from an inner courtyard; faint breathing. The camera pans across the windows opposite on the same floor, then looks down from the sixth floor to the courtyard far below.

JULIETTE as a little girl. She steps out onto the narrow ledge that runs all around the sixth floor. She places her feet in second position like a ballet dancer. Her eyelashes brush against the wall. She begins to move along the ledge.

The rest of the scene is through Juliette's eyes: she looks through the neighbours' windows, then the wall and downpipes appear as she passes on to the next window.

– A sparsely furnished room: a man and his wife staring at each other glumly across a table, eating.

– Wall.

– A soldier's uniform hung on the back of a chair; the foot of an unmade bed with a woman's clothes draped across it.

– Wall.

– A little boy holding a teddy bear, looking straight at the camera. He holds the bear out to the camera.

– Wall and drainpipes.

– A room full of packing crates and luggage.

– Juliette's plimsolled feet and the courtyard below. Sound of breathing continues.

– A woman with a cat on her lap, under the photograph of a cat. She looks vacantly at the camera as though watching someone go past on the ground floor.

– Wall.

– An old man sitting very close to the window, mending a watch.

– Wall.

– A hand comes out, pulls Juliette into the room, and slaps her across the face.

Mme GRÉCO: I'll kill you if I catch you doing that again!

Black screen.

15. INTERVIEW ROOM.

Bare walls. Short MAN in jaunty suit and polka-dot tie behind a desk, with papers in front of him; JULIETTE on a wooden chair.

MAN, *prodding the papers*: Your papers aren't in order. What's your *real* name?

JULIETTE: Gréco. Juliette.

MAN: You're lying. These are false papers. What is your real name?

JULIETTE: My real name? Juliette … What's yours?

Close up: the man's face, his eyes narrowing, moves towards the camera.

Black screen.

16. PRISON CELL.

Juliette sitting on her camp-bed, her knees pulled up to her chest. Her face is badly bruised. (Film her in this position for ten minutes. Reduce to fifteen seconds with dissolves.)

17. FRESNES.

View of the prison walls from the road, as in scene 8, but stationary. Sound of rooks cawing. Five seconds.

Black screen, fading to light grey. Sounds of the city and the chattering of sparrows.

18. AVENUE FOCH.

JULIETTE sitting, clutching her knees, but this time on a bench, wearing a coat. She looks up.

Creamy mansions on the Avenue Foch and the tall trees in the lovely light of morning. Juliette, dressed as in the opening scene, stands up

and begins to walk along the avenue. *Faint trumpet music. Passers-by look at her. (Do not use extras.)*
(*MUSIC: This should not interrupt the images but seem to accompany Juliette along the street: something like Miles Davis's 'Générique' – long, lonesome notes. If possible, show him the whole take, uncut, and get him to improvise.*)

19. HÔTEL CRYSTAL, BEHIND SAINT-GERMAIN-DES-PRÉS.

Natural sound.
Full-frame shot of the dingy hotel entrance: grubby, half-length curtains; dirty windows; bucket of detergent outside.
Zoom out: JULIETTE walks into shot. She stands looking into the dark brown interior of the hotel.

20. HÔTEL CRYSTAL, INTERIOR.

JULIETTE climbs the staircase (iron banister, brown carpet, embossed velvet flock wallpaper). The hotel owner (shirtsleeves, stained waistcoat) appears at the bottom of the stairs.
HOTELIER: Where do you think you're going?
JULIETTE, *descending the stairs*: I've come for my things.
HOTELIER *disappears, comes back with battered suitcase; dumps it on the hall carpet*: There . . .
JULIETTE: Is that all?
HOTELIER: Hey! 'Is that all' . . . Who does she think she is? . . . Try the pawn-shop . . .
JULIETTE *stares at the hotelier.*
HOTELIER: What am I? A Sister of Mercy? You left without paying.
JULIETTE *kneels on the carpet, and opens the suitcase.*
Close up: countless tiny moths flutter out of the suitcase; the remains of a dress are just visible.

21. STREETS AROUND
SAINT-GERMAIN-DES-PRÉS.

*Long take: camera follows JULIETTE, who is carrying her suitcase.
Rue Saint-Benoît, left along Boulevard Saint-Germain, past the
church and the little park. People are talking animatedly. Three
young German soldiers go by, looking like nervous schoolboys in their
cheap wool uniforms. Posters have been pasted on the tree-trunks:*
AVIS À LA POPULATION, *with 'FFI' daubed over it in black
paint;* TOUS AU COMBAT! *and* LA VICTOIRE EST
PROCHE!, *with a printed red band pasted across it signed by
General von Choltitz threatening the destruction of Paris.*
*Juliette turns left down Rue de Buci and threads her way through the
market stalls towards the building on the corner of the Rue de Seine.*
Close up: the severed, golden horse-head of the boucherie chevaline
*next door to the hotel. A plaque beside the door advertises 'Chambres
à la journée'.*
*Juliette looks away from the head and walks into the dark hallway. The
screen continues to show the hotel entrance for four seconds.*
Loud explosions and shouting.

22. HOTEL ROOM.

JULIETTE opens the sixth-floor window, steps out onto the leadwork.
Rooftop view. Smoke rising from certain parts of the city.
*Archive footage: posters being torn from walls; civilians in suits and ties
carrying rifles; barricades; people taking cover in doorways; a tricolor
flying from the Préfecture de Police, and the towers of Notre-Dame
from a sandbagged window in the Préfecture; armoured cars racing
along the Rue de Rivoli; bodies and debris lying on the Place Saint-
Michel; General von Choltitz emerging from the Hôtel Meurice,
lighting a cigar and having it crushed into his face by a woman in
the crowd; American tanks festooned with cheering girls.*
Rooftop view of Paris.

JULIETTE *withdraws into the room and lies down on the bed, staring
at the ceiling.*
*White plaster ceiling and light-bulb. Sounds of gunfire and cheering.
Ceiling fades to bright sky with white clouds.*

23. JOËL'S APARTMENT.

Medium close up: a mountain of miscellaneous clothes.
*Zoom out: a large studio apartment that looks like the property room of
an abandoned theatre. Joël, a very tall, myopic young man, quite
camp, opens the door:*
JOËL: My God! Is it really you?
JULIETTE, *smiling faintly*: I don't know … Perhaps it is … Can I
come in?
Joël ushers her in. They sit; he hands her a cigarette.
JOËL: Where have you been? No one's seen you for ages!
JULIETTE: On vacation … at Fresnes … (*Silence.*) They took my
sister. And my mother, because, you know, my mother liked
adventures … (*Shrugs her shoulders, pulls on her cigarette and
blows out a torrent of smoke.*) But she's only my mother, and she
always said she bought me from the gypsies …
JOËL, *inspecting Juliette with amiable distaste*: Yes, and she bought
your clothes from the gypsies, too. I can see that. Now we shall
have to see what we can do for you. (*Waves an arm at the clothes
racks and the mountains of material.*) My family, too … Their
business was confiscated, and now (*in a posh, 16th-arrondissement
accent*) I have come into possession of the family fortune! …
(*Pulls a green loden overcoat from the racks.*) The only problem is,
they specialized exclusively in men (*arches his eyebrows*). It runs
in the family, you know! But now that we've all been 'liberated',
we don't have to worry ourselves about such petty distinctions!
… Here, try this on!
JULIETTE *tries on the coat and shrugs it onto the floor. Then she
explores the racks and piles of clothes, and 'models' various outfits: a
khaki uniform, a black gabardine, which she takes off again quickly*

after looking in the full-length mirror; then a hefty pullover and a large tweed jacket which she pulls about her and smells with an air of contentment.

(NB: this is not the Juliette Gréco of later years. She looks more like a chubby, street-wise teenager than a fashion model, but she wears even the most ludicrous combinations with a certain style.)

Two of her girlfriends enter and join in the fashion parade. Improvised, saucy conversation on the subject of men's clothes. (Interview the actors; film in a single take, and edit out the interviewer's questions.)

JULIETTE: I'll never get used to buttoning it up the wrong way.

JOËL: You'd be surprised, my dear ...

Juliette plunges back into the coat-racks. Before she re-emerges, the camera turns to the smiling faces of her two friends, applauding:

LUISA, *laughing, in mock-indignation*: You're not going out dressed like that! ...

24. PLACE SAINT-GERMAIN-DES-PRÉS.

Two WOMEN of a certain age, swathed in funereal black, carrying handbags, looking scandalized.

JULIETTE and her two FRIENDS standing in front of a bar, all three wearing men's jackets with wide shoulders, and trousers with the legs rolled up. Juliette begins to unbutton her jacket.

Close up: a pair of boots on display outside a shoe shop; legs walking past on the pavement. From one pair of legs to the next, the boots disappear.

JULIETTE buttoning her jacket over something bulky, and the three girls walking smartly away into the crowd on the Place Saint-Germain-des-Prés.

25. LUXURIOUS DRAWING ROOM, FAUBOURG SAINT-GERMAIN.

Ironic, light chamber music.
An elegantly dressed LADY in pearls and turban, looking supercilious
but alarmed. Sitting opposite her: JULIETTE, with very long,
uncombed hair, wearing a black figure-hugging woollen dress and the
leather boots from the previous scene.
LADY, *to Juliette*: Do you have much experience in the
profession?
JULIETTE: Oh yes, a lot of experience.
LADY: You have worked as a maid before?
JULIETTE, *looking around the drawing room*: Yes … Have you?
Close up: horrified look on the lady's face.

26. STREETS AROUND SAINT-GERMAIN-DES-PRÉS.

A wet evening; lights shining on the pavement. JULIETTE and her
FRIENDS walk along, discussing films. The camera follows the
conversation as though it is one of the group.
JOËL: … But it's about a capitalist. It's a glorification of
America.
LUISA: Can't a communist make a film about a capitalist? In any
case, it's allegorical.
ANNE-MARIE: So is practically everything! … Lang, Welles,
Renoir … It's all allegory.
JOËL: Allegory of *what*, might one ask?
They reach the corner of the Rue Dauphine and the Rue Christine, and
stop in front of a bar.
JULIETTE, *looking up at the plastic letters above the entrance, 'Le*
Tabou': It's *all* real … And when you go outside into the rain,
you start to fade away, because the film was more real than you
are …
LUISA, *cheerfully*: Poor thing! She doesn't know who she is, do

you, darling? This afternoon, she thought she was a
chambermaid ...

JOËL, *pushing open the door, dramatically*: Scene Two: they enter a
disgusting little bar called 'Le Tabou', where Joël buys everyone
an exotic cocktail, and Juliette thinks she's in Tahiti ...

27. 'LE TABOU'.

*Inside: bulky men drinking at the bar – warehouse porters and
newspaper-delivery drivers in fur-lined jackets. They look round at
the group entering.*

*JULIETTE and FRIENDS walk to a stairwell and descend to a long,
vaulted cellar full of little stools and tables. Lights shine through
African masks on the wall. They sit down at one of the tables.*

28. RUE DAUPHINE.

*Close up of bar entrance outside. It looks cleaner and snazzier than before.
The sign, 'Le Tabou', is now in blazing neon. A cat runs across the
street as a car pulls up. Well-dressed people are entering the bar.
Crescendo of voices and jazz music.*

29. 'LE TABOU'.

*In the vaulted cellar: women dressed in New Look clothes, and their
lounge-suited chaperones. They look inquisitive and slightly
apprehensive. Some of them are pointing at people in the cellar and
especially to a motley group of intellectuals at the far end, bathed in
smoke.*

*JULIETTE and LUISA stand near the entrance, apparently invisible to
the people coming in. They pinch the ladies' bottoms and point
derisively at their expensive clothes. A po-faced man in black-rimmed
spectacles enters the club. Juliette slides a notebook out of his back
pocket. Luisa takes it from her and reads ...*

LUISA: 'Le Tabou, 33 Rue Dauphine, Tel. DANTON 53–28. *All night* … (imagine!) … drunken philosophers, illiterate poets, Africans, long-haired adolescents …' (*To Juliette*:) That's you! I bet he's got a photographer with him! Try to look like a savage … You should go and sit with your intellectual friends over there. You're their little pet! …

They walk over to a table where a black man is playing records. Men stare at Juliette; she stares back. She bends over the turntable and tries to read the label.

Close up: a blurred reflection of her face on the black vinyl. The record is Miles Davis – something casual and hypnotic ('Deception').

BORIS VIAN (*realistically larger than life, debonair and slightly manic; leans over, close to Juliette*): It's Miles Davis … He's in Paris, for the jazz festival. Do you want to go and hear him?

JULIETTE *looks up at Vian.*

VIAN: We'll take you if you like. He's rehearsing at the Salle Pleyel.

JULIETTE *nods her head.*

VIAN, *hands on hips*: She never speaks! Why do you never speak? (*Fixes his eyes on her.*) We'll take you there on one condition: you have to let us hear your voice.

JULIETTE *shakes her head, looks awkward.* No.

VIAN: OK. You can use someone else's words. It's like ventriloquism … (*Taking her over to the smoke-shrouded table.*) You know these alcoholics, don't you? (*They greet Juliette. Vian gestures grandly*:) Mademoiselle Gréco is in search of a song.

BEAUVOIR (*striped pullover, hair tied back, red fingernails; to Sartre*): You said Gréco ought to be a singer. Why don't you give her a song?

SARTRE, *thinking*: What about 'La Rue des Blancs-Manteaux'? I wrote it for *Huis Clos*, but (*raising his vodka glass to Juliette*), I hereby offer it to Mademoiselle.

BEAUVOIR: That's nice! A song about an executioner … Find something better … Imagine her on the stage.

SARTRE, *inspecting Juliette*: 'Juliette' … rhymes with … *fillette* … Ah! … 'Si tu t'imagines, fillette'. Raymond Queneau. (*To Juliette*:) You know Queneau?

JULIETTE *nods her head.* Yes.

BEAUVOIR, *leaning over the table towards Juliette, smiling tipsily*: 'Your rosy cheeks', 'your slender waist' ... (*To Sartre*:) What else? ...

SARTRE, *merrily*: 'Your twinkling feet, your sylph-like thighs ...' We can get Kosma to write the music.

All look at JULIETTE. Contra-zoom: she suddenly appears, as if in her mind's eye, in the pose of a singer standing at a microphone. She stares at the camera with the shadow of a smile. The music has segued discreetly into something more gentle and romantic – 'Moon Dreams' or 'Générique' again.

The merry group at the table continue reciting phrases of the poem: 'A triple chin, a muscle turned to flab . . .'; 'Gather the roses, the roses of life!'; 'If you think they'll last forever, you've got another think coming, little girl!'

30. SALLE PLEYEL.

The dilapidated, art deco facade of the Salle Pleyel. Music, at first indistinct and echoing, becomes gradually louder during the following sequence.

The camera moves through the white columns of the foyer.

The auditorium. On the distant stage: a bass-player, a drummer and the pencil-thin figure of Miles DAVIS (23 years old). He wears a white shirt, black tie and a sharply tailored linen suit. His dazzling trumpet catches the light.

Seats in the auditorium and scattered listeners; JULIETTE sitting a few rows from the front, her hands clasped around her left knee, listening intently. She is dressed simply but strikingly in black, with more mascara than before.

Dissolve: people here and there in the auditorium, this time in different seats; JULIETTE as before. During the dissolve, the music changes to a slow, poignant tune reminiscent of the opening sequence. While the music plays: close up of Juliette staring past the camera.

Music stops.

DAVIS *and the other musicians resting between numbers; a photographer taking pictures of Davis, a journalist scribbling notes.*

DAVIS, *to one of the musicians, jerking his head*: Hey, who's that girl over there? The one with the long black hair?

MUSICIAN: That one over there? What do you want with her?

DAVIS: What do you mean, what do I want with her? I want to get to know her. She's been sitting there all day …

MUSICIAN: She's not for you, man. She came with Boris Vian and that crowd. She's one of those 'existentialists' …

DAVIS: Man, I don't care about all that shit. She's beautiful. I want to get to know her. (*Quietly.*) I ain't never seen a woman look like that before.

Davis beckons to Juliette with his index finger. She walks slowly up to the stage and climbs the steps. They stand looking at each other, smiling warily.

DAVIS: You like the music?

JULIETTE: *Si j'aime la musique?* … (*She looks closely at his trumpet, then runs her finger softly along the tubing.*) *Comme vous voyez* …

DAVIS, *readjusting his stance*: OK, so you don't speak English, huh? That's cool … We'll improvise! … (*Waves the trumpet.*) You play? You play an instrument?

JULIETTE *purses her lips, mimes playing a trumpet*: *Montrez-moi* . . .

DAVIS: Here, put your fingers here.

Close up: Juliette presses the valves as Davis blows the trumpet. Beautiful, brazen sounds come out. Her face lights up; she laughs out loud.

DAVIS, *laughing*: That's not bad at all! (*To musician, swaggering:*) Hey, man! I just played a duet with an existentialist! (*To Juliette:*) You wanna go for a coffee? … *Café?*

JULIETTE: *Oui, mais pas ici* … (*Takes his hand silently and leads him off the stage.*) *Venez* …

MUSICIAN: Hey, Miles!

DAVIS, *turning round*: You just keep working on those changes, man!

31. BANKS OF THE SEINE.

Close up: a pigeon pecking between the cobblestones. The pigeon flies off.

Zoom out – camera close to the ground: a beggar with a crutch, chasing away the pigeon. Legs and feet of JULIETTE and DAVIS – her sandals, his shiny leather boots, walking along the Seine embankment, upstream of the Pont des Arts. Sound of walking feet.

Zoom out: a bridge at an oblique angle, half-hidden by the branches of a willow; Juliette and Davis in a tight embrace; Davis with his back to the river. A coal barge comes into shot. On the barge, standing by the geranium-bedecked cabin, a little girl watches the lovers.

They continue their walk along the embankment. Silence.

DAVIS *starts to say something.*

JULIETTE, *glancing down: Je n'aime pas les hommes ... mais vous, (looking at Miles) vous, c'est différent ...*

DAVIS: You don't like men? Is that what you said? Well, I'll tell you, in America, I ain't a man. (*Displays his fingers.*) I'm a nigger! (*Juliette strokes his fingers.*) I'm an *entertainer* ... (*Davis flaps his hands, minstrel-style.*) An Uncle Tom – you know what I mean?

JULIETTE: La Case de l'Oncle Tom, *oui, je sais ...*

DAVIS, *looking almost shy; walking on*: There's some kind of special smell here I ain't smelled anywhere else. (*Sniffs the air. Juliette looks amused and surprised.*) It's like coffee beans ... and coconut and lime and rum all mixed together, and ... like eau de cologne ... Heh! This must be 'April in Paris' ... (*singing*) pap, pap, pap, pap, pap ...

JULIETTE *stops, pulls his arm, points at his face: La trompette ... tu fais comment? ...*

DAVIS *mimes trumpet playing; JULIETTE stands on tiptoe and kisses him on the lips.*

Long take: they continue walking along the Seine. A few people pass – no one pays any attention to them (use extras), except an angler worried about his jars of bait.

Music: faintly recognizable improvisation on the tune of 'April in Paris'.

They reach the steps that lead back up to the street near Place du
  Châtelet. Davis looks out along the river, then runs to catch up with
  Juliette.
DAVIS, *taking her hand*: Say, what *is* an existentialist, anyway?
JULIETTE *smiles inscrutably.*
Music continues as they walk up to the busy street.

32. NEWSREEL.

(Faster film stock; grainy.)
Blank screen, numbers counting down. 7, 6, 5, 4, 3 …
Voice-over: suave, becoming increasingly sarcastic.
NARRATOR:
The *quartier* of Saint-Germain-des-Prés …
The square and the church. Close up of crumbling, ivy-covered walls.
The remains of the oldest abbey in Paris. A corner of the provinces
  in the heart of the city. Here, time passes more slowly.
Place de Furstemberg; pushchairs; an old woman feeding pigeons,
  another knitting on a park bench.
In this quiet little square, one can visit the studio where Delacroix
  revolutionized the art of his time. Sometimes, it seems as
  though nothing has changed …
Pavement in front of café. Respectable bourgeois men and women
  reading newspapers, stirring cups of coffee.
There's the Café de Flore …
A teenage girl and boy walk past: she wears a sweater, Capri pants,
  sandals laced above the ankle, pony-tail; he has an open-neck shirt,
  beard, cigarette dangling from his mouth. The camera lets them pass,
  then swivels quickly to follow them. Lingering shot of girl in centre of
  screen. She tears the wrapper from a chocolate ice cream and drops it
  on the pavement.
Did I say nothing had changed? … The Café de Flore is now a
  temple – a temple whose high priests are called Jean-Paul
  Sartre and Simone de Beauvoir.
Café table with empty coffee cup and overflowing ashtray, and two books:
  Le Deuxième Sexe *and* Les Mains sales.

And the name of this cult? EXISTENTIALISM!

Frantic trumpet and cymbal.

Bookshop: young people picking through books; handwritten posters –
    'Are you for or against?', etc.

The Club Saint-Germain, underground dance-floor. Men in sunglasses,
    women in split skirts. Fast jazz music.

Close up: crude painting on wall based on le Douanier Rousseau's The
    Muse Inspiring the Poet: *Sartre in dinner jacket with pipe in*
    mouth, next to a long-haired figure resembling Juliette Gréco.

Some say that this misty philosophy, which no one understands,
    not even its exponents, is essentially Germanic; others that
    Sartre and his acolytes are the Trojan Horse of 'the American
    way of life'. And who could deny it?

More scenes of dancing.

Jazz … the jitterbug … American cigarettes …

Relaxed, laughing faces, chewing gum.

Those GIs feel quite at home at the Club Saint-Germain!

Close up: young man wearing flat cap, sunglasses, toothy smile.

'*Homo existentialis*' wears sunglasses and lives underground. His
    bookstores, bars and, yes, his 'discothèque', are all several
    metres below sea-level – probably because of his morbid
    fascination with the Atom bomb. And, of course, he – and she –
    wears black … Black (*slight cough*) is his favourite colour …

Black American enjoying the music and the dancing.

Cut to: Sartre walking along a pavement talking to an earnest
    admirer.

Who is that man who looks like a gargoyle come to life, or a
    grocer going back to his shop? . . . You don't know? Why,
    that's the man who started it all! – Jean-Paul Sartre. He's the
    one those long-haired adolescents call 'master'. The author of
    . . . 'Being and Nothingness', 'Nausea', 'Dirty Hands' – well,
    you get the picture …

News footage of Sartre talking to Simone de Beauvoir at a literary
    party.

Ask any of the young women who've been invited up to the
    master's room … I'm told on reliable authority that there's a
    distinct smell of Camembert chez Jean-Paul Sartre …

Po-faced NARRATOR *of documentary sitting at café table: chequered suit, black-rimmed glasses, trying to look older than he is; waiter removes his cup. Narrator speaks to camera: zoom from across the street – vehicles and pedestrians pass in front of him in a blur.*

Well, it's not what I was brought up to think of as French literature … The only thing resembling an idea I could find in all this 'philosophy' seems to be this: we're all free to do whatever we like … Well, then … (*Picks up the books from the table.*) I, too, am an existentialist … (*Stands up, tosses the books into a dust-cart, and walks off down the street.*)

Jazz music.

Blur of windows: camera whizzes back along the shop-fronts to:

33. CAFÉ DE FLORE.

(*Higher quality film stock, as before the newsreel.*)

SARTRE, BEAUVOIR, DAVIS, JULIETTE. A continual stream of words. The conversation goes on, almost too fast to be followed, above the sound of other customers (including the director), the garçons *shouting orders, twirling trays;* mobylettes, *car horns, police whistles, etc.*

JULIETTE follows the conversation but also looks around at the other tables and the life of the street. Her silence and facial expressions are a continual counterpoint to the conversation.

SARTRE talks with DAVIS in English. He speaks grammatically but with an atrocious accent. The cigarette is never far from his mouth. (*No subtitles.*)

SARTRE: . . . because your music has a political resonance …

DAVIS: I just blow the trumpet, man. I blow that trumpet and the sounds come out and the cats dig it … Or they don't dig it; it's all the same to me. (*Long fingers flutter.*) Politics is what I'm getting away from.

SARTRE: From my point of view, this is a political act.

DAVIS, *leans forward*: It's just music, man.

SARTRE: Yes, jazz music, which is an expression of liberty.

DAVIS, *leans back; forced smile*: That's a white man's word – jazz. White men always want to put a label on everything. They're

[307]

just tunes, man. I take the tunes to pieces and I put them back together in different ways, without the clichés ...

SARTRE: Yes, and then no one can hear the tune without really hearing it. (*Stubs out cigarette; taps another from the packet.*) For example: here is a glass. A glass on the table.

DAVIS *picks up his glass, drinks, puts it back on the table*: Uh huh.

SARTRE: I say, 'glass', and the glass is exactly the same as before. Nothing happens to it, except perhaps it oscillates, but not very much. It is as if the glass does not give a shit.

DAVIS: Heh! This is existentialism, right?

SARTRE: No, Gréco is *existentialisme* if you believe the *journalistes*. (*Smiling.*) '*La Muse de l'existentialisme.*'

All look at JULIETTE. *She watches a woman in Dior clothes walking past with a poodle, which lifts its leg at a tree.*

SARTRE: This is not existentialism. This is a man who is talking to another man ...

DAVIS looks intently at Sartre.

SARTRE: But when I say the word 'glass', something *has* happened. The glass is not any more in the shadows. It is not ... (*looks at Beauvoir*) ... *perdu dans la perception globale des choses* ... lost in the global perception? ... When I name something, this is not without consequence, which is what the man who uses violence – *la torture* – (*Juliette looks up*) what he understands when he forces another man to say a name or a telephone number or an address. (*To the* garçon.) *Oui, apportez-nous une bouteille.* (*To Davis.*) This is why we can say that the writer and, in a certain sense, the musician, removes the innocence of things.

DAVIS, *laughing*: Yeah, that's what I do, man, I 'remove the innocence of things'!

SARTRE: So, for example, in the Alabama, the oppression of the Negroes is nothing until somebody has said, 'The Negroes are oppressed.'

MILES *cocks his head; looks doubtful.* That's a place I ain't never gonna see ...

SARTRE: Or, a better example: in *La Chartreuse de Parme* by Stendhal – *Vous la connaissez, Gréco,* La Chartreuse de Parme?

(*Juliette smiles noncommittally.*) Mosca, le comte Mosca, is very worried by the feelings – the feelings he cannot define – which his lover and Fabrice have for one another. And he sees them go away in the carriage, sitting one next to the other, and he says, '*Si le mot d'amour ...*', *euh*, 'If the word *amour* – love – is pronounced between them, I am lost ...' (*Blows out smoke.*) So you have, when you name something, a responsibility.

DAVIS *places his hand on Juliette's.*

BEAUVOIR, *smiling at Davis and Gréco*: *Oui, la responsabilité!* ... But do you know when he said this, when Sartre said this, about *la responsabilité de l'écrivain*?

SARTRE, *emptying his glass, titters.*

BEAUVOIR: He was invited to give a *conférence* at UNESCO. It was the first meeting of UNESCO, two or three years ago, in 1946. At the Sorbonne. The evening before, we went to the Schéhérazade, with Koestler and Camus. And Sartre – you remember? – danced with Mme Camus, which was like watching a man lugging a sack of coal. He was very drunk, and he had to give his talk in the morning, but he had not written a line.

DAVIS, *pointing a finger at Sartre*: The teacher hadn't done his homework!

BEAUVOIR: Yes, and Camus, who was also drunk, said, 'You will have to do it without my help,' and Sartre said, 'I wish I could do it without *my* help.'

SARTRE, *stubby fingers spread on the table, giggles.*

BEAUVOIR: And then – he does not remember this – we had breakfast Chez Victor at Les Halles: *soupe à l'oignon, huîtres, vin blanc* – and then it was dawn, and we stood on a bridge over the Seine, Sartre and me, and we were so sad about *la tragédie de la condition humaine – eh oui!* – that we said we should throw ourselves into the river. But instead of that, I went home to my bed, and Sartre, he went to the Sorbonne to talk about *la responsabilité de l'écrivain* ...

DAVIS: That's cool, Jean-Paul. They knew you were talking straight because you hadn't prepared ...

BEAUVOIR, *shaking her head*: No, Sartre, he had everything already in his head.

SARTRE, *with his wall-eyed stare, purses his lips, looks serious*: What can we do? We can only try not to make ourselves guilty. That is what I said at the Sorbonne. It was after the Libération. (*The* garçon *arrives with the next bottle. Sartre fills the glasses. To Davis, suddenly:*) Why don't you and Gréco get married?

DAVIS, *looking at Juliette*: Responsibility, man ... I love her too much to make her unhappy.

BEAUVOIR, *to Juliette, smiling*: Il vous aime trop pour vous rendre malheureuse.

JULIETTE *kisses Davis on the cheek.*

They look at each other. Close up: both in profile.

JULIETTE (*to Beauvoir*): Il ne veut pas m'emmener avec lui aux États-Unis.

DAVIS: Ayta-Zoony? Oui, mauvais, très mauvais pour les Negroes. Et très très mauvais pour les femmes blancs avec les Negroes.

SARTRE: But you can remain in France, where everybody loves your music.

JULIETTE, *to Sartre and Beauvoir, looking at Davis*: Vous ne trouvez pas qu'il ressemble à un Giacometti?

DAVIS: Jacko Metti?

WAITER: Je vais vous débarrasser ... Vous allez dîner?

BEAUVOIR: Will you have dinner?

DAVIS, *looking at Juliette*: No, we gonna find ourselves a bridge and look at the river, and then maybe we'll jump in ... Shit, I just came here to play music, I wasn't expecting none of this.

A CUSTOMER (*the director*) *at one of the neighbouring tables, folds his newspaper, stands up and leaves.*

JULIETTE pours some sugar into a cone of paper, reaches over and takes an empty ashtray from the next table, and puts both items into her bag. Stands up and takes Davis's hand.

SARTRE, *to Juliette*: 'Si tu t'imagines ...' You haven't forgotten, Gréco?

JULIETTE, *leaving with Davis, looks back, shakes her head.*

Zoom back: 'existentialist' young man in street looking into dust-cart, takes out a book and leafs through it. Walks off down the street, reading the book.

34. EXT. HÔTEL LA LOUISIANE, RUE DE SEINE.

Camera pans slowly from ground floor to top floor of the hotel – grimy shutters, window boxes, balcony railings. Pause at the top floor.

35. INT. HÔTEL LA LOUISIANE.

Hotel room. DAVIS in bed; JULIETTE sitting cross-legged on the bed, looking at him.
Silence.
DAVIS: She's called Irene. She's a good girl. I care for her a lot. But she's like . . . She's not like you. She doesn't have your independence … She doesn't have your style … I mean …
JULIETTE, *looking sad but not distraught; it is unclear how much of Davis's talk she understands:* Tu vas rester ici (*pointing down*), à Paris … en France?
DAVIS: I dunno … I could get used to being treated like a human being … He's right, Jean-Paul. Everybody likes my music. But that ain't good. Anything I play, the audience cheers. It gets so I'm not even sure it's me who's playing … But if I go back to the States, I sure as hell ain't gonna find another woman like you.
JULIETTE, *getting back into bed:* Tu reviendras un jour. Et tu m'enverras tous tes disques …
Mellow trumpet music.
The following sequence is an accompaniment to the music rather than the other way about. (As in scene 18, ask Davis to improvise – but without showing him the sequence. Show some of the unedited take of scene 31 along the banks of the Seine.)

36. OPPOSITE THE HOTEL, RUE DE SEINE.

(This is the same location as Juliette's childhood home in scenes 12 and 14.) The view of windows across the street. Dissolves, showing sunlight on the face of the building, from morning to late afternoon.

37. PLACE SAINT-GERMAIN-DES-PRÉS.

JULIETTE and DAVIS. His arm around her shoulders – his tall body
towards the camera, his face in profile, kissing Juliette. Her face,
also in profile, her head tilted back, her body arched like a musical
instrument. (Copy the pose from a Robert Doisneau photograph.)
The spire of the church of Saint-Germain-des-Prés appears in the
background. The angle of the shot makes it look as though they
stopped to kiss among the traffic while crossing the square.
A car pulls up just behind them. Sound of a door banging.
JULIETTE, *quietly:* Voilà ... Il est toujours plus facile de partir que
de rester ...
DAVIS *gets into the taxi. He turns round and stares through the rear*
window at Juliette (at the camera) with the look of a man being
taken to jail.
JULIETTE *watches the taxi disappear into the traffic towards the Rue*
Bonaparte. She stands still for a long moment, then turns around and
looks over at the church spire ...

38. PLACE SAINT-GERMAIN-DES-PRÉS.

... which now appears in colour.
(All the final scenes are in colour.)
Long take; hand-held camera. Medium zoom at distance: the life of the
square: people, cars, bicycles.
Black screen.
Title: 'Five years on ...'

39. WALDORF-ASTORIA, NEW YORK.

The grand hotel facade on Park Avenue; yellow taxis, doormen, etc.
Expensive hotel carpet; door with shiny brass fittings and a spy-hole.
Door opens.

JULIETTE; *her face is powdered and almost emaciated compared to her pudgier adolescent face; her nose is artificially thinner. She holds out her arms (speaking in English):* Miles! I am so glad ...

DAVIS, *features taut, eyes bulging, visibly stoned; dressed in a shapeless sports jacket:* Yeah, right. (*Looks nervously down the corridor, both ways.*) What did I tell ya? (*Looks past her into the room.*) They gave you a whole suite? (*Swaggering like a pimp. Looks back down the corridor.*) Here's your room service.

Man in blue Waldorf-Astoria uniform arrives with trolley; sees Juliette and Davis, and freezes.

DAVIS, *taking the bottle from the ice-bucket:* What's the matter with you, motherfucker? (*To Juliette:*) What did I tell ya? I told ya I never wanna see you in this country. (*Jerking his head. Unconvincing swagger.*) You got some money? I need some money right now!

JULIETTE, *looking shocked, searches in her bag, hands Davis some dollar bills.*

DAVIS *grabs the money, pushes past the man. He heads along the corridor, takes a swig from the bottle.*

40. HOTEL ELEVATOR.

DAVIS *in the elevator, surrounded by mirrors, staring wild-eyed at his feet; looks up, tears in his eyes.*

41. CONCERT ROOM, WALDORF-ASTORIA.

JULIETTE *on stage – a slim, dark figure, and the microphone stand. She is dressed in black and her hair is long and straight, but it now looks designedly artless, and the stage lighting gives her an air of sophistication. She sings the whole song, 'Si tu t'imagines, fillette' – from the orchestra intro to the audience reaction at the end. (Three minutes.) She gives a muted rendition, ice-cool and slightly winsome. The emotions on her face are those required by the song.*

(*Subtitles:* If you think, little girl ... They're going to last forever ... The days of love and passion ... You've got another think coming, little girl ...)

Cut twice during the song to DAVIS, *in the hotel lobby, arguing with the clerk and being asked to leave.*

End with JULIETTE, *engulfed in applause, looking straight at the camera. A lingering close up of her face and fluttering false eyelashes.*

Black screen.

42. PLACE SAINT-GERMAIN-DES-PRÉS.

During this scene, the credits appear.

Film crew on the square. JULIETTE, *wearing a corseted Dior coat; otherwise much the same as in the previous scene.* ACTORS *in gabardines and fedoras standing around, chatting and smoking.*

Slowly fade in trumpet music, as in the title sequence.

MAKE-UP WOMAN *powdering Juliette's face.*

DIRECTOR, *with megaphone:* À vos places!

JULIETTE, *pointing to two men, standing close by; she raises her hands at the director.*

Close up: po-faced critic in black-rimmed spectacles talking to another critic:

CRITIC 1: That's not how she looked! She was just a *girl* ... In fact, she looked like a juvenile delinquent ...

CRITIC 2: What do you expect? This is what they call 'reality'! ... (*They laugh conspiratorially.*)

DIRECTOR, *to man with clipboard:* Get those idiots off the set! ... (*Looking round, in exasperation:*) Where are the Gestapo?! (*To the actors in gabardines:*) Messieurs, when you're ready ...

ACTORS *drop their cigarettes, crush them under their jackboots, and walk towards a black Citroën. One of the actors, as he passes* JULIETTE, *tickles her waist. She turns, laughing, towards the camera. Despite the make-up, she looks happy and natural.*

Freeze frame.

Fade out.

Credits continue.

THE DAY OF THE FOX

1. SNIPER FIRE

No one who was there that day ever forgot what he saw. The ceremony would have been memorable enough on its own; the dire emergency that plunged it into chaos gave it the aura of a truly exceptional, almost supernatural event. It was as though God had decreed that, at the end of the latest episode of the saga titled 'France', every plot-line should converge at Notre-Dame-de-Paris on the 26th of August 1944. The leading actor, appropriately named de Gaulle, was placed where he could be seen from every angle. He seemed to belong to the same field of vision as the towers of the cathedral. As the great bell tolled, dinning each historic moment into the collective memory, ten thousand brains whirred like movie cameras, recording every sight and sound for the benefit of future grandchildren whose procreation struck them there and then as a sacred obligation. The race would continue undiminished, massed behind a leader whose invulnerability had been tested before the eyes of the civilized world.

The man whose voice had resonated from the tomb of exile and emboldened his cringing listeners in their darkened rooms had stridden into Paris like a giant. Though his gauntness bore poignant testimony to four long years of London fog and English food, he still had the bearing of a leader. He had stooped beneath the Arc de Triomphe and laid a cross of white roses on the Tomb of the Unknown Soldier. He had walked the full length of the Champs-Élysées, cheered from every tree and lamp post, saluted by officers whose cratered cheeks were moist with tears, and kissed by pretty girls who darted from the crowd waving handkerchiefs and ribbons. The tanks of General Leclerc had rumbled along at his side like the chariots of myrmidons. Only occasionally had he been obliged to ask his comrades at the front of the procession to remain a few steps behind him.

On the Place de la Concorde, the smiling generals climbed into cars and were whisked along the Rue de Rivoli to the Hôtel de Ville, where de Gaulle was received by the Liberation Committee as head of the provisional government. When he emerged on the balcony to address the crowd, the surge of officers behind him almost sent him tumbling over the edge. One of his subordinates later described how he had squatted at the General's feet, embracing his knees to prevent him from falling headlong into the sea of faces. 'The enemy is teetering', said de Gaulle to the crowd, 'but fights on on our soil. We who shall have seen our history's finest hour must prove ourselves worthy of France to the very end.'

From the Hôtel de Ville, de Gaulle and his government-to-be crossed the river and reached the cathedral of Notre-Dame at 4.20 in the afternoon for the service of thanksgiving.

As so often happens when thousands of people witness the same event, no two accounts are the same. There is even some doubt about the identity of the villains who nearly ruined the hour of triumph. The file remains open to this day, but since disaster was averted and the final outcome has never been in doubt, even the most determined conspiracy theorists have shown little interest in the case.

The BBC's Robert Reid, who had arrived from Saint-Lô a day before with the US Army, was well placed to observe the critical moments. He was sitting cross-legged on the ground, near the west door of the cathedral, holding his microphone. As soon as the emergency was over, he rushed to find his recording man, who was staring at the disc on his turntable: it was covered in tiny fragments of medieval stone. The two men hurried over to the Hôtel Scribe to submit the recording to the censors. There was a heated discussion about the desirability of telling the world that General de Gaulle had nearly been assassinated. Finally, permission was granted, and the recording was broadcast the next day on the BBC's *War Report*, then retransmitted by CBS and NBC.

Spellbound listeners heard Reid's hoarse, high-pitched voice above the cheers of the crowd: '*The General is being presented to people. He is being received ... He's being received ...* ' Suddenly, there was the crackle of gunfire, voices crying out and the sound of a Yorkshireman and his microphone being trampled by a crowd of Parisians. There followed a few moments of silence. Then the mutedly ecstatic voice of Reid returned. He might have been narrating a novel by John Buchan, but the sounds of commotion all around him confirmed the veracity of his report:

> That was one of the most dramatic scenes I have ever seen! . . . Firing started all over the place . . . General de Gaulle was trying to control the crowds rushing into the cathedral. He walked straight ahead into what appeared to me to be a hail of fire from somewhere inside the cathedral . . . But he went straight ahead without hesitation, his shoulders flung back, and walked right down the centre aisle, even while the bullets were pouring around him. It was the most extraordinary example of courage I have ever seen! There were bangs, flashes all about him, yet he seemed to have an absolutely charmed life.

Years later, Reid wrote a more detailed account of the incident. It was published by his grandson in 2007. The snipers appeared to have taken up position inside the cathedral – in the upper galleries and behind the great organ – and also on the roof. A man standing very close to Reid was hit in the neck, and others were injured as they tried to hide behind pillars and under chairs. Estimates of the number of casualties vary from one hundred to three hundred. He remembered the reek of cordite mingling with the smell of incense, and 'the crazy scene' of modern warfare in a twelfth-century cathedral. And, like everyone else, he marvelled at the sight of General de Gaulle standing bare-headed before the altar like a man sent from God: 'There were blinding flashes inside the cathedral, there were pieces of stone ricocheting around the place.' 'Heaven knows how they missed him, for they were firing the whole time.'

In the immediate aftermath of the shooting, two questions were asked: who were the snipers, and – a largely rhetorical question – how on earth did General de Gaulle survive the hail of bullets? Eventually, when peace had returned to Europe and the heroes of the

Liberation were mired in domestic politics, a third, insidious question was asked, though only in private: was the identity of the snipers somehow connected with de Gaulle's miraculous survival?

None of these questions has ever been answered to everyone's satisfaction. Reid himself saw four 'raffish-looking' gunmen being led from the cathedral: they were dressed in grey flannel trousers and white singlets, and appeared to him 'very obvious Germans'. Meanwhile, across the square, a nine-year-old boy, whose father worked as a chauffeur at the Préfecture de Police, had climbed out of the window of his fourth-floor apartment onto a sloping zinc roof. Crouching behind the stone parapet, he looked over at Notre-Dame and observed shots being fired from the top of the towers. Some moments later, 'a few suspects' were marched onto the square. The boy, whose name was Michel Barrat, identified them as '*miliciens*', which is to say, members of the French paramilitary force that had served as auxiliaries of the Gestapo. As he leaned over and peered down at the square, he saw one of the arrested men being beaten up, and perhaps killed, by the crowd. 'That brutal scene is still engraved on my memory', he wrote in 1998.

While these arrests were taking place, sporadic gunfire was still scattering the crowd, though no one could tell whether the shots were being fired by German snipers or by trigger-happy soldiers of the Résistance.

The Liberation of Paris was a bloody and protracted affair. On 26 August, when de Gaulle marched down the Champs-Élysées, the city was still swarming with German soldiers, Gestapo officers, Vichy militia and other *collaborateurs*. Some of those desperate men may have hidden in the cathedral, seeking sanctuary or vowing to die in a blaze of vengeful glory. Anyone familiar with the story of Quasimodo would have known that, apart from the sewers, there was no better hiding place in Paris. When he was asked why no one had thought to conduct a search of all the stairways and galleries of the cathedral before the service of thanksgiving, the *gardien* of the towers replied, 'It's like the catacombs in there!' A thorough search *was* conducted after the shooting, but according to a lieutenant-colonel serving with the Second Armoured Division, the officers who were sent up into the towers to investigate 'found no one there but policemen'.

20. Juliette Gréco and the church of Saint-Germain-des-Prés.
By Georges Dudognon.

21. Barricade on the Boulevard Saint-Germain near Rue Hautefeuille, May 1968. By Alain Dejean.

22. Jean-Paul Sartre and Simone de Beauvoir selling *La Cause du peuple*, 1970.

23. The Arc de Triomphe, from 'Le Plitch', in *Mémoires d'outre-espace* (1983) by Enki Bilal. 'The Government and I shall soon be in a position to offer you rational explanations for this delicate problem! . . .'

24. The Sacré-Cœur de Montmartre and the route of the Eurostar, looking west from the Col de la Chapelle.

25. President Nicolas Sarkozy inaugurating the 'Historial Charles de Gaulle' at Les Invalides, 22 February 2008. By Melanie Frey.

Historial Charles de Gaulle
Hôtel national des Invalides - 22 février 2008

De Gaulle himself suggested a third possibility in his *Mémoires de guerre*. He, more than anyone else, was aware of the dangerous vacuum created by the retreating tide of fascism. He knew that yesterday's comrades might be tomorrow's political rivals, and that, despite the presence of the American army, a coup d'état might occur at any moment. In his memoirs, written in the 1950s, when he was preparing his return to power, he asked himself and his readers, 'Why would a German soldier or a *milicien* have shot at chimneys instead of aiming at me, when I was exposed and in the open?' He hinted, none too delicately, that the mysterious snipers were members of the French Communist Party: 'I have the feeling that this was a put-up job, perpetrated with the political aim of spreading panic in the crowd and justifying the continued imposition of a revolutionary power'.

If the communists had been hoping to prove themselves indispensable by maintaining a state of terror, the attempt failed completely. The gun-battle at Notre-Dame only established Charles de Gaulle as the uncontested political and spiritual leader of the new republic. By striding up the aisle and standing at the altar in a hail of bullets, he had written himself into every future history of France. Some of the men who were trying to elbow their way into the new regime thought that de Gaulle had effectively conducted a coup d'état of his own, but any sly insinuations were silenced by the glorious outcome, and the unanswered questions would soon be of purely academic interest: What had those policemen been doing in the towers, and how had the snipers in the cathedral eluded the search party? Who were the arrested men seen by Robert Reid and the boy on the roof? And why did the official inquest that was held immediately afterwards find no trace of any arrest?

Only a man who begrudged de Gaulle his hour of glory would have bothered to ask such questions, and only a man who hoped to emulate his triumph might have wondered what lessons could be learned from his masterly manipulation of what appeared to be a totally unpredictable event.

2. OBSERVATORY GARDENS

LATE IN THE EVENING of 15 October 1959, a man who looked rather pleasantly self-satisfied, though perhaps a little nervous, sat in the famous Brasserie Lipp on the Boulevard Saint-Germain, guarding the remains of a delicate sauerkraut and a bottle of Gewürztraminer. The waiters who buzzed about his table showed by the swift discretion of their gestures that this was a regular and honoured customer. He had the good looks of a man who, though well into his forties, is cheered by the sight that greets him in the shaving-mirror every morning. In the evening (as on that evening), the merest hint of dilapidation – a kink in his thin black tie, a slightly rumpled collar, the five-o'clock shadow on his upper lip – suggested a day devoted to matters that transcended personal appearance but without posing any serious threat to elegance. He had what he might have called an air of quiet dignity. An occasional crinkling of the eyes and a boyish pout that a novelist might have described as 'sensual' and 'indicative of a strong will' endowed him with a certain charm that, until recently, had served him well.

The Brasserie Lipp was François Mitterrand's favourite eating-place. It was half a mile from the Senate and half a mile from the apartment that he occupied with his wife and two sons in the Rue Guynemer on the quiet side of the Jardin du Luxembourg. Though he enjoyed a reflective stroll through the streets of the Left Bank, he had apparently decided that evening, for safety's sake, not to walk home. His blue Peugeot 403 was parked across the road, ready to be driven away at a moment's notice. It was close to midnight, and, although the Flore and the Deux Magots were still busy, the traffic had thinned out and there was little danger of his being trapped in one of those interminable Chinese puzzles of tightly parked cars which, to foreign visitors, are one of the wonders of Paris.

He sat downstairs, near the door, in the brittle, tinkling light of mirrors and ceramic tiles depicting huge, fleshy green leaves and parrots paradoxically camouflaged by their vivid colours. On the ceiling, smoke-cured Cupids twisted their little brown bodies to aim their arrows at invisible targets. Even at this late hour, he was half-expecting his former colleague, Robert Pesquet, to turn up at the Lipp. For a moment, a man with Pesquet's build had stood in the shadow of a doorway across the road, but then had disappeared. It would not have been surprising if he had changed his mind. With the confusion that now prevailed, one often found oneself associating with unreliable, slightly sinister fools like Pesquet.

Fifteen years had passed since the day he had saved the General from falling off the balcony of the Hôtel de Ville. Naturally, de Gaulle had not looked to see who had saved him, and Mitterrand himself had told the story so many times with slightly differing details that he was not even sure that it had actually happened. On the following day, General de Gaulle had summoned him to the War Ministry and, recognizing the man who had refused in 1943 to merge his own resistance group with the Gaullists, had said, like an impatient headmaster, 'You again!' Instead of confirming him as the self-appointed Minister for Prisoners of War, de Gaulle had informed him that his services would not be required in the new government.

With de Gaulle's retirement from politics in 1946, his own career had taken off. He already had the velvety charm that later earned him the nickname 'the Fox'. The devious road-map of his past, which had taken him from xenophobic nationalism to almost simultaneous distinction in the Vichy regime and the Résistance, and then to that broad domain of opportunity called the centre-left, now looked almost like a bold itinerary based on long-held convictions. He had been the youngest Minister of the Interior in French history. Recently, he had served as Minister of Justice, which had enabled him to amass a considerable treasure of experience, friends, contacts and compromising dossiers on all sorts of people, though not, as it happened, on Robert Pesquet. But then Pesquet was able to compromise himself without anyone's assistance.

Pesquet, too, had lost his seat in the recent elections, when de Gaulle had returned triumphantly to power. Yet while Mitterrand himself had been salvaged by the centre-left and given a seat in the Senate, Pesquet was still in the political wilderness. He was thought to have links with the secret paramilitary units that waged a war of terror on the 'traitors' who wanted to abandon Algeria to the Arabs. In fact, Pesquet was simply a victim of his political philosophy: 'Keep your eyes on the bottom of the leading sheep', he liked to say, 'and look neither left nor right.' Evidently, he had chosen the wrong sheep. His so-called friends on the right had hardly leapt to his defence when he was accused of planting the bomb that was found in the toilets of the Assemblée Nationale. And Pesquet's clownish retort had scarcely served his cause: 'Why the hell would I have tried to blow the bogs up when it's the only useful place in the whole building?'

He peered out at the street, distinguishing the dark figures outside from the reflections that flitted across the screens and mirrors. From a certain angle, a man who seemed to be heading for the Place Saint-Germain-des-Prés would suddenly vanish into himself and set off in the opposite direction. Sitting in the window of the Lipp, one could inspect a passing woman from the front and then, without turning one's head, complete the assessment from the rear. Robert Pesquet materialized from neither direction. He looked up at the wall above the telephone and the humidor. The clock, for once in agreement with its reflections, said midnight. He waited another twenty or thirty minutes, then walked out into the street, feeling the car keys in his pocket.

The October nights had turned chilly. He climbed smartly into the driving seat, turned the key and started the engine at the first attempt.

The Peugeot 403 had been the result of a careful selection process, like a stylish outfit that appeared to owe its elegance to chance. It was the perfect car for a prominent centre-left, anti-Gaullist politician with a foot placed quite firmly in the socialist camp. With its (purely hypothetical) top speed of 128 kph and its neat but almost dowdy corporation, it exuded robustness and reliability; yet it also had a certain modestly aspirational quality. The leather trim, the cigarette lighter and the fog lamps, which came as standard, looked to a future of international travel and freedom from material cares. The gear lever was mounted on the steering column, which provided an extra seat up front. Despite the folding armrests and the reclining front seats, the 403 seemed more likely to be used for holidays with a medium-sized family than for escapades with a mistress.

He drove across the square, heading east, then signalled right to turn into the Rue de Seine.

At that moment, according to what was, for a time, the only available account, a small dark car took the same corner rather too tightly and almost wedged him up against the kerb. There was nothing unusual in this, but, as he told reporters shortly afterwards, it made him 'vigilant'. These were, after all, troubled times. He was hardly the most faithful advocate of decolonization – as Minister of Justice, he had called for Algerian liberation movements to be crushed by military might – but as the would-be champion of whatever an anti-Gaullist party would have to represent, he was more or less obliged to be in favour of withdrawal, and there were many in France who were murderously opposed to any politician who even hinted at Algerian independence. Only three days before, *Paris-Presse* had reported that a pro-French-Algeria hit squad had crossed the Spanish border and was operating somewhere in France.

He accelerated gently along the Rue de Seine, which turns into the Rue de Tournon. Up ahead, he could see the dome of the Senate. A right turn would take him to the corner of the Rue Guynemer, where he lived. But when he glanced in the rear-view mirror, the other car was still there, and so, instead of heading for home, he turned left, as he later explained, 'in order to give myself time to think'. The Boulevard Saint-Michel lay ahead; the railings of the Luxembourg were to his right, the silent bookshops of the Rue de Médicis to his left.

By his own account, the following sequence of events, from start to finish, must have taken little more than two minutes. On the Square Médicis, the dark car surged alongside and tried to run him off the road. There was no longer any doubt in his mind. He jammed the accelerator to the floor; the 403 responded almost instantly and shot along the boulevard. In the rear-view mirror, he saw the other car fall behind. At the first turn – the dimly lit Rue Auguste-Comte, which runs between the Luxembourg and the Observatoire – he flung the car to the right, pulled over to the left and opened the door. He vaulted the metal railings, took four or five strides across the grass and flattened himself on the ground.

As he lay face down on the damp grass, he heard the sound of skidding tyres and a rattle of shots from an automatic weapon. It would have been an ironic end for a man who had escaped six times from prisoner-of-war camps to be gunned down in a Paris park. In 1940, when he had been wounded near Stenay on the Meuse, the stretcher party had had to leave him in the open, exposed to the strafing of a German fighter plane. Perhaps it was that experience that gave him the sangfroid to stand up, run across the lawn and jump over the hedge that borders the Avenue de l'Observatoire. He squeezed himself into the corner of the entrance of no. 5, and rang the bell. As he did so, he heard the assassins' car roar off into the night.

By now, the whole *quartier* was awake. The police were on the scene in no time at all, closely followed by journalists. Television cameras were set up and flash-bulbs blazed. The seriousness of the incident was plain to see: seven bullet holes in the front and rear doors of the 403. The senator showed exemplary calm but was obviously shaken.

It was now just after one o'clock. After taking down the details – the chase along the boulevard, a small car containing two, maybe three armed men – the reporters dashed to all-night bars to telephone their news-rooms or raced back across the river to offices in the second *arrondissement*. They were just in time for the night editors to insert brief reports: 'Senator In Foiled Assassination Attempt'. Next day (Saturday, 17 October), it was front-page news in all the papers. For once, the political news was as thrilling as a crime novel, and the sub-editors had an easy job:

DEATH CHASE IN THE OBSERVATORY GARDENS!

TWO HEADLIGHTS IN THE NIGHT . . . IT WAS THE KILLERS!

There were maps and diagrams, with dotted lines and arrows showing exactly where the senator had jumped the hedge on the Avenue de l'Observatoire and where he had been standing when the killers drove away. There were photographs of the bullet holes in the bodywork, and of the garden railings, which appeared to be about four feet high. (The senator was obviously a man who had kept himself in trim.)

Fully aware of the danger, as he continued to drive along, M. François Mitterrand was devising a plan that would give his pursuers the slip ... He was able to survive the premeditated assassination attempt thanks to his extraordinary calm under fire, his presence of mind and his encyclopedic knowledge of the Latin Quarter.

The shooting in the Jardins de l'Observatoire rang alarm bells all over France. New security measures were introduced. French-Algeria sympathizers were visited by the police and had their apartments searched. Border controls were tightened. Moderate left-wing politicians and commentators warned of a possible fascist coup d'état and demanded swift and effective reprisals. The Republic was in danger. The crackdown was so sudden and severe that some right-wing politicians claimed that it was all a cunning attempt to justify political repression and to discredit the patriotic cause of French Algeria.

Senator Mitterrand himself showed admirable restraint. Even at the height of his parliamentary career, he had never been so much in demand. He was besieged by news photographers and pestered for interviews. However, in statements to the press, he confined himself to a few careful words: 'Since feelings are running high at the moment, I do not want to say anything that might inflame the situation, though simple logic would suggest that the explanation for this attack lies in the climate of political passion that has been created by extremist groups.'

For a man who had been sliding down the greasy pole, it was an extraordinary turn of events. From one day to the next, he became the leading champion of the fight against right-wing terrorism. Messages of sympathy and support reached him from all over France. An assassination attempt was scarcely something to celebrate, but a good politician knows how to profit from adversity. François Mitterrand was back where he belonged. De Gaulle would no longer be able to ignore him, and the socialists who had shunned him because of his dubious past would welcome him as a battle-hardened hero in the long struggle against the Gaullists.

3. CLOT

AT THAT TIME, there was, realistically, only one man who could be entrusted with the delicate and potentially dangerous job of tracking down the terrorists. Only one man commanded the respect of politicians, criminals and the media, and had sufficient public prestige to ensure that the investigation would be seen as exhaustive and fair.

Commissioner Georges Clot, head of the Brigade Criminelle, was an affable and modest man, who found his own dazzling reputation something of an embarrassment. He had been featured in so many crime magazines, under titles such as 'Commissioner Clot Against Dédé la Gabardine', that some people believed him to be a fictional character. A year before the attempted assassination of Senator Mitterrand, Clot had appeared on a television programme devoted to Simenon, the creator of Maigret, and had tried to explain exactly how the adventures of Inspector Maigret differed from the unexciting drudgery of real detective work. But since Clot himself was one of the models for Maigret, he had failed, despite the convincingly dreary setting of metal file cabinets and plastic chairs, to dampen the romance.

It was precisely because Clot had known the allure of criminal investigation that he was such an effective policeman. He came from a large family in the heart of the remote Aveyron. His father, a village postman, had destined Georges for the teaching profession, but one day, a cousin had arrived from Paris with a friend who worked for the Sûreté. Young Clot had listened to the man's tales of impenetrable enigmas and brilliant, retrospectively obvious solutions, and discovered his true vocation.

A long time passed before he was able to get his teeth into a genuine mystery. It was four or five years before the Second World War. He was a junior detective in the Grandes-Carrières precinct in the north of Paris when the sort of case he had always dreamt of finally landed on his desk. A concierge in the Rue de Damrémont had reported the mysterious death of an old Russian officer. The body was lying on the bed, dressed in the uniform of a hussar. When his dolman was unbuttoned, the man was found to have died from a deep stab-wound. A blood-smeared sabre, which matched the wound, had been hidden in a cupboard. Strangely, there was no damage to the dolman. Its gold braid was intact and nothing had pierced the cloth.

That night, Clot examined the puzzle with mounting excitement. A shadowy tale began to form in his mind: a murder disguised as a natural death; a murderer who simultaneously covered his tracks and left incriminating evidence. Perhaps the murder in the Rue de Damrémont was the obscure dénouement of a drama that had its roots in the darkest days of Czarist Russia ...

Next morning, a letter arrived at the police station. It had been written and posted the day before by the dead man. Having decided to kill himself, he had administered the fatal blow and used the last seconds of his waning life to replace the sabre in the cupboard and to button up the splendid uniform in which he wished to be buried. For Clot, this was a huge disappointment but a salutary lesson: nine times out of ten, ingenious reasoning was a complete waste of time.

Then came the war, which saw Clot digging a tunnel for six months in a Moravian prisoner-of-war camp only to be caught a few yards before the end. He was repatriated, and spent the rest of the war as a policeman in Paris, pretending to root out members of the Résistance but in fact supplying them with false passports. After the war, he accepted the nightmarish task of arresting and interviewing policemen who had collaborated too closely with the Nazis, and showed an admirable determination to distinguish force of circumstance from malice.

Since then, Clot had run the Brigade Criminelle too efficiently for any Sherlock-Holmesian excitement. He was happily married to his job and immune to the allure of mystery. He did however allow himself an occasional furtive expedition to Montmartre and the Marché aux Puces. By posing as an art-collector, he uncovered hundreds of forged paintings – mostly Picassos and Utrillos. When the canvasses began to clutter up the corridors, he hung them on his walls and lent them to his colleagues. After five years of undercover bargain-hunting, the offices on the Quai des Orfèvres housed the world's largest collection of bogus masterpieces. No doubt, among those objects of beauty and desire lurked some genuine, priceless originals that should have been sent across the river to the Louvre. But since experts and even the painters themselves could not always tell the difference, there was little sense in troubling the art world with futile mysteries.

WHEN NEWS OF the shooting in the Jardins de l'Observatoire reached him that night in October 1959, Georges Clot felt the old stirrings of detective fever. Not only was this a matter of national importance, it also promised to be a satisfyingly tricky hunt for professional killers who must have covered their tracks in interesting ways. The police car raced along the boulevard and stopped where some people were listening to a man in a dark overcoat. The man was pale and trembling but evidently able to keep an audience hanging on his every word.

Commissioner Clot greeted his former boss (he had known the senator as Minister of Interior), and took his statement. The details supplied by Mitterrand were understandably sketchy, but there were peculiarities about the case that – experience told him – would soon resolve themselves into definite leads. In fact (perhaps it was the late hour or the eminence of the victim), it had the slightly skewed, dreamlike quality of the most seductively enigmatic cases. Even before he had sent his best men to interview the waiters at the Lipp and the inhabitants of the *quartier*, a thousand questions were taunting his mind with tantalizing ambiguities.

For instance, it was well known that French-Algeria activists planned their operations with military precision, for the excellent reason that most of them were high-ranking officers in the French army. Why, then, had they – or their hired assassins – used a vehicle that was unable to keep up with a 403, which was hardly a gazelle among motor cars? Assuming the information to be correct, the whole thing had taken an inordinate amount of time: at least ten minutes to drive 1.6 kilometres. It would have been the slowest car chase in history. Perhaps the senator had lingered in the vicinity of the Lipp, or perhaps the assassins had waited – but why? – before riddling the 403 with bullets.

Discrepancies like these were often explained as the investigation proceeded. Even a man with Mitterrand's self-possession was likely to misremember things that immediately preceded such a shocking event. Apart from his vagueness about the time, it was impossible not to be struck by the fact that he had mentioned a Square Médicis, which, strictly speaking, did not exist, at least not under that name. Insignificant details, no doubt, but details that established the possible unreliability of the victim's own testimony.

The forensic team raised a new set of questions. They festooned the senator's car with metal rods that made it look like a wounded boar – one rod for each bullet hole. There were seven in all, poking out of the front and rear doors of the passenger side in a neat arc. One thing was immediately obvious: all the rods were at right angles to the doors, which meant that, when the shots were fired, the assassins' car had not been moving.

He was, in short, dealing with professional killers who had had the self-assurance to stop their car and shoot a man whom they presumed to be lying flat across the front seats or cowering on the floor. One of the bullets had in fact punctured the driver's seat. But these were also professional killers who had failed, twice, to run their target off the road and then almost lost him on the Boulevard Saint-Michel. And if they were such confident and cold-blooded killers, why had they not taken the obvious precaution of peering into the car and then looking to see whether their target was lying on the ground a few yards away or – stupidly, it had to be said – standing up, running across the grass and jumping over a hedge?

Then there was the matter of the seven bullet holes. According to the forensic team, the killers had used a Sten gun, probably left over from the war. Four years of Nazi occupation had filled the cellars and tool sheds of France with illicit weapons and produced a generation of men who considered illegal activity an expression of personal freedom. It was an odd choice of weapon all the same: Sten guns were notoriously unreliable. But even a Sten could fire thirty rounds in three seconds. Why, then, had only seven shots been fired? (There was no sign that any bullets had missed the car.) Was this the work of some previously unknown and under-rehearsed group of poorly funded terrorists? Was it intended simply as a warning? (But there were easier and safer ways to intimidate a politician.) Or was it – Clot dreaded to think – a covert operation carried out by French intelligence agents with the aim of influencing public opinion?

All in all, it was a captivating case. Phone taps and searches of suspects' homes turned up nothing; the hit squad from Spain gave no sign of life; there were witnesses who had heard the shooting, but no one had actually seen it happen. And yet, as the days passed, Clot felt a strange reluctance to pursue the investigation. It looked increasingly like the sort of case that would be solved by the sudden appearance of a piece of evidence that no amount of ingenuity could have produced. The more he saw of it, the less enticing it became. It is entirely to Georges Clot's credit as a policeman that the anticipated joy of discovery had already begun to fade when, on 22 October, he stuffed the files into his metal cabinet and slammed the drawer shut with a bang that had the fake Picassos and Utrillos dancing on their hooks.

4. POSTE RESTANTE

THE MÉDICIS POST OFFICE stands opposite the Senate on the Rue de Vaugirard, at a point where the wind always seems to be blowing up a storm, probably because of the inordinate length of the street (the Rue de Vaugirard is the longest in Paris), which funnels the south-westerlies into the heart of the Left Bank.

Just after lunch, the ladies who sat behind the counters saw the doors swing open and a posse of men burst into the building as though blown in by a gust of wind. One was a lawyer, dressed in his robes; another – who seemed to be the focus of attention – looked too silly and fidgety to be genuinely important. This, and the presence of several cameramen, convinced some of the *postières* that a film was being made, and they reached for their combs and powder compacts.

Few would have suspected that the weaselly little man in the disreputable-looking raincoat had ever sat on the benches of the Assemblée Nationale. On the other hand, the smirk on his face and his curiously flinching gait made it easy to imagine him creeping into the parliamentary toilets with a bomb. He stubbed out his cigarette, walked up to the counter labelled 'Poste restante', and asked for any mail addressed to M. Robert Pesquet. An envelope was produced, which he left lying on the counter. Then he turned around and said, like a bad actor, 'Maître Dreyer-Durfer, kindly take this letter, which I have not touched, place it in your briefcase and deposit it in a safe for the examining magistrate.'

The lawyer slid the letter off the counter, held it up between thumb and forefinger, and addressed the post office at large: 'I am taking this letter, M. Pesquet, untouched by yourself, which I shall place in a safe, as you have just requested, in which it shall remain at the disposal of the examining magistrate.' Then, turning to the flustered clerk, he said, in the same stentorian voice, 'I, Maître Dreyer-Durfer, request that you make a note of all that has just occurred.'

'Yes, sir,' stammered the woman, 'Do you want me to make a note of the words, too?'

A look of inexhaustible patience appeared on the lawyer's face. 'The words above all, my good lady, if you please.'

With that, Maître Dreyer-Durfer led the way out of the post office, followed by his smirking client, who quickly lit another cigarette in the lee of his black robe.

ROBERT PESQUET, former carpenter, former *député*, stool-pigeon of the far right and member of several thuggish 'patriot' groups, had single-handedly solved the mystery of the assassination attempt. Two days before, a group of journalists had heard him make his astonishing claim in his lawyer's chambers in the Rue de la Pompe. Naturally, Senator Mitterrand had denied everything. But now, Pesquet had played his trump card: a letter written and posted to himself forty-eight hours before the events.

The letter was read out to the lawyers and their two clients in the chambers of Judge Braunschweig at the Palais de Justice. '*I shall describe in exact detail the bogus assassination attempt of the Jardins de l'Observatoire that will take place on the night of 15–16 October according to the plan devised by M. Mitterrand . . .*'

According to Pesquet's letter, Mitterrand had come to him with a scheme that would save them both from political obscurity. The letter went on to describe everything, in the future tense, exactly as it had occurred, from the Brasserie Lipp to the Jardins de l'Observatoire. Pesquet had followed in his Simca with a dim but playful peasant who worked on his estate at Beuvron-en-Auge. The Sten gun had been borrowed from a friend. The only changes Pesquet had to point out to the judge concerned the few minutes during which Mitterrand had been lying on the wet grass, waiting to be assassinated. First, two lovers had been kissing under the trees; then a taxi had dropped off a fare. After driving around the block several times, the Simca had stopped alongside the 403, and Pesquet had heard a voice coming from the darkness: 'Shoot, for God's sake! What the hell are you doing?' Everything else had gone according to plan: the Sten gun sputtered and banged; Pesquet drove on to the Boulevard du Montparnasse, parked the car and returned on foot in time to admire Mitterrand's suave performance in front of the cameras.

The judge laid down the letter and looked up to see the unusual spectacle of half a dozen speechless lawyers. For the first and only time, François Mitterrand appeared to lose his self-control. He turned pale and made a sound that might have been a sob. He could hear the cackling of his enemies and the hysterical laughter of twenty-six million voters. His career was in ruins. Whether or not Pesquet was telling the truth, this was the kind of humiliation from which no politician ever recovered.

Even in this, his darkest hour, 'the Fox' remembered the lessons he had learned in the war. A man who had escaped six times from prisoner-of-war camps was not so easily defeated. It was unfortunate, of course, that Pesquet had accused him of faking the assassination attempt before revealing the letter, and that Mitterrand had accused Pesquet of slander. It was also unfortunate that he had allowed himself to bask in all the praise and sympathy. After Pesquet's *poste restante* trick, he could hardly claim to be entirely innocent. And yet, there was one possible explanation that just might be accepted as the truth ...

This was the version of events that Mitterrand gave to Judge Braunschweig and the nation. He confessed that he had indeed met

Pesquet once or twice before the shooting. Pesquet had come to him with a terrible tale: his old French-Algeria friends, to whom he owed a great deal of money, had ordered him to assassinate Mitterrand. If Pesquet refused, he would certainly be killed, and so he had begged Mitterrand to help him out. A faked assassination attempt would let Pesquet off the hook and make it less likely that anyone else would try to kill Mitterrand. In a spirit of Christian charity, Mitterrand had agreed to play along. Their last meeting was to have taken place at the Brasserie Lipp. Though Pesquet had not shown up, the rest of the operation had gone as planned. It was only when Pesquet had accused him publicly of organizing the whole charade that Mitterrand realized what had happened: he was the victim of a right-wing plot to destroy his political career.

Though not entirely convincing, this would at least present him in a slightly better light. The newspapers were unimpressed. No one expected politicians to obey the law, but they were supposed to retain a certain dignity and savoir-faire. One of the least insulting headlines appeared in *L'Aurore*: 'To think that this booby used to be Minister of the Interior!'

JUDGE BRAUNSCHWEIG made the best of a bad job. Somehow, the guilty had to be punished, but without causing further damage to the international standing of the French Republic. The world must know that Paris was not Shanghai or Casablanca. Pesquet and his sidekick were charged with possession of an illegal weapon, while Mitterrand, having wasted the time of Commissioner Clot with a pointless investigation, was charged with contempt of court. These were comparatively minor charges, which would probably be dropped in any case.

Surprisingly, the Senate voted to strip Mitterrand of his senatorial immunity, but by then the case had entered the boundless, foggy realm of judicial procedure whose decaying files are occasionally washed away by a tide of indifference and secret negotiations. Biographers and historians who have gone in search of the unrecognizable fragments of truth have seen various oily personalities emerge from the mist: Prime Minister Debré, who had been accused of ordering an illegal execution in Algeria; Pesquet's lawyer, Tixier-Vignancour, who defended right-wing terrorists and stood as a presidential candidate; and Tixier-Vignancour's bullish campaign manager, Jean-Marie Le Pen. These were some of the men whom Mitterrand suspected of plotting his downfall. None of them ever confessed to any involvement in the affair.

Pesquet himself was forced to leave the country and has since invented so many different versions of the incident that even if he now made an honest confession, it would be worthless. In a letter published by *Le Monde* in 1965, he unexpectedly lent support to Mitterrand's presidential campaign by confessing that Mitterrand had organized the fake assassination attempt in good faith. Later, however, he retracted his statement, claiming that friends of Mitterrand had paid him forty thousand francs to write the letter. The retraction itself earned him a few more francs when he published it in a book titled *My Genuine-Fake Assassination Attempt on Mitterrand: The Truth at Last*.

The 'Affaire de l'Observatoire' reached its practical conclusion that winter, when, in a seemingly needless reconstruction arranged by Commissioner Clot, Senator Mitterrand's Peugeot 403 was taken to a quiet avenue in the Bois de Vincennes, peppered with bullets and crashed into a tree. The original shooting had left it relatively unscathed. After the 'reconstruction', all that remained was a tangled, windowless wreck.

'The Fox' now entered the period that came to be known as his 'crossing of the desert'. Having first demanded that Mitterrand be prosecuted, President de Gaulle changed his mind and decided that the incident should never again be mentioned, and that his own party would never try to profit from it. Some said that he was trying to protect his Prime Minister, Michel Debré, from any embarrassing revelations that Mitterrand might make about his role in the murder of a general in Algeria. Others, close to de Gaulle, said that he wanted to uphold the dignity of the office, since – incredible as it seemed at the time – Mitterrand might one day be President. Of course, de Gaulle knew full well that Mitterrand would never be allowed to forget. For years afterwards, though the *députés* of the Assemblée Nationale maintained a courteous silence on the subject, it was extraordinary how often the word 'Observatoire' cropped up in their speeches.

5. PETIT-CLAMART
(EPILOGUE)

A WEDNESDAY EVENING in late August 1962: it was the time of year when a parking space, a taxi or an empty telephone box were easy to find. Cafés were filled with stacks of chairs and barricaded with pinball machines. Traffic was at such a low ebb that the obelisk in the centre of the Place de la Concorde could be reached on foot. In the Rue du Faubourg Saint-Honoré, the usual group of white-gloved policemen stood around the pillared entrance of no. 55, making it possible for tourists to identify it as the Élysée Palace, the official residence of the President of the French Republic.

A man holding a motorcycle helmet who had been examining the window display of a Russian antiques shop on the other side of the street looked through the iron gates and saw General de Gaulle walk down the steps of the palace. (It *was* the General, not the man who sometimes impersonated him.) He watched de Gaulle usher his wife into a black Citroën DS before joining her in the back seat. The officer who climbed in next to the chauffeur was the de Gaulles' son-in-law, Alain de Boissieu. Behind them, in another DS, were four 'gorillas' or 'super-cops'. Their names, too, were known to the man who was watching from the street.

The meeting of the Council of Ministers had just ended. The entire meeting had been devoted to the question of Algeria. In June, the Évian Accords had been approved by a referendum, and Algeria was now an independent state, but some of the Algerian-born French-men who were incensed at de Gaulle's betrayal of the *pieds noirs* had vowed to continue the struggle. There had been a spate of bank robberies that bore the mark of the right-wing commando group, the Organisation de l'Armée Secrète. A high-ranking OAS official, André 'the Monocle' Canal, had been arrested in Paris by undercover policemen pretending to clean the facade of his building. He was carrying a letter in which the treasurer of the OAS was asked to make available a sum of one million francs; evidently, a big operation was being planned.

Faced with this army of embittered patriots and mercenaries, the government was trying to come up with a convincing package of anti-terrorist measures and to decide what to do with the thousands of disgruntled refugees who were flooding into Marseille. The meeting had ended only when glazed eyes and rumbling stomachs made further discussion pointless. Several ministers had rushed away immediately to go on holiday before the next emergency. Despite the late hour, the President, his wife and son-in-law were to be driven to the aerodrome at Villacoublay, sixteen kilometres to the south-west. From there, they would be flown to their home at Colombey-les-Deux-Églises.

The usual precautions had been taken, which is to say, not as many as de Gaulle's security officers would have liked. The longest-serving police commissioner attached to the Élysée, Jacques Cantelaube, had recently handed in his resignation in protest at de Gaulle's abandonment of the colony. There were fears that too many people knew the routes that the motorcade usually took. Sometimes, de Gaulle managed to slip out of the Élysée with his chauffeur and had himself driven through the city with the presidential pennant flapping in the breeze for the convenience of any madman with a rifle. Even when he was in a cooperative mood, he accepted only the lightest protection: two outriders in front, another DS behind, with two policemen on motorbikes bringing up the rear. This was the small convoy that scrunched across the gravel and swerved smoothly out into the Rue du Faubourg-Saint-Honoré that Wednesday evening at 7.55 p.m.

The man who had been watching from the other side of the street walked towards his motorbike, which was parked outside a café. At the same moment, inside the Élysée, someone picked up a telephone, dialled the number of an apartment at 2, Avenue Victor-Hugo in Meudon, and said, '*It's number two.*'

So MANY ATTEMPTS had been made on de Gaulle's life that he was beginning to look like a fantastically lucky character who happens to move just when the chimney falls from the roof or who bends to tie his shoelace when the custard pie is launched. In September 1961, the presidential motorcade had been heading for Colombey-les-Deux-Églises along *route nationale* 19. It had passed Pont-sur-Seine at 110 kph and was descending towards the village of Crancey through a landscape of open fields and small woods. Road-menders had left a large pile of sand by the side of the road. Inside the sand was a propane cylinder packed with forty-three kilograms of plastic explosive and a fuel can containing twenty kilograms of petrol, oil and soap flakes. A man was watching through binoculars. He pressed the button on his remote-control unit. A storm of sand and gravel engulfed the DS. De Gaulle shouted, *'Marchez! Marchez!'*, and the driver accelerated through a wall of flames. No one was hurt. For some reason, the detonator had become separated from the plastic explosive and only the fuel can had ignited. With this arrangement, the forensic expert explained, 'it was like trying to set fire to a tree trunk with a sheet of paper'.

Since then, the attacks had become more frequent. Though there was no longer any hope of changing the political situation, the OAS was bent on revenge. Even in the heart of Paris, de Gaulle was being hunted like a rabbit. It seemed to be only a matter of time before he was shot or blown up. A whole division of the Brigade Criminelle was working night and day to find the faceless enemy. They scanned the *fiches* that were filled in by hotel guests. They photographed suspects using periscopes poking through the roof vents of trades-men's vans – an idea they had borrowed from the OAS. They analysed mysterious acronyms and other political graffiti that appeared in the corridors of the Métro. As the ministers had just been told, the intelligence services were drowning in data and had to spend most of their time eliminating useless information.

The OAS, meanwhile, had some excellent sources of its own – a cleaning lady at the Élysée Palace and (it later transpired) Com-missioner Jacques Cantelaube. They knew the different routes that were taken by the motorcade. They knew that sometimes the black car was a decoy and that de Gaulle was riding in the yellow or the blue DS. Even if the informer in the Élysée failed to ascertain the route, they had simply to post someone in the street outside or at the Villacoublay aerodrome with access to a telephone. Fortunately, so far, something had always gone wrong.

Earlier that year, the killers' van – a Renault *estafette* – had managed to pull alongside the presidential DS as it approached the Pont de Grenelle along the Quai Louis Blériot. They were winding down the windows when a little 4CV slipped in between the two vehicles and the DS was lost in traffic. On another occasion, the OAS commandos known as 'the Limp', 'the Pipe', 'Angel-Face' (a Hungarian mercenary) and 'Didier' (Lieutenant-Colonel Bastien-Thiry) had been waiting for the tip-off in the cafés that surround the Porte d'Orléans Métro station, unaware that a postal strike had put the phone system out of action. Even the multi-pronged operation that was planned for de Gaulle's visit to eastern France (involving a booby-trapped level-crossing and trained dogs carrying remote-controlled explosives) had been comprehensively wrecked. As 'Didier' later confessed before his execution, 'All along, we had the impression of coming up against what you'd have to say was sheer bad luck. It dogged us to the very end.'

The closest they had come to hitting 'the Big Target' was one of the operations code-named 'Chamois'. (This was the name used by the OAS for any operation requiring a long-range rifle.) On the evening of 20 May, a search of an apartment in one of the new blocks that had been built on the site of the former Vel' d'Hiv at 13, Rue du Docteur-Finlay turned up a package labelled 'Algiers – Paris Orly'. It contained a bazooka and three rockets. The secret services knew the target – de Gaulle – but not the place and the time. The OAS had discovered that, between eight and nine o'clock every evening, the old painter who lived above the antiques shop at 86, Rue du Faubourg-Saint-Honoré closed his shutters for the night. The windows of his living room looked directly through the gateway opposite and, in a slightly descending line, at the entrance of the Élysée Palace. On 23 May, de Gaulle was to receive the visit of the President of Mauritania. The protocol for such visits never varied. When the visitor's car entered the courtyard, de Gaulle emerged from the palace and stood still at the top of the steps for at least ninety seconds. On 21 May, the plot was discovered; on 22 May, the painter closed his shutters and went to bed as usual; and on 23 May, de Gaulle stood on the steps and welcomed the Mauritanian President into the Élysée Palace.

That Wednesday evening, after leaving the Élysée at 7.55 p.m., the motorcade slid through the August evening traffic, crossed the Pont Alexandre III and headed into the low sun and the south-western suburbs. Seven minutes later, it left the city at the Porte de Châtillon. With an occasional blast of sirens, it would cover the next eight kilometres at over 70 kph before turning sharp right for the aerodrome.

At that moment, seven and a half kilometres down the road, the owner of the Ducretet-Thomson television showroom in Petit-Clamart was winding down his steel security grating before going to collect his car from the garage.

Trapped between the outer suburbs and the girdle of expressways, Petit-Clamart consisted of the jumbled remnants of every phase of its development since the days when it was a zone of quarries and vegetable fields. There were some pebble-dash houses, an Antar station, some shops and vacant lots. Village life – what remained of it – was represented by a few clumps of privet hedge, a pot of geraniums and a birdcage on a sooty windowsill. Petit-Clamart was not a place where anyone stopped on purpose, which is why the owner of the showroom was surprised later on not to have noticed the car that was parked across the road in the Rue du Bois.

The car was a Citroën ID. Two hundred metres up the avenue, in the direction of Paris, a Peugeot 403 was parked on the pavement. On the other side of the road, a yellow *estafette* faced south-west, its rear windows pointing towards Paris. Together, the three vehicles formed a triangle. The time was 8.08 p.m. A man had just rattled open the sliding door of the *estafette* and was urinating behind a hedge, his head turned in the direction of Paris. A few cars went past with their wipers on. The light rain made the evening unusually gloomy for August, and some of the cars in the distance coming from Paris had turned on their headlights.

He ran with his trousers still undone, shouting something at the van. '*Itt vannak!*' He hooked his hand on the edge of the door and swung himself in, still yelling, '*ITT VANNAK!*', which is Hungarian for 'They're here!'

The motorcade was approaching the crossroads at 90 kph, sounding its sirens like an express train. A driver who was heading for Paris pulled over and saw a barrier of tiny flames crackle across the road before he felt his index finger leap off the steering wheel. Alain de Boissieu shouted to his parents-in-law, 'Get down!' a split second before the men in the 403 and the *estafette* opened fire. Television screens exploded in the showroom. In the Trianon café, which was closed for the season, bullets punctured the vinyl seats. For a second or two, the scream of accelerating engines drowned out the racket of four M1s, an MP40 and two FM24/29 machine-guns.

Immobilized by the crossfire, de Gaulle's DS would be exposed to the direct fire of the gunmen who were waiting at the corner of the Rue du Bois. This was the plan that had been worked out in the apartment at Meudon with toy cars on a table.

Their machine-guns juddering in their hands, they saw the outriders swerve and surge; they saw the flickering imperfections of a scene suddenly sprayed with bullets; they saw the flash of chrome and lacquered fuselage as the DS, driven by the man who had accelerated through the wall of flames near Pont-sur-Seine, shot past with a slur of tyres and roared into the sunset, leaving Petit-Clamart looking even tattier than usual.

Three minutes later, President de Gaulle stepped out of the DS onto the runway at Villacoublay. Little cubes of glass trickled from his suit onto the tarmac. His wife said, 'I hope the chickens are all right.' She was thinking of Thursday's lunch, which was in the boot of the DS, but the policemen thought she was referring to them, since a *poulet* is a 'cop'. De Gaulle, who was never effusive, thanked his driver and his son-in-law, and said calmly, 'It was a close thing this time.' He seemed more upset by what appeared to be the pitiful ineptitude of the OAS: '*Ils ont tiré comme des cochons.*' ('They couldn't hit a barn door at ten paces.')

Less than an hour later, the *estafette* was found in the Bois de Meudon. The machine-guns were still inside it, along with a bomb that was supposed to have destroyed the evidence. The fuse had been lit but for some reason had gone out. Most of the conspirators were rounded up within a fortnight and only 'the Limp' was never caught. At the crime scene, the investigators found a hundred cartridges scattered about the crossroads. It seemed incredible that only one person had been hurt. (The driver bound for Paris had to have his index finger bandaged.) About ten bullets had hit the car, and most of them had been fired too low to do much damage. Despite the mole in the Élysée, no one had told the killers that the presidential DS was equipped with bullet-proof tyres and hydraulic suspension. Even so, they seem to have suffered almost unbelievable bad luck. Two of the machine-guns had jammed, and 'the Limp' had had to change his clip in mid-volley.

Amazed by de Gaulle's good fortune, and embarrassed by their failure, some members of the OAS came to suspect that this and other attacks had been orchestrated by secret-service agents with the aim of discrediting the OAS and turning the President into 'a living miracle'. This also appeared to be the view of television commentators, according to Prime Minister Pompidou, who was told of their sarcastic reporting by a friend who owned a television set. How else, the journalists seemed to say, could one explain the rapid capture of the culprits, the self-extinguishing fuse, de Gaulle's invincibility and all the other minor miracles?

No evidence of secret-service involvement has ever come to light, and even if it had done, it would only have enhanced de Gaulle's reputation for extraordinary competence and guile. In all the emergencies he had faced in the last twenty years, he had never made a secret of the fact that it was sometimes necessary to deceive the electorate in the interests of the nation. Most of the electorate admired him for saying so. It was commonly believed that without a leader who knew how to fool his enemies, France could never survive in a world of treachery and violence.

FOUR WEEKS AFTER the outrage, on the evening of Thursday, 20 September, the funereal form of the living miracle flickered out at the passing traffic at the crossroads in Petit-Clamart. President de Gaulle had decided that the time had come to deliver an important message to the electorate. The irony was probably not lost on the owner of the recently repaired Ducretet-Thomson television showroom: historic broadcasts like this were always good for business.

President de Gaulle sat in the Salon Doré at the Élysée Palace. A cartoonist might have depicted him as a human lighthouse in a storm. His eyebrows plunged and soared like seagulls; his vast hands reached out as though to salvage that fragile infant, the French Republic. Behind him were massed the silent representatives of French culture in their leather bindings.

> *Françaises, Français* . . . You and I have lived through so much toil, tears and blood, we have known the same hopes, the same passions and the same triumphs, that there exists between us a unique and special bond. This bond which unites us is the source of the power that is vested in me, and of the responsibility that comes with that power . . .

In his apartment in the Rue Guynemer, François Mitterrand was listening to the broadcast with a mixture of rancour and admiration. De Gaulle delivered his address with impressive, agonizing slowness. His tone suggested long deliberation rather than a reaction to passing events. A wave of sympathy had followed the outrage, and de Gaulle was now on the highest pinnacle of his career since the Liberation. No one would accuse him of weakness if he decided to retire to the peace of Colombey-les-Deux-Églises and to leave the Élysée to a younger, more vigorous man . . .

> . . . In spite of everything, personal liberty has been preserved. The grave and painful problem of decolonization has been solved. Enormous labours lie ahead of us, for a nation that continues to live continues to progress. But no one seriously believes that progress can occur if we renounce our solid institutions. The nation would be cast into the abyss . . .

It was perhaps at this point that François Mitterrand found the title of his next book. It would be a searing indictment of Gaullist policies and practice, and of the 'uncrowned dictator' himself . . .

> The keystone of our régime is the presidency. It follows that, instead of being chosen by a relatively small constituency of elected

representatives, the President must receive his mandate directly from the people . . .

He would call his book '*Le Coup d'état permanent*' . . .

I have therefore decided to propose that henceforth the President be elected by universal suffrage . . .

It was, one had to admit, a master stroke. The Senate and a broad coalition of *députés* were opposed to the institution of a 'Bonapartist' régime. Too much power would be vested in one man ... But the voters, oblivious to the long-term consequences, would inevitably turn out to glorify the living miracle, just as their great-grandfathers had rushed to the ballot boxes to ratify the coup d'état of Napoleon III.

A month later, de Gaulle's proposal was accepted by almost two-thirds of the electorate. The national elections that followed were a triumph for the Gaullists. There were also some small but significant victories for the anti-Gaullist coalition. In the Nièvre *département*, a man who, only three years before, had – for reasons that remained obscure – prostrated himself on a wet lawn in the Latin Quarter while a Norman peasant fired a machine-gun at his 403, regained his seat in the Assemblée Nationale. He would have to sit out the next few years on the opposition benches, enduring taunts and sly allusions to hired assassins and observatories. But even de Gaulle was not immortal. In five, ten or fifteen years, age would achieve what several thousand guns, bombs and hand-grenades had failed to do. De Gaulle would enter the realm of legend, and the skies over Paris would seem to darken with his death. Then, perhaps, in that twilight, the Fox would finally have his day.

EXPANDING THE DOMAIN OF THE POSSIBLE

I. A. i.

THE CAMPUS OF Nanterre-Paris X had been built among shanty-towns beyond the western edge of the city, on seventy-nine acres of former *terrain militaire*. The origin of the name 'Nanterre' is Nempthor, from Nemptodurum, meaning 'hill-fort of the sacred wood or clearing'. The earth consisted mainly of compacted garbage and builders' rubble. Cars circulated easily, but not pedestrians. Thirteen thousand students were housed in buildings made of concrete blocks and windows that were always dirty. Some of the rooms looked down on shacks where immigrant workers from Portugal and North Africa lived under sheets of corrugated iron. It was 1967. On beaches in the south of France, naked breasts and perfect tans were a common sight. Women used sun-tan lotion; men lay on their stomachs in the sand. Some people went to naturist colonies in pine forests and formed temporary *ménages* based on sexual excitement and socio-economic equality.

At Nanterre-Paris X, male and female students were housed in separate buildings. They had yet to see the benefits of the Neuwirth Law of 28 December 1967, which legalized the contraceptive pill, but many of them had read or had heard about D. H. Lawrence, the Surrealists, Wilhelm Reich, Aldous Huxley, Herbert Marcuse and Simone de Beauvoir. Publicity campaigns by holiday providers such as Club Méditerranée proved that sexual liberation was available to the salaried, middle-class population independently of ideology. In three or four years, the majority of students at Nanterre would

[349]

occupy positions assigned to them by the state and, as they had learned to conceptualize the matter, contribute to the exploitation of the proletariat.

Since 1965, women had been allowed to work and to open a bank account without the permission of a father or a husband. Their mothers had been granted the right to vote in 1944. Sexual liberation was only part of what was known as 'expanding the domain of the possible'. Pregnancy remained a serious risk and abortion was illegal, but a wide range of other options was available. The monthly magazines *Elle* and *Marie-Claire* had already broached the subjects of heavy petting, oral sex, orgasm, love in a physical relationship and the use of 'beauty products'. Almost half of each issue was devoted to advertising. The models were depicted in positions of sexual availability. Bodies engaged in unorthodox sexual acts could also be discerned in photographs of bottles of mineral water and vermouth. The total wattage available to the average household had more than doubled since before the Second World War, and women were said in the advertisements to have been 'liberated' by household electrical items.

The chief impediment to interpersonal sex at Nanterre was a regulation banning male students from female premises. The academic authorities were thought to have imagined nocturnal orgies, though intercourse was just as likely to occur in the early morning when the banging of garbage trucks and the scream of two-stroke motorcycle engines brought the partners to mutual semi-consciousness. It seemed a ridiculous restriction of individual freedom. A concrete tower containing several hundred hypothetically liberated young females, some of whom wore miniskirts and synthetic pullovers, seemed a throwback to the Middle Ages. The Americans were fighting an imperialist war in Vietnam. Radical thinkers were questioning the bases of Western civilization. Some rock stars were not much older than students at Nanterre.

I. A. ii.

IT WAS IN MARCH, when the weather improved, that the trouble began. The doors to the girls' dormitory were locked, but only in a ritual fashion, because the janitorial staff knew that they could be opened with moderate force within thirty seconds. The doors were forced open, and soon afterwards, boys were circulating freely in the girls' dormitory.

The action was welcomed by most of the professors at Nanterre, because they disapproved of the segregation of students, and the majority of them were sociologists, political scientists and authorities on Romantic and Post-Romantic literature. Apart from radio, television and newspaper reporters, no one beyond the campus gave the dormitory revolt much thought, except of a speculative, mildly pornographic nature. The commonly expressed view at Nanterre was that structures had to be changed on several levels to reflect changing mentalities. Some students decided to postpone their political involvement until they had spent a year or two reading and reflecting; others stressed the need to adapt to what they saw as a public service (the university). It was generally agreed, however, that the academic authorities, who represented the government and the capitalist system, should grant them certain rights. The abrogation of a rule was almost insignificant. It was not as if mind-expanding drugs and gratuitous acts of violence had been legalized.

For a time, instead of creeping through ground-floor windows, boys infiltrated the female blocks without impediment. They brought wine, cigarettes, Tunisian pâtisseries, hot dogs and erections. Some girls became lonelier as a result, and the structure and conduct of discussions changed. Boys were able to generate larger quantities of discourse proportionate to the amount of text they had read. Socially, the change was small. The *ciné-club* was just as well attended. Girls remained more active in the provision of amenities and entertainment than in political committees. It is probably true, as some historians insist, that the dormitory revolt at Nanterre in 1967 should not be seen as the prologue to the more serious events that followed.

I. B. i.

THE FOLLOWING YEAR, 8 January (a Monday) was marked by the opening of an Olympic-size swimming pool at Nanterre by the Minister for Youth and Sport.

In 1968, an Olympic-size swimming pool on a university campus was an overdetermined space characterized by a complex network of social structures and global capitalist tendencies. On one level, it was a place where boys and girls could enact a visual exchange without implicating themselves in a contractual obligation. Swimwear exposed up to nine-tenths of the body, and packaged and commodified the remaining parts. Exchanges took place, however, not in the quasi-natural setting of a beach or a pine forest, but in a refrigerative environment of laminated tiles and chlorinated water. Boys who went to a swimming pool with the thought of picking up girls (a practice known as *draguer*, which means 'to dredge' or 'to trawl') found their penises reduced to prepubescent dimensions. Moreover, use of the swimming pool implied a certain competitiveness in the interests of the state: health and healthiness, national athletic dominance, and so on. The Minister for Youth and Sport had recently launched his 'thousand clubs' policy, which promised to fund places of recreation and to give young people administrative control over the clubs. They would be able to tailor the clubs' services to local demand by providing ping-pong, *flipper*, *baby-foot* and coffee produced by the high-pressure brewing process. The minister had published a thick report titled *Le Livre blanc de la jeunesse*, in which the positive views of young people were recorded.

I. B. ii.

THE OPENING CEREMONY took place in the evening, after classes. The minister's speech was interrupted by a red-haired student with an open collar and a cheeky, pugnacious face. He was afterwards known as 'Dany le Rouge' and identified as the son of German Jews who had fled to France. 'M. le Ministre,' he said, 'I have read your

White Book on Youth. In three hundred pages, there is not one single mention of the sexual problems of young people.'

The Neuwirth Law had come into effect eleven days before. The cost of the pill was not covered by social security, and any woman who had started taking the pill on the day the law was passed was still impregnable. The minister's retort was not widely reported, because the chief point of interest was felt to be the student's audacious interruption. 'With a face like yours,' said the minister, 'you must be quite familiar with such problems. I cannot recommend too highly a dip in the swimming pool.'

Document 1: Conclusions of *Le Livre blanc de la jeunesse*

The young French person hopes to marry young but worries about bringing children into the world before he has the means to bring them up correctly. His number one objective is professional success. In the meantime, he saves what he can from his modest earnings – the young man hopes to buy a car, the young girl to make her trousseau. The young French person takes an interest in all the big problems of today but has no desire to rush into politics. 72% of young people are of the opinion that the right to vote should not be given to the under-21s. They do not believe that war is imminent, and think that the future depends above all on industrial efficiency, internal order and the cohesion of the population.

I. C. i.

THE NANTERRE swimming pool incident, rather than the dormitory revolt, is now thought to be a significant forerunner of the later troubles. Many other acts of rebellion could be cited. For example, during the traditional New Year's reception, the Dean of Nanterre, his wife and their four guests left their seats of honour to collect food from the buffet when (as the dean recalled twenty-five years later) they noticed four young sociology professors removing their bags and belongings and taking their seats. The dean then remembered the warning given by his friend Raymond Aron, when he had learned that Nanterre was to have a sociology department: 'By its very nature, this discipline will engender action groups that will create tensions and agitation. Beware of sociologists! They'll make a mess of everything!'

I. C. ii.

As examinations loomed, rebellious behaviour began to affect the educational process itself. Previously, professors had delivered their lectures to fifteen hundred or two thousand students packed into an amphitheatre. The students scribbled notes, chatted and read the newspaper. One professor likened the experience to 'talking in the concourse of the Gare Saint-Lazare'. Sometimes, the professors saw their students at an oral examination, and were struck by their 'encyclopedic ignorance'. Now, lectures were being interrupted by students who demanded the right to speak and then lectured the professor on his pedagogical backwardness and his role as a tool of state repression.

The media took a keen interest in youthful rebellion, and so, before long, television viewers (potentially half the population) were treated to the unusual spectacle of students holding press conferences. The students sat like examiners behind a trestle table, talking into microphones. They blew out clouds of smoke, wagged their fingers at the audience and used terms from sociology and political science which, to many viewers, seemed incongruously professorial. They expressed themselves in the form of questions, to which they supplied the answers, following a rhetorical model to which they were accustomed. 'Why are we in revolt? Because the ruling class is trying to condition our daily life. Why is it trying to do that? Because Western imperialism is opposed to all forms of popular culture. Why is it opposed to popular culture? Because, in the final analysis, this is a class struggle.'

This form of exposition, commonly used with passive audiences, allowed objections to be answered before they were raised by an antagonist: 'Are we not members of the bourgeoisie ourselves? Yes, but, as such, we must use our freedom to criticize and, if need be, to overturn the state. What would be the result of such a revolution?

The result would be, not the simple *embourgeoisement* of the proletariat and the insertion of the sons of the proletariat into managerial positions, but the abolition of the distinction between labour and management.'

Despite superficial differences, this was roughly in line with Gaullist policy, which, since 1945, had striven to increase the involvement of workers in the running of factories (a practice known as *cogestion*). For the *téléspectateurs*, the interest of such conferences lay in the exciting usurpation of institutional authority, the flouting of generational power structures and in the references to media manipulation, which added a degree of self-reflection and unpredictability not normally seen in government-controlled public broadcasting. Furthermore, whereas representatives of the government and the university were distinguished by drab items of clothing purchased as *ensembles*, the students' clothing (knitwear, scarves, second-hand jackets, etc.) showed signs of what the anthropologist Lévi-Strauss termed *bricolage* – the improvisational use of manufactured objects for purposes other than those for which they were intended, normally associated with primitive, pre-capitalist societies.

I. C. iii.

ON 20 MARCH, students protesting against the war in Vietnam smashed the windows of the American Express offices near the Opera and daubed slogans on the walls. Two days after that, six Nanterre students were arrested in a pro-Vietcong demonstration. This confirmed the view of many commentators that '*nanterrisme*' was part of an international youth movement rather than a specifically French phenomenon.

On returning to Nanterre that evening, militant students filed through a small door marked 'Entrance reserved for administrative staff and professors'. Pushing past a pair of startled administrators, they climbed to the top floor of the highest building on the campus and entered the Council Chamber. Its dominant position was felt to reflect the authoritarian nature of the educational régime. They sprayed some slogans on the walls ('Teachers, you are old, and so is the culture you teach') and passed a resolution. The students agreed to called themselves the 22nd of March Movement, by allusion to Fidel Castro's 26th of July Movement. Shortly afterwards, they were given an assembly room in which to hold their political meetings and renamed it the Che Guevara Room.

I. D. i.

FOR THE *téléspectateurs* who saw these images of student revolt, this was indeed, as the commentators insisted, 'a strange new phenomenon'. The youth of Paris had been subtracted from the city as though by a bureaucratic Pied Piper and placed in a 'learning factory'. They had been parcelled up and ejected en masse along the line of the Champs-Élysées to land in the former *terrain militaire* in the far west of the conurbation. Once there, they were fed on predigested information marketed as 'knowledge' and dispensed by professors who were little more than vending machines. Most of the students were in their early twenties and came from the sixteenth, seventeenth and eighteenth *arrondissement*s of Paris. More than ninety per cent of them were of bourgeois parentage (upper and middle management, liberal professions, civil service), but their parents were either unwilling or not wealthy enough to provide them with better accommodation. A 'concrete cube' at Nanterre cost ninety francs a month; an unfurnished room in Paris with no water or gas cost one hundred and fifty francs a month.

I. D. ii.

BECAUSE OF an administrative failure to anticipate the explosion in the student population, the range of activities at Nanterre was comparatively small. There was the *ciné-club*, the subsidized restaurant, a cafeteria with a hundred seats, the possibility of taking a train to Paris, hitchhiking out to 'the country' or cooking a pot of stew in a communal kitchenette and sharing it with friends. Some of the students volunteered to work with children of the shanty towns.

They helped them with their French and taught them to recognize parts of speech and the different tenses. Many of their contemporaries were riding Vespas or Vélosolex, buying records, practising macramé and *scoubidou* to produce items such as key-strings and lampshades; they visited shopping centres and airports, and lived in situations more conducive to the cultivation of sexual or romantic relationships. At Nanterre, friends were either an obtrusive presence or a prophylactic against anxiety and alienation. Services aimed at young people, such as the popular radio programme and magazine *Salut les Copains* ('Hi, Gang'), were seen as a form of paternalism and were largely devoid of intellectual content.

The student revolt promised to enlarge the range of activities and to target services more accurately. However, in the absence of capital, these activities were often of a symbolic nature: displaying pictures of Trotsky or Mao Tse-tung, eating sandwiches in a lecture hall, carpeting an office floor with cigarette-ends, organizing political *'groupuscules'*.

Ironically, the student leaders appeared on television not just as 'people in the news' but as consumers and objects of visual consumption. They were, to quote the subtitle of Jean-Luc Godard's film of 1966, *Masculin Féminin*, 'the children of Marx and Coca-Cola'. They possessed the marketable qualities of youth, elegance and wit. Their long hair conformed to commercial models of youth such as the Beatles and Alain Delon. Although the students' ideological referents were specialized and professional – Marx, Nietzsche, Freud, etc. – their sentiments were recognizable as those of the *yé-yé* songs that dominated the hit parade, which, as yet, showed few signs of the market segmentation that was so noticeable in Britain and America: '*Il ne restera rien*' ('There'll Be Nothing Left'), '*Je ne sais pas ce que je veux*' ('I Don't Know What I Want'), '*Ma jeunesse fout le camp*' ('My Youth Is Going Out The Door'). The interviewers tended to ignore the politico-philosophical debate and sought out female students whose faces and clothing corresponded to the tastes of the *téléspectateurs*. They did not try to belittle or humiliate them, though they did often flirt with them in order to produce a telegenic reaction or to implicate the viewer in the process of seduction.

[357]

Document 2

A documentary on Nanterre and '*nanterrisme*' was screened by the public broadcasting agency, ORTF, on 26 March 1968. It gave a sympathetic view of the range of student opinions, and aroused feelings in the audience that affected initial perceptions of the May revolt. Much of the documentary was filmed in a small, crowded room in which a dozen sociology students were sharing a pot of stew served in two stainless-steel pans and a Le Creuset cooking pot. The atmosphere, at first, was noisy and convivial.

A traditional anthropologist might not have considered the film a particularly valuable document because of the male interviewer's interference with the principal interviewee – an attractive female student dressed in a thin, striped pullover and a short skirt. She appeared eloquent, affable, rather timid, but keen to answer the questions accurately. The camera showed her face in close-up and made her eyes and mouth the centre of attention. In the cramped conditions, the interviewer occasionally obtruded in the form of a wave of dark hair or a black-sleeved arm suddenly raised to consult a gold wristwatch. The student sat with her bare knees clutched to her chest and appeared to be slightly overshadowed by the interviewer. At first, the hubbub in the room almost drowned out some of her answers, but as the interview proceeded, the room became noticeably quieter.

You're a student of what?
Last year, I was in sociology; and this year, I'm doing a diploma on
  demographics. In fact ... I'm doing a study of the research that's
  been carried out into the fertility of oppressed women.
That's a very serious subject ...
Yes. It's a subject I find really interesting because it's about women.
You used to live in Reims, I think you told me.
Yes, I was living in Reims.
And you've been at the hall of residence ...
I've been here ... it's my second year ... When I first got here, in
  January, I was living here in secret.
How do you mean, 'in secret'?
With a boyfriend ... because I didn't have a room.
With a boyfriend?
A boyfriend.
Whom you got to know ...

Whom I got to know last year ... I've been with him since last year.
You met him here?
I met him here.
How is it that a young girl from the provinces turns up in Nanterre and ...
There are lots of provincials here at Nanterre ... You see, you get
   here, and at first you're a bit lost ...
You didn't know anyone.
No, I didn't know anyone. The first month, I spent hardly any time
   here. I arranged to spend the night with friends in Paris ... I didn't
   want to live here. It was really frightening.
Why?
First, because I'd never lived in an HLM* like this – these little
   pigeon-holes and boxes. And I was afraid to live here ... As soon as
   the boys find out there's a new girl, they pounce on you ...
What do you think causes that?
Well, it's caused by the fact that they're bored, obviously. They're
   looking for something new, that's all; it doesn't go any further than
   that ... It's the problem of ... of boredom. When you come out of
   the restaurant in the evening, you don't know what to do. You're
   fed up. There's the cafeteria ...
And since you first met this boy ... you're still with him.
Yes.
Is that usually the case?
No. It's very difficult for a couple to succeed.
Why?
Because it's impossible to live like a couple here. It's not a normal sort
   of life. And you can never get away from friends. . . . There are lots
   of interchangeable couples. They live together for a week and then
   they change partners.
Do you think that has to do with Nanterre?
No ... I think it has to do with any student residence.
It has to do with living in a hall of residence?
Look, if you have fifteen hundred girls and fifteen hundred boys living
   face to face, there are going to be problems ... problems to do with
   couples, problems with ... I don't know ...
Doesn't that worry you?
(*Quietly.*) Yes, it does ...

---

* HLM (pron. *ash-el-em*): *Habitation à loyer modéré* (low-cost public housing).

Do you think that the boy you're living with is sensitive to these problems?
Of course ... of course ... Especially now that there's a sort of
collective madness and people are leaving ... You start out as a
well-balanced group of individuals, and then suddenly it all falls
apart, and your friends go off just like that.
(Pause.)
Are there evenings when you feel really fed up?
Of course ... Just now it's every evening.
Even though you're with Jacques? ...
(Pause.)
Yes ...

The room has now fallen silent. The girl to the left of the interviewee, who at first looked cheerful, seems depressed and uncomfortable. A male student bites his nails and is visibly agitated. No
conclusions are drawn from the interview. The scene then changes
abruptly, and the documentary ends with four male students in Spanish
costume playing gypsy music on guitars and mandolins at the foot of a
concrete tower.

Questions and sample answers

• *What did the students fear?*
That they might invest their youth in hard study and then fail to find
a job. (The risk of unemployment remained high.)

• *What might the consequences have been?*
Their spending power would be negligible, affecting not only marriage prospects but also lifestyle, and leading eventually to social
déclassement.

• *How were the students affected by the increasing social mobility of
the late 1960s?*
Social mobility was a mixed blessing. It meant not only that children
of the proletariat could aspire to managerial positions, but also that
children of the bourgeoisie might find themselves descending into a
kind of neo-proletariat.

II. A. i.

ON 2 MAY, as a result of continued protests and damage to university property, the authorities decided to act. Government ministers were afraid that the troubles at Nanterre would spread to other sections of the university. That evening on television, with an air of stern regret, the Dean of Nanterre announced the suspension of classes.

For this complex struggle on the new terrain of public relations, Dean Grappin appeared sadly unprepared, like a gladiator in a minefield. He used sentences, the syntax of which, in order for their meaning to be grasped, called for an unusual degree of concentration. He accumulated nouns and pronouns with which he would have to be heard to have made the proper grammatical agreements before the end of the sentence. He was, in effect, sitting a small public examination set by himself. He concluded his address; the screen turned grey; students continued to make the journey from Nanterre and to file into the chlorinated corridors and amphitheatres of the Sorbonne.

The revolt had now migrated from the wasteland on the western horizon into the most famous, telegenic and overdetermined space in continental Europe: the Paris Latin Quarter and its main commercial artery, the Boulevard Saint-Michel.

Next day, marching into the minefield, the authorities asked the police to evacuate the Sorbonne.

II. B. i.

THE STUDENTS who assembled in the courtyard of the Sorbonne on 3 May were inspired by similar protests at Nantes, Strasbourg, Berlin and Berkeley. Using picks and hammers, they converted parts of the building and its furniture into 'anti-fascist equipment' (sticks and stones). They were anticipating an attack by an anti-communist student group called Occident, which had been infiltrated by former terrorist paratroopers of the OAS. Occident members wearing motorcycle helmets and brandishing axe handles were demonstrating a few yards away on the Boulevard Saint-Michel, demanding that the protesters be sent to Peking.

At about four o'clock that afternoon, instead of helmeted fascists spoiling for a fight, the students saw, entering from the Place de la Sorbonne, a battalion of men who would normally have spent Friday afternoon directing traffic, arresting burglars, importuning beggars and expressing admiration for the sexually interesting parts of the bodies of Parisian women and, to a lesser extent, of foreign female tourists.

These policemen, incorrectly identified by the students as members of the CRS,* having little experience of crowd control, performed their task clumsily. They bundled three hundred students into the 'salad shakers' (police vans). One of those arrested was Daniel Cohn-Bendit, known as 'Dany le Rouge', who was due to appear at a meeting of the University of Paris on 6 May, charged with 'agitation'.

The university and the government believed that the 'extremists' in the Sorbonne represented a minority, and that all the other students were busy in their concrete cubes preparing for examinations, which they were due to sit in three weeks' time.

II. B. ii.

DESPITE THE increasing use of non-gender-specific clothing and hairstyles, the police successfully distinguished male from female students. Avoiding contact with the female students, they herded the male students into the waiting vans.

What happened next was more significant than it might appear at a distance of forty years. Female students surrounded the police vans and began to chant '*CRS – SS*', equating the police with the Gestapo (a historically dubious but ear-catching slogan), and '*Libérez nos camarades!*' To the policemen, the girls were not Trotskyites, Leninists, Stalino-Christians or Maoists; they were child-bearing ornaments and objects of desire. Their use of the noun *camarades*, which can be

---

* CRS (pron. *say-air-ess*): Compagnie Républicaine de Sécurité.

either masculine or feminine, reoriented the conflict and induced a dangerous degree of semiotic confusion in the forces of order.

Seven days later, on the first 'Night of the Barricades' (see sections III. A.–B.), the police would go on the attack. They charged the poorly made barricades on the Rue Gay-Lussac and unlawfully broke into apartments in pursuit of rioting students. In a street near the École des Mines, a girl wearing almost nothing came rushing out of a building and stopped in the street like a hunted rabbit. She was passed along a line of policemen, beaten up and dragged to a 'salad shaker' that was waiting in the Rue des Fossés-Saint-Jacques. Local people who witnessed the violence were horrified.

Questions and sample answers

• *How had the conflict changed?*
The conflict had been radicalized and polarized. The policemen, who were of predominantly proletarian, artisan and petit-bourgeois origin, had reasserted the power of institutional authority over individual, bourgeois self-expression. They did this, however, without the blessing of their bourgeois superiors. The Prefect of Police, Maurice Grimaud, having witnessed the scenes of violence on television, sent a circular to all his agents: 'Striking a demonstrator who is on the ground is the same as striking oneself.' It was an aphorism rather than an order, and was evidently greeted with incomprehension or derision.

• *Who was at fault?*
a) The police, who had offered to allow the students to leave the Sorbonne peacefully but then arrested them as they tried to leave. This gave rise to a violent demonstration, which the police repressed with greater violence, which led in turn to yet more violent demonstrations.

b) No one was at fault. Although the flames of rebellion were fanned by the police, the conscious intentions of individuals and groups were subsumed in a power struggle which was in turn determined by long-term historical trends. The nature of this struggle remained obscure to most of the participants.

• *What was the nature of the struggle?*
The students had been conducting a form of consumer protest, focused on staff reductions, poor facilities, gender segregation and a law (the

Loi Fouchet) that would have restricted access to university education. When the police became aggressors, the students found themselves opposing a rebellion of armed members of the lower classes. This rebellion corresponded more closely to underlying historical trends (monopolization of surplus value by the bourgeoisie, alienation of the proletariat, etc.) and thus became the new focus of agitation.

III. A.

DEMONSTRATIONS took place in Paris on 6, 7 and 8 May. On 9 May, the Government announced that the Sorbonne was to remain closed. On the night of 10 May, barricades appeared at several key points of the Latin Quarter for the first time since 1944.

Although their composition differed from that of their predecessors (cars instead of carriages, café chairs instead of domestic furniture), these barricades were associated by newspaper readers and *téléspectateurs* with moral rectitude and sexual adventure: Cosette and Marius in Victor Hugo's *Les Misérables*, the bare-breasted 'Liberty' figure in Delacroix's *Liberty Leading the People*, and countless romantic serials loosely based on episodes of the Paris revolutions of 1789, 1830, 1832, 1848 and 1871.

The barricades offered a seemingly unique opportunity to participate in 'history', and their sudden appearance in the Latin Quarter contributed to the media success of the riots. In the short and long terms, they enhanced the attraction of the Latin Quarter as a tourist destination. During a lull in the fighting, a Belgian tour bus stopped next to a crumbling barricade; a young man got out and stood on the barricade with a stone in each hand while his father took a picture.

May '68 was a revolution with its own theme park. A graffito that appeared on the walls of various public buildings advertised the sites of historical interest even before the historical events had occurred: '*Ici, bientôt, de charmantes ruines*' ('Coming soon: picturesque ruins.')

III. B. i.

PARTLY BY CHANCE, and partly by imitation of guerrilla movements, the students evolved a crude communications network,
using bicycles, mopeds, walkie-talkies and transistor radios. With
their light-weight footwear, they could out-run booted policemen
and were able to dodge about the city in small groups, avoiding road
blocks, setting fire to cars and urinating on the flame of the Unknown
Soldier. Live reports on the youth-oriented stations Europe 1 and
Radio Luxembourg had the effect of coordinating the riots. Radios
were placed on windowsills, and the commentaries cascaded down to
the streets in stereo. Reporters exaggerated the numbers involved and
brought even more people onto the streets.

Despite attempts by politicians and the police to identify ringlead-
ers, there was no recognizable command structure. Confusingly, the
students failed to conform to the model of earlier bourgeois protesters (duffle coat, baggy blue pullover, yellow 'Boyard' cigarette). The
subsequent re-education of the police would concentrate, therefore,
on the free-floating signifiers of adolescent bourgeois culture:
'Eschew all prejudgements! A good policeman does not categorize
people according to their clothing or physical appearance: a black
leather jacket is not necessarily the costume of a hooligan; a hippie is
not always a drug addict; long hair is not the external symbol of
delinquency.'* Deprived of these simple keys to social status, many
policemen found their duties increasingly difficult to perform.

III. B. ii.

BY NOW (10–11 May), the 'anti-fascist equipment' of the Sorbonne
occupiers had been upgraded to a more efficient, paramilitary arsenal.
The police used tear-gas grenades, stun grenades, water cannon,
truncheons, rubber batons and booted feet. The students employed a

---

* *Le Policier et les jeunes* ('The Police and Young People'), distributed by the
Préfecture de Police; still in print, in a slightly modified form, in 2008.

greater variety of weapons: projectiles, including building rubble, cobblestones and iron bars; catapults; a sand-blaster; planks of wood with protruding nails; smoke bombs and tear-gas produced by chemistry students; Molotov cocktails containing metal pellets or topped up with motor oil to produce an effect similar to that of napalm.

Burning cars – especially the lightweight Simca 1000 and Citroën 2CV – were both defensive and offensive weapons. (The owners of these cars, being sympathetic to the students, covered by insurance and coveting more recent or prestigious models, were not generally opposed to their use in barricades.)

The effectiveness of the students' weaponry can be gauged by the number of casualties. After the Night of the Barricades, three hundred and sixty-seven people had been injured, of whom two hundred and fifty-one were policemen and other service personnel. Eighteen policemen but only four students were seriously wounded. Sixty cars were destroyed and a hundred and twenty-eight severely damaged. The absence of fatalities, which is still felt to be a remarkable feature of the riots, may reflect a certain degree of ritualism in the use of these weapons. It should be noted, however, that, with road blocks, cratered streets, almost two hundred cars *hors de combat* and many others safely stored away in underground car parks, inhabitants of the Latin Quarter were less likely to die a violent death in May 1968 than at other times.

III. B. iii.

RITUALISM WAS particularly evident in the use of cobblestones – cubes of blue-grey or pinkish granite from quarries in Brittany and the Vosges weighing approximately two kilograms and laid in fan-shaped patterns by skilled manual labourers to provide a durable and easily repaired road surface. Many were covered with a thin layer of tarmac but could soon be dislodged with a pick or a road-drill. Hurled with sufficient force, a cobblestone could seriously injure even an armoured policeman.

The cobblestones (*pavés*) were not just weapons, they were symbolic objects, representing the essence of the city ('*le pavé de Paris*' is a metonymical expression with romantic overtones). Furthermore, cobblestones represented the hard, back-breaking labour of the proletariat and the paternalistic provision of undifferentiated communal services by the state. The slogan, '*Sous les pavés, la plage*',* asserted the underlying truth of individual consumer choice and the freedom to engage in leisure pursuits. (The sand, in fact, was not the geological 'beach' beneath Paris but imported industrial sand that was compacted and levelled to provide a smooth base for the stones.)

The commercial availability in 2008 of cobblestones used in the May 1968 revolt suggests that many were collected at the time as valuable commodities and investments. Prices vary according to historical significance and the aesthetic properties of the stone.

Document 3: Cobblestones advertised on eBay.fr in May 2008.

(a) 'Genuine cobblestone, witness of French history': 1 euro; 10 euros postage and packing.

(b) 150 cobbles marked 'Quartier Latin, Mai 68' in red and blue paint: 'memorable souvenirs that can be used as book-ends or paperweights'.

(c) 'Decorative display object', currently in a flower-bed at Boussu (Belgium): a 'witness of the events of May 68, which passed through the windshield of my father-in-law's 2CV, which was parked at the time in the Latin Quarter'. 10 euros.

(d) 'Parisian cobblestone in its original state, with traces of tar', collected 'as a souvenir' by a fireman on the night of 23–24 May, 'subsequently used as a book-end'. 27 euros.

IV. A. i.

AFTER THE Night of the Barricades, the conflict could no longer be seen as a simple rebellion against the government and its agencies.

A new protagonist, whose emergence had been anticipated and, it might be said, desired by the students, now appeared on the scene. The CRS had been founded after the Liberation as a special force to fill a gap between the regular police and the army. They were trained

---

* 'Under the cobbles, the beach.'

in crowd control and mountain rescue. They patrolled motorways in urban areas and served as lifeguards at lakes and beaches.

CRS recruits had a relatively low level of education. Many came from deprived areas where physical violence was a form of personal expression as well as a form of defence. They did not have homes of their own but were housed in special barracks. They were strangers to the areas they policed, partly because, as sons of the proletariat, they might otherwise have found themselves, during a workers' strike, opposed to members of their own family or clan.

The men of the CRS were poorly paid and unappreciated. Many suffered from social alienation and psychological problems related to insecurity. They compensated for this by developing a tribal sense of loyalty and tradition, sharpened by a perception that the misdemeanours of all the forces of order were blamed on the CRS. In May 1968, they often worked several shifts in a row and were kept on duty overnight, cooped up in armoured coaches parked in side streets.

IV. A. ii.

THIS OSTENSIBLY proletarian and provincial force became 'the enemy' to a much greater degree than the bourgeois, Parisian authorities. As usual in such conflicts, propaganda was used to dehumanize the enemy, enabling combatants to overcome moral or aesthetic objections to physical violence. For example, a cartoon in a student paper showed an injured CRS man being prepared for a heart-transplant operation: the heart was to be supplied by an anaesthetized '*vache*'* in the neighbouring bed.

The CRS fostered sympathy for the students by attacking innocent bystanders and allowing their actions to be guided by a simple form of class consciousness. According to one eye-witness, a teacher leaving a bookshop in the Latin Quarter was beaten up by a group of CRS. When the officer in charge ordered his men to stop, observing that the victim looked too respectable to be a student, one of them objected, 'But, chief, he was carrying books!'

* *Vache*: 'cow', equivalent here to British or American 'pig'.

IV. B.

IT WAS NOW that the student revolt revealed its unexpected capacity to redefine market segments. In streets and boulevards that were already saturated with commercial signifiers, the revolt carved out its own niche, and proved that the market's ability to commodify ideas as well as products had been drastically underexploited. Shops that stood in riot zones sold red bandannas, Che Guevara T-shirts and other revolutionary paraphernalia from the very beginning of the revolt. Students of the École des Beaux-Arts flooded the new market with screen-printed posters and called on striking school-children to help paste them up. Slogans appeared on walls throughout the Latin Quarter and branded the revolt so successfully that these slogans are still being used in 2008 to describe and analyse the conflict.

Document 4: Questions and sample answers.

Analyse the following slogans:

• *'Sous les pavés, la plage'*.
   (*Related slogan*: *'Je jouis dans les pavés'*: 'I come in the cobbles.')
The 'beach' symbolizes leisure and self-gratification. After a predominantly urban existence as students and then as managers and civil servants, many of the rioters would acquire or rent properties in rural or semi-rural parts of France with access to a lake or a beach, developed and managed for the purposes of recreation, with lifeguards, retail outlets and other amenities. This would form part of a lifestyle associated with certain ideas of freedom, which in turn would be associated nostalgically with the revolt of May '68.

• *'Soyez réalistes: demandez l'impossible'*: 'Be realistic: ask for the impossible.'
   (*Related slogan*: *'Prenez vos désirs pour la réalité'*: 'Treat your desires as reality.')
A serious-ironic invitation to assert consumer-control over the market and to redefine liberty in terms of personal preference. Cf. *'Soyez exigeant: demandez le cognac Hennessy!'* ('Be demanding – ask for

Hennessy!'); '*Parce que je le vaux bien*' ('Because I'm worth it'). Cf. also the CGT's* call to workers: 'Match your desires to reality.'

- '*Baisez-vous les uns les autres, sinon ils vous baiseront*': 'Fuck, or be fucked.'
  (*Related slogans*: '*Déboutonnez votre cerveau aussi souvent que votre braguette*': 'Unbutton your brain as often as your trousers.' And: '*Faites l'amour et recommencez*': 'Make love and start again.')

These slogans reflect familiarity with the theories of Reich, Foucault and Lacan. Erotic activity is conceptualized as a form of socio-political competition. The '*baisez-vous*' slogan, blasphemously derived from John 15:12, would later be applied in other forms to professional activity in business and financial markets.

- '*Si tu rencontres un flic, casse-lui la gueule*': 'If you meet a cop, smash his face in.'
  (*Related slogans*: '*Si tu veux être heureux, pends ton propriétaire*': 'Happiness is a landlord with a noose round his neck.' And: '*Ne dites plus: Monsieur le Professeur; dites: Crève, salope!*': 'Don't say, "Professor", say, "Drop dead, bitch!"')

These slogans represent an appropriation of proletarian forms of discourse and their rebranding with bourgeois irony. The feminine noun *salope*, applied to a male, is supposed to intensify the insult. Only the first of these slogans was intended as a practical recommendation.

V. A. i.

ON MONDAY, 13 May, in what appeared to be a victory for student propaganda, workers joined the revolt. The unions were caught off guard and pretended to have called for a one-day general strike. The government itself was in a state of chronic indecision. The student demonstrations had given rise to a mass revolt that directly threatened the power of the unions and the economic well-being of the state. This spontaneous alliance of workers and intellectuals was worryingly reminiscent of the successful revolutions of 1830 and 1848.

The students gathered at the Gare de l'Est and marched along the

---

* CGT: Confédération Générale du Travail. The most powerful trades union federation, dominated by the French Communist Party.

Boulevard de Magenta. As the demonstration passed in front of the Socialist Party's headquarters, some elderly socialists appeared on the balcony, displaying a hastily made banner proclaiming 'Solidarity with the Students'. The students chanted back, 'Op-por-tun-ists!' and 'Bureaucrats – into the street!' Confused by this anarchic scorn for political tradition and the respect due to age, the socialists shrank back behind the windows in embarrassment. The socialist politician François Mitterrand, however, joined the march and offered himself as a compromise candidate in the event of presidential elections.

At Place de la République, the students joined the workers. The crowd (officially estimated at two hundred thousand) surged along the Rue de Turbigo towards Place du Châtelet and the Left Bank, instead of following the traditional route of workers' marches (République to Bastille). Several hours would pass before the head of the march reached Place Denfert-Rochereau via the Boulevard Saint-Michel.

V. A. ii.

THE COMMUNIST newspaper *L'Humanité* had been denouncing the students as 'dubious elements' and 'bourgeois leftists'. The communist-dominated CGT called them 'pseudo-revolutionaries in the service of the bourgeoisie'. But young workers at the big Renault factory at Boulogne-Billancourt in the south-western suburbs had been impressed by the students' spontaneity. Although they thought it odd that anyone should complain about a university education, they empathized with their cheerful anarchy. Some of the young workers had been arriving for work without their blue overalls: some wore leather jackets, others were in shirtsleeves, which was a uniform strictly reserved for the higher ranks of management. They were tired of the unions' insistence on following 'the party line', and had no particular objection to becoming bourgeois themselves.

The demonstration passed through the Temple district, where smiling Algerians, some of whom had seen members of their family murdered by Paris policemen in 1961, joined in the chants of '*CRS – SS*'. Thousands of schoolchildren marched in perfect order, divided into *arrondissement*s, with neatly painted banners calling for 'Democratic Reform of the Education System'. They passed through the Marais, where militant workers and impoverished bourgeois intellectuals inhabited the crumbling palaces of a forgotten civilization. The activists of the third and fourth *arrondissement*s were used to spending their weekends at the police station after writing the latest issue of their 'mural newspaper' on the walls of the Marché des Enfants Rouges on the corner of the Rue Charlot. Many of them had temporary jobs – they worked for construction and removal companies or (as unemployed sociology graduates) conducted surveys for polling organizations – and could barely afford to be on strike.

Having reached an agreement with the police, the CGT stewards controlled the march, which the unions had decreed would be peaceful, and kept a watchful eye on the schoolchildren, the anarchists and the action committees of workers and students. The students chanted, 'Power to the Workers!' and, 'Adieu, de Gaulle!' The unions' banners said, 'Defend Our Purchasing Power'.

V. A. iii.

WHEN THE HEAD of the march reached Denfert-Rochereau at 5.30 p.m., something happened that seemed at the time to be a turning point, though it can now be seen as a confirmation of the essentially bourgeois tendency of the revolt. CGT stewards locked arms and prevented the students from continuing the march. The students had been intending to hold the biggest rally held on the Champ de Mars since Robespierre's Feast-Day of the Supreme Being in 1794. Loudspeakers told the crowd to disperse, recommending 'order, calm and dignity'. When the students refused to go home, the CGT stewards knocked them to the ground and tore the banners from their hands.

Only a few thousand students made it to the Champ de Mars. After sitting on the grass by the Eiffel Tower, listening to speeches, the students re-occupied the Sorbonne, while the union leaders went home and prepared for negotiations with the government.

V. B. i.

PARIS NOW entered a period of festive chaos. In spite of the unions, the general strike continued. Soon there were petrol queues, and the streets were reclaimed from Citroëns, Fords, Peugeots, Renaults and Simcas. Parisians rediscovered their city and talked to one another in the street. Deserted railway tracks shone in the sun, and anglers on the Seine and the Canal Saint-Martin were undisturbed by the wash of passing barges. Even Monoprix, whose basement supermarkets had caused something of a retail revolution by staying open on Mondays, remained closed.

After two weeks of general strike, the spectre of a cigarette shortage hung over the city, but the workers and the students stood firm. They organized the manufacture and distribution of cigarettes made from discarded butts, sold in packets of four at a generally agreed price of fourteen centimes.

V. B. ii.

DURING THE strike the protests continued, but there was already an air of anticipated nostalgia about the riots. The night of 23–24 May was called the Second Night of the Barricades. The students had been hoping to commemorate the anniversary of the Paris Commune by torching the Hôtel de Ville, but spies dressed in kaftans and Mao jackets had alerted the authorities, and the police brought out the giant high-speed bulldozer that they had borrowed from the army. Instead, students, workers and the unemployed assembled at the Gare de Lyon and set off in separate groups for the Right Bank, where they set fire to the Bourse and attacked the firemen who came to extinguish the fire.

Impressions of these events would later be treasured as memories of a transcendent experience and recounted many times over to children, grandchildren and researchers: the Doppler shift of sirens, the thump of helicopters surging over rooftops, booted feet marching parallel to the main arteries, the acrid smell of tear gas, the shiny black plastic of capes and truncheons, the slippery sludge of flattened sandwiches. The sense of a priceless, unrepeatable experience was enhanced by the physical transmutation of the students: they looked ragged, sleepless and disreputable. Their faces were covered in talc or masked with handkerchiefs soaked in lemon juice as a defence against the gas. In the swirling clouds of chemicals, the streets of modern Paris looked like parts of the old revolutionary *faubourgs* or, with a stretch of the imagination, like scenes of the Vietnam War in *Paris-Match*.

For two hours on the Second Night of the Barricades, large parts of Paris were in the hands of the students. It had often been said that a population brainwashed by television would never have taken the Bastille, because everyone would have rushed home to watch it on the box. But now, as if by accident, the students (or rather, eight million striking workers) had brought the Fifth Republic to the brink of collapse.

In the absence of leaders, they were unable to capitalize on their advantage. That day, and in the days that followed, the CRS and the police, who were terrified of being lynched by angry citizens, grabbed students and schoolchildren as they rode past on bicycles, punctured their tyres and emptied their satchels onto the street. They lined them up against the 'salad shakers' and kicked them in the genitals. They arrested people who had dirty hands, dark skin or (remembering Dany 'le Rouge' Cohn-Bendit) red hair. For the same reason, they arrested people who had a foreign name or accent. They punched them in the throat and made them walk between lines of CRS who broke their ribs and noses. At Beaujon Hospital, which served as a detention centre, they threatened them with further beatings and prevented them from calling their families or receiving medical attention. Before releasing them, they confiscated one shoe from each detainee.

Traffic lights in the Latin Quarter changed from red to green and seemed to serve a purely decorative function. Towards the end of May, Paris began to resemble the set of a science-fiction film. When the Métro was running, squads of CRS who looked like Martian robots waited for students to emerge from the underground at Cardinal-Lemoine, Mabillon or Maubert-Mutualité. A few enclaves of hedonistic mayhem survived like post-nuclear colonies. The Sorbonne and the Odéon theatre were run by anarchist collectives and overrun by rats. Many of the occupiers were seeing the inside of a university or a theatre for the first time. In the Sorbonne, the smells of incense and patchouli had overcome the disinfectant. The early slogans had disappeared under the tide of anarchist inscriptions and stains. Girls and boys lost their virginity in the corridors. They discovered Jimi Hendrix, Janis Joplin, hashish and LSD. The mood of casual optimism was maintained by student spokesmen who assured everyone that, at the end of the academic year, they would be deemed to have passed the non-existent examinations.

Document 5: Slogans of late May '68.

'*Examens = servilité, promotion sociale, société hiérarchisée*': 'Examinations = servility, social advancement and hierarchical society.'

'*Même si Dieu existait, il faudrait le supprimer*': 'Even if God existed, he would have to be abolished.'

'*Quand le doigt montre la lune, l'imbécile regarde le doigt (proverbe chinois)*': 'When the finger points at the moon, the idiot looks at the finger (Chinese proverb)'.

'*Réforme, mon cul*': 'Reform, my ass.'

VI. A. i.

AFTER THREE WEEKS of dazed exhilaration, the end of May '68 was bound to be an anti-climax.

President de Gaulle had mysteriously disappeared at the height of the general strike. He was rumoured to have gone to Baden-Baden to assure himself of the army's support in the event of a coup d'état. Meanwhile, the unions negotiated a deal with the government. The minimum wage was to be increased by 36%, the working week reduced to forty hours and the unions were to have more say in the running of factories.

To the union leaders' astonishment, the proposals were rejected by the rank and file. It was then that President de Gaulle returned

to Paris. On 30 May, he sat at his desk in front of a radio microphone and spoke of 'intimidation, intoxication and tyranny'. He also
appeared on television, and his appearance alone was worth a thousand tanks: old man's ears, sagging, watery eyes like flooded mine
shafts, and the long, grey face of a badly weathered municipal statue.
The majority of the voting population found this reassuring. The
President announced the dissolution of the Assemblée Nationale.
Legislative (but not presidential) elections were to be held in June.

VI. A. ii.

THE EFFECT was almost instantaneous. Unions abandoned the
workers to the CRS and turned their full attention to the election
campaign. 'May '68' was glamorous and theatrical. 'June '68' was
bloodier and less appealing to the *téléspectateurs*, especially since most
of the key events did not take place in Paris. It was in June that the
forces of order, battling against members of their own class, lived up
to their reputation. On 11 June, at the Peugeot factory at Sochaux in
eastern France, two workers were killed and a hundred and fifty-one
were seriously wounded. The government enacted emergency legis-
lation: many left-wing organizations were outlawed, demonstrations
were banned and paramilitary Gaullist groups were given carte
blanche to 'encourage' the workers to end the strike.

VI. A. iii.

ON 14 JUNE, the Sorbonne, the École des Beaux-Arts and the
Odéon theatre were cleared out by the police and disinfected by
immigrant cleaning women. Citizens who were unaware of the
underlying historical process were surprised to learn that the government intended to satisfy the students' principal demands. In a
private meeting with the Dean of Nanterre, the new Minister of
Education, Edgar Faure, outlined the new policy of placating the
protesters by enhancing their access to capital: 'Give them money,
and they'll shut up.'

Even as the decrees were being drafted, producers were re-positioning their brands to take account of changes in customer engagement. A special edition of *Elle* magazine (17 June) congratu-lated female students on their 'amazing courage' and stressed the growing importance of interactivity: 'We want to participate much more closely in your preoccupations of today, and your cares of tomorrow, and to get you to participate in ours.'

Female students had participated mostly by distributing tracts, organizing crèches and by lying unconscious on the ground, being filmed by cameramen. Only a few of them had thrown missiles, and none of them had appeared on television as leaders of the revolt. Their equal treatment by the forces of order, however, had given them a sense of civic importance and consumer rights. A poster produced by the École des Beaux-Arts, titled 'Beauty is in the Street', showed a young woman launching a cobblestone rather wildly but with graceful, trousered legs and the flapping skirts of a knee-length duffle-coat. This charming, iconic design anticipated some of the fashions that would be unveiled in the summer collections, notably by Yves Saint-Laurent, who dedicated his range of duffel coats and fringed jackets to the students of May '68.

VI. B.

'MAY '68' came to stand for personal liberation and the bankruptcy of a paternalistic, gerontocratic system. However, it is important to remember that the biggest manifestation of popular feeling in May '68 did not involve the students: when General de Gaulle returned to Paris on 30 May, more than half a million people marched up the Champs-Élysées. This huge demonstration of support for the Gaullist régime was organized by Gaullists, but the numbers far exceeded expectations. In the subsequent national elections, the Gaullists won a crushing victory. Left-wing parties had never had such a small share of the vote.

Not long afterwards, the Dean of Nanterre saw huge consignments of furniture and educational equipment arriving on the campus. Gigantic projects of no apparent worth were afoot. Cafeterias and language laboratories sprang up all over the campus, and the builders who constructed them – at vast expense to the government but very little to themselves – joked openly about their imminent early retirement. To a mind unschooled in the dynamics of capital flow and long-term growth, this could only be described as 'waste'. It was a small comfort to the dean to be told by the Minister of Education that no questions would be asked about education spending until 1970.

Questions

- *How did the student revolt of May '68 lead to the biggest popular demonstration of support for an existing regime in the history of France?*
- *Did everyday life change as a result of May '68?*
- *Were the students right to see examinations as the tool of a repressive, hierarchical society?*
- *Summarize the conclusions according to the foregoing analysis.*

In May 1968, children of the bourgeoisie provoked a proletarian revolt. The revolt took two forms: a) a violent rebellion of the forces of order, which turned them into public enemies; b) a general strike that defied union leaders and led to a split between unions and workers.

The consequences of this were: a) rapid improvement in living conditions and services for the young bourgeoisie; b) the discrediting of non-consumer-oriented educational methods; c) devaluation of age as a marker of social status; d) public endorsement of capitalist aspirations by union leaders; e) the effective eradication of the Communist Party as a major force in French politics.

- *Describe the legacy of May '68 in the light of public opinion polls.*

After May 1968, 62% of French people declared themselves 'quite satisfied' with things in general, more satisfied than not with relationships, housing and work, but only slightly satisfied with leisure – perhaps a sign of greater customer awareness. Only 32% described themselves as pessimistic (16% didn't know, or perhaps didn't want to think about it). More people aged between fifteen and twenty-one were happy in 1969 than in 1957. 71% felt 'free' when making purchases, either because they had sufficient spending power or because the range of products was adequate to their desires. 77% thought themselves lucky to be living in the late 1960s.

In 2008, most people who responded to opinion polls believed that May '68 had revolutionized French society, especially in the realms of sexual equality and workers' rights, and that the revolt had made the government more accountable to public opinion. Asked to name the May '68 slogan most relevant to today's world, almost half the respondents chose 'It is forbidden to forbid', while only 18% voted for 'Be realistic: ask for the impossible.'

PÉRIPHÉRIQUE

Gan, 1972–1977

IT WAS A SCENE that might have come from a comic book – some preposterous, graphic assemblage imposed on the city by a megalomaniac *bande dessinée* artist with a limitless budget and a nasty sense of humour.

The Finance Minister had just emerged from a meeting in the Louvre. He glanced along the avenue to the west-north-west; his jaw dropped, and he said to himself, 'What the hell is *that*?!'

Something thin and vertical bisected his eye. Then a memory attached itself to the ghastly image, and he thought: 'It was, yes, supposed to be big, but not *that* big ...' (Too tall for the artist to fit it onto one eyeball.)

Seen from behind, he was quite tall himself: buttress-shouldered, with light tracery around the neck, delicately cupola'd with baldness; early English rather than flamboyant. But *that* ... (It seemed to come out of the top of his head.) No one could possibly miss it. He stood at one end of the sacred alignment where Parisians took their bearings: Louvre, Obelisk, Arc de Triomphe – civilization's compass needle. The historic Grand Axis was a thin straight line at the centre of the globe: in one direction, the Great Pyramid of Giza; in the other, the island of Manhattan. And now, just up the road – that hulking great tower: La Tour GAN – so tall it would never look exactly perpendicular.

The *bande dessinée* artist might have drawn it in between one frame and the next.

Rising in the west, it reduced the Arc de Triomphe to the size of a mousehole. It redefined horizons and called the shots on perspective. In his mind's eye, he saw a long, thin shadow fall across Paris, turning the city into a passive sundial. Even before the building was finished, the drawings were coming to life: the scratchy trees, a gratuitous bird, a woman with a pram, businessmen in shiny blue suits and vertically striped shirts, resembling the building they worked in – in effect, fittings.

Corporate aspirations were written all over its glassy facade. Anyone who saw those three enormous letters at the top of the tower might have mistaken them for the name of the city. Gath, Ashkelon, Athens, Babylon, Gan. Groupe des Assurances Nationales.

Faced with this towering obscenity, the Minister of Finance – already considering his options – cast his mind back to 1960 and the Rue Croulebarbe . . . *Croulebarbe*: it sounded like a name from a fairy tale. No. 33 Crumblebeard Street had set the pattern for the next twelve years. First, the project was a drawing on a display board in a refitted Second Empire drawing room. An innocuous address identified it as a normal part of the city. The architects talked of 'integration', as though the monster were to make its home in a convivial and accommodating neighbourhood of the sort depicted in children's books: the chequered tablecloths of a restaurant, a cat snoozing under a concierge's knitting, the casual intimacy of clothes hanging in the *blanchisserie-pressing*. Next, there was a hole in the ground with men and machines moving about inside it. And then, suddenly, it shot up like an elevator, the living-cubes materializing around it as it went, from one floor to the next, in a single day.

The friendly neighbourhood was gone for good. As for the monster, there were no words to describe it – or very few: a steel tube, a blank panel, then another steel tube followed by a window, in a row of eight panels and eleven windows, with minor variations, multiplied vertically by twenty-three.

It had more glass in it than the Hall of Mirrors at Versailles. Standing outside 33, Rue Croulebarbe, you could see the setting sun in both directions. Now, after twelve years of *urbanisme*, it seemed a midget by comparison.

As Minister of Finance, he had been present at most of the

meetings. There had been much talk, he recalled, about transparency: transparent government, transparent buildings. (He could see through the men who sat around the table.) Symbols and metaphors would be brought to life. Why? This was the talk.

He had serious reasons to doubt the transparency of glass. Twelve years after the scandal of Crumblebeard Street, a man couldn't walk through Paris without seeing himself everywhere. The city had never been so opaque. Pairs of Parisians everywhere, and every paired pedestrian a self-hating Narcissus.

It was time to draw the line. And he was the man to draw it … Or his name was not Valéry Giscard d'Estaing.

FIVE YEARS LATER, after becoming President of the French Republic, he drew the line at twenty-five metres, which was for the centre of the city, and for the periphery he set it at thirty-seven metres. This was thirteen and nineteen heights of Giscard respectively – excluding the Eiffel Tower, the Tour Montparnasse, three or four other towers and the rest of La Défense and the Front de Seine, which were already under way. Twenty-five and thirty-seven metres were the new vertical dimensions of the city, and it was a highly popular measure. Almost everyone could see the point of it.

The Black Prince, # 1

NORTHERN PARIS at night: the slag-grey hills of Belleville, Ménilmontant and Charonne, overgrown with aerials and chimneys. A lopsided building somewhere near the Porte des Lilas.

A window on the fourth floor, under the eaves: a young woman sleeps under a wind-blown sheet, dappled by the moonlight or the yellow streetlamp.

Sounds come through the open window. Something like the wail of a tom cat – *Nyeeoooowww!!!* – draws a ribbon of sound around the outskirts of the city, marking its perimeter. She stirs on the bed, and moves her legs as if to release the tension. For a moment, she is out there with him on the motorbike.

There are no lights on in the building but it has patches of dirt or shade that almost look like human faces. A man walks past on the pavement below with no discernible features on his face. He turns a corner, slowly, as though he has a long way to go. His shoes are expensive but well worn. The artist shows him leaving a faint trail of white dust.

Quai de Béthune, 1971

WHEREVER GISCARD looked in Paris, he saw the works of his predecessor: Pompidou the banker, Pompidou the poetry-lover, Pompidou the President; some might have said the visionary. The chortling, two-faced peasant who kicked him out of the Ministry of Finance. – '*Pom-pi-dou*', like the peeping of a car horn.

If he hadn't died in 1974, after less than five years in office, who knows what he might have done?

Pompidou came from the land of the Arverni, where volcanic plugs jut out of the landscape like ancient, eroded skyscrapers, and the granite pastures are so bleak that an unsilenced engine is like the song of the skylark or the bleating of a calf. When he drove his car in Paris, he wanted buildings to disappear, which, in a sense, they did. He said, 'It is up to the city to adapt itself to the automobile, not the other way around. We must renounce an outmoded aesthetic.' His body had already adapted: he had a driver's sagging hips and jittery legs.

In 1971, the architects who had won the competition to design the Centre Beaubourg came to see him at the Élysée. First, they saw the President of the French Republic in a suit; then he went away, changed into something more casual and came back smoking a Gauloise, saying, 'I'm glad I'm not an architect. It must be the most difficult job in the world – all those building regulations!'

He did not pretend to be an expert, though he did have opinions. Asked about modern urban architecture, he said, 'Without towers, it can't exist.' The reporter from *Le Monde* looked through the windows of the President's office and saw the skyline changing as he spoke. 'Like it or not,' said Pompidou, 'you can't get away from towers.' Then he added, as though in confidence, 'And I know I shouldn't say this, but the towers of Notre-Dame ... they're too short!'

His wife Claude was better on the details. It was she who decided that the largest ventilation components of the Centre Beaubourg (the roof-top cooling towers and the street-level air intakes) should be white instead of blue.

THE POMPIDOUS lived in what, to judge by the coffered entrance door with its lions' heads and wreaths, was a beautiful old town-house on the Île Saint-Louis, at 24, Quai de Béthune. Three hundred years before, property speculators had developed the Quai de Béthune and renamed it Quai des Balcons for marketing purposes. Parisians who passed that way in their powdered wigs thought the exclusive water-front development an eyesore: balconies spoiled the classical simplicity of the facades and induced the wives of rich financiers to display themselves like prostitutes. In 1934, one of the balconied houses was bought by Helena Rubinstein, the cosmetics millionairess. She tore it down and replaced it with a characterless mansion boasting a fashionable porthole window. All that remained of the original building was the entrance door. This was no. 24, where the Pompidous lived.

The Île Saint-Louis was so quiet in the evenings that one could almost believe that there were still toll-keepers on the bridges and chains to prevent anyone from reaching the island after dark. Next door, at no. 22, Baudelaire had lived as a young dandy with his hookah and his coffin-bed and the old paintings that he bought on credit from a curiosity shop on the island. Pompidou was an admirer of Baudelaire, and of poetry in general. 'I remain convinced', he wrote in his memoirs, 'that the face of a young girl and a soft, supple body are among the most moving things in the world, along with poetry.' His anthology of French poetry included several poems from *Les Fleurs du Mal*.

> 'The shivering dawn, in her pink and green dress,
> Slowly advanced along the deserted Seine ...'

> 'Evenings on the balcony, veiled in pink mist!
> How soft your breast seemed, and how kind your heart!'

It was some weeks after the judging of the architectural competition and the first excavations for the Beaubourg, which sent tremors to the most distant parts of Paris (but not to the Île Saint-Louis). Pompidou and Baudelaire looked out of their respective windows, smoking cigarettes, blowing thought-bubbles of smoke towards the Left Bank. Only the Rue Poulletier and one hundred and thirty years separated them. The silvery wake of a river rat pushing through sewage could be seen under both windows.

Baudelaire gazed at the 'watery suns and muddled skies' above the Montagne Sainte-Geneviève and thought of his mulatto girlfriend's 'lying eyes'. He saw the branch of the Seine where the water burbles under the Pont de Sully. He saw the grubby barges and laundry boats, and imagined himself in a city of canals where 'vagabond vessels from the ends of the earth have come to satisfy your slightest desire'.

Next door, Pompidou imagined things that no one had ever imagined in that location: a forest of high-tensile steel and cross-bracing girders blotting out the view; a multi-lane overpass soaring through the rooftops, and space-age cars that seem to bulge and contract like tigers as they take the swerves. Where lovers strolled and beggars dreamed, he saw a limited-access freeway, just like the one that already runs along the Right Bank – the Voie Georges-Pompidou – and a thousand windscreened faces shooting out of an underpass, stunned by a sudden vision of beauty (golden domes, turrets, etc.) until a screech of brakes jerks them back to the present.

The Black Prince, # 2

POMPIDOU FLICKS his burning cigarette onto the street below. A faceless man walks along the *quai*. His black shoe extinguishes the butt as he passes. He wears a long coat, from which small amounts of what looks like builders' rubble trickle out onto the pavement. He reaches the other side of the island and looks up towards the hunched suburbs and the Saturn Vs of the Sacré-Cœur. The clouds are red. Wailing sounds arc over the sky. Somewhere in the hills near the Porte des Lilas, the young woman sits up in bed.

She thinks of the time when she fell asleep on the saddle, resting her head on her lover's back, leaning on the black leather. Through the bow of his shoulder, she could feel every bump and tremor, every syncopated rumble of the tarmac. His stillness never worried her. He said, 'Danger comes from other people.'

They were already in their mid-twenties, which made it seem as though everything had gone very quickly. At high speed, the changes came slowly and easily – a slight bulge yielding, a readjustment of their twinned bodies. He always said, 'When something changes, it has to be rediscovered.'

Seven hours from now, he would try to break the record, which stood at twelve minutes and a few seconds. He would see a Paris that no one had ever seen before, because everything looks different at speed. She slips back under the sheet and stretches out. She dreams of falling asleep on the bike, waking up in a favourite part of Paris: the leafy banks of the Canal Saint-Martin, the Place du Tertre, the Forum des Halles. A false dawn floods the room with yellow light.

Beaubourg, 250 BC – AD 1976

THAT NIGHT, Louis Chevalier had walked all the way from the heights of Belleville to the Île Saint-Louis, then back across the river to the Place de l'Hôtel de Ville. On a map devoid of other markers, his trail would have suggested a network of capillary paths that had grown up haphazardly, or constrained by ancient habits and accidents of geography. He had walked for five miles, through two thousand years of history. Now, he stood on a tiny hill of debris, staring at the 'Plateau Beaubourg'.

He knew the area like the back of his hand. Or rather, he knew it as it had been before he was born. (Anything too recent made only a faint impression and met with a blank stare.) He had lectured at the Sorbonne on the history of Paris, to students barely out of the womb, beginning with the Gauls who periodically annihilated their settlement to prevent it from falling into the hands of their enemies. Invited to give his expert views on the city's modern redevelopment, he had written one of his history books in a room at the Hôtel de Ville above the office where Baron Haussmann had planned the destruction of Paris. He had been a contemporary of Pompidou at the École Normale, and had sometimes lunched with the President and a few other *normaliens* at a little restaurant in the Rue Haute-feuille, where Baudelaire was born, but he had never dared voice his true opinions.

Now, Chevalier was writing a book called *L'Assassinat de Paris*. It was the fruit of long walks and readings that had left him up to his knees in the past. He would show the city succumbing to planners and financiers, and, if indignation left him room, he would recon-struct the Paris of his studious memory: 'Left to itself, History would forget. But fortunately, there are novels – loaded with emotions, swarming with faces, and constructed with the sand and lime of language.'

He liked to feel the filth of the Beaubourg *quartier* permeate his body: its smut was an essential part of its history. The original village, built on a mound above the riverside swamp, had been named Beaubourg (Pretty Place) in a spirit of medieval sarcasm. Three of the nine streets in which Louis IX had allowed prostitutes to operate were in Beaubourg, which had once had the rudest street names in Paris: Rue Maubuée (Dirty Washing Street), Rue Pute-y-Muse (Streetwalker Street), Rue du Poil-au-Cul (Hairy Bottom Street), Rue Gratte-Cul (Arsescratcher Street), Rue Troussevache (Cow-shagger Street), Rue Trousse-Nonnain (Nunfucker Street) and Rue Tire-Vit (Cocktugger Street), where Mary Queen of Scots was said to have asked her guide, 'What street is this?', to which the guide had euphemistically replied, 'Rue Tire-Boudin, Your Highness.' And 'Tug-Sausage Street' it remained until the 1800s, when it was renamed Rue Marie-Stuart.

Architectural pearls were forever being found in this squalid zone: curious lintels and casements, a Renaissance staircase in a sordid vennel, the embedded vestiges of turrets and gables, cellars belonging to houses of which no stone survived. Until 1950, hovels had squatted on the roof of the church of Saint-Merri, separated from one another by the flying buttresses.

The Plateau Beaubourg, where Chevalier stood, was now a '*parking sauvage*'. The rectangular patch of wasteground was used by motorists and by truck drivers serving the local shops. Painted transvestites and other creatures of the night hung around until they were replaced, just before dawn, by the muscular unemployed, looking for odd jobs at what remained of the markets.

In the days when buildings were thought to be incurable carriers of disease, the area had been designated *Îlot insalubre n° 1*. It was the first of seventeen Unhygienic Precincts identified by government commissions in 1906 and 1919. In 1925, Le Corbusier had produced a plan – sponsored by a car company – that would deal with insalubrity once and for all. Much of the Right Bank would be flattened and the 'tubercular' buildings (and all the other buildings too) would be replaced by eighteen cruciform towers. East–west arteries would allow motorists to cross what had once been Paris in a matter of minutes. Le Corbusier's secretary, who came in from the suburbs, would never be late for work again. The plan had been shelved, but the idea remained as a dream: Paul Delouvrier, 'the Haussmann of the suburbs', who had discovered Paris from the driving seat of his Studebaker convertible, decreed that Parisians should be able to travel about their city at 50–60 kph.

Several streets in Unhygienic Precinct No. 1 had been swept away in the 1930s as part of the programme of rationalization and sanitization, leaving the area of wasteground, which every night was carpeted afresh with broken glass, condoms and hypodermic needles.

THIS WAS THE SITE that Pompidou had chosen for a cultural centre and modern art museum. ('It has to be modern art because we already have the Louvre,' he explained.) Six hundred and eighty-one teams of architects had submitted designs of bewildering variety: a cube, a bent prong of glass and metal, a discombobulated rhombus, an inverted pyramid, a giant egg and something resembling a wastepaper basket. The winning design was compared to an oil refinery, which pleased the architects. It made radical use of steel, plastic and colour-coded utility tubes: green for plumbing, yellow for electricity, blue for ventilation, red for hot air. Specially designed seats, ashtrays and noticeboards were an integral part of the design, until they were stolen as souvenirs. Best of all, there was to be an escalator running up the outside in a perspex sheath.

Most of the local inhabitants were not opposed to the new building. 'Who wants to live next to *that*?' they would ask, pointing

at the neighbouring slum from their own section of Unhygienic
Precinct. They looked forward to the oil refinery. It would 'regener-
ate' the *quartier*. All the money went to the west of Paris, and it was
high time that the east enjoyed some prosperity. There would be new
shops and better drains, and the cafés would once again be full of
cheerful customers heaping scorn on the municipal authorities, the
President, technocrats, artists, builders, tourists and the young.

Louis Chevalier hated people for liking Paris in ignorance of what
it once had been. To him, Paris was a composite place built up
over the ages, a picture book of superimposed transparencies, overpopulated with the dead and haunted by the ghosts of the living.
No sooner was a building demolished and replaced than his mind
rebuilt it.

A light rain had begun to fall. His trouser legs felt heavy with the
damp; his muscles turned to mud. He walked to the corner of the
Rue de la Verrerie and stood in the doorway of Saint-Merri, where,
in 1662, the sister of Blaise Pascal had waited for the very first
omnibus. (The service was her brother's idea.) Five buses went by,
but all were full, and at last she had turned to walk home in a huff.
He retraced her steps a short distance, then entered a side street near
the Place Sainte-Opportune. On either side of the street, there were
sounds of patient industry. A cobbler was sitting on his doorstep,
tapping at a piece of leather. Market traders were passing with their
baskets, handcarts, mules, tricycles and gas-fuelled trucks of a kind
that was no longer manufactured.

At the end of the street was the 'Grand Trou des Halles' where
the central markets, known as 'the Stomach of Paris', had been cut
out. Tourists and Parisians were leaning on the barriers, gazing at
the exposed strata and thinking about dinosaurs and Gauls.

In this ravaged zone, the crowd of inter-epochal Parisians was
especially dense. By a wall that seemed to buckle with posters and
stickers, gouged by knives and chisels, a man in a short blue coat had
been crouching, two centuries before, clutching a door key, carving
something on the stone. Restif de la Bretonne had already defaced
every parapet on the Île Saint-Louis when he began to etch his way
through the *quartier* Beaubourg. Years later, 'to make the past live
like the present', he returned to read these messages to his future self

and remembered his exact state of mind at the time: '*10 jun. Reconci-liatio: cubat mecum*' ('Reconciliation: she slept with me').

A historian claimed to have discovered some of Restif's graffiti, but many of the stones had long since been chopped out and replaced, and the door key had never bitten very deeply. Now, there were transfixed hearts and genitals, cave paintings and cartoon faces, and skulls whose eyes grew wider and deeper as the rain and petrol-laden air ate into them. The letters of old slogans had blurred with age, and the ringed *A*s of anarchists were as soft as ancient crosses carved on menhirs.

The Black Prince, # 3

THE RAIN IS a bad sign, but it will pass with the night. From Belleville, one hundred and thirty metres above sea level, Paris is becoming more distinct, like a coastline. It might almost be Nice or Constantinople. She looks out towards the centre, where tall cranes flash their red lights at aeroplanes, and waits for the dawn's slow light to find the edge of the city.

This time, he will be alone – a *chevalier* or a prince leaving on a heroic expedition. But they will all be there to send him on his way, the riders who know each other only by their sound. They call him 'Pascal', but this is just a name they use to show familiarity. Soon, he will be known to the world by another name. A camera crew is already setting up at the Porte Maillot, and one of the riders is trying to explain to a reporter: 'It's like the new radar detectors: you know they exist, but you don't know where they are.'

She is dressed in her leathers, and what might be a skirt of chainmail. She stands for another moment at the window, taking a last look at Paris, a helmet under her arm.

Beaubourg, 31 January 1977

HERE, THE POET had sat in a wine shop with a bottle of Burgundy and a saucer of walnuts, writing on the back of a letter – '*New palaces*, *scaffolding, blocks of undressed stone, / Decrepit suburbs, everything becomes an allegory of something else, / And my cherished memories are heavier than rocks.*' Now, in the Paris that Louis Chevalier was forced to inhabit, the sign above the wine shop said 'Pier Import – All the Orient at a Price You Can Afford'. He headed for the Rue de Rivoli, which still seemed new to him, past snickering neon signs that he could barely decipher: Drugstore, Snack, FNAC, Mic-Mac, Sex-Shop, Self, Le Petit Prince, Halles-Capone.

Near the corner of the Rue de l'Arbre-Sec, he gave directions to a young lieutenant who was looking for a hotel that no longer existed in a street that had changed its name.

Chronological anomalies were a normal part of life for Louis Chevalier. But since the redevelopment of the *quartier* had begun, even people who lived in the present had been noticing an inappropriate coincidence of historical periods. Families who came to see the work in progress were confronted with veteran prostitutes slouching on purpose-built stone staircases that led directly up from the street. Mothers averted their children's heads and shot a glance at their husbands. Drunken clowns from circuses that had gone bankrupt after the war competed with graduates of the Marcel Marceau School of Mime. Beaubourg summoned up its ancient past, and over the whole Unhygienic Precinct – even when almost nothing remained of it except facades – and all through the corridors of the Châtelet-Les Halles RER-Métro station, there was the potent smell of the centuries: mould, sodden limestone, vomit, cabbage, corpse and cleaning fluid. A deodorizing unit had analysed its composition, but to no avail. Long after the renovation of the *Îlot insalubre* and the removal of Les Halles to Rungis, the authentic stench of the *quartier* Beaubourg hung on.

He made his way back to the Plateau Beaubourg, where he stood, a witness from another age, staring at a blazing wall of light. He had seen the building going up, tube by tube, until now, at last, it appeared to be permanently unfinished.

His cupola gleaming in the spotlights, Giscard stooped as though entering a crypt. Baudouin I, Princess Grace, Presidents Mobutu and Senghor, and all the other personalities and heads of state had long since settled into their seats of chrome and leather when he arrived in the vast aquarial foyer with the wife of Pompidou. It was Claude Pompidou's first outing since the death of her husband. The late President's face hung over the foyer in the form of a hexagonal moon made of strips of metal. Even in his fragmented state, he appeared to be chortling like a peasant.

The guests, who numbered five thousand, had spent the last hour pushing one another towards the escalators and from one floor to the next, looking for the buffet. (Giscard had ordered that no food or drink should be served at the grand opening.) Then the escalators had been stopped, and 'the Beaubourg' had filled with sounds of exasperation and the clicking of heels on metal steps.

Outside, on the tarmac apron that had been the Plateau Beaubourg, a man stood among the onlookers, the world-class buskers and the qualified clowns. If *L'Assassinat de Paris* had carried illustrations, the artist would have shown him holding a thought-bubble in which Baudelaire's poem, 'Parisian Dream', had been traced in a spidery hand:

> A terrible sight, never seen by mortal eye . . .
> Irregular vegetation had been banished.
> An intoxicating monotony of metal, marble and water;
> A Babel of stairs and arcades; a palace,
> Infinite, with neither entrance nor exit.
> A tamed ocean passed through a tunnel of jewels.
> The colour black itself had an iridescent sheen.
> No star, no vestige of the sun, even low in the sky:
> All those wondrous things had their own source of light . . .

Inside, Giscard picked his way to the see-through podium. He had hoped that the project, starved of cash, would die a natural death. But then Pompidou's protégé, *'le Bulldozer'*, Jacques Chirac – whose jutting jaw resembled the blade of a bulldozer – had put his weight behind the Centre Pompidou and pushed it through the committees.

The Centre had, however, proved useful in an unexpected way. On entering the private apartments at the Élysée for the first time as President, Giscard had found himself in the eerie but oddly irritating presence of a stainless-steel sphere. All around him was something like the insides of a transistor radio seen by a man who had shrunk to the size of a flea. This 'environmental salon' had been commissioned by Pompidou: polymorphic murals in over five thousand colours changed as one moved about the room, synaesthetically suggesting – and eventually causing – a severe headache. On Giscard's orders, the 'kinetic space' had been removed to the Centre Pompidou where it belonged.

It was, therefore, with a mixture of relief and distaste that Giscard delivered his muddled and insulting speech of inauguration under the chortling, hexagonal moon:

> Now, and for decades to come, a vast crowd will flow through this Centre. Long waves of humanity will batter the dyke of the museum's canvasses, decipher the books, gape at the images, and listen to the slippery tonality and syncopation of the music.

As he spoke, he looked up into the vacuous circuitry of girders and tubes – green for plumbing, blue for ventilation ...

There was, he could see it now, something entirely fitting about the Centre Pompidou. All that rubbish had to go somewhere, and where better than an architect-designed eyesore on a patch of waste-ground? It had, moreover, united the Parisian bourgeoisie in loathing and fear of change. The very next day, eighteen thousand people came to see it, exceeding everyone's expectations.

AFTER HIS LONG WALK through the centuries, the historian slept an agitated sleep on the rumpled debris of his bed. Like many Parisians, he would leave his shutters closed, even in the daytime. Only the maid would open them, when she came to wash away the grime. Baudelaire, who had moved from the Quai de Béthune to the other side of the island, had taken the extra precaution of having the lower panes of his window frosted 'so I can see nothing but the sky'.

> And then I woke up . . . eyes aflame.
> The horrid slum, the stab of care, the brutal clock –
> Midday! – It was raining shadows and the world was numb.

The Black Prince, # 4–5   •
(SEPTEMBER 1989)

SHE HAS STOPPED where the cobbles of the Place de l'Étoile meet the cobbles of the Avenue Foch, on the brow of what was once the Colline du Roule. The view down the avenue is a Joan Miró of bleary ochre light and pink splotches in which she sees his red light growing fainter. Few Parisians are about at that hour on a Sunday morning. The road surface glistens with the breath of the night but it will dry out in the breeze. Out beyond the old fortifications, conditions are very different. She catches the sound of the circular wind, and the wash of the traffic sweeping in from the south and the west.

They have come from all over Paris to see him off. A flotilla of halogen beams escorted 'the Black Prince' – a.k.a. 'Pascal' – to the great tidal river of the Champs-Élysées. Halfway up, they stopped at the Pomme de Pain for a *chausson pomme* and a coffee. It was there that they took the vow of silence a week before. They all have names that might have come from comic books or boutiques – Philou, Coyote, Karolus, Titi, Obelix, Pandore, Princesse.

She accompanies him as far as the Arc de Triomphe, then watches him embark on the gentle incline of the Avenue Foch. It is five minutes past seven. Just before the Porte Dauphine intersection, he slows down and stops at a light: someone crosses the road in front of him, cautiously, but without looking up.

From the other end of the avenue, she senses the acceleration as he descends the slip-road, past the rider with the stopwatch.

GISCARD FELT LIKE a tiny cathedral in a Sempé cartoon, dwarfed by ominous towers. He had saved the Gare d'Orsay and put a stop to the hundred-and-eighty-metre-tall Tour Apogée by the Place d'Italie. He had given the city a perimeter of frustrated skyscrapers truncated at thirty-seven metres. But there was nothing that he could have done to prevent the biggest architectural imposition of all.

From Porte de la Plaine, it had moved east to Place d'Italie. Advancing at a rate of twenty-three centimetres an hour for eighteen years, it had followed the outer line of the nineteenth-century fortifications, which the Director of Parks and Gardens had ear-marked in the 1950s for a 'Green Belt' of promenades and play-grounds that would be 'a reservoir of clean air'. The last section had been completed shortly before Pompidou's death: from Porte d'Asnières to Porte Dauphine. It was now the most obvious feature of Paris on a map: a wobbly, amoebic circle, in which the monu-ments of the old city were featureless particles awaiting digestion in their vacuoles.

Before the Revolution, the tax-wall of the Fermiers-Généraux had raised howls of protest. Surrounded from within, the city had laid siege to itself, and an anonymous wit had penned the memorable line, '*Le mur murant Paris rend Paris murmurant*': Parisians were muttering about their immurement, bewailing the wall that walled them in. Now, the saying was literally true: Paris was surrounded by a contin-ual murmur, a whispering wall of tyres and tarmac, a caterwauling of combustion engines.

The Boulevard Périphérique – shortened to 'le Périph' – made no difference whatsoever to traffic inside the city. The exogenous blood system pumped its corpuscles into a dead body clogged with inert cells. It was called 'the Ring of Death' and 'the Circle of Hell'. It boasted one accident per kilometre per day, and it was thirty-five kilometres all the way round.

EVEN AT THAT HOUR, there is a surge and purpose about the traffic. It is essential to reach a safe speed – 190–200 kph – as quickly as possible. Drivers nearly always leave a gap of at least a metre, which is all he needs.

A red light is winking: at some future moment on a different time-scale, that vehicle will begin to change lanes. He allows the machine to relax into its natural velocity: 210, 220 kph …

The pillars of a tunnel, blazing orange, riffle past like a flick book cartoon. A walkway tilts 25 degrees and vanishes. – 0' 45". – The next exit, Porte Maillot, is coming up already: the camera on the fuel tank sees the gigantic, maligned tower of the Palais des Congrès craning its neck. Other, inferior towers lean back to let him pass.

He knows the Périph like a lover's body: the roughness and bumps between La Villette and Pantin; the surprising curve near the Porte des Lilas, where the road ahead will be invisible for maybe two seconds. He changes down, then back up into fifth.

A suspension bridge flexes its cables and flounces away. Cars – going where? – flash past in reverse. A tall partition blocks his view: a truck – it has no right to be in that lane – pulls out in front of him, suddenly grows taller, and all at once he is in the same time-zone as the truck. The deck of a bridge begins to rotate on its axis. A line of trees caught in a hurricane or some catastrophic stalling of the planet shoots overhead.

Perhaps, from where she is waiting, she will hear the scream of acceleration.

A WHITE PARTITION has been pulled across the room. Here, as Pompidou once complained, less than three hundred yards from the Champs-Élysées, the sounds of the city are muffled and distorted. In front of the partition is a model of the new national library. It consists of four towers, which are said to resemble open books, but without spines or pages.

No one who enters the office could fail to notice it. Ten million books, in their original, undigitized form, will fill the windows of the towers. In the present state of technology, the books will be destroyed by sunlight, but things move so quickly that – according to what will later be known as the Law of Accelerating Returns – by the time the towers are built, someone somewhere will have invented a special glass that will neutralize the effects of light without dimming its radiance.

Giscard's successor is called 'Mitterramsès', and this is the ninth year of his reign. He is also known as 'Tonton' ('Uncle'), and hence as 'Tontonkhamoun'. He comes from Jarnac (*sic*), on the River Charente. Not since the days when the Parisii cowered behind their wooden stockade has the kingdom been so clearly marked off from the outer world. Nowadays, 'Inside the Périphérique' is another way of saying 'Paris'.

Every few weeks, Mitterramsès has himself and his advisers taken through the inner city on a ritual itinerary. Sailing down the Seine, within the sacred perimeter, it is noticeable how these 'Grands Projets' – those he initiated himself and those he inherited from

Giscard – go in pairs, on either side of the river, as though the delineated zone were a vast temple complex: Bibliothèque de France and Parc de Bercy, Opéra-Bastille and Institut du Monde Arabe, Musée d'Orsay and Pyramide.

'When I was a student', he tells the television reporters who interview him in front of the sloping panes of the Louvre Pyramid, 'I was already rebuilding Paris'. Sandblasted, returfed, repopulated, its windows filled with monitors and cables, the heart of Paris has never looked so new. But the age of monuments is passing. A building is now an obstacle, a reinforced ego, a magnified piece of street furniture. A generation of towers is already marked for demolition, and, standing between the two reporters, Mitterramsès seems to age and shrivel. The Périphérique is no longer a limit; it is the principal avenue of a city that has yet to be identified – according to architects who have seen it from the air. Either that, or it is the centre of the vast new conurbation of Periphopolis.

Speed is eating away at the urban fabric, altering the shape and density of things. Skateboarders are plying routes of staggering complexity and length, instinctively rediscovering geological events and two thousand years of urban planning. Practitioners of parkour flip and spring about the city faster than cars, just as Quasimodo scrambled over the face of Notre-Dame.

'The form of a city changes faster, alas, than a human heart!'

It was time to change the human heart ...

A TRUCKER'S FACE pushed up against the glass, jawbone on the steering wheel, eyes boggling ... *Nyeeooowww!!!* –

A city falls away to the right, and he descends towards a curved horizon. Concrete ceilings fly overhead like some futuristic dungeon complex. – 7′ 46″. – A satellite estate blinded by sound barriers, then a shanty town that has slipped between the carriageways. To the north, behind the gantries that name the invisible suburbs, a colony of towers grows more distant. Contracted by speed, the Périph has a rhythm and integrity that its million daily users will never know.

The sun rises behind him and then to his right: cars are entering the 'Circle of Death' in greater numbers, and there are the first signs of the turbulence that will lead to gridlock later in the day. On the straight section after Gentilly – Montrouge, Malakoff, Porte de la Plaine – the corrugation rattles out a measure of his speed, and he feels the acceleration before it happens. – 10′ 10″.

Two tunnels separated by a heartbeat, then the ribbed carcass of the Parc des Princes dancing down like a space invader – too big to see him shooting underneath, through the long tunnel of the Bois de Boulogne, the echoes catching up and overtaking, before the little road ascending, the streetlamps' blessing, and the traffic from another, more leisurely age, circling the leafy carousel of the Porte Dauphine.

11′ 04″ – Porte Dauphine and back again, all the way around. This is a record that will last for years.

SHE DID HEAR the scream. She circled the Place de l'Étoile, then rode down the Champs-Élysées, stopped on the square with the courtyard of the Louvre and the Pyramid as her backdrop, and returned just in time to the Pomme de Pain, which the *motards* have virtually taken over. A moment in history …

He says just this: '11′ 04″.'

She places her hands on either side of his helmet. The face is a blur, a city hurtling backwards into a forgotten future.

SARKO, BOUNA AND ZYED

1. Bondy

TWO CENTURIES AGO, for those who had the means to travel in what passed for comfort, Paris began and ended at 28, Rue Notre-Dame-des-Victoires. Number 28 had once been part of a town house belonging to the Marquis de Boulainvilliers. In 1785, the property was sold to the King for six hundred thousand livres, and the garden was converted into the central terminus of the national coaching and posting service, the Messageries Royales, whose yards and booking offices had previously been scattered across the city. At seven or eight in the morning, and at five or six in the evening, the coaches known as *turgotines*, painted with the gold insignia of the Messageries, left for all corners of the kingdom; at various other times throughout the day, incoming coaches, ghostly with the dust of distant parts, tipped their benumbed occupants out into the miscellaneous crowd.

Whatever else they had on their minds – a lover left behind or ardently awaited, the luxuries of Paris or the looming monotony of the provinces – all but the most innocent or debonair of travellers who boarded the east-bound coach shared the same apprehension, especially if, having failed to book a seat on the morning service, they were forced to leave Paris when the lamps were lighting up the boulevards.

Like other passengers, they examined the carriage and the horses, assessed the resilience of the straps that held their luggage, and inspected the driver for signs of inebriation. They peered at the rectangle of sky above the rooftops and worried about the weather and the state of the roads. When the postilion called them to board, they noted the age, profession, size and smell of their fellow travellers, and prepared for delicate negotiations, the result of which would determine the congeniality of the next four or five days.

Along with all these vital considerations, travellers bound for the east had an additional cause for anxiety. After leaving Paris by the Porte Saint-Martin, their coach would follow the Canal de l'Ourcq across a level plain dotted with churches and attractive villas. Forty minutes into the journey, they would reach the little village of Bondy, which marked the edge of the smiling landscape of lanes and meadows between the Seine and the Marne where Parisians went for walks and picnics. Then, after the château and the staging post, they would enter a region of wooded hills which, like some ghastly cul-de-sac in the sunless heart of the city, had escaped the influence of civilization.

Although it took less than half an hour to cross it in a stagecoach, the Forest of Bondy was a large, dark blot in the mental geography of Parisians. It was one of those half-imagined places, like the Gorges d'Ollioules on the road from Toulon to Marseille, or the frontier passes of the high Pyrenees, that made city-dwellers feel safe in their crime-ridden metropolis. Barely two leagues from the glittering boulevards, the Forest of Bondy was believed to be swarming with brigands who thought nothing of leaving coach passengers dangling from improvised gibbets for the sake of a few coins and trinkets. Since 675, when King Childeric II and his wife Bilichilde had been murdered in the forest, so many travellers had perished at the hands of highwaymen that '*forêt de Bondy*' had entered the language as a synonym for 'den of thieves'. It was there that unspeakable things were done to the heroines of the Marquis de Sade, and scarcely a year went by without a Bondy Forest, thick with black and green paint, being trundled onto the stage of a boulevard theatre to provide an evocative backdrop for yet another hapless maiden dressed in white.

The horrors of the Forest of Bondy were no doubt exaggerated, but drivers and their passengers were always glad to see the other side of it, and it was only when the villages of Livry and Clichy had been left behind in their clearings that the passengers tucked into the provisions they had brought from Paris and began to sing the songs that would help to shorten the interminable journey.

Though partly mistaken in their object, their fears were not entirely unfounded. The Forest of Bondy had once formed part of the double belt of dense woodland that supplied Paris with timber and fuel, and offered it illusory protection from invaders. Beyond the wooded boundaries of the Île-de-France lay the windy plains of Champagne and Lorraine, and beyond them, the vast expanse that stretched all the way to Asia, whence came barbarians and the plague. In 1814, it was from the wooded heights of Livry and Clichy that the Cossacks saw Paris for the first time, and it was in the Château de Bondy that Tsar Alexander menacingly reminded the municipal delegation of Napoleon's unprovoked attack on Moscow. More than half a century later, the Prussian army laid waste to the same woods and villages as it encircled the defenceless city.

Apart from the blacksmiths and innkeepers who plied their trade along the post road, the inhabitants had remained as obscure as savages in a remote colony. Parisians who knew every cobblestone of their *quartier* and who could detect the slightest variation in a neighbour's routine had only the foggiest notion of human life. beyond the boulevards. The people of the forest had first come to the attention of Parisians on the eve of the Revolution, when every town and village in the kingdom was invited to record its grievances. The villagers who lived by the Forest of Bondy turned out to have fears of their own. They were constantly in danger of starvation. The roads to local markets were unusable for half the year, the horses, hunting dogs, pigeons and rabbits of wealthy landowners destroyed their crops and they were cruelly burdened with taxes. The people of Aulnay-lès-Bondy complained that their property was not respected: 'It seems only just that each individual should be free within his own enclosure and should not be troubled by incursions.'

Even in that quiet dawn of the industrial age, the villages of the forest were unloved satellites of the great city. They felt its gravitational pull but not its warmth. Paris had always been terrified of its *banlieue*. Exploiting its labour and resources, the city tried to keep it at a distance and even to abolish it altogether. In 1548, Henri II had ordered that the new houses in the *faubourgs* should be demolished at their owners' expense. In 1672, when it was too late to stop the *faubourgs* from snaking into the countryside, all building beyond the outer perimeter was banned. It was feared that Paris would suffer the fate of ancient cities that had grown so huge that they could no longer be policed. But the wealth and needs of Paris drew ever larger armies of migrant labourers. They came on the roads, canals and railways that were centred on the capital like the spokes of a wheel. They repaired and serviced the city that treated them as serfs. When a ring of fortifications was placed around Paris in the 1840s, an anarchic zone of overpopulated suburbs quickly filled the belt between the fortifications and the old tax wall. To neutralize the threat to public order, the new suburbs were incorporated into the city in 1859. Yet still the city grew, and every year another group of farms, dairies, vineyards and allotments was engulfed by the tide.

Lying just beyond the limits of the metropolitan area, the villages of Clichy, Livry, Aulnay and Bondy preserved their rural appearance. The last known highwaymen were executed in 1824, by which time the business had become less profitable: railways drained the great east road of traffic, and most of the outsiders who passed through the villages belonged to a vanishing world. They followed much older routes in search of comforts that a modern city could not provide. They came on pilgrimages to the forest chapel of Notre-Dame-des-Anges, where the Virgin Mary had descended from heaven in a flash of light and rescued three merchants from robbers on her birthday in 1212: the stream that ran nearby was found to possess miraculous healing powers. Even when highwaymen had become as scarce as wolves, it was easy to picture those villages as they had been a thousand years before. In fact, the region might have escaped the urban flood entirely were it not for an administrative decision that made the Forest of Bondy a place to be feared with good reason.

FOR CENTURIES, the city's main abattoirs and refuse dump had occupied the site of the Montfaucon gibbet, where a massive medieval tower had stood, each of its gaping windows occupied by a crow-pecked corpse suspended from a chain. As it seethed out towards the Buttes Chaumont and the village of La Villette, the city had spread around its own waste, and the stench had become intolerable. In 1817, a decision had been taken to move the abattoirs to Aubervilliers and the festering mound of filth to the ill-famed Forest of Bondy. By

1849, long, heavy barges were sliding out of Paris every day along the Canal de l'Ourcq to dump the city's excrement on Bondy.

Only when several years' worth of waste had been floated out to the forest did the danger become apparent. Bondy was once again a spectre on the north-eastern horizon. It was as though administrative convenience had been the unwitting servant of an ancient curse. In 1883, a group of concerned citizens alerted the authorities to the new menace with a book titled *L'Infection de Paris*. Every year, as soon as the weather turned warm, 'foul odours' descended on the north-eastern quarters of Paris. The cover of the book showed the city divided into its twenty *arrondissement*s. A small black rectangle at the top right, labelled 'Bondy', was irradiating Paris with pestilential rays. The five *arrondissement*s facing Bondy – tenth, eleventh, eighteenth, nineteenth and twentieth – were black; the others were grey or white depending on their distance from the source of infection. Inside the book, the diagram appeared again, this time with a little table showing the annual death rate to be highest in the *arrondissement*s closest to Bondy, and a terse caption: 'This map speaks for itself.'

The old Forêt de Bondy seemed pathetic by comparison. Modern-day Bondy was killing Parisians by the thousand. 'Sewage men, knackers and other industrial workers are blockading Paris and growing rich at its expense.' And who were these lethal parasites who lived in a blighted landscape of rust and demolition, where normal people retched as soon as they drew breath? Had anyone seen their identity papers? According to the book, the unregistered workers who made a living from the city's waste were 'a transient population of foreigners, mostly Germans and Luxembourgeois of dubious origin' ... It was unclear whether the threat to Paris was believed to come from its own excrement or from the alien population that processed it.

In 1911, braving the stench, an ethnologist went out to see what was left of the old way of life. He travelled to the Forest of Bondy on the anniversary of the Virgin's birth. There, between the villages of Clichy and Montfermeil, he found pilgrims still flocking to the little chapel of Notre-Dame-des-Anges. But the ancient traditions had been infected – or so it seemed to the ethnologist – by what he took to be the modern world. The simple piety of the medieval peasant was nowhere in evidence. The sickly smell of fried food hung over the wooden shacks that housed the pilgrims, and many of the faithful were clearly inspired by something other than religious fervour: 'One may be quite certain that, for most of the thousands who visit the chapel, the water of the miraculous fountain is not their principal source of liquid refreshment.' The chapel itself had recently been burgled, which seemed to prove that nothing was sacred any more.

Despite the growth of their enormous neighbour, change came slowly to the hills of the north-east. As the pestilential odours succumbed to modern technology, ever larger sections of the forest were carved into plots and sold to Parisian tradesmen looking for cheap retirement homes in the country. They brought with them their garden forks and pruning shears, and their proletarian ideals and organizations. As the old hierarchy of landlord and peasant dissolved, the villages became part of a 'Red Belt' of socialist and radical councils that seemed to present yet another threat to the security of Paris. But the rural past hung on, and even at the outbreak of the Second World War, the owner of one of those modest plots could still collect manure for his rose bushes from the cows that ambled along the main streets of Livry and Clichy.

It was only a matter of time before the area was engulfed by Greater Paris. Urbanization spread along the Canal de l'Ourcq, bringing its own trees and topsoil as a final insult to the forest. The neat little houses with their iron railings began to look as quaint and vulnerable as the cottages they had replaced. The first blocks of flats were built in 1960, then came the social housing projects with names that might have been chosen in desperation from a municipal catalogue: the Hamlet, the Village, Temple Wood, the Old Mill. Soon, the original terrain with its mounds and hollows was bulldozed into irrelevancy and was noticeable only to pedestrians with heavy shopping or arthritis. The pilgrims' chapel was stuck on a patch of hard-wearing grass beside the four-lane Boulevard Gagarine, and the miraculous stream was led off through a culvert. Later, the sacred well became polluted and was stopped up. More tower blocks were erected on what were now the exposed and windy heights: 'Les Cosmonautes', 'Allende', 'La Tour Victor Hugo'.

The immigrant workers, who had once come from Alsace and

Germany, and then from Brittany and the south, now came from even further afield – Turkey and the Middle East, the Maghreb and Equatorial Africa, China and south-east Asia. Parisians who had moved to the suburb a generation before, and who had looked down their noses at the rustic locals, asked themselves, as they stood at the bus stop next to black, brown or yellow-skinned people dressed in brightly coloured prints and camel-skin jellabas, whether they still lived in a country called France.

It would be hard to say exactly when the region was severed from its rural past forever, and when the wilderness returned to the Bondy Forest in a different guise. The ridge of gypsum above Clichy and Montfermeil continued to produce plaster of Paris until 1965, and there were still some market gardens supplying the local grocers who held out against the supermarkets. On the other side of the canal, at Aulnay-sous-Bois, even when most of the population was commuting into Paris, there were fields of wheat, oats, barley, beetroot and potatoes. But the farmland was shrinking, and the rich smells of pigs and ploughed earth, which had reminded some of the newcomers of villages they had left behind, became ever fainter. The old world ended without anyone noticing. One day in the 1960s, when the Eiffel Tower could still be seen from the higher ground, the last farmer reached the end of his field, turned his tractor back towards 'the Village', and left his land to the developers.

2. Valley of Angels

THE SOUND OF the engines faded, and for a moment, they seemed to be safe. A steel gate that was supposed to close off a patch of wasteground had been left open. The three boys darted through it and into the undergrowth. Scraggy trees had grown up there like squatters in a condemned building. Their thin branches were tangled with creepers, and their roots clung on to old rubbish. It was a little remnant of forest in which three boys could hide from their pursuers.

There had been ten of them at the sports ground playing football, and not just playing: half the boys from Clichy-sous-Bois were technical wizards for the simple reason that there wasn't much else to do in the holidays apart from wasting time on the PlayStation and hanging about at the *centre commercial* or the Muslim Burger King listening to zouk and American rap on pirated CDs. They knew how to curve the ball in from the corner to the head of a Zidane or a Thierry Henry who would knock it down through the goalkeeper's fumbling feet. One of them – Bouna's little brother – had been spotted by a scout and sent for a trial at Le Havre. They were agile and tricky, and these three in particular were fast and had an instinctive understanding of each other. Bouna was black and came from Mauritania; Muhittin was Turkish and a Kurd; Zyed was an Arab from Tunisia, and a kind of legend in the suburb: he was known as 'Lance-pierre' ('Slingshot') because he could throw a chestnut and hit a window on the sixteenth floor.

They had noticed the dimming of the light before they looked at the time. It was the last week of Ramadan, and none of them had eaten since morning. Their parents were very strict about the six-o'clock rule. All ten of them had started to run when they heard the police sirens, but most of them had been caught, and now there were just the three boys, heading back to the monolithic forest of towers where the wind that never stopped blowing filled the entrances with litter.

Once, there had been marble in the foyers, and janitors who took out the rubbish and made sure the lifts were working. A generation later, the towers were like derelict buildings. Water ran down the walls and the corridors stank of urine. The planes coming in to land at Roissy Charles-de-Gaulle always missed them, but the towers were falling apart anyway. Children's bikes and old furniture that had been pushed onto the balconies made the apartment blocks look ragged, as though they had been eviscerated by a bomb blast. Some of the families who lived there never went out, and since the names on the letterboxes downstairs had been torn away or defaced, it was as if they didn't exist. Years before, they had fled from persecution by the FLN or the Khmer Rouge. Now, they were terrorized by teenagers: Clichy-sous-Bois had the youngest population in France, and one of the highest rates of unemployment.

The sirens swirled around on the gusty wind, rushing through gaps between buildings, bouncing off walls. A man who worked at the crematorium had seen the boys crossing the building site – wearing hoods and headphones, their Nikes flashing in the gloom – and had telephoned the police, because they might fall into a hole and hurt themselves, or because they must be thinking of stealing something.

As a precaution, none of them carried identity papers (it had taken their families years to get those papers), but a boy without papers was liable to be arrested, and Zyed had been told by his father that if he was picked up by the police for whatever reason, he would be sent back to Tunisia, which would be a fate worse than death.

A policeman or a bourgeois would have found their route irregular and suspicious. Knowing the lie of the land, they were heading for home in a logical straight line from the football pitch – across the building site and the 'Pama' (Parc de la Mairie) after Avenue de Sévigné, towards the towers of Le Chêne Pointu and La Vallée des Anges, where Zyed lived. The glare of security lamps darkened the twilight. They ran to the rhythm of the music in their ears. '*La FranSSe est une garce . . . comme une salope il faut la traiter, mec! . . . Moi je pisse sur Napoléon et leur Général de Gaulle . . . Putain de flics de fils de pute.*'

The sucking sound of the police sirens came through loud and clear. One of the other boys, crouching behind a burned-out car, had seen the policemen go by. Some of them were in plain clothes, which was not a good sign, and they were carrying flash-ball guns (marketed as 'the less lethal weapon' – because the bullets were not supposed to penetrate a clothed body). Bouna, Zyed and Muhittin had run like wingers on a break in the closing seconds of the game to the other side of the park, hared across the road and dived into the wooded wasteground. This was, in police parlance, 'an extremely hilly sector', and since the policemen came from Livry-Gargan, where only French people lived, they might soon give up and go home.

The wasteground was a no-man's-land, somewhere on the edge of Clichy-sous-Bois, which itself was nowhere in particular.

NOW THAT IT HAD been swallowed by Greater Paris, the north-eastern *banlieue* was further than ever from the boulevards. Many of its inhabitants had never been to Paris and had never seen the Eiffel Tower. Clichy-sous-Bois had no railway station. Its transport links with the centre were tenuous and inconvenient. The area was 'enclaved'. Clichy wasn't even on the RER map: it lay somewhere in the out-of-scale empty space between Sevran-Livry and Le Raincy-Villemomble-Montfermeil, which looked like insignificant outposts, even though a quarter of a million people lived there. In *Les Misérables*, when Jean Valjean rescued Cosette from her foster parents at Montfermeil and brought her back to Paris by way of Livry and Bondy, he was able to take a direct service from the centre of the city: a bus for Bondy left from the Rue Sainte-Apolline near the Porte Saint-Martin. But in 2005, Bouna's father, who was a dustman, like Zyed's, spent an hour on the RER every morning on his way home from work and then had to wait for the 601 which wandered about for six miles before dropping him off near Notre-Dame-des-Anges.

In any case, a *renoi* or a *rebeu* (a Black or an Arab) from the suburbs was no more likely to tour the sights than a nineteenth-century inhabitant of the Faubourg Saint-Marceau would have gone for a stroll in the Faubourg Saint-Germain. For a boy from the *banlieue*, Paris was one of the big railway stations or the Forum des Halles, where French boys and girls spent thousands of euros on designer clothes and CDs, took drugs and kissed in public, as though they had no brothers to look out for them and didn't know the meaning of respect.

Paris was also known to be extremely dangerous. On the day he received his first diploma, a Moroccan boy had gone to Paris to visit his aunt. He had been arrested at the Gare de Lyon and beaten up by four policemen in a cell, then released without charge. Everyone had similar tales to tell. The police would stop a boy in the street, force him to take off his jeans and insult his family or what they took to be his religion. Sometimes, they pretended they were going to kill him or grabbed him by the balls and said things that must have been written down somewhere in a police manual. '*T'aimes ça, petite pédale, qu'on te les tripote, hein? Allez, vas-y, là, chiale un coup devant tes potes!*' ('You like having them tickled, don't you, you little poof? Go on, show your mates what a cry-baby you are!') It happened in the *banlieue* too, but at least in the *banlieue* there was a sense of community, and there were places where the police never went.

This is why they had taken to their heels when they heard the sirens, and why they began to panic when they heard another car pulling up on the other side of the wasteground.

The wasteground sloped down steeply to the south. There were soft mounds of earth where trees had fallen over as though they had been trying to get away. It had once been a plaster quarry, and then a municipal dump. Before that, it had belonged to the Abbey of Clichy. They were standing somewhere above the old abbey cellars, in the magical place that Mme de Sévigné had loved to visit. She had written from there to her daughter in 1672: 'It is hard for me to see this garden, these alleys, the little bridge, the avenue, the meadow, the forest, the mill and the little view, without thinking of my darling child.'

They hurried through the trees and found the edge of the wasteground marked by a concrete wall. On the other side of the wall was an enclosed area full of metal structures and windowless buildings. Beyond that was the row of little houses with tidy front gardens and security gates along the Rue de l'Abbaye. The neighbourhood dogs were barking, excited by the sirens and the flashing lights. The boys could hear the crackle of the police radios just a few yards away. At least one other car had pulled up, and the wasteground seemed to be surrounded. The only place to go was over the wall. There were notices on the wall – as there were all over the *banlieue*: a skull-and-crossbones, some writing, and a raised black hand that looked like a stencilled graffito. Another sign showed a cartoon face with lightning bolts for hair. They climbed the wall, too scared to worry about the height, and dropped down on the other side.

TWO RINGS OF CABLES surround the City of Light – one at a distance of twenty-four kilometres, the other at sixteen kilometres from the centre. Though no one would ever go to see them, these two enormous rings are as important in the history of Paris as the walls and ramparts that mark the stages of the city's expansion. The outer ring carries 400,000 volts. The inner ring, which reached Clichy-sous-Bois in 1936, carries 225,000 volts. In France, this dual configuration is unique to Paris. If one substation is affected, some of the power can be made up by the next substation along, and in this way, the Paris region, which consumes one-fifth of the electricity used in France, is protected from major power cuts.

The three boys had taken refuge in the Clichy substation, which reduces the incoming voltage to 20,000 volts and feeds it into the distribution network. First, they tried a door in the main building, but the door was locked. Then they climbed a gate into a compound within the enclosed area, and went to stand as far from the gate as possible: if the policemen tried to get in, they could still try to hide behind one of the transformers.

Bouna and Zyed stood on one side of the compound, Muhittin on the other. There was no longer any hope of getting home by six o'clock. The best thing was to wait for the police to go away. Ten minutes passed, then another ten minutes. The policemen sat in their cars, their blue lights flailing across the trees. They were talking to the operator at Livry-Gargan: 'Yeah, *Livry, we've located the two individuals; they're climbing into the EDF* site ...*' '*Repeat end of message ...*' '*Yeah, I think they're going into the EDF site. Better get some back-up so we can surround the area.*' '*OK, got that.*' At one point, one of the policemen was heard to say, '*S'ils rentrent sur le site EDF, je ne donne pas cher de leur peau*': 'I don't fancy their chances (literally: 'I wouldn't give much for their skin') if they go into the EDF site.'

Four cars and eleven policemen had taken up position around the compound. No one called the electricity company or the fire brigade. The boys had entered the substation at about half-past five. At twelve minutes past six, one of the boys – Bouna or Zyed – raised his arms in a gesture of desperation or impatience, hoping for a miracle or trying to work off some nervous energy. It is likely that, by then, the police had left the scene, since no one reported the brilliant flash of light that danced above the walls and disappeared.

3. Immigrant

TWENTY HOURS BEFORE, the Minister of the Interior had visited the north-western suburb of Argenteuil after dark. It was a deliberately provocative visit. Some stones were thrown by local youths and bounced off the security guards' hastily opened umbrellas. A woman

---

* Électricité de France.

called down to the minister from the balcony of a tower block and asked if he was going to do something about the *racaille* ('scum'). The television camera showed the minister looking up at the balcony. For a moment, he was eclipsed by the shaven head of a boy who was jumping about, trying to get his grinning face on TV. Then the minister jabbed his finger aggressively over his shoulder, and said to the woman on the balcony, 'You want someone to get rid of those gangs of scum, don't you? . . . We'll get rid of them for you.'

A short man dwarfed by his security officers, he nonetheless looked like a man who was not to be trifled with. He had removed his tie, and he wore an expression that was something between a scowl and a leer – the face of the cowboy vigilante who knows that the bad guy is out of bullets. There was a lunge and swagger about his gestures that made it easy to edit the videos and make him look like a rapper – '*When I hear de word* banlieue, *I get muh flash-ball out!*' (The joke was that the minister had ordered the prosecution of a rapper for defamation of the French police.)

These walkabouts in the *banlieue* were important opportunities. The minister's popularity rating always soared after a visit to the *banlieue*, and he played his role to perfection. He was the decent man who has finally had enough, who stands up to the hooligans and tells them who's in charge. In June, he had gone to the suburb of La Courneuve, where a child had been shot, and promised that the area would be 'cleaned up with a *Kärcher*', which is a high-pressure hose used to blast the filth off paving stones. He made 'no apology' for using inflammatory words. 'The French language is rich. I see no reason why I shouldn't use its full range.'

As he explained in his manifesto-autobiography, he had had to be tough to survive. In the beginning, he was on his own: 'I had no network, no personal fortune, and I was not a civil servant.' He was a lawyer in the wealthy suburb of Neuilly-sur-Seine. He was also the son of an immigrant, and he had an unusual, foreign-sounding name: Sarközy de Nagy-Bocsa. It might have been Jewish or perhaps Romany, but in any case not French. 'With such a name, many people would have deemed it wise to melt away into anonymity rather than seek the limelight.'

'Sarko' – as he was known to enemies and allies alike – loved his job as Minister of the Interior: 'Day and night, drama and passion rise up at the office door: hostage crises, terrorist threats, forest fires, demonstrations, raves, bird flu, floods, disappearances – the responsibility is overwhelming.' He saw himself at Sangatte, in the hangar where illegal immigrants were penned: 'Three thousand pairs of eyes imploring me and threatening. None of them spoke a single word of French. They expected everything of me, but I had so little to give.' He increased the fingerprint database from 400,000 to 2.3 million, and allowed foreign prostitutes who betrayed their pimps to remain in the country.

Out of devotion to his job, he had neglected his wife: there were sacrifices that had to be made. The country was falling apart. Rural France was being colonized by the British, and French businessmen were emigrating to London. His own daughter-in-law had gone there to work for a bank. Middle-class people saw their investments losing value, while unionized workers thought they had a God-given right to a minimum wage.

He remembered how, as a fifteen-year-old boy, he had laid a flower under the Arc de Triomphe on the day of General de Gaulle's funeral. No one cared about the nation any more. French football supporters booed the 'Marseillaise'. Cowards who had been shot in the First World War were rehabilitated. Napoleon Bonaparte was likened to Adolf Hitler, and colonization was seen as a criminal enterprise.

As a professional politician, he did whatever he could to earn the respect of the police. He allowed them to carry flash-balls and, since 'the biggest problem is housing', he gave them better barracks and police stations. When a police officer married or had a child, the officer received a personalized bouquet from the minister. The minister's own Labrador, Indy, had been sent for training with the counter-terrorist RAID unit of the national police. Policemen would no longer have to work with their hands tied behind their backs: the old 'defensive strategy' would be replaced with an 'offensive philosophy' that would 'bring firepower to zones of lawlessness'.

His speeches were played to members of the public assembled by a public-relations firm. The members of the public held joysticks connected to a computer, and twitched the sticks in response to what they heard: left for negative, right for positive. The word '*racaille*' had produced a significant jerk to the right.

The woman on the balcony at Argenteuil on the evening of 26 October had unwittingly uttered a vote-winning word. Journalists would always find some elderly white woman with shopping bags or a well-dressed social worker to say that things were not so bad in the *banlieue*, that young people had nothing to do and were poorly treated. But no politician could ignore the fears of ordinary people when they saw the beautiful city of Paris besieged by the *racaille*.

4. City of Light

AT TWELVE MINUTES past six on 27 October 2005, the lights went out in Clichy-sous-Bois. There were howls of dismay in a hundred thousand households. Then the emergency backup supply kicked in, and the lights came back on. This was the sort of service people had come to expect in the rundown *banlieue*.

A teenage boy came shambling into town, looking like some kind of alien. He was heading for La Vallée des Anges and Le Chêne Pointu. His face was a nasty shade of yellow, and his clothes were smouldering as though he was about to burst into flames. He slumped along, eyes glazed, muttering something incomprehensible.

He reached the shopping centre at 6.35. The first person he saw was Bouna's older brother, Siyakha Traoré. Muhittin could barely speak, as though his tongue was too big for his mouth. Siyakha made out just two words, which he repeated over and over again: *Bouna ... accident ...*

He had clambered over the wall in a dream. The policemen were nowhere to be seen. He had noticed that his clothes were burning, which seemed incredible. His friends had disappeared in a flash of light. For a moment, the air had been on fire. The next thing he knew, his jacket was being pulled up over his head by Siyakha's friend.

The friend phoned for an ambulance while Muhittin led Siyakha through the park. He was saying, 'They chased us ...'

They reached a place near a mound of trees that Siyakha, in all the years he had lived in Clichy-sous-Bois, had never noticed. He could feel the heat coming off the concrete walls, and there was a smell that reminded him of a sick room. He asked, 'Where are they?' Muhittin covered his face with one arm and pointed with the other: 'In there.'

Later that night, Muhittin lay on the operating table and then in a sterile room at the Hôpital Saint-Antoine, watched by his father, an unemployed brick mason, who spoke to him through the Hygiaphone. The news was spreading through the *banlieue*, first by word of mouth, then by television and radio, and then, more slowly, like incessant, heavy rain, through the blogosphere.

The sequence of events became muddled almost immediately. The crucial pieces of information were carried along by an overwhelming narrative that had the unmistakeable appearance of truth. No matter how often the facts were cut and pasted, edited and translated into the evolving language of the *banlieue*, they always came out the same. The police had caused the death of two boys in Clichy-sous-Bois. The Minister of the Interior had called them 'scum'. Another boy was fighting for his life. The victims were a Black, an Arab and a Kurd. They were boys from the *banlieue*, no different from anyone else. One of them was only fifteen years old.

On the following night, twenty-three cars were set alight in Clichy-sous-Bois, and there were pitched battles with the police. Cars were always burning somewhere in the suburbs, but now the fires were like hilltop beacons signifying an invasion or a festival.

From his hospital bed, where he had to lie very still because of all the skin grafts, Muhittin could watch a television that was bracketed to the wall. Sometimes, he was in tears; at other times, he trembled with rage. Politicians were feeding the flames with their lies. On his second day in hospital, he was questioned by the police, who brought a computer and a printer and spoke to him without using the Hygiaphone. 'Look what you've done now,' they said. 'Thirteen cars were set on fire yesterday.' They told him to sign the statement, and since he was unable to write with his burned hands, they made him sign with a cross.

The signed statement was leaked to the press. Muhittin Altun was said to have confessed that the police had not been chasing them, and that they had been fully aware of the danger of entering an EDF site.

Furthermore, the Prime Minister and the Minister of the Interior announced that according to information received from the police, the boys who died had been in the act of committing a burglary.

On 30 October, a tear-gas grenade launched by the police exploded outside the Bilal mosque at Clichy-sous-Bois and the fumes wafted into the building. The mosque was full because it was near the end of Ramadan. The congregation tumbled into the street to see policemen pointing their guns and shouting. Then the situation 'stabilized': that night, only twenty cars were set on fire. But the violence was spreading, at first in a tight arc around the northern suburbs, then fanning out to the west and the south.

In the days when Northmen had sailed down the Seine to plunder Paris, chroniclers had exaggerated the calamity to match the magnitude of the offence. In 2005, television news performed a similar function. A map of France, less accurate than the charts of medieval geometers, appeared on CNN, showing Lille on the coast and Toulouse in the Alps. Commentators analysed the situation and warned of a cataclysm of international dimensions: the burning of the Paris *banlieue* was connected with racial tension, terrorism, fundamentalist Islam, the practice of polygamy and the wearing of the veil. Paris was no longer the enchanted enclave of biscuit-tin memorials preserved by architects and politicians for the benefit of the admiring world. It was something vast and shapeless, ugly, unruly and uncharted. Its population of intellectuals, café waiters and *femmes fatales* had vanished. A new population of Parisians appeared in the international media, their hooded faces flaring out of the apocalyptic gloom when police cars passed with flashing lights or another petrol bomb exploded.

At the beginning of November, the capital was ringed with fire. From Clichy-sous-Bois, the inferno seemed to be heading for the centre of Paris along the Canal de l'Ourcq, through Bondy, Bobigny, Pantin and La Villette. On 6 November, civil disorder had spread to twelve other cities from Brittany to the Mediterranean.

The Minister of the Interior talked of 'extreme violence such as is rarely seen in France', but the people at the centre of the eruption knew that they were witnessing something that was practically a speciality of Paris. The police intelligence service was preparing a confidential report: the troubles had nothing to do with religion, race or country of origin. No terrorists or gangs were involved. The violence was entirely spontaneous. This was not juvenile delinquency, it was an 'urban insurrection' and a 'popular revolt'.

The revolutionary spirit of the *faubourgs* was still alive, and old Parisian traditions were being upheld by the *racaille*. On 8 November, paying tribute to the City of Light, hundreds of towns and cities were in flames, from Perpignan to Strasbourg, and a state of national emergency was declared.

Those unsightly quarters of Paris called the *banlieue* were proving themselves worthy of the capital. One day, perhaps, like other popular revolts, the riots would be seen as the birth pangs of a new metropolis. Paris had been expanding since the Middle Ages, pouring over the plains and flooding the valleys of the river system, as though it would eventually fill the entire Paris Basin. Each eruption had threatened to destroy the city, but each time, a new Paris had risen from the ashes. In the glowering hills that could be seen from Montmartre and the Eiffel Tower, a world was taking shape, and the millions of people who had known and loved Paris would have to return to discover the city again. Meanwhile, tour companies and hotels were reporting mass cancellations. From their concrete canyons and eyries, the inhabitants of the *banlieue* were sending out their electronic messages, which were translated by the world's press from a *banlieusard* patois composed of French, Arabic, Romany, Swahili and American English.

Their Paris was a rap litany of place names that only the most exhaustive guide book would have recognized as the City of Light: Clichy-sous-Bois, La Courneuve, Aubervilliers, Bondy … This was the city that had grown from an island in the Seine until it stretched to the horizon in all directions. The *racaille* were marking their tribal territories in that great grey mass of buildings between the wooded massif of Meudon and the plains of the Beauce and the Brie. They, too, were children of Paris, and, like true natives of the city, they expressed their pride in angry words that sounded like a curse. And since, by some miracle, the world was reading their messages, they wrote of the perilous adventures and the unforgettable education that awaited anyone who dared to visit the wilds of the undiscovered city: 'If you come to Bondy, you won't get out alive! …'

TERMINUS:
THE NORTH COL

WE REACHED BONDY on our touring bikes just as the sun was turning the Canal de l'Ourcq into a ribbon of grey steel. That morning, we had set off from the Col du Donon, which lies nine hundred and eighty feet below the highest peak of the Vosges mountains in north-eastern France. For centuries, the col was used by Celtic tribes and Roman legions passing between Germany and Gaul. Its importance as a crossing-point is marked by the remains of a temple to Mercury and, on the southern ascent, by a memorial to the *passeurs* who helped French prisoners to escape from the Nazis. From there, we had spiralled down through the pine forests, over the Grendelbruch Pass, to the valley of the Rhine and the city of Strasbourg, then crossed the plains of northern France. By the time we reached Paris, we had covered five hundred and eighty-one kilometres at an average speed of 92 kph, according to my GPS unit, which, in the excitement of reaching Strasbourg railway station on time, I had forgotten to turn off.

A canalside bike path starts near the Gare de l'Est. It crosses the toy-town science park of La Villette, and passes under the baleful eyes of the neo-Gothic flour mills, the Grands Moulins de Pantin, which, until 2003, sucked in all the wheat of the Brie and the Beauce to feed the *boulangeries* of Paris. After Pantin, the *piste cyclable* wanders through a maze of half-demolished buildings, past the hulks of abandoned factories inexplicably 'under video surveillance', every window smashed and every surface covered by graffiti-artists as resourceful and determined as property developers. Then, rejoining the canal, it straightens out, and the speed picks up enough to change

[425]

into the big chain-ring. Suddenly, approaching Bondy and the bridges that carry the Périphérique de l'Île-de-France, which marks the heliopause of the Paris system, we were pedalling alongside the Métro. A train was slowing down before veering into the Bobigny–Pablo Picasso station, and we could see the faces of passengers staring out at the open air.

At that time of evening, the north-eastern *banlieue* looked like a promotional film for home-buyers and investors. A Black African was walking along the tidy embankment with a friend who appeared to be Kurdish; a little girl was gleefully escaping from her parents on a tricycle. There was a startling absence of broken glass on the towpath; the only danger was a fast dog chasing the figures-of-eight of a fresh smell. After Bondy, where the canal swings north-east, in the cavernous gloom of yet another road bridge, three teenage boys were standing, looking tough and nervy, deep in some shared concern but obviously open to distractions. When they saw us coming, they moved to one side, and, with a shout of recognition, cheerfully saluted Margaret because she was wearing the red cap of a French cycling team, Brioches la Boulangère.

We left the canal at a pedestrian bridge and rode for two kilometres through the streets of Aulnay-sous-Bois. The Hôtel du Parc was a five-storey concrete dormitory with a view of a car park. The Senegalese man at the reception desk sent us down to the cellar to store our bikes; then he asked us where we had come from 'like that'.

Every cyclist enjoys the chance to shrug off an epic expedition and to extol the miraculous efficiency of the bicycle, and so I told him, 'This morning, we were on top of the Vosges mountains; we cycled down to Strasbourg and took the TGV to the Gare de l'Est.'

The man looked slightly puzzled, his question evidently unanswered. 'No, no,' he said, 'I mean, how did you get here from the Gare de l'Est?' 'We cycled out along the canal.' His eyebrows shot up, and he almost shouted, 'You came all the way here from the Gare de l'Est – on your bikes?!' – 'Yes ...' – '*Oh là là! C'est fort, ça!*' ('Blimey! That beats everything!') Shaking his head, he handed us our room key, and said again, '*Ah! C'est fort, ça!*'

It was not the fact of having cycled seventeen kilometres that amazed him but the thought of actually traversing that solidified ocean of shunting yards, building sites, cemeteries, schools, hospitals, stadiums, advertising space and infrastructure that joins Paris to the *banlieue*. For some reason – personal challenge, GPS malfunction or an inappropriate foreign way of doing things? – we had spurned the merciful oblivion of the transport network to pursue our unimaginable course through the great abstraction.

Next morning, with the rain bucketing down, the expedition may well have appeared to verge on the eccentric. We cycled across the canal and the unfenced railway tracks to Clichy-sous-Bois. After exploring the area around the EDF site where the two boys had died, we headed back towards Paris. During one of the heavier downpours, we stopped under a bridge where a dead smiley face in blue paint announced the supremacy of 'The Canal Brotherhood' and the boys of 'North Bondy', all of whom had sensibly remained indoors. We left the canal near the Périphérique de l'Île-de-France and splashed along the main street of Drancy to the hideous apartment blocks of La Muette. It was here that Jews from the Vel' d'Hiv had been incarcerated in 1942. The buildings had been completed after the war as though nothing had happened. The U-shaped block around the central courtyard survived the demolition of the towers in the 1970s and is now used as 'social housing'. Most of the five hundred people who live there are waiting to be moved to less squalid accommodation. Some of them were standing under the concrete awnings as though they were ready to leave at any moment.

On a photograph taken that morning in Drancy, a complex expression on Margaret's usually sunny face suggests that this would never be counted among our favourite springtime trips to Paris. Fortunately, the visit to the *banlieue* was just a prelude: we were returning to Paris on a mission. Three months before, a chance discovery in a Paris bookshop had turned up a tantalizing trace of something that had been lost for many centuries. It had been one of the most important sites in Paris, and was in some ways the foundation of all the city's future glories.

The rain eased off as we reached the edge of the eighteenth *arrondissement*. Patches of eggshell-blue sky appeared above the Sacré-Cœur. It seemed as though the conjunction of personal adventure and historical discovery would occur. Foolishly, I uttered the ritual phrase, 'Paris will never look the same again.' Almost immediately, as though the demon twin of Saint Christopher who accompanies every traveller had been listening, we were lost. The eighteenth *arrondissement*, where I had lived as a teenager, did not look the same, and the elementary GPS unit showed only a dithering line of dots on a blank background. The streets that were crammed in between the railway lines in the 1930s surreptitiously change direction whilst appearing to run straight. On what turned out to be the tiny, disproportionately confusing Place Hébert, I unfolded the flapping map of Paris, and, after a few more ritual phrases, we set off again in the direction of the Porte de la Chapelle.

COMING FROM GRENOBLE, where the Alps rise up 'at the end of every street', Stendhal was 'disgusted' by his first sight of Paris in 1799: 'The environs struck me as horribly ugly – there were no mountains!' The capital of France was a geographical anti-climax, a city built on sand and puddles. One of its grandest *quartier*s was called 'the Marsh' (le Marais); its original name, Lutetia, was thought to be derived from a Gaulish word for 'mud' or 'swamp'. Every thirty years or so, the Seine, suffering from senile amnesia, flooded half of Swampville in an attempt to get back to its old bed, which lies a kilometre and a half to the north of the Île de la Cité, along the line of the Grands Boulevards. The knobbly mounds of gypsum that rimmed the city were like a botched imitation of the Seven Hills of Rome. During the nineteenth century, some of them were even rounded off and flattened, as though town planners had taken Isaiah's prophecy to heart: 'Every mountain and hill shall be made low: and the crooked shall be made straight'.

In 1899, the popular geographer Onésime Reclus found some ironic consolation in the fact that the Paris meridian exactly bisects the peak of Mount Bugarach, six hundred and sixty-four kilometres to the south. He declared Mount Bugarach to be a Parisian Pyrenee, 'the Metropolitan Pic du Midi': Paris had a mountain after all ... But a mountain that was invisible even from the Eiffel Tower on a clear day was a part of the Parisian landscape only in the most abstract sense. Pending future upheavals of the Paris Basin, the capital would have to be content with its grandly named little lumps: Montmartre,

Montparnasse, Montrouge, Montsouris and the Montagne-Sainte-Geneviève.

It was in January 2008, while browsing in a Latin Quarter bookshop, that I discovered what appeared to be a mountain in one of the most densely populated parts of Paris. It was such an unlikely discovery that I wanted to leave the shop at once, with the precious information stored away and preserved, at least for a few days, from the inevitable disappointment. Like every visitor to Paris, I had made 'discoveries' that were known already to millions of people – the mysterious little attic room on the south face of Notre-Dame overlooking the Seine, or the crenellated brick tower that hides in a shrubbery near the western foot of the Eiffel Tower (a chimney left over from the old hydraulic lifts). Then there were the discoveries that were purely archival – things that had vanished so completely that the imagination had no purchase on the present: the unmarked location of the guillotine that beheaded Marie-Antoinette, or the little-known Isle Merdeuse ('Shitty Island') that used to lie in the Seine in front of what is now the seat of the French parliament. And finally, there were all the discoveries that weren't discoveries at all, because, despite plausible real equivalents, they existed only in a writer's imagination: the seedy boarding house 'in that vale of flaking plaster and streams of black mud' behind the Panthéon where Balzac's *Le Père Goriot* begins, or the curiosity shop on the Quai Voltaire where Raphaël de Valentin in *La Peau de chagrin* acquires the magical ass's skin that makes his every wish come true.

This time, I felt sure that something real lay behind the excitement, and that, for once, instead of simply hoarding the memory of its treasures, I would be giving something back to Paris. The clue was an engraving made in 1685 by an anonymous artist. It shows the village of La Chapelle (now part of the eighteenth *arrondissement*) strung out along a ridge, its little houses silhouetted against a white sky under billowing, rococo clouds. A hedge-lined road climbs up through neatly furrowed fields to a small church tower that stands at the highest point: it was there that the road from Paris crossed the main street through the village before dropping down on the other side.

To anyone who has walked or cycled through France with a vision of the map's lines and symbols superimposed on the landscape, the engraving is instantly recognizable as the picture of a col. Cols or mountain passes are a kind of international velocipedal currency: the difficulty of a ride – or a stage of the Tour de France – is measured by the number of cols it crosses, and even if the cols are only a few hundred metres above sea level, a rider who has crossed them is entitled to feel that mountains have been conquered. Often, they are marked by a chapel, a cross or a standing stone, and, if officially recognized as cols, by a special road sign. A col – also known as a *pas* (or a *porte* if it straddles a frontier) – is a gateway to another world. At cols, as at river confluences and tribal boundaries, human history and physical geography are in closest conjunction.

Ever since hearing of a cyclists' organization called the Club des Cent Cols, I had been keeping a list of the cols we had crossed on our travels, accidentally or on purpose. The Donon was number 215 on the list, and the Grendelbruch Pass number 216. A cyclist who has crossed at least a hundred different cols, 'for personal pleasure' rather than in a spirit of competition, can submit a complete list, and, provided that all the cols appear in the club's catalogue, the new member receives a colourful diploma stating that the holder has, 'on a cycle propelled by muscular force alone, climbed at least 100 cols, including 5 over 2000 metres'.

As Stendhal might have guessed, Paris lies in the middle of a col desert. While the mountainous borderlands and the Massif Central have thousands of cols, there are barely ten between the Vosges mountains and the hills of Normandy, and only one within a day's ride of Notre-Dame. This seems particularly sad since the introduction of the 'Vélib' self-service scheme in 2007. Every day, on lumpy grey bikes that might have materialized from a children's cartoon, thousands of Parisians rediscover their city's topography: the Avenue des Champs-Élysées is once again a hill, and 'Montagne Sainte-Geneviève' is no longer a misnomer. Yet there is no official recognition of the exploits of *vélibistes*, and nothing that allows pedalling Parisians to celebrate the eminence of their city.

The hypothetical pass at La Chapelle seemed to promise reparation. If the summit of the road that climbs up from the Seine to cross the northern ridge was a col, then the hills on either side of it –

Montmartre and the Buttes-Chaumont – could legitimately be counted as mountains ...

In January, a preliminary investigation on foot produced some encouraging evidence. At the church of Saint-Denys-de-la-Chapelle, opposite the Hollywood Video shop and the Sex in the City club, the road slopes down on either side. The old Roman road from the south and the Rue du Faubourg-Saint-Denis converged at what is now the Marx Dormoy Métro station. In the other direction, the road descends gently to the plain of Saint-Denis where the gigantic medieval fair of Lendit was held. Some historians believe that this convenient plateau above the marshes of Lutetia was the sacred 'centre of Gaul' where, according to Caesar, Druids came from as far away as the Mediterranean and Britannia to elect their supreme pontiff.

La Chapelle still has the bustle and turbulence of a major crossing point. The main street is a continual two-way procession of cars and trucks. With its jostling crowds and tatty shops, it has more of the big city about it than the delicate stage sets of central Paris. Across the road from the church, at the end of the Impasse du Curé, there is a view through iron railings of the Sacré-Cœur on its ant-hill of roofs and chimneys. Far below, trains from Picardy, Flanders and the Channel coast rattle through the deep cutting towards the Gare de l'Est and the Gare du Nord.

In the whispering gloom of the church, a parish history in the form of a small brochure explained that this was the site where Saint Denis, who brought Christianity to Lutetia, was buried along with his severed head: a shrine was raised there in 475 by Saint Geneviève, the nun from Nanterre who had a genius for organizing military resistance and famine relief. Evidently, she knew that martyrs should be buried at places such as cols, through which travellers are forced to pass. Next door to the church, the Joan of Arc basilica marks the site where, in 1429, the Maid of Orleans spent the night before riding down to the gates of occupied Paris, and where she rested the following night after receiving a crossbow bolt in the leg. The parish history was offered as 'a message of welcome and friendship'. We read it by the light of some votive candles. At the top of page two, we discovered that someone had been there before us:

[431]

The church was erected by the side of the great Gaulish road which, after crossing the Seine by the Île de la Cité, passes through a col between Montmartre and Ménilmontant, and proceeds to the town of Saint-Denis and beyond.

The thrill of finding the first piece of corroborative evidence overcame the mild disappointment of being beaten to the col. Three months later, this time with our bicycles, we made what we thought was the first conscious two-wheeled ascent of Paris's only col. At the Porte de la Chapelle, we turned to face south, and set off up the slope with a thousand other road-users. To mark the historic moment, I looked over at the chapel as we reached the summit, but a furniture van was squeezing past, blotting out the view, and the narrow strip of asphalt between its tyres and the kerb was of more immediate interest. A lapse of concentration, and the expedition would have ended, without even the consolation of an official commemorative plaque: 'Died crossing the Col de la Chapelle.'

Then began the real challenge: how to have the col ratified by the Club des Cent Cols. I knew this would not be easy. Every year, the club's 'Ethics, Reflection and Proposal Committee' publishes a list of 'Rejected Cols'. Ridiculous as it might appear to non-cyclists, some tourist offices try to attract *cyclotouristes* by exaggerating the hilliness of their region. Some of them even conjure up non-existent cols and invite cycling clubs and journalists to come and celebrate the erection of a sign. The Club des Cent Cols has no patience with this sort of trickery. Typical entries in the list are:

'Col des Cantonniers' (Var): Invented, without local evidence, for promotional purposes. Contravenes article 11.

'Col des Cyclotouristes' (Savoie): Indistinct topography. Fabricated by local cyclists. Contravenes article 11.

It turned out that there had been some discussion of the Parisian col after a member of the club, on a visit to the 'archaeological crypt' of Notre-Dame, had noticed the words 'Col de la Chapelle' painted on a papier-mâché relief map of ancient Paris. The experts on the committee had decided that there was insufficient evidence, and the case had been closed. The President answered my email as swiftly and efficiently as a racing cyclist swerving past a pothole:

This col has never been accepted. It is not shown on a map, nor is it named by a sign.

At least his message left a glimmer of hope: 'This col...' Its existence was not explicitly denied. Logically, then, the next step was to try to have the col inscribed on a map and printed on a road sign.

I wrote to the Institut Géographique National, electronically and then on paper, including the proper coordinates, and some further evidence from research in the library. It seemed that, back in the days when Prefects Rambuteau and Haussmann were replacing murky alleyways with gas-lit boulevards, an archaeologist called Théodore Vacquer, who resembled 'a permanently curled hedgehog', was snuffling through the debris, trying to piece together a mental image of Lutetia. He found the Roman forum under the Rue Soufflot, and the Roman arena by the Rue Monge. Vacquer was a digger, not a writer, but a study extracted by a geographer from his enormous nest of notes and sketches appeared after his death in 1912. There, for the first time, the existence of a 'Pas de la Chapelle' was revealed. Since then, a few geographers (but not cartographers), stalking into the increasingly uncluttered past of Paris, across Precambrian river beds and hills still wet with ancient seas, have written of the col that lay on the prehistoric 'tin route' from Britannia to the Mediterranean.

Weeks passed. Either an expedition to the lost col had set out from the IGN's headquarters at Vincennes and never returned, or my letter had continued its journey to a recycling centre. In the meantime, I wrote to the mayor of the eighteenth *arrondissement* and to the civic authorities at the Hôtel de Ville.

A month later, a letter arrived from the IGN. It confirmed the 'geographical and topographical' existence of a Parisian col – 'the lowest point between the Butte Montmartre and the Buttes Chaumont'. However, 'until now', the writer teasingly went on, the col has never appeared on an IGN map for two reasons: first, 'the urban fabric is very dense in this area'; second, 'its name is not currently used by the local inhabitants'. In other words, there were already too many place names on the map, and if an explorer arrived at La Chapelle, asking for the col, he would be met with blank stares (unless, of course, he happened to ask a geographer or the man who wrote the parish history).

I waited in vain for replies from the municipal officials, who might not have shared the cartographic scruples of the IGN. But by then, it no longer seemed to matter. A galvanized col sign embedded in the asphalt of La Chapelle would have been nothing but a quaint impediment, a photo opportunity for *vélibistes*, a slightly more durable form of graffiti – assuming that room could have been found for it among all the other sobering statements of urban fact: '*PASSAGE INTERDIT*', '*FIN DE ZONE TOURISTIQUE*', '*VOUS N'AVEZ PAS LA PRIORITÉ*', etc.

Something had been obvious all along: the city, built by human beings, is indifferent to their desires. It shows them the solid form of their fictions, their tales of intimacy and glory, of love and everlasting pride, the legends and stories that only one person ever knew or that recruited generations to their make-believe. It educates even the most successful megalomaniacs in the smallness of their dreams. Paris shows its true face from the top of the Tour Montparnasse, where guards patrol the suicide fence. Most of that galactic scatter of illuminations reaching out to the horizons is darkness.

Every living city is a necropolis, a settling mountain of populations migrating downwards into the soil. Kings, queens and emperors are only its servants. They help it to erase even the possibility of memory. The sites of commemoration built by Napoleon III buried acres of history. A boulevard named after a battle obliterated the mementos of a million lives, and, at the end of his reign, the Archives Nationales went up in flames.

Five thousand miles from Paris, on an island in the South Atlantic, Napoleon Bonaparte dreamed of what he might have done, 'given only twenty years and a little spare time'. In the telescopic eyes of exile, Paris was an orb that he had held in his hand. If only time had served him, the old city would have vanished: 'You would have looked for it in vain. Not even vestiges would have remained.'

On Saint Helena, Napoleon rummaged through his past: the docking of the riverboat under the towers of the Île de la Cité, the crowds that clogged the narrow streets, the École Militaire and the Palais-Royal. He remembered a day in the terrible year of 1792. The alarm bells were ringing, and there were rumours of a great upheaval. A ragged army was surging out of the *faubourgs* towards the

Tuileries. He left his hotel in the Rue du Mail and headed for the *quartier* of slums and ruined mansions between the Louvre and the Carrousel. An ugly gang of ruffians was parading a pikestaff on which a head had been impaled. Noticing the young captain with his clean hands and laundered clothes, they challenged him to shout '*Vive la nation!*' – 'which, as you can imagine, I hastened to do'.

He went on to the Place du Carrousel, where he entered the house of a friend. The building had been turned into a kind of warehouse: it was packed with the belongings of aristocrats who had fled the country, taking whatever money was offered for their furniture, their trinkets and their family portraits. He made his way upstairs, through the debris of the world that was passing away, and looked out of a window: the rabble were storming the Tuileries Palace, butchering the Swiss Guards. From that window, as though from the balcony of a theatre, he witnessed the end of the French monarchy. Years later, on evenings when the Emperor prowled the streets of Paris in disguise, eavesdropping, inspecting the faces of Parisians for clues to the world he was creating, he looked for the house where so much history had been emblazoned on his mind. But his orders for the renovation of the *quartier* had been so swiftly carried out, and 'so many great changes had taken place there that I was never able to find it again'.

THE COL DE LA CHAPELLE is still unrecorded on the map, and there is still no mountain in Paris. Unlike human beings, an accident of geography requires no commemoration, and perhaps, as the IGN's letter suggested, it no longer exists. In the nineteenth century, the railways passed through the col, almost flattening it as they went. The cutting changed the landscape; white steam erupting from the locomotives formed new skies above La Chapelle, fashioning new routes for the imagination – a strand of pavement, a palace of chimneys, a procession of ghosts on a black canal. In 2010, only the volume of traffic testifies to the col's importance. This brainstem of the future city, where travellers passed even before there was a settlement on the island in the Seine, is now the route that is taken by the Eurostar from London. Anyone curious to know the site should look for it on the left side of the Paris-bound train, shortly after the engine sheds marked 'Gare du Landy' (from the 'Lendit' fair at the fabled centre of Gaul). As the train reaches the summit, there is a faint sensation of the motors' tug and release, but the col is easy to miss, since the carriages pass over it when the announcement has already been made – *'Nous arriverons dans quelques instants à la Gare du Nord'* – and it is time to put away the book, gather up the luggage and prepare to meet the miraculous creation where even the quietest street is crowded with adventures.

Chronology

c. 4500 BC Neolithic settlements on the Seine (on the site of modern Bercy).

c. 2nd century BC The Celtic Parisii tribe settles on an island in the Seine.

52 BC Defeat of the Parisii by Caesar's second-in-command, Labienus.

1st century AD Development of the Gallo-Roman city of Lutetia on the left bank of the Seine: forum, aqueduct, baths (Cluny), theatres, amphitheatre (Arènes de Lutèce).

late 3rd century Saint Denis brings Christianity to Lutetia.

360 Julian II proclaimed emperor in Lutetia.

451 Saint Geneviève saves the city, now known as Paris, from Attila the Hun.

508 Clovis, King of the Franks, makes Paris his capital.

543 Foundation of the abbey of Saint-Germain-des-Prés in fields outside the city.

639 The basilica at Saint-Denis becomes the royal necropolis.

885–86 Viking siege of Paris.

10th and 11th centuries Decay of public buildings; shrinking of Paris and its population.

1108–37 Reign of Louis VI, who makes Paris the main royal residence.

c. 1140–1307 Temple fortress: headquarters of the Knights Templar.

1163–1345 Building of the cathedral of Notre-Dame-de-Paris on the site of the Saint-Étienne basilica.

1190– Building of the Louvre and the Philippe-Auguste Wall. Land area of Paris: 2.53 km^2.

1248   Consecration of the Sainte-Chapelle.

1257   Foundation of the Sorbonne.

1328   Population: 61,098 hearths (over 200,000 people). Paris the largest city in Europe.

1356–83   Charles V Rampart and Bastille. Land area of Paris: 4.39 km².

1407   Assassination of Louis d'Orléans, brother of King Charles VI, in the Marais. Start of civil war.

1420   Paris occupied by English and Burgundians.

1429   *September* – Joan of Arc launches an attack on Paris.

1437   *November* – Charles VII recaptures Paris.

1515–47   Reign of François I: development of Louvre; new Hôtel de Ville on the Place de Grève.

1560–74   Regency of Catherine de Médicis. Building of Tuileries Palace.

1572   *23–24 August* – Saint Bartholomew's Day massacre of Protestants.

1588   *12 May* – Day of the Barricades (revolt against Henri III).

1589–1610   Henri IV King of France (crowned 1594). Completion of Pont Neuf, development of the Marais and the Faubourg Saint-Germain.

1635   Académie Française founded by Cardinal de Richelieu.

1648   *26 August* – Day of the Barricades (beginning of Fronde civil wars).

1658   *February* – Flooding of the Seine.

1661–1715   Reign of Louis XIV. Construction of Observatory (1667) and Les Invalides (1671); ramparts replaced by boulevards (1676).

1665–83   Ministry of Jean-Baptiste Colbert: development of road system centred on Paris; creation of Académie des Sciences (1666); creation of post of Lieutenant-Général de Police de Paris (1667), with responsibility for public safety, street-cleaning, etc.

1682   The royal court moves to Versailles.

1686   Opening of the first successful coffee-house, the Café Procope.

1700   Population: c. 515,000.

1702   *12 December* – Paris is divided into twenty *quartiers*.

1715–74   Reign of Louis XV.

1722–28   Palais Bourbon (Assemblée Nationale).

1740   *December* – Flooding of the Seine.

1751–88   École Militaire and Champ de Mars.

1755–75   Creation of the Place de la Concorde.

1775–91   First completely accurate map of Paris, by Edme Verniquet.

1779   First pavement (sidewalk) in Paris, Rue de l'Odéon.

1770s and 80s   Building boom: development of Chaussée-d'Antin and riverbanks, commercial development of Palais-Royal (1781–84), urbanization of outlying villages.

1782   Théâtre-Français (Odéon).

1783   *21 November* – First untethered balloon flight, by Pilâtre de Rozier, from Château de la Muette to the Butte-aux-Cailles.

1784–89   Tax wall of the Fermiers Généraux. Land area of Paris: 33.7 km².

1786   Catacombs built by Charles-Axel Guillaumot.

1789   Population: c. 650,000. *14 July* – Fall of the Bastille. *15 July* – Appointment of first Mayor of Paris. *5–6 October* – Louis XVI forced by popular demonstration to return to Paris from Versailles.

1790   Completion of Église Sainte-Geneviève (Panthéon). *15 January* – France divided into eighty-three *départements*. Paris forms a *département* in its own right.

1791   *21 June* – Arrest of Louis XVI and Marie-Antoinette at Varennes.

1793   *21 January* – Execution of Louis XVI. *10 August* – Opening of Louvre Museum. *16 October* – Execution of Marie-Antoinette.

1794   *17 July* – Office of Mayor of Paris abolished (recreated briefly in 1848 and 1870–71). *28 July* – Execution of Robespierre.

1795 *11 October* – Paris is divided into twelve *arrondissements*, each with its own mayor, and forty-eight *quartiers*.

1799 *November (18 Brumaire)* – Coup d'état: Napoleon Bonaparte First Consul.

1801 First official census – population (underestimated?): 547,000.

1802–26 Canal de l'Ourcq and Bassin de La Villette.

1804 Coronation of Emperor Napoleon I at Notre-Dame; creation of Père-Lachaise cemetery.

1804–14 Renovation and development of Paris, notably on nationalized Church property: first section of Rue de Rivoli, Place du Châtelet, Bourse (Palais Brongniart), continuation of La Madeleine, Arc de Triomphe (completed 1836); new bridges (Ponts des Arts, d'Austerlitz, d'Iéna); system of covered sewers.

1805 First consistent numbering and naming of Paris streets.

1811 Creation of Brigade de la Sûreté.

1814 *31 March* – Paris occupied by Allied armies.
   11 April – First abdication of Napoleon.
   May – First Restoration.

1815 *18 June* – Battle of Waterloo.
   9 July – Second Restoration.

1815–24 Reign of Louis XVIII.

1824 Accession of Charles X.

1828 First successful omnibus service in Paris.

1829 Rue de la Paix becomes the first gas-lit street in Paris.

1830 July Revolution; abdication of Charles X; coronation of Louis-Philippe.

1832 *March–September* – Cholera epidemic.
   June – Repression of popular revolt.

1833–48 C.-P. Barthelot de Rambuteau Prefect of the Seine *département*: renovation and completion of squares and monuments, provision of public fountains, the first tarmac-covered streets and the first street urinals (*vespasiennes*).

1834 *14 April* – Popular insurrection: massacre of men, women and children at 12, Rue Transnonain by the National Guard.

1837   First railway station in Paris: 124, Rue Saint-Lazare.

1841   Population: 935,000 (50% born in Paris; almost 3% of French citizens live in Paris).

1841–44   Adolphe Thiers's ring of fortifications.

1843   Île Louviers joined to the Right Bank of the Seine.

1845–64   Renovation of Notre-Dame by Viollet-le-Duc (inaugurated on Christmas Day, 1862).

1848   February Revolution. *June* – Repression of popular revolt.

1851   *2 December* – Coup d'état of Louis-Napoléon Bonaparte (Emperor Napoleon III, 1852–70).

1853–70   Georges-Eugène Haussmann Prefect of the Seine *département*: 20,000 houses demolished; 44,000 houses and apartment blocks built; roads widened and network extended by 106 km (including four new bridges and 664 km of *trottoirs*); 21,000 more street-lights; drainage system increased from 107 to 561 km; three new parks and eight '*squares*'; thirteen new churches and two synagogues; five new theatres.

1854–57   Landscaping of Champs-Élysées and Bois de Boulogne.

1855   *21 September* – Haussmann's circular on the harmonization of Paris: all buildings in the same block to have the same continuous balconies, cornices and roofs.

1855–59   Creation of a north–south axis from the Gare de l'Est to the Observatoire. (Inauguration of Boulevard de Sébastopol: 5 April 1858.)

1859   *November* – Annexation of suburban *communes* and reorganization of Paris into twenty *arrondissements*. Population before annexation: 1,174,000; after: 1,696,000 (4.6% of French population). Land area: 78.02 km².

1850s and 60s   *Grands magasins* (department stores): Bon Marché (1852), Grands Magasins du Louvre (1855), Bazar de l'Hôtel de Ville (1860), Printemps (1865), Belle Jardinière (1866), Samaritaine (1869).

1860–68   Bibliothèque Nationale, by Henri Labrouste.

1865–66   Demolitions on the Île de la Cité, whose resident population falls from 20,000 to 5,000.

1866   Pneumatic post network (until 1984).

1870   *September* – Defeat of France by Prussia at Sedan; Siege of Paris; proclamation of Third Republic.

1871   *March* – Election of Paris Commune; National Government at Versailles. *May* – Destruction of Hôtel de Ville (rebuilt 1874–82) and Tuileries Palace (not rebuilt); defeat of Commune by government troops.

1875   Inauguration of Opéra designed by Charles Garnier (Avenue de l'Opéra completed 1878).

1875–1914   Building of Sacré-Cœur basilica at Montmartre.

1879   National Government returns from Versailles to Paris.

1889   Universal Exhibition and inauguration of Eiffel Tower.

1891   *15 March* – Paris time imposed on the rest of France.

1895   *December* – First public screening of motion pictures, by the Lumière brothers, at the Grand Café, Boulevard des Capucines.

1898   *13 January* – Zola's letter on the Dreyfus Affair.

1900   *April–November* – Universal Exhibition; inauguration of Gare d'Orsay, Grand and Petit Palais, Pont Alexandre III. *19 July* – Opening of first Métro line in Paris.

1903   *July* – The first Tour de France bicycle race begins and ends in Paris suburbs.

1906 and 1919   *Îlots insalubres* identified for slum clearance.

1910   *January* – Worst flooding since 1658. *4 November* – Opening of first Nord–Sud underground railway line.

1911   Population: 2,888,000 (7.3% of French population; 18%, including suburbs).

1914   *31 July* – Assassination of Jean Jaurès at Café du Croissant. *1 August* – France orders general mobilization. *30 August* – First aerial bombardment of Paris (Gare de l'Est).

1915   *20–21 March* and *29 January* 1916 – Zeppelin raids on Paris.

1918   *January–September*: Occasional bombardment by Gothas and long-range cannon. *11 November* – Armistice.

1919   Opening of Le Bourget airport. Demolition of Thiers's fortifications begins.

1921 Population: 2,906,000 (7.4% of French population; 15%, including suburbs).

1925 Exposition Internationale des Arts Décoratifs et Industriels Modernes.

1930 Land area (now including Bois de Boulogne and Bois de Vincennes): 105.4 km².

1937 International Exhibition and inauguration of Palais de Chaillot.

1939 *3 September* – Declaration of war.

1940 *June* – German army enters Paris; French government leaves for Tours, then Bordeaux.
July – Establishment of Vichy régime. Paris, in the Occupied Zone, remains the capital of France.

1942 *July* – 'Rafle du Vel' d'Hiv' (biggest round-up of Jews in Paris).

1944 *August* – Liberation of Paris.

1946 Population: 2,725,000 (6.8% of French population); of Seine *département*: 4,776,000.

1950 Creation of HLMs (rent-controlled public housing) and the first 'dormitory towns'; opening of new Port of Paris at Gennevilliers.

1952 Orly replaces Le Bourget as the main civil airport for Paris.

1958– Development of business quarter, La Défense.

1959–69 Presidency of Charles de Gaulle.

1961 Creation of 'District de la Région Parisienne' (renamed 'Île-de-France', after the former province, in 1976).
17 October – Massacre of Algerians by Paris police.

1962 *July* – Algeria granted independence. *4 August* – Loi Malraux creates conservation areas in central Paris.
22 August – Attempted assassination of President de Gaulle at Petit-Clamart.

1964 *July* – Seine *département* divided into Paris, Seine-Saint-Denis, Val-de-Marne and Hauts-de-Seine.

1965 'Schéma Directeur de la Région Parisienne': creation of five satellite '*villes nouvelles*' – Cergy-Pontoise, Évry,

Marne-la-Vallée, Melun-Sénart and Saint-Quentin-en-Yvelines.

1968   *May–June* – Student protests and general strike.

1969   Work begins on Tour Montparnasse (completed 1972) and a regional express train network (RER); the central markets, Les Halles, moved out to Rungis.

1969–74   Presidency of Georges Pompidou.

1973   Completion of Boulevard Périphérique.

1974   Opening of Roissy-Charles de Gaulle airport.

1974–81   Presidency of Valéry Giscard d'Estaing.

1975   Population of Paris: 2,317,000; of metropolitan area: 9,879,000 (4.4% and 18.7% of French population).
1 July – Launch of flat-rate ticket for entire Paris transport network (*Carte orange*).

1977   *31 January* – Centre Georges-Pompidou ('le Beaubourg').
28 February – Height limit of twenty-five metres imposed on all new buildings in central Paris.
March – Jacques Chirac first Mayor of Paris since 1871.

1979   Demolition of wine warehouses at Bercy.
September – Forum des Halles.

1981–95   Presidency of François Mitterrand.

1981   *September* – First TGV rail service: Paris–Lyon.

1984–87   Parc de la Villette.

1986   *December* – Musée d'Orsay.

1989   *March* – Grand Louvre and Pyramid.
July – Opéra Bastille.

1991   Discovery of neolithic tools and dugouts at Bercy.

1992   *April* – Opening of Disneyland Paris.

1994   *14 November* – The first Eurostar train leaves the Gare du Nord for London Waterloo.

1995–2007   Presidency of Jacques Chirac.

1996   *December* – Opening of Bibliothèque Nationale de France.

1998   *12 July* – French national football team wins the World Cup in the Stade de France at Saint-Denis.

1999　Population: 2,125,000; of metropolitan area (Île-de-France): 10,947,000 (18.7% of French population; 6.9% born outside European Community).

2001–　Bertrand Delanoë Mayor of Paris.

2002　*July–August* – 'Paris-Plage': creation of temporary 'beaches' on the banks of the Seine.

2005　*October–November* – Popular revolt in the *banlieue* and in towns and cities throughout France.

2006　*March* – The Sorbonne occupied by students; evacuated by CRS.

2007–　Presidency of Nicolas Sarkozy.

2007　*July* – Introduction of Vélib bike rental scheme.

2008　*1 January* – Smoking banned in cafés and restaurants.

2010　Projected completion of Périphérique de l'Île-de-France.

Sources

ONE NIGHT AT THE PALAIS-ROYAL

Abrantès, Laure Junot, duchesse d'. *Mémoires de Madame d'Abrantès*. Ed. A. Ollivier. 1958.

Arrêté des demoiselles du Palais-Royal consfédérés [sic] pour le bien de leur chose publique. c. 1790.

Balzac, Honoré de. *Le Colonel Chabert.* 1832.

Balzac, Honoré de. *Splendeurs et Misères des courtisanes.* 1838–47.

Bertin, Le Chevalier. 'Voyage de Bourgogne'. In *Voyages des poètes français*. 1888.

Blagdon, Francis William. *Paris As It Was and As It Is.* 1803.

Boudon, Edmée-Marie-Claude de. *Lettres . . . ou Journal d'un voyage à Paris.* 1791.

Carroll, Charles Michael. 'The History of "Berthe": A Comedy of Errors'. *Music & Letters*, July 1963, pp. 228–39.

Chateaubriand, François-René de. *Mémoires d'outre-tombe.* Ed. J.-C. Berchet. 1989–98.

Hurtaut, Pierre-Thomas-Nicolas and Magny. *Dictionnaire historique de la ville de Paris et de ses environs.* 1779.

Isherwood, Robert. *Farce and Fantasy: Popular Entertainment in Eighteenth-Century Paris.* 1986.

Kotzebue, August von. *Souvenirs de Paris en 1804.* Tr. G. de Pixérécourt. 1805.

Lamothe-Langon, Étienne-Léon de. *Voyage à Paris, ou Esquisses des hommes et des choses dans cette capitale.* 1830.

Lefeuve, Charles. *Les Anciennes maisons de Paris.* 1875.

Mercier, Louis-Sébastien. *Tableau de Paris.* 1782.

Napoleon I. *Manuscrits inédits, 1786–1791.* Ed. F. Masson and G. Biagi. 1907.

Sources

Parent-Duchâtelet, A.-J.-B. *De la prostitution dans la ville de Paris*. 3rd ed. 1857.

Restif de la Bretonne, Nicolas-Edme. *Le Palais-Royal*. 1790; 1988.

Salgues, Jacques-Barthélemy. *Mémoires pour servir à l'histoire de France sous le gouvernement de Napoléon Buonaparte*. Vol. I. 1814.

Wild, Nicole and David Charlton. *Théâtre de l'Opéra-Comique, Paris: répertoire, 1762–1972*. 2005.

Winter, Edward. 'Napoleon Bonaparte and Chess'. 1998. http://www.chesshistory.com/winter/extra/napoleon.html

Young, Norwood. *Napoleon in Exile: St. Helena, 1815–1821*. 1915.

THE MAN WHO SAVED PARIS

Blagdon, Francis William. *Paris As It Was and As It Is*. 1803.

Clément, Alain and Gilles Thomas. *Atlas du Paris souterrain*. 2001.

Dulaure, Jacques-Antoine. *Histoire physique, civile et morale de Paris*. 1829.

Dunkel, Jean-Timothée. *Topographie et consolidation des carrières sous Paris*. 1885.

Guillaumot, Charles-Axel. *Mémoire sur les travaux ordonnés dans les carrières de Paris*. 1797; 1804.

Guillaumot, Charles-Axel. *Remarques sur un livre intitulé 'Observations sur l'architecture', de M. l'abbé Laugier*. 1768.

Héricart de Thury, Louis. *Description des catacombes de Paris*. 1815.

Hurtaut, Pierre-Thomas-Nicolas and Magny. *Dictionnaire historique de la ville de Paris et de ses environs*. 1779.

Jenlis, Suzanne de. 'Charles Axel Guillaumot'. *ABC Mines*, April 2004. http://www.annales.org/archives/x/guillaumot.html

Journal des Mines, XXXV (1814), p. 194.

Lefrançois, Philippe. *Paris souterrain*. 1950.

Mercier, Louis-Sébastien. *Tableau de Paris*. 1782.

Mercier de Compiègne, C.-F.-X. *Manuel du voyageur à Paris*. 1798–99.

Pétition des ouvriers employés aux carrières de Paris, adressée au Conseil d'État. c. 1790.

Pinkerton, John. *Recollections of Paris, in the Years 1802–3–4–5*. 1806.

Simonin, Louis-Laurent. 'Les Carriers et les carrières'. In *Paris-Guide, par les principaux écrivains et artistes de la France*. Vol. II. 1867.

Thépot, André. *Les Ingénieurs des mines du XIXe siècle*. 1998.

Lost

Maps: Roussel, *Paris, ses fauxbourgs et ses environs* (1730); Louis Bretez ('Plan Turgot'), 1739; Guillaume Dheulland, *Ville, Cité et Université de Paris* (1756?); Jean Delagrive, *Plan de Paris* (1761); Robert de Vaugondy, *Plan de la ville et des faubourgs de Paris* (1771); Hurtaut and Magny, 'Plan de la ville et fauxbourgs de Paris', in *Dictionnaire historique [. . .]* (1779); Edme Verniquet (see Pronteau, below).

Angoulême, duchesse d'. *Mémoire écrit par Marie-Thérèse-Charlotte de France sur la captivité des princes et princesses ses parents.* 1892.

Anon. *Almanach du voyageur à Paris.* 1787.

Anon. 'Paris'. In Pierre Larousse. *Grand Dictionnaire universel du XIXe siècle*, XII (1874), p. 243 ('Rues').

Barberet, Joseph. 'Cochers et loueurs de voitures'. *Le Travail en France*, IV (1887), pp. 199–324.

Berty, Adolphe. *Topographie historique du vieux Paris: région du Louvre et des Tuileries.* 1885.

Bouillé, François-Claude-Amour, marquis de. *Mémoires sur la Révolution française.* 1797.

Bouillé, Louis-Joseph-Amour, marquis de. *Souvenirs et fragments.* Ed. P.-L. de Kermaingant. Vol. I. 1906.

Campan, Madame. *Mémoires sur la vie privée de Marie-Antoinette.* 1823.

Cointeraux, François. *Paris tel qu'il étoit à son origine, tel qu'il est aujourd'hui.* 1798–99.

Convention Nationale. *Procès-verbaux du Comité d'instruction publique de la Convention nationale.* Vol. IV. 1794.

Fontanges, François. *La Fuite du Roi (20 juin 1791): relation du voyage de Varennes.* 1898.

Gauthier, V.-Eugène. *Annuaire de l'imprimerie.* 1853.

Hillairet, Jacques. *Dictionnaire historique des rues de Paris.* 10th ed. 1997.

Lavallée, Théophile. *Histoire de Paris, depuis le temps des Gaulois jusqu'à nos jours.* 1857.

Lefeuve, Charles. *Les Anciennes maisons de Paris.* 1875.

Louis XVI, Marie-Antoinette and Marie-Élisabeth. *Lettres et documents inédits.* Ed. F. Feuillet de Conches. 1864–73.

Mercier, Louis-Sébastien. *Tableau de Paris.* 1782.

Moustier, François-Melchior, comte de. *Relation du voyage de Sa Majesté Louis XVI lors de son départ pour Montmédi.* 1815.

Pinkerton, John. *Recollections of Paris, in the Years 1802–3–4–5.* 1806.

Pronteau, Jeanne. *Edme Verniquet, 1727–1804, architecte et auteur du 'Grand Plan de Paris'*. 1986.

Pronteau, Jeanne. *Les Numérotages des maisons de Paris*. 1966.

Prudhomme, Louis-Marie. *Voyage descriptif et philosophique de l'ancien et du nouveau Paris*. 1814.

Rousseau, James. 'Rue sans nom'. In Louis Lurine. *Les Rues de Paris*, II (1844), pp. 207–20.

Tourzel, Louise-Élisabeth, duchesse de. *Mémoires de madame la duchesse de Tourzel, gouvernante des enfants de France*. 1883.

Valori, François-Florent, comte de. *Précis historique du voyage entrepris par S. M. Louis XVI, le 21 juin 1791*. 1815.

Weber, Joseph. *Mémoires concernant Marie Antoinette, archiduchesse d'Autriche, reine de France*. 1804–09.

RESTORATION

Balzac, Honoré de. *La Peau de chagrin*. 1831.

Beaugrand, Émile. 'Cordonniers (hygiène industrielle)'. *Dictionnaire encyclopédique des sciences médicales*, XX (1877), pp. 429–32.

Dumas, Alexandre. *Le Comte de Monte-Cristo*. 1845–46.

Échard and Michaud Jr. 'Peuchet (Jacques)'. *Biographie universelle (Michaud) ancienne et moderne*. 2nd ed. XXXII (c. 1856), pp. 631–33.

Marx, Karl. 'Peuchet: vom Selbstmord' ('Peuchet on Suicide'). *Gesellschaftsspiegel*, January 1846.

Pacca, Bartolomeo. *Mémoires du Cardinal Pacca*. Tr. L. Bellaguet. 1833.

Peuchet, Jacques. *Mémoires tirés des archives de la Police de Paris*. 1838.

Peuchet, Jacques. *Du Ministère de la Police Générale*. 1814.

Peuchet, Jacques. 'François Picaud'. *Le Monte-Cristo* (ed. A. Dumas), 23 and 30 June 1859.

Reichard, Heinrich August Ottokar. *Guide des voyageurs en France*. 1810.

Thiers, Adolphe. *Histoire de la Révolution française*. 1839.

FILES OF THE SÛRETÉ

Parts of this story appeared in a different form in the *London Review of Books*: G. Robb, 'Walking Through Walls', *LRB*, 18 March 2004.

Anon. 'Juin 1832 (Insurrection des 5 et 6)'. In Pierre Larousse. *Grand Dictionnaire universel du XIXe siècle*, IX (1873), pp. 1096–97.

Sources

Chenu, A. *Les Conspirateurs*. 1850.

Cooper, James Fenimore. *A Residence in France*. 1836.

Grasilier, Léonce. 'Les Policiers officiels adversaires de Vidocq'. *L'Intermédiaire des chercheurs et curieux*, 1910, pp. 827–29.

Hugo, Victor. *Les Misérables*. 1862.

Kalifa, Dominique. *Naissance de la police privée*. 2000.

Merrick, Jeffrey. '"Nocturnal Birds" in the Champs-Élysées: Police and Pederasty in Prerevolutionary Paris'. *GLQ* (2002), pp. 425–32.

Roguet, Christophe-Michel. *Insurrections et guerre des barricades dans les grandes villes*. 1850.

Stead, Philip John. *Vidocq: A Biography*. 1953.

Vidocq, Eugène-François. *Mémoires de Vidocq, chef de la Police de Sûreté, jusqu'en 1827*. 1828–29.

Vidocq, Eugène-François. *Les Voleurs: physiologie de leurs moeurs et de leur langage*. 1837.

A Property in Bohemia

Baldick, Robert. *The First Bohemian: The Life of Henry Murger*. 1961.

Boisson, Marius. *Les Compagnons de la vie de bohème*. 1929.

Caron, Jean-Claude. *Générations romantiques: les étudiants de Paris et le quartier latin, 1814–1851*. 1991.

Champfleury. *Souvenirs des Funambules*. 1859.

Champfleury. *Souvenirs et portraits de jeunesse*. 1872.

Claretie, Jules. *La Vie à Paris*. 1880.

Delvau, Alfred. *Henry Murger et la Bohème*. 1866.

Du Camp, Maxime. *Paris, ses organes, ses fonctions et sa vie*. 1875.

Dufay, Pierre. 'Des Buveurs d'eau à la "Vie de Bohême"'. *Mercure de France*, 1 April 1922.

Héricault, Charles d'. *Souvenirs et portraits*. 1902.

La Bédollière, Émile de. *Le Nouveau Paris: histoire de ses 20 arrondissements*. 1860.

Montorgueil, Georges. *Henri Murger, romancier de la Bohème*. 1928.

Murger, Henry. *Propos de ville et propos de théâtre*. 1875.

Murger, Henry. *Scènes de la vie de bohème*, ed. P. Ginisty. 1924.

Murger, Henry. *Scènes de la vie de bohème*, ed. L. Chotard and G. Robb. 1988.

Nadar et al., *Histoire de Mürger* [sic]. n. d.

St John, Bayle. *Purple Tints of Paris: Character and Manners in the New Empire*. 1854.

Sources

Schanne, Alexandre. *Souvenirs de Schaunard*. 1887.

Toubin, Charles. 'Souvenirs d'un septuagénaire'. In *Baudelaire devant ses contemporains*. Ed. W. T. Bandy and C. Pichois. 1995.

Vitu, Auguste (?). *Le Corsaire-Satan en Silhouette*. Ed. G. Robb. 1985.

MARVILLE

Annuaire-almanach du commerce et de l'industrie, ou Almanach des 500,000 adresses. 1861.

Annuaire de la librairie, de l'imprimerie, de la papeterie, du commerce, de la musique et des estampes. 1860.

Avice, Jean-Paul. 'Marville et les fantômes du réel'. In *Naissance du fantôme*. Ed. J.-D. Jumeau-Lafond. 2002.

Baudelaire, Charles. *Correspondance*. Ed. C. and V. Pichois. 1973.

Baudelaire, Charles. *Œuvres complètes*. Ed. C. Pichois. 1975–76.

Carmona, Michel. *Haussmann*. 2000.

Davanne, A. *Rapport sur les épreuves et les appareils de photographie*. In Ministère de l'Agriculture et du Commerce. *Exposition Universelle Internationale de 1878 à Paris*. 1880.

Delvau, Alfred. *Les Dessous de Paris*. 1860.

Disdéri. *Manuel opératoire de photographie sur collodion instantané*. 1853.

Haussmann, Georges-Eugène. *Mémoires*. Ed. F. Choay. 2000.

Kerouac, Jack. *Satori in Paris*. 1966; 1985.

Lazare, Félix and Louis. *Dictionnaire administratif et historique des rues de Paris et de ses monuments*. 1844–49.

Lecouturier, Henri. *Paris incompatible avec la République: plan d'un nouveau Paris où les révolutions seront impossibles*. 1848.

Le Gray, Gustave. *Traité pratique de photographie sur papier et sur verre*. 1850.

Maréchal, Henri. *L'Éclairage à Paris*. 1894.

Musée Carnavalet. *Eugène Atget: itinéraires parisiens*. Ed. D. Harris. 1999.

Ollivier, Émile. *L'Empire libéral*. Vol. III. 1898.

Paris, ses curiosités et ses environs avec un nouveau plan. *Annuaire parisien, contenant 25.000 adresses des fabricants, négociants et commerçants les plus importants*. 1850.

Pichois, Claude. *Baudelaire à Paris*. 1967.

Pichois, Claude and J.-P. Avice, *Baudelaire – Paris*. 1994.

Texier, Edmond. *Tableau de Paris*. 1852–53.

Thézy, Marie de. *Marville, Paris*. 1998.

Sources

Van Zanten, David. *Building Paris: Architectural Institutions and the Transformation of the French Capital.* 1994.

Le Véritable conducteur parisien, 1828.

Viel-Castel, Horace de. *Mémoires . . . sur le règne de Napoléon III.* 1883–84.

REGRESSION

Bullard, Alice. *Exile to Paradise: Savagery and Civilization in Paris and the South Pacific.* 2000.

Daeninckx, Didier. 'La Marque de l'histoire' (lecture). 2003. http://www.editions-verdier.fr/v3/oeuvre-cannibale-3.html

Dousset-Leenhardt, Roselène. *Terre natale, terre d'exil.* 1998.

Du Camp, Maxime. *Les Convulsions de Paris.* 1881.

Edwards, Stewart. *The Paris Commune 1871.* 1971.

Exposition Universelle Internationale de 1889 à Paris. Catalogue général officiel. 1889.

Forbes, Archibald. *Camps, Quarters, and Casual Places.* 1896.

Garnier, Jules. 'La Nouvelle-Calédonie à l'Exposition universelle de 1878'. *Bulletin de la Société de Géographie,* January–June 1879.

Gayet de Cesena, Amédée. *Le Nouveau Paris: guide de l'étranger.* 1864.

Grousset, Paschal and François Jourde. *Les Condamnés politiques en Nouvelle-Calédonie.* 1876.

Hans, Ludovic and J.-J. Blanc. *Guide à travers les ruines.* 1871.

Horne, Alistair. *The Fall of Paris.* 1989.

Lissagaray, Hippolyte-Prosper-Olivier. *Histoire de la Commune de 1871.* 1876.

Michel, Louise. *Légendes et chants de gestes canaques.* 1885.

Michel, Louise. *Mémoires.* 1886.

Paris libre, journal du soir, April–May 1871.

Pierotti, Ermete. *Rapports militaires officiels du Siège de Paris.* 1871.

Rochefort, Henri. *Les Aventures de ma vie.* 1896.

Roujou, Anatole. 'Sur quelques types humains trouvés en France'. *Bulletins de la Société d'anthropologie de Paris,* 1872, pp. 768–82.

Schreiner, Alfred. *La Nouvelle-Calédonie depuis sa découverte (1774) jusqu'à nos jours.* 1882.

Société d'anthropologie de Paris. *La Société, l'École et le laboratoire d'anthropologie de Paris à l'Exposition universelle de 1889.* 1889.

Topinard, P. 'Discussion sur les moyennes'. *Bulletins de la Société d'anthropologie de Paris,* 1880, pp. 32–42.

Sources

MADAME ZOLA

Alexis, Paul. *Émile Zola, notes d'un ami*. 1882.
Anon. 'Chronique de l'Exposition'. *Le Temps*, 31 March 1889, p. 2.
Anon. *Les Merveilles de l'Exposition de 1889*. 1890 (?).
Bloch-Dano, Evelyne. *Madame Zola*. 1997.
Brown, Frederick. *Zola: A Life*. 1996.
Goncourt, Edmond and Jules de. *Journal: mémoires de la vie littéraire*. 1989.
Hemmings, F. W. J. *The Life and Times of Émile Zola*. 1977.
Laborde, Albert. *Trente-huit années près de Zola*. 1963.
Maupassant, Guy de. *La Vie errante*. 1890.
Mitterand, Henri. *Zola*. 1999–2002.
Say, Léon. 'Les Chemins de fer'. In *Paris-Guide, par les principaux écrivains et artistes de la France*. Vol. II. 1867.
Zola, Émile. *Correspondance*. Ed. B. H. Bakker. 1978–95.

MARCEL IN THE MÉTRO

Albaret, Céleste and Georges Belmont. *Monsieur Proust*. 1973.
Basset, Serge. 'Sur le Métropolitain'. *Figaro*, 20 July 1900, p. 3.
Bechmann, Georges. *Salubrité urbaine, distributions d'eau, assainissement*. 1898–99.
Biette, Louis. 'Le Métropolitain'. *Revue de Paris*, 15 April, 1 and 15 May 1906.
Carter, William C. *Marcel Proust: A Life*. 2000.
Davenport-Hines, Richard. *Proust at the Majestic*. 2006.
Galipaux, Félix. 'Le Métro, monologue'. *Je sais tout*, 15 June 1916, p. 671–75.
Lamming, Clive. *Métro insolite*. 2005.
Ossadzow, Alexandre and Claude Berton. *Fulgence Bienvenüe et la construction du Métropolitain de Paris*. 1998.
Petitjean, Narcisse-Nicolas. *Les Grands travaux de Paris: l'Exposition de 1900, le Métropolitain, la démolition des remparts, la nouvelle enceinte, le tout-à-l'égout*. 1895.
Proust, Marcel. *À la recherche du temps perdu*. Ed. J.-Y. Tadié. 1987–89.
Proust, Marcel. *Correspondance*. Ed. P. Kolb. 1970–93.
Proust, Marcel. 'Journées de lecture'. *Figaro*, 20 March 1907, p. 1.
Rearick, Charles. *The French in Love and War: Popular Culture in the Era of the World Wars*. 1997.

Tadié, Jean-Yves. *Marcel Proust*. 1996.
Vuillaume, Maxime. *Paris sous les Gothas*. 1918.

THE NOTRE-DAME EQUATION

A scholar without Fulcanelli's mystical insights might have identified 'The Alchemist' as the Wandering Jew: see M. Camille, *The Gargoyles of Notre-Dame* (Chicago, 2009).

Aubert, Marcel. 'La Maison dite de Nicolas Flamel'. *Bulletin monumentale (Société française d'archéologie)*, 1912, pp. 305–18.

Bottineau, Yves. *Notre-Dame de Paris et la Sainte-Chapelle*. 1966.

Chancel, Jacques. Interview with Eugène Canseliet. 'Radioscopie'. France Inter, 23 June 1978.

Choquette, Leslie. 'Homosexuals in the City'. *Journal of Homosexuality*, 2001, pp. 149–68.

Comptes rendus hebdomadaires des séances de l'Académie des Sciences, CCXXVI (24 May 1948), pp. 1655–56; CCXXIX (7 November 1949), p. 909.

Dillon, Emile Joseph. *The Inside Story of the Peace Conference*. 1920.

Edwards, Henry Sutherland. *Old and New Paris*. 1893–94.

Figuier, Louis. *L'Alchimie et les alchimistes*. 1860.

Fulcanelli. *Le Mystère des cathédrales et l'interprétation ésotérique des symboles hermétiques du Grand Œuvre*. Ed. E. Canseliet. 1964.

Fulcanelli. *Les Demeures philosophales et le symbolisme hermétique . . .* Ed. E. Canseliet. 1965.

Gobineau de Montluisant, Esprit. Explication très-curieuse des énigmes et figures hiéroglyphiques au grand portail de l'église cathédrale et métropolitaine de Notre-Dame de Paris. 1640; 1954.

Hugo, Victor. *Notre-Dame de Paris. 1482*. 1831.

Ibels, André. 'Les Faiseurs d'or'. *Je sais tout*, August 1905, p. 185–94.

Jollivet-Castelot, François. *Comment on devient alchimiste*. 1897.

Jollivet-Castelot, François. *Le Grand-Œuvre alchimique*. 1901.

Levenstein, Harvey. *We'll Always Have Paris: American Tourists in France Since 1930*. 2004.

MacMillan, Margaret. *Peacemakers: the Paris Conference of 1919*. 2001.

Pauwels, Louis and Jacques Bergier. *Le Matin des magiciens*. 1960.

Phaneg, G. *Cinquante merveilleux secrets d'alchimie*. 1912.

Pitollet, Camille. 'Où est la momie de Cléopâtre?'. *L'Intermédiaire des chercheurs et curieux*, 1935, pp. 6–9, 387–91 and 832.

Richelson, Jeffrey T. *Spying on the Bomb: American Nuclear Intelligence from Nazi Germany to Iran and North Korea*. 2006.

Sources

Sclove, Richard E. 'From Alchemy to Atomic War: Frederick Soddy's "Technology Assessment" of Atomic Energy, 1900–1915'. *Science, Technology, & Human Values*, Spring 1989.

Soddy, Frederick. *The Interpretation of Radium and the Structure of the Atom.* 1920.

Tiffereau, Cyprien-Théodore. *Les Métaux sont des corps composés: mémoires présentés à l'Académie des Sciences.* 2nd ed. 1857.

Viollet-le-Duc, Eugène. *Du style gothique au XIXᵉ siècle.*1846.

Viollet-le-Duc, Eugène and Jean-Baptiste Lassus. *Projet de restauration de Notre-Dame de Paris.* 1843.

Weber, Eugen. *The Hollow Years.* 1995.

Weiss, Louise. *La Résurrection du chevalier.* 1974.

White, Watson. *The Paris That Is Paris.* 1926.

A LITTLE TOUR OF PARIS

Anon. 'Last Days'. *Time*, 24 June 1940.

Below, Nicolaus von. *At Hitler's Side: the Memoirs of Hitler's Luftwaffe Adjutant.* Tr. G. Brooks. 2001.

Bormann, Martin. *Hitler's Table Talk, 1941–44. His Private Conversations.* Tr. N. Cameron and R. H. Stevens. 1953; 1973.

Breker, Arno. *Im Strahlungsfeld der Ereignisse, 1925–1965.* 1972.

Cobb, Richard. *French and Germans, Germans and French.* 1983.

Cocteau, Jean. *Journal, 1942–1945.* Ed. J. Touzot. 1989.

Dietrich, Otto. *The Hitler I Knew.* Tr. R. and C. Winston. 1957.

Engel, Gerhard. *Heeresadjutant bei Hitler, 1938–1943: Aufzeichnungen des Majors Engel.* Ed. H. von Kotze. 1974.

Giesler, Hermann. *Ein anderer Hitler: Bericht seines Architekten*, 2nd ed. 1977.

Hitler, Adolf. *Reden und Proklamationen, 1932–1945.* Ed. M. Domarus. 1987.

Krob, Melanie Gordon. 'Paris Through Enemy Eyes: the Wehrmacht in Paris, 1940–1944'. *Journal of European Studies*, 2001, pp. 3–28.

Langeron, Roger. *Paris, juin 40.* 1946.

Paul, Elliot. *The Last Time I Saw Paris.* 1942; 2001. (British edition: *A Narrow Street.*)

Pryce-Jones, David. *Paris in the Third Reich.* 1981.

Schroeder, Christa. *Er war mein Chef: aus dem Nachlaß der Sekretärin von Adolf Hitler.* Ed. A. Joachimsthaler. 1985.

Shirer, William L. *The Collapse of the Third Republic.* 1969.

Sources

Speer, Albert. *Inside the Third Reich*. Tr. R. and C. Winston. 1971.
Sweeting, C. G. *Hitler's Personal Pilot: The Life and Times of Hans Baur*. 2000.
Warlimont, Walter. *Inside Hitler's Headquarters*. Tr. R. H. Barry. 1964.

OCCUPATION

I am particularly indebted to *La Grande rafle du Vel d'Hiv* by C. Lévy and P. Tillard. Nat Linen (Anatole Linenstein) was arrested and deported in 1944; he was interviewed in 1965. Anna Lichtein and her mother returned from Auschwitz.
Alary, Eric. *La Ligne de démarcation*. 2003.
Amouroux, Henri. *La Vie des Français sous l'Occupation*. 1961.
Cocteau, Jean. *Journal, 1942–1945*. Ed. J. Touzot. 1989.
Colette. *Paris, de ma fenêtre*. 1944.
Diamond, Hanna. *Women and the Second World War in France, 1939–48*. 1999.
Grynberg, Anne. *Les Camps de la honte*. 1999.
Guéno, Jean-Pierre and Jérôme Pecnard. *Paroles d'étoiles*. 2002.
Laloum, Jean. *Les Juifs dans la Résistance et la Libération*. 1985.
Langeron, Roger. *Paris, juin 40*. 1946.
Lazare, Lucien. *Rescue as Resistance*. Tr. J. M. Green. 1996.
Lemalet, Martine. *Au secours des enfants du siècle*. 1993.
Lévy, Claude and Paul Tillard. *La Grande rafle du Vel d'Hiv*. 1967.
Marrott-Fellag Ariouet, Céline. 'Les Enfants cachés pendant la seconde guerre mondiale'. 2005. http://lamaisondesevres.org/cel/celsom.html
Ousby, Ian. *Occupation: the Ordeal of France*. 2000.
Sartre, Jean-Paul. 'Paris sous l'Occupation' (1945). In *Situations, III*. 1949.
Veillon, Dominique. *La Mode sous l'Occupation*. 1990.
Zeitoun, Sabine. *Ces enfants qu'il fallait sauver*. 1989.

LOVERS OF SAINT-GERMAIN-DES-PRÉS

The imaginary screenplay is based closely on the autobiography of Juliette Greco, several interviews, and Miles Davis's unsparing account of himself in *Miles: the Autobiography*.
Anon. 'L'Existentialisme à Saint-Germain-des-Prés' (documentary). *Les Actualités françaises*, 20 September 1951.
Beauvoir, Simone de. *La Force des choses*. 1963.

Beevor, Antony and Artemis Cooper. *Paris After the Liberation, 1944–1949.* 2004.

Carles, Philippe. Interview with Juliette Gréco. Tr. R. Williams. *Guardian*, 25 May 2006.

Charbonnier, Jean-Philippe. 'Juliette Gréco & Miles Davis – Paris 1949' (photograph).

Davis, Miles and Quincy Troupe. *Miles: the Autobiography.* 1990.

Gréco, Juliette. *Jujube.* 1982.

Gréco, Juliette. Interview. 'Gros plan'. ORTF, 13 July 1962.

Queneau, Raymond. *L'Instant fatal.* 1946; 1948.

Sartre, Jean-Paul. *La Responsabilité de l'écrivain.* 1946; 1998.

The Day of the Fox

Barrat, Michel. 'Scènes de la libération de Paris en 1944'. 1998. http://adminet.tv/barrat/liberation.html

Belvisi, Armand. *L'Attentat: indicatif Écho-Gabriel.* 1972.

Cocteau, Jean. *Journal, 1942–1945.* Ed. J. Touzot. 1989.

Crang, Jeremy A. 'General de Gaulle under Sniper Fire in Notre-Dame Cathedral, 26 August 1944: Robert Reid's BBC Commentary'. *Historical Journal of Film, Radio and Television*, August 2007, pp. 391–406.

Delarue, Jacques. *L'O.A.S. contre de Gaulle.* 1981.

Duprat, François. *Les Mouvements d'extrême-droite en France depuis 1944.* 1972.

Gaulle, Charles de. *Mémoires de guerre.* 1954–59.

Giesbert, Franz-Olivier. *François Mitterrand ou la Tentation de l'histoire.* 1977.

Lacouture, Jean. *Mitterrand: une histoire de Français.* 1988.

Larue, André. *Les Flics.* 1969.

Mackworth, Cecily. 'Letter from Paris'. *The Twentieth Century*, December 1959.

Marton, Lajos. *Il faut tuer de Gaulle.* 2002.

Méfret, Jean-Pax. *Jusqu'au bout de l'Algérie française.* 2003; 2007.

Nay, Catherine. *Le Noir et le Rouge, ou l'Histoire d'une ambition.* 1985.

Pesquet, Robert. *Mon vrai-faux attentat contre Mitterrand.* 1995.

Peyrefitte, Alain. *C'était de Gaulle.* 1994.

Tiersky, Ronald. *François Mitterrand, the Last French President.* 2000.

Williams, Philip M. *Wars, Plots and Scandals in Post-War France.* 1970.

Expanding the Domain of the Possible

Dark Star Collective. *Beneath the Paving Stones: Situationists and the Beach, May 1968.* 2001.

Daum, Nicolas. *Mai 68 raconté par des anonymes.* 2008. Revised ed. of *Des révolutionnaires dans un village parisien.* 1988.

Franco, Victor and Claude Ventura. 'Les Résidents de Nanterre'. 'Tel Quel'. ORTF, 26 March 1968.

Gallant, Mavis. *Paris Notebooks.* 1968; 1988.

Grappin, Pierre. *L'Île aux peupliers, de la Résistance à Mai 68: souvenirs du doyen de Nanterre.* 1993.

Grimaud, Maurice. *En mai, fais ce qu'il te plaît.* 1977.

Kidd, William. 'Liberation in Novels of May '68'. In *The Liberation of France.* Ed. H. Kedward and N. Wood. 1995.

Labro, Philippe, Michèle Manceaux et l'équipe d'*Édition spéciale. Mai/juin 68: 'Ce n'est qu'un début'.* 1968.

Marwick, Arthur. *The Sixties: Cultural Revolution in Britain, France, Italy and the United States, c. 1958 – c. 1974.* 1998.

Quattrocchi, Angelo and Tom Nairn. *The Beginning of the End: France, May 1968.* 1968; 1998.

Reynolds, Chris. 'May 68: A Contested History'. *Sens public,* October 2007.

Rioux, Lucien and René Backmann. *L'Explosion de mai.* 1968.

Ross, Kristin. *May '68 and Its Afterlives.* 2002.

Seidman, Michael. *The Imaginary Revolution: Parisian Students and Workers in 1968.* 2004.

Singer, Daniel. *Prelude to Revolution: France in May 1968.* 1970.

Speter, Ludwig. 'La Crise de mai-juin 1968 dans *le Figaro*'. Institut d'Études politiques de Rennes, 2005.

Veillon, Dominique. 'Esthétique et représentations de la femme à travers la presse féminine'. *Les Années 68: événements, cultures politiques et modes de vie.* Lettre d'information, 26. 1997.

Périphérique

Agence Trévelo & Viger-Kohler. 'La Question de la limite'. In 'Paris Métropole'. 2006. www.paris.fr/portail/accueil

Agulhon, Maurice. 'Paris: la traversée d'est en ouest'. In Pierre Nora, ed. *Les Lieux de mémoire.* Vol. III, 3. 1992.

Bernard-Folliot, Denise and Société Anonyme d'Économie Mixte d'Aménagement et de Restauration du Secteur des Halles (SEMAH). *Les Halles – Beaubourg*. 1980.

'The Black Prince' ('Le Prince Noir'). *Paris Périphérique, 11.04: The Illegal Record* (DVD). 2008.

Brassaï. *Graffiti*. Tr. D. Radzinowicz. 2002.

Charnelet, Patricia and William Leymergie. 'Midi 2'. Antenne 2, 4 March 1988.

Chevalier, Louis. *L'Assassinat de Paris*. 1977; 1997.

Evenson, Norma. *Paris: a Century of Change, 1878–1978*. 1979.

Fierro, Annette. *The Glass State: the Technology of the Spectacle*. 2003.

Flonneau, Mathieu. *L'Automobile à la conquête de Paris*. 2003.

Jamet, Dominique, et al. 'Les Paris de François Mitterrand': Institut François Mitterrand. 2003. http://www.mitterrand.org/Les-Paris-de-Francois-Mitterrand

Joffet, Robert. 'Le Point de vue du Conservateur des Jardins de Paris'. *Urbanisme*, XXI, 3–4 (1952), pp. 109–24.

Le Corbusier. *La Ville radieuse*. 1935. (*The Radiant City*. 1967.)

Maspero, François. *Roissy Express: A Journey through the Paris Suburbs*. Tr. P. Jones. 1994.

Mollard, Claude. *Le Centre National d'Art et de Culture Georges-Pompidou*. 1975.

Périer, Gilberte *née* Pascal, et al. *Lettres, opuscules et mémoires*. 1845.

Poisson, Georges. *Histoire de l'architecture à Paris*. 1997.

Pompidou, Georges. *Entretiens et discours*. 1975.

Pompidou, Georges. *Pour rétablir une vérité*. 1982.

Quatremère de Quincy, Antoine. *Encyclopédie méthodique: Architecture*. 1788–1825.

Restif de la Bretonne, Nicolas-Edme. *Mes Inscripcions*. Ed. P. Cottin. 1889.

Roussel, Éric. *Georges Pompidou*. 2004.

Silver, Nathan. *The Making of Beaubourg: a Building Biography*. 1994.

Sutcliffe, Anthony, *Paris: an Architectural History*. 1993.

SARKO, BOUNA AND ZYED

Barron, Louis. *Les Environs de Paris*. 1886.

Black, Robert. *The History of Electric Wires and Cables*. 1983.

Bonnier, Louis. *L'Évacuation des matières de vidanges à Paris*. 1910.

Bromberger, Dominique. *Clichy-sous-Bois, vallée des anges*. 2006.

'Cahier des très-humbles remontrances, supplications, plaintes et doléances de la paroisse d'Aulnay-les-Bondis' (1789). In *Archives parlementaires . . . États Généraux*, I, IV (1879), p. 326 ('Paris; hors les murs').

Cazelles, Christophe, et al. *Les 'Violences urbaines' de l'automne 2005*. Centre d'analyse stratégique, 2007.

Chaigneau, Rafaël. 'Un pèlerinage en forêt de Bondy'. *Revue du traditionnisme français et étranger*, 1913, pp. 156–8.

Chemin, Ariane. 'Le Dernier jour de Bouna Traoré et Zyed Benna'. *Le Monde*, 8 December 2005.

Counil, Émilie, et al. 'Petite histoire de la commune d'Aulnay-sous-Bois'. In *Étude de santé publique autour d'une ancienne usine de broyage d'amiante*. 2007.

Dorré, L. *L'Infection de Paris et de la banlieue*. 1883.

Faure, Alain. 'Villégiature populaire et peuplement des banlieues'. In *La Terre et la Cité: Mélanges offerts à Philippe Vigier*. 1994.

Guillerme, André, et al. *Dangereux, insalubres et incommodes: paysages industriels en banlieue parisienne*. 2004.

Hugo, Victor. *Les Misérables*. 1862.

Initiatives Pour un Autre Monde (IPAM). *Le Soulèvement populaire dans les banlieues françaises d'octobre – novembre 2005*. 2005. http://www.reseau-ipam.org/IMG/pdf/Dossier_IPAM_Revoltes_urbaines.pdf

Louette. *Itinéraire complet de la France*. 1788.

Mignard, Jean-Pierre and Emmanuel Tordjman. *L'Affaire Clichy*. 2006.

Monsieur R. 'Fransse'. *Politikment Incorrekt* (CD), 2005.

Perrignon, Judith. 'Muhittin Altun'. *Libération*, 31 December 2005.

Recasens, Olivia, Jean-Michel Décugis and Christophe Labbé. *Place Beauvau: la face cachée de la police*. 2006.

Rouquette, Jules. *La Forêt de Bondy, ou les Misères du peuple*. 1887.

Sarkozy, Nicolas. *Témoignage*. 2006.

Sévigné, Marie de Rabutin-Chantal, Mme de. *Lettres*. Ed. M. Monmerqué. 1862–66.

Slooter, Luuk. *Cité Dreams: An Analysis of the French Suburban Riots of 2005*. Utrecht University, 2007.

Stovall, Tyler. *The Rise of the Paris Red Belt*. 1990.

TERMINUS: THE NORTH COL

Abeillé, Anne. *Dictionnaire du Vélib'*. 2007.

Bastié, Jean. *La Croissance de la banlieue parisienne*. 1964.

Beaujeu-Garnier, Jacqueline. *Paris: hasard ou prédestination? Une géographie de Paris*. 1993.

Bonnardot, Alfred. 'Note sur un des îlots de la Seine'. *Bulletin de la Société de l'Histoire de Paris et de l'Île-de-France*, 1879, pp. 29–30.

Bourgon, Anne. 'La Cité de la Muette à Drancy'. In *Place, Memory, Meaning: Preserving Intangible Values in Monuments and Sites.* ICOMOS, 14th General Assembly, 2003.

Chenay, Christophe de. 'L'Ancien camp de Drancy devient monument historique'. *Le Monde*, 1 August 2005.

Chevalier, Louis. *Montmartre du plaisir et du crime.* 1980.

Club des 100 cols (journal). Articles by A. Collonges (1981), C. Guitton (1982) and J. Briot-Giraudin (1989).

Dion, Roger. 'Paris dans la géographie'. *Revue des Deux Mondes*, 1 January 1951, pp. 5–30.

François, Jacques. *Histoire du village de La Chapelle.* 2002.

Jones, Colin. 'Théodore Vacquer and the Archaeology of Modernity in Haussmann's Paris'. *Transactions of the Royal Historical Society*, 2007, pp. 157–83.

Las Cases, Emmanuel, comte de. *Mémorial de Sainte-Hélène.* 1842.

Lombard-Jourdan, Anne. '*Montjoie et Saint Denis!': le centre de la Gaule aux origines de Paris et de Saint-Denis.* 1989.

Pachtère, F.-G. de. *Paris à l'époque gallo-romaine.* 1912. (From the papers of Théodore Vacquer.)

Planhol, Xavier de. *Géographie historique de la France.* 1988. (Tr. J. Lloyd: *An Historical Geography of France.* 1994; 2006.)

Reclus, Onésime. *Le Plus beau royaume sous le ciel.* 1899.

Rouleau, Bernard. *Le Tracé des rues de Paris.* 1988.

Stendhal. *Vie de Henry Brulard.* 1835–36; 1890.

Index of Paris and Conurbation

General Index

General Index

Acknowledgements

I am grateful to my cherished editors – Sam Humphreys at Picador and Starling Lawrence at Norton – and readers: Gill Coleridge of Rogers, Coleridge and White, Melanie Jackson of the Melanie Jackson Agency, Alison Robb, Stephen Roberts and Margaret, who appears as a protagonist but is present on every page. I would also like to thank the following people and institutions: Morgan Alliche, Paul Baggaley, Ian and Ruth Bird, Nicholas Blake, Wilf Dickie, Camilla Elworthy, David Fawbert, Sudhir Hazareesingh, James Hiddleston, Henry Johnson, Cara Jones, Andrew Kidd, Laurence Laluyaux, Josine Meijer, David Miller, Claude and Vincenette Pichois, Gerald Sgroi, Peter Straus and Isabelle Taudière; the Social Science Library, the Taylor Institution and the History Faculty Library of Oxford University, the Bodleian Library, the Bibliothèque Nationale de France, the Bibliothèque Historique de la Ville de Paris, the Musée Carnavalet, the Institut Géographique National, the Club des Cent Cols and the RATP.